GUARDIANS OF EMPIRE

BRIAN MCALLISTER LINN

Guardians

of Empire

The U.S. Army and the Pacific, 1902–1940

The
University
of North
Carolina
Press

Chapel Hill
& London

© 1997 The University of North Carolina Press

All rights reserved

Manufactured in the United States of America

The paper in this book meets the guidelines for
permanence and durability of the Committee on
Production Guidelines for Book Longevity of the
Council on Library Resources.

Library of Congress
Cataloging-in-Publication Data
Linn, Brian McAllister.
Guardians of empire : the U.S. Army and the
Pacific, 1902–1940 / by Brian McAllister Linn.
p. cm. Includes bibliographical references and
index. ISBN 0-8078-2321-X (alk. paper) 1. United
States—Military policy. 2. United States. Army.
I. Title.

UA23.L5768   1997   96-24200
355'.033073—dc20   CIP

01 00 99 98 97   5 4 3 2 1

To Diane Kamins Linn

CONTENTS

MAPS & ILLUSTRATIONS

Maps

Illustrations

The central question for any study of the U.S. Army in the Philippines and Hawaii is why, with almost four decades to prepare, these military forces proved unable to defend the nation's Pacific possessions against Japan. Traditionally, the approach to this question has been to focus on the events immediately preceding the Japanese attacks of 7–8 December 1941. Historians, both academic and popular, have culled through mountains of documentation seeking to piece together the chain of events—or the web of deceit—that led to the "day of infamy." In the process, they have created new mountains of documentation on the "Bomb Plot" or "winds execute" messages, blaming or defending anyone from President Roosevelt to obscure radar operators, and offering explanations ranging from simple human error to international cabals or the fundamental differences in Japanese and American culture. The annual appearance of yet another best seller demonstrating some dark conspiracy, predicated on some heretofore overlooked radio broadcast or cocktail conversation, indicates the enduring interest in the genesis of the attack. But fixing on the period immediately before it unfairly casts the nation's forces in Hawaii and the Philippines in the role of somnolent victims passively awaiting the onslaught. Historians, preoccupied with investigating the event, have largely overlooked the decades that preceded it.

This book seeks to offer a somewhat longer perspective through a narrative history of the U.S. Army in Hawaii and the Philippines from 1902 to 1940. Its focus is restricted to the military forces in the two Pacific territories—there is little mention of the troops in China or Panama, or of naval and diplomatic issues, or of the events immediately preceding the outbreak of war—and its task is not to delineate the road to Pearl Harbor, but to illuminate the numerous paths the army trod in its long search for a viable Pacific defense. Contrary to popular belief, the Japanese attack did not catch soldiers unaware. Indeed, the army was like the boy who cried wolf. For years it had foreseen both the threat and its own inability to ward it off. The history of the Pacific

Army is, in many respects, a history of why the obvious did not happen—of why sensible precautions were omitted, why prescient solutions died stillborn, why evident protective measures were ignored—as Sherlock Holmes astutely noticed, why the dog did not bark. Thus it seeks less to explain what the U.S. Army should have done, than what it did, or failed to do, and why. For that reason, it is as concerned with Honolulu and Manila as with Washington, as interested in beach defense tactics as grand strategy, as curious about how the army dealt with threats that never materialized as how it failed to deal with the one that did.

To facilitate this inquiry, the book focuses on five major themes. The first of these is an exploration of the U.S. Army's strategic thinking about the Pacific. It discusses not only the various twists and turns in this thought—as evidenced by declarations of policy, war plans, and projects—but also the constant tension between those who saw defense of the Pacific possessions as one of the army's primary missions and those who insisted that overseas considerations be subordinate to continental defense. Imperialist officers such as Leonard Wood and Douglas MacArthur argued that the security of the United States depended on trade and power projection in the Far East, which in turn depended on a strong permanent presence in the western Pacific and on military forces ready for immediate deployment overseas. They recognized that only possession of the archipelago, or at least Manila Bay, would allow the United States to avoid a prolonged and perhaps indecisive Pacific war and to launch immediate operations against the Japanese Empire. Often they developed an emotional commitment to the territories and considered themselves honor bound to protect a dependent and vulnerable people. Thus the Philippines were valuable not just for strategic or commercial reasons, but as transfer point for American values and institutions to Asia, and Hawaii was essential as an assembly site for ships and troops moving into the western Pacific. Their opponents sought to restrict the American defense perimeter to Hawaii and perceived the Philippines as a dangerously exposed and strategically unimportant outpost. Hawaii, in this view, was essential not as a staging area, but as the outer bastion of continental defense. In part a reflection of the much broader argument between isolationism and interventionism, in part a very specific military debate over the utility of forward deployment and overseas bases, it remains a problem to this day.

The second theme concerns the practical, or tactical, aspects of Pacific defense. For almost four decades the central question in the Pacific was unchanged: how to defend distant, militarily weak possessions against a strong and aggressive regional power. Although the source of the threat remained constant, its appearance changed repeatedly: no sooner had the army resolved the problem of ship bombardment than it was threatened with land invasion; no sooner had it developed tactics for guarding the beaches than it faced the specter of aerial raids. Moreover, American political leaders insisted on retaining foreign garrisons and pursuing active, even confrontational policies against Japan, but refused to fund either the armament or manpower required to make these policies good. The U.S. Navy proclaimed that a Pacific fleet was essential to protect vital economic and strategic interests, and that this fleet depended on bases in the Philippines and Hawaii; but it refused to guarantee their safety or even commit itself to their defense. Unable to secure sufficient support from either its political superiors or its naval colleagues, the army's role in the Pacific was all too accurately summarized by a senior officer in 1907 as to "hold the bag" for the nation's venture into imperialism and seapower.

The third theme is closely tied to the second, and reflects the Pacific Army's role as guardian of empire. Whom were the guardians guarding against? From their inception, the overseas garrisons were charged not only with protecting the nation's new wards, but controlling them. This was especially true in the Philippines, but applied as well in Hawaii, where the large Japanese American population provided a constant source of worry to ethnocentric officers who distrusted "natives," and viewed them as unreliable at best, subversive at worst. But the fidelity to the United States exhibited by Filipinos and Hawaii's Japanese in 1941 does not, by itself, prove that this loyalty existed in 1911 or 1921 or 1931, or that army suspicions were merely racist or paranoid. There was ample documentation—however ambiguous, inconclusive, and biased—to suggest that the local populations must be watched. Thus, the U.S. Army in the Pacific had to look inward as well as outward, to guard as much against rebellion and sabotage as invasion.

The army's inability to trust the very people it was supposed to protect led to a fourth problem: how to utilize local manpower without risking an uprising. By the end of the first decade of the century, army planners recognized Japan's ability to concentrate overwhelming force against any American garrison in the Philippines. Even more disturbing, there was a strong likelihood that by launching a surprise attack, the Japanese could crush the defenders before reinforcements could arrive from the United States. Clearly more manpower was necessary, but the only possible source lay in the polyglot, indifferent, and possibly disloyal inhabitants. To recruit, arm, and train them as a counterforce to the Japanese was to run the risk of creating an equally dangerous opponent.

The fifth, and perhaps dominant, theme is the disparity between military policy and its practice, between what plans call for and what can actually be accomplished. It may be argued that a policy that lacks the means of achievement is no policy at all. Certainly in the case of the Pacific Army, the nation's declared policy to defend the overseas territories was confounded by a dearth of resources to do it. But this book is not intended as yet another exposé of the U.S. government's failure to honor its commitments. Rather, its question is why the U.S. Army failed itself in not developing a realistic answer to the major strategic problem it faced between 1902 and 1940: the protection of Hawaii and the Philippines from Japanese attack. In part, this book is an account of well-conceived ideas falling victim to institutional inertia, financial constraints, parochialism, paranoia, tunnel vision, face-saving, egotism, and accidents of timing. But it is also a study of how modern military institutions, staffed by intelligent and committed professionals, can work devotedly, and generate sophisticated projects and plans, but still not address the central issues that confront them. Time and again the underlying assumptions of the current military defense plan for Hawaii or the Philippines would be exploded, only to be replaced by a new plan based on equally questionable preconceptions. Challenged by a strategic dilemma, army officers tinkered with technicalities: they placed their faith in unproved technology such as the airplane, or in hazardous relief plans, or in implausible tactical plans based on nonexistent manpower. Whether because of a commendable "can do" spirit or less laudable overoptimism, or "not-on-my-shift" careerism, army officers refused to admit defeat, refused to challenge their civilian superiors to provide realistic policies, refused to insist that overseas commanders subordinate local plans to the country's strategic necessities. If, as Douglas MacArthur and others have charged, America's leaders failed to provide the guardians of the nation's Pacific empire with the means to perform their duty, then it was a failure for which the guardians themselves bear much of the responsibility.

This project began in 1989 as a study of the Pulahan and Moro conflicts, funded by a National Endowment for the Humanities Summer Stipend. The bulk of the research was done as a John M. Olin Postdoctoral Fellow in Military and Strategic Studies at Yale University during the 1990–91 academic year. A Peace Fellowship at the Hoover Institution of War, Revolution and Peace during the 1993–94 year allowed me to write and revise the manuscript in a most supportive environment. My own institution, Texas A&M University, has been exceptionally generous with leave time and financial support. The Program to Enhance Scholarly and Creative Activities Grant provided summer funding in 1993 and a Faculty Development Leave in 1995 allowed time for revisions. Texas A&M's Research and Graduate Studies Faculty Mini-Grants allowed me to conduct research in 1992 and 1993 and its Military Studies Institute furnished research grants in 1991 and 1992. Without such assistance, it would have been impossible to conduct the archival research upon which this book is based.

So many individuals have given me the benefit of their advice and support that I must apologize in advance for omissions. I would especially like to acknowledge Allan R. Millett, Edward M. Coffman, and David F. Trask, three preeminent military historians who from the outset have been both mentors and friends, unstinting in their professional assistance. At Texas A&M, Larry D. Hill and Julia Kirk Blackwelder of the History Department and Charles Johnson and Ben Crouch, associate deans of research at the College of Liberal Arts, worked exceptionally hard to secure me leave time. My colleagues in the History Department have been very supportive, particularly R. J. Q. Adams, Terry Anderson, Joseph Dawson, Roger Beaumont, and James Bradford. Special thanks to Mary Johnson and Walter, Vickie, and C. Davis Buenger. Thomas Hendriksen, Ramon Myers, and the incomparable Wendy Minkin treated me with great kindness and consideration at the Hoover Institution. At Yale University, I benefited from the support of Sir Michael Howard, Paul Kennedy, and Howard Lamar. My co-Fellows, Rich Muller,

John Caldwell, James Schepley, Semion Lyandres, and Wen-hsin Yeh, took an active and beneficial interest in my work.

From the beginning, veterans provided invaluable support and advice. Their letters and comments greatly assisted my understanding of the Pacific Army's social history. I was impressed by the veterans' candor and honesty and touched by their hope that I could portray their experiences with accuracy. In particular, I wish to thank Russell A. Eberhardt, Howard C. Fields, Robert W. Keeney, Walter Maciejowski, and Thomas J. Wells. I trust this work provides some small reward for their selflessness in answering my questions.

My work at libraries and archives was greatly assisted by the kindness and support I received. In particular, I would like to thank Tim Nenninger, Mitch Yockelson, Will Mahoney, and Rich Boylen at the National Archives; Richard Sommers, David Keough, Louise Arnold, and John Slonaker at the U.S. Army Military History Institute; Graham Cosmas, Edgar Raines, and Andrew Birtle from the U.S. Army Center of Military History; Judith Bowman and Thomas Fairfull of the Army Museum of Hawaii; and Leatrice R. Arakaki of the 15th Air Base Wing History Office, Hickam Air Force Base. I appreciate the help of archivists and staffs at the Special Collections of the U.S. Army Military Academy Library, the Manuscripts Division of the Library of Congress; the South Carolina Historical Society; the Southern Historical Collections at the University of North Carolina at Chapel Hill; Perkins Library at Duke University; the Dwight D. Eisenhower Presidential Library; the Yale University Library; the Archives of the Hoover Institution of War, Revolution and Peace; Green Library at Stanford University; the Massachusetts Historical Society; the U.S. Air Force Historical Research Agency; the U.S. Army Command and General Staff College Library; the Hawaii State Archives; Hamilton Library at the University of Hawaii at Manoa; and the Texas State Archives.

Drafts of the manuscript were read by Edward M. Coffman, Allan R. Millett, Peter Maslowski, Carol Petillo, Edward Miller, A. J. Bacevich, Mark Peattie, Roy Flint, and William R. Braisted. Their comments and suggestions improved it greatly and constantly challenged me to explain my conclusions better; the mistakes that remain are mine alone. Finally, I would especially like to acknowledge the support of my father, James R. Linn, who applied his exceptional editing skills to what were often confused and fragmented drafts. To my wife, Dinny, I have an obligation that is beyond words. Since 1985, she has moved five times—living on both coasts, in the Midwest, and in the South—and leaving friends, employment, and the comfort of a home to start anew. She has had to endure a one-year commuter marriage and several summers of separation and reading and correcting innumerable grant proposals and chapter drafts. I owe her a debt for which the dedication of this book is only a small repayment.

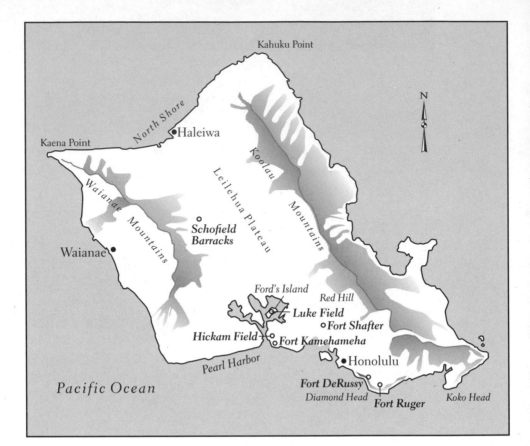

Oahu

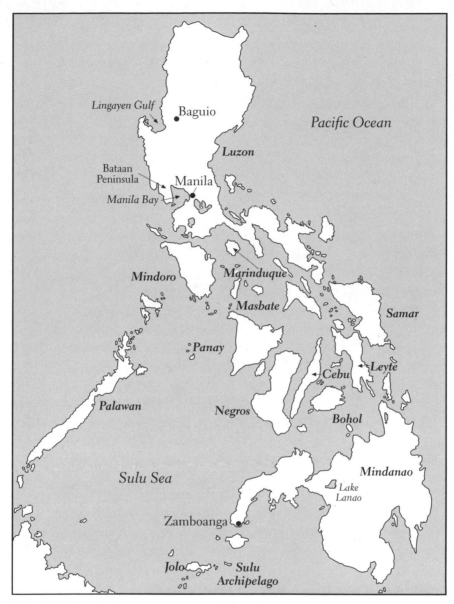

The Philippines

3

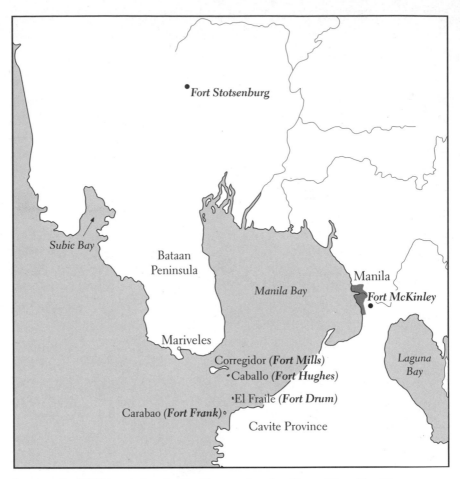

Luzon's Military Installations, Including Manila Bay Defenses

CHAPTER 1

The Guardians Arrive

The United States Army was a primary instrument in the acquisition of a Pacific empire in 1898, but its participation was hardly the result of careful planning. Indeed, prior to the dispatch of troops during the Spanish-American War, its officers had given virtually no thought to permanent service overseas. Because the War Department possessed neither a general staff nor a war college charged with determining policy, military personnel exchanged views on national security issues largely through the armed forces' journals. In contrast to the navy, which produced several advocates of American expansion into the Pacific, the army showed little interest. Officers might accept contemporary views of the need for foreign markets and overseas coaling stations, but they did not incorporate these goals into the mission of the U.S. Army. Their focus was on the transformation of the old Indian-fighting constabulary into a modern military force—a shift that required them to devote their attention to the militia, the integration of new weapons and tactics, professional education, strike duty, and the concentration of army units into larger posts. When the possibility of international conflict was discussed, their thinking was continental and they anticipated only a limited role for ground forces outside the nation's borders. The army's primary duty would still be the defense of the vulnerable Atlantic ports and harbors from raids and attacks. Neither tradition, nor military theory, nor its interpretation of its role under the Constitution prepared it for imperialist ventures; as Lieutenant George W. Van Deusen put it in 1894: "It is contrary to all the principles of our government to engage in foreign wars."[1]

Concerned with continental defense and internal reform, the army paid little attention to areas outside of the Americas and Europe. In 1875 General

William T. Sherman deplored the fact that "Asia . . . remains to us, in America, almost a sealed book, though we know that the reflux tide of civilization is setting back from Europe to those very lands."[2] Sherman was especially interested in the methods used by the European colonial powers to defend their distant frontiers. He dispatched Brevet Major General Emory Upton and two other officers to study the armies of the Far East. But in accordance with Upton's own preconceptions, the mission sped through the colonial and Asian military systems, devoting most of its attention to Germany and France. A more prescient study was Captain Arthur MacArthur's 1883 "Chinese Memorandum." Already something of an economic imperialist, MacArthur advocated overseas expansion: "we cannot attain our natural growth, or even exist as a commanding and progressive nationality, unless we secure and maintain the soverignty [sic] of the Pacific."[3] MacArthur's views attracted no attention at the time; they were pigeonholed in the War Department, where they remained unread for almost a century.

Much of the army's complacency about the Pacific may be explained by the absence of discernible threat. The incomplete harbor defenses on the West Coast caused some concern, but even their critics recognized that they were sufficient against any thrust from the Americas. Moreover, it was unlikely that Great Britain, the only opponent capable of attacking from the Pacific, would concentrate its resources in such a remote theater. Japan, which by 1907 would emerge as the primary danger, was then admired as a plucky nation pursuing the "civilized" ways of the West. Naval officers and such civilian expansionists as Theodore Roosevelt might foresee conflict, but there is little indication that the army shared their concern.[4]

The only Pacific area that attracted army interest was Hawaii, and here its attention was peripheral at best. The islands were occasionally visited by troop transports on the California route, and some Hawaiian-born soldiers fought in the Civil War; there was little else. The first War Department study did not occur till 1873, when Major General John M. Schofield and Lieutenant Colonel Burton S. Alexander inspected Hawaii's harbors, fortifications, and military resources. Schofield concluded that Pearl Harbor's value to the United States and world commerce was "too manifest to require discussion. It is the key to the Central Pacific Ocean, it is the gem of these islands, valueless to them because they cannot use it, but more valuable to the United States than all else the islands have to give." In any conflict with a "powerful maritime nation"—specifically Great Britain—Hawaii could serve either as a base for an attack on the United States or as a bastion to protect it. Annexation was premature, but that in a few years it would be relatively easy: "When that time comes, it will so far as can now be foreseen, depend only upon the United

States to decide the question of annexation; the voice here will be decidedly in favor of it, unless some new cause arises to change the current of opinion."[5] Like Schofield, Alexander stressed nonintervention, "I feel sure that the Department would not suppose for a moment that I would presume, or wish, to inaugurate any scheme looking to the annexation of these Islands to the United States."[6]

Not even Hawaii's political upheavals or the growing clamor from expansionists created much response within the army. It was sheer coincidence that in 1893, the year a coup overthrew the Hawaiian monarchy and established a republican government committed to annexation, the War Department's newly created Military Information Division (MID) published *The Hawaiian Islands*. This thirty-four-page pamphlet, the first in an MID series on areas of strategic interest to the nation, examined Hawaii's political situation, communications, geography, climate, population, economy, and social structure. It noted that the military defenses of the Hawaiian Republic were negligible and that its armed forces consisted of little more than sixteen soldiers assigned to guard the deposed queen. Moreover, the Hawaiians were now in decline and "except politically as the one-time owners of the islands, the natives are but an unimportant element of the people and their consent or opposition could have but little influence upon the course of events. They are a peace-loving race, and, in a military sense, are not worth consideration, but they are brave individually. . . . Little resistance could be anticipated from them even in defense of their country."[7] In this ethnocentric dismissal of native rights and capabilities, the MID study probably reflected the biases of the majority of U.S. Army officers in 1893. But beyond noting the Hawaiian Islands' military weakness and accurately predicting that an invader would encounter ineffectual opposition, the report made no argument for annexation.

The pamphlet was briefly reviewed in two service journals, one of which remarked that it would be invaluable to a commanding general should the United States ever invade "the land of the Kanaka." Too much should not be made of this statement, for the main point of both reviews was that thanks to the MID project the army would soon have comparable information about "every country with which we are liable, at any time, to be brought into conflict, in the extension and protection of our rapidly growing foreign commerce."[8] The Cleveland administration's decision to withdraw the treaty to annex Hawaii virtually ended discussion both in the army's official correspondence and in the military periodicals, which provided an unofficial source of communication.

Not until 1898, following President William McKinley's resubmission of the annexation treaty, did tangible evidence of army interest in the Hawaiian

Islands appear. By that time General Schofield had become convinced that the islands were not only "essential military and naval outposts" but that they could legally be assimilated under the existing territorial system. Believing the indigenous population unprepared to fulfill the obligations of citizens, Schofield suggested the nation follow the precedent of Reconstruction and make the army responsible for governance.[9] An article by Lieutenant S. L. Slocum pushed the case for annexation in terms to make any jingo rejoice: national expansion was necessary both for economic survival and because the "spirit of unrest and ceaseless energy . . . [which] have ever characterized the Anglo-Saxon race, pervade this country now and clamor for expansion and more intimate relations with the outer world."[10] Not only did military and economic self-interest justify immediate annexation, there was a moral obligation to those Americans in Hawaii. But in an article immediately preceding Slocum's, Lieutenant J. H. Reeves disclaimed any interest in annexation, insisting he wrote on Hawaii only to provide information to military men concerned with the major issues of the day.[11]

The army's cautious approach to Pacific matters was overtaken by Commodore George Dewey's victory at Manila Bay on 1 May 1898. Uncertain as to Dewey's situation, the War Department hurried troops to relieve him and seize Manila. The department's initial plan called for a small 5,000-man expedition to capture and occupy the weakly defended capital, but this was challenged almost immediately by the expedition's commander, Major General Wesley Merritt, who believed he must be strong enough not only to capture Manila but to occupy the entire archipelago. President William McKinley refused to commit himself to either position, but the War Department increased the expedition's authorized strength to 15,000. The first soldiers of Merritt's newly designated 8th Army Corps left San Francisco for Manila on 25 May, to be followed by two additional contingents, a total of some 11,000 officers and men. Although efficiently organized and rapidly embarked, the troops sailed away with only a vague idea of what they were supposed to accomplish.[12]

Dewey's triumph and the dispatch of supporting forces refocused attention on Hawaii. McKinley's annexation treaty was still languishing in the Senate when the Spanish-American War began. Although officially neutral, the young Hawaiian Republic immediately offered its facilities, and lavishly entertained the 8th Corps' soldiers on their way to the Philippines. In Washington, a joint resolution to annex the islands was introduced on 4 May. In the ensuing debate, annexationists repeated their standard contention that Hawaii was essential to the defense of the West Coast, and added a significant new one: that it was necessary for the successful prosecution of military operations in the Philippines. Both arguments were of dubious validity, but the desire to succor Dewey contributed greatly to both houses' ratification by 7 August. On 12 August the Hawaiian Islands formally became part of the United States, and four days later a small garrison—the 1st New York Volunteer Infantry Regiment and a battalion of the 2nd U.S. Volunteer Engineers— arrived in Honolulu. After an enthusiastic reception, the soldiers marched to the newly established Camp McKinley at the foot of Diamond Head and set up tents and shanties. The "somewhat disorderly" New Yorkers soon began an "incessant growling" that they had been abandoned by the army without sufficient money, food, or shelter, and that hundreds were sick.[13] Together with soldiers en route to the Philippines, they raided local gardens, bilked merchants, and harassed the army's provost guards. More serious were a number of attacks on local Chinese, which prompted a strong protest from the Chinese consul and an army investigation.[14] Following Spain's request for an armistice in August, the 1st New York withdrew, leaving only a small force of engineers, to be joined in June 1899 by four batteries of the 6th Artillery.

Despite isolated incidents of fraud and violence, relations between the army and the Hawaiian population were quite good. Local entertainers greeted troop transports, and the newly formed Hawaiian Red Cross assisted soldiers during their stay. There was little civil-military tension, in part because the appointment of the republic's former president, Sanford B. Dole, as the new territorial governor insured a smooth transition of power and obviated any need for military interference. The most serious test faced by the soldiers occurred in January 1900, when bubonic plague broke out in the Chinatown section of Honolulu. At the request of the Board of Health, Major Samuel M. Mills took over the supervision of the area next to Camp McKinley and stationed troops at the mountain passes to prevent entry to the city. On 20 January a fire set by officials to clear a plague-infested area spread through Chinatown, destroying 4,000 homes and sending thousands of quarantined inhabitants into hitherto safe areas. Upon the urgent plea of Governor Dole, who feared riots and looting, Mills deployed his small force of artillerymen until the end of the crisis. The entire incident was of importance only in that it set the tone for later civil-military relations in Hawaii. Mills sought both to cooperate fully and to avoid any appearance of interference in civilian concerns. For their part, civil officials had no hesitation in requesting military assistance. Shortly afterward, this cooperation was formalized when an army surgeon was appointed to a committee on bubonic plague.[15]

In contrast to the enthusiastic "aloha" they had received in Hawaii, American soldiers were greeted with suspicion when they arrived in the Philippines at the end of June. Almost a month earlier, Filipino nationalists and local political leaders had overthrown Spanish control in the countryside and bottled up most of the Spanish forces in Manila. Emilio Aguinaldo, exiled for his leadership in an earlier revolt, had been returned to the islands on one of Dewey's dispatch boats; and on 24 May he had declared himself dictator of an independent Philippine government, which he hoped would be recognized by the United States. The arrival of the first contingent of the 8th Corps aborted his plans to take the capital free of outside aid. Although he cooperated with the Americans, Aguinaldo could not help but notice their reluctance to confirm either his 12 June declaration of independence or his assumption of the presidency of a new national government. As for Merritt, his instructions gave him complete political authority in the islands; but perhaps recognizing the discrepancy between his theoretical and his practical powers, he neglected to publicize those instructions or to establish formal relations with the Filipino rebels until Manila had been taken. Once in possession of the city he could deal with Aguinaldo from a position both of military and political strength.

The capture of Manila did not simplify the situation, for the American victory was duplicitous at best. Terrified that Aguinaldo's irregulars might avenge themselves on their former masters, the Spanish commander negotiated an informal agreement with Dewey: after a token battle to satisfy honor, the Spanish would surrender to the Americans, who agreed to protect them from Filipino vengeance. In the ensuing Battle of Manila, on 13 August, Merritt's forces secured the city; then, under the muzzles of American rifles, the Filipino troops resumed their positions in the trenches, and an uneasy truce followed which neither side cared to violate. Aguinaldo busied himself consolidating his position and overcoming internal resistance, hoping Congress would reject the treaty with Spain and, with it, the United States's claim to the Philippines. McKinley was persuaded that abandoning the islands would result in internecine war and draw the imperialist powers into a potentially explosive struggle. Optimistic reports from the 8th Corps's new commander, Major General Elwell S. Otis, led him to believe that many Filipinos distrusted Aguinaldo and needed only the assurance of American goodwill to shift their allegiance. The president thus urged patience and delay, while at the same time outlining a policy of "benevolent assimilation," which called on the army to act as a force for law, order, and reform. Motivated partly by the president's orders, partly by concern for its soldiers' health, and partly by a reforming urge to convey the benefits of American rule to the Filipinos, the army began a thorough renovation of Manila. It inspected slaughterhouses, reorganized refuse collection, established new medical services, and reopened schools.[16]

The five months of uneasy truce ended on 4 February 1899, when a minor altercation between patrols touched off widespread fighting. The 8th Corps swept into the Filipino trenches, mauling its opponents, and soon captured the Republican capital at Malolos, some twenty-five miles northwest of Manila. Still intent on demonstrating the legitimacy of its government, at first the Republican Army employed conventional European tactics. But despite the individual courage of its soldiers, it never overcame the handicap of outmoded weaponry, poor leadership, and personal and sectional rivalries. What saved Aguinaldo was the weakness of the Americans, who lacked both the manpower and the logistical base strong enough to sustain their offensives. Campaigns quickly assumed a numbing similarity: Otis would dispatch a column, which would soon find the Filipinos dug in across a rice paddy or river crossing. The soldiers would deploy and attack; the Filipinos would withdraw. After regrouping and resting, the column would then push on, only to encounter another entrenchment a few miles up the road. After a few days the cumulative effects of fever, lack of water, and heat exhaustion would force the column, still undefeated but no longer capable of offensive operations, to turn back. As one veteran noted, these sweeps through the countryside were "like passing a finger through water"; after the troops were gone, Aguinaldo's soldiers returned to the old battlefields, rebuilt their trenches, and punished those who had collaborated with the invaders.[17] By the time the summer monsoons arrived to shut down active operations, the 8th Corps—some of its regiments reduced by 60 percent from disease and fatigue—had achieved little more than a standoff. These early campaigns demonstrated that U.S. authority could be imposed only where territory was permanently held, and this, in turn, implied the conquest and occupation of the entire archipelago.

A substantial number of the Americans who fought in the first six months of the Philippine War were volunteers who had enlisted for the duration of the Spanish-American War. With the ratification of the Peace of Paris in April 1899, their military obligations expired, and they demanded their immediate discharge. By then it had become clear that America's newly won empire entailed considerable expense: not only the Philippines but Cuba needed additional troops for occupation duties. The Army Act of 2 March 1899 increased the Regular Army to 60,000 men and added a temporary force of 35,000 U.S. Volunteers specifically for service in the Philippines. The act's manpower provisions were to expire in July 1901, for Congress assumed that by then everything would be in order and the U.S. Army could be reduced to its 1898 level of 28,000. These newly raised Regulars and Volunteers began to arrive in Manila in September 1899 and were deployed almost immediately. Despite Otis's fussy demeanor, he had considerable strategic ability, as his northern offensive demonstrated. Major General Arthur MacArthur's division was to drive the main Filipino army back up the Central Luzon Plain toward Lingayen Gulf; meanwhile, cavalry would swing around Aguinaldo's left flank, blocking his retreat into the hills, and a joint army-navy expedition would land two infantry regiments at Lingayen Gulf, sealing off escape routes into the mountains of northern Luzon. The operation was nearly a complete success: within a few weeks Aguinaldo's army evaporated, but the determined Filipino president eluded his pursuers and remained a symbol of continued resistance.

With Aguinaldo's army destroyed, U.S. forces turned south and by the end of February 1900 virtually every important town in the archipelago lay under the U.S. flag. Yet even as the Americans tasted victory, the Philippine War entered a new phase. On 13 November 1899, with his conventional forces collapsing, Aguinaldo had proclaimed that resistance would continue as guerrilla warfare. He divided the Philippines into military districts under regional commanders and outlined a strategy for protracted war. The *insurrectos*, as they were soon termed by the troops, would no longer engage the U.S. Army in direct combat. Instead, they would prevent the Americans from governing the Filipino people. Accordingly, through appeals to patriotism—as well as intimidation and terrorism—they discouraged collaboration, and obtained money, food, recruits, and information. At the same time, they struck at isolated U.S. patrols, ambushed ration wagons, fired into troops' quarters, and, mission accomplished, reverted to "amigos," strong in loyalty to the new colonial masters. Rather than win victory, the Filipino nationalists hoped to wear down the occupation forces, frustrate benevolent assimilation, and so demoralize the American people that they would vote for the antiannexationist William Jennings Bryan in the 1900 election.

From the perspective of the senior officers in Manila, the war had ended with the collapse of the Republican Army. Reflecting the common belief that "if we give the natives peace and prosperity, they will be content; and opposition will cease"; the army would establish justice, administrative efficiency, and economic stability.[18] General Otis therefore reorganized his tactical units into geographic districts; he broke up his brigades into battalions and companies and stationed them in hundreds of towns throughout the islands. Their primary task was to restore order in the countryside and prepare the Filipinos for their new role as U.S. subjects. Not only would the army return to its historic mission of chasing down hostiles on the frontier, but in addition— through the establishment of efficient civil administration, through the formation of cooperative town governments and police forces, through the construction of roads and schools, and through the encouragement of local industry and trade—it would secure the allegiance of the population. The commanding general of the Division of the Philippines was also the military governor, and a similar integration of civil and military duties flowed down throughout the occupation forces. Colonels and majors ruled provinces, and an individual company commander might serve also as customs collector, auditor, sanitary inspector, judge, police chief, school superintendent, and mayor. MacArthur, who succeeded Otis in May, maintained his predecessor's emphasis on restoring law and order to the countryside.

By February 1900, military operations had degenerated into an endless series of ambushes, desultory volleys at distant opponents, skirmishes, and, very occasionally, desperate close-in fighting. Tactically, the army adapted well to these challenges: with the exception of a few defeats—the surrender of a company on Marinduque Island, the bloody skirmishes at Mabitac, Catubig, and Cusucus Canyon, the massacre at Balangiga—the army repeatedly overcame the *insurrectos*. The practical field training given Regulars and Volunteers, the open-order formations adopted in 1891, and the excellent Krag-Jorgenson rifle proved effective against poorly armed and untrained opponents. The guerrillas' ambushes and hit-and-run attacks were frustrating, but soldiers soon learned to avoid spike-lined pits and mantraps, to surround and search villages and barrios, to operate in the jungles and mountains, to station strong point and flank units on patrols, and to "comb the bamboo" with volleys. Transported by a diverse collection of steam vessels and native canoes, they became adept at amphibious raids. Coastal garrisons coordinated defense with patrolling gunboats, and several guerrilla attacks were shattered by a torrent of rifle and cannon fire from ship and shore. Cavalry and mounted infantry scoured the countryside, gathering intelligence, raiding guerrilla hideouts, and relieving beleaguered garrisons. Filipino collaborators, some of them former partisans, accompanied army patrols, uncovering camps, confiscating food and supplies, identifying tax collectors and spies, and sometimes fighting as auxiliaries. As post commanders purged the insurgent logistical network in the villages and as patrols cordoned off the population, the guerrillas were slowly driven into the "boondocks," denied food and shelter, hunted alike by Filipinos and Americans, and ultimately forced to surrender.[19]

By the end of 1900, the progress in regional pacification and the reelection of McKinley had shifted the momentum to the Americans. MacArthur issued the internationally accepted Civil War regulations, General Orders 100, which authorized deportation, imprisonment, and land confiscation to punish guerrillas and their supporters. American patrols, often assisted by Filipino militia, pressed into the countryside with new aggressiveness, destroying enemy food caches and camps. MacArthur also ordered increased attention to the destruction of the civilian infrastructure in the towns that supplied the guerrillas with food, information, and shelter. As a price for their own freedom, captured guerrillas were forced to cooperate with the authorities: serving with the colonial government, leading local auxiliaries, negotiating the surrender of their former comrades. A daring raid captured Aguinaldo in March 1901. His highly publicized capitulation to American authority made collaboration respectable and inspired several of his lieutenants to surrender. As more and more provinces were declared pacified and turned over to the civilian Philippine Commission and its enforcement arm, the Philippine Constabulary, more soldiers were freed for active operations in the last remaining centers of resistance: the southwestern Luzon provinces of Batangas, Laguna, and Tayabas and the Visayan island of Samar.

Unfortunately, these final pacification campaigns were characterized by an unusual degree of ferocity. In both areas, the guerrillas pursued a strategy of protracted war, seeking less to control territory than to disrupt the imposition of American authority; they were willing and able to continue the conflict for years. In southwestern Luzon the active participation of the provincial elite in the guerrilla movement gave it a cohesion and level of popular support that was lacking in most of the archipelago. On Samar, the island's jungles, mountains, swamps, and hellish climate frustrated U.S. attempts to close with the enemy. The butchery of a U.S. infantry company at Balangiga, Samar, on 28 September 1901, not only brought home the strength of the Filipino resistance in these two areas, it also provided officers with justification to enact harsher methods than had previously been tolerated. In southwestern Luzon, Brigadier General J. Franklin Bell relocated much of the population into "protected zones" and made the principal citizens responsible for any acts of resistance in their areas. Although successful in severing the guerrillas' ties to the population, Bell's tactics seemed all too similar to those pursued by the Spanish in Cuba, and were blamed for creating epidemics and famine. On Samar, the incompetent and unstable Brigadier General Jacob H. Smith openly sanctioned retaliatory policies. He reportedly told one subordinate to "kill and burn" and that he wanted the interior of the island turned into a "howling wilderness." The severe, and atypical, campaigns in Samar and southwestern Luzon dragged on until mid-1902, prolonging the war by almost a year.[20]

The U.S. Army's achievement in the Philippine War should not be underestimated. It had fought resourcefully in exotic terrain against unconventional and sometimes barbarous tactics. Its success was all the more notable because it was achieved by an army without a formal counterinsurgency doctrine and

with no experience in Asian guerrilla warfare. Although there were commanders who cited both Indian and European colonial warfare in advocacy of
specific measures, most junior officers, on whom the brunt of the decisions
and adaptations fell, relied on their own grasp of shifting, sometimes evanes-
cent, military objectives, on their hard-won knowledge of local conditions and
practices, and, above all, on their native ingenuity and their sense of decency,
in order to bring peace and accord to their area of operations.[21]

The imperial wars of 1898 to 1902 transformed the U.S. Army. Between 1899
and 1902 the Philippine War alone required some 125,000 Regular and Volunteer soldiers—necessitating an almost threefold expansion of the small and
self-contained Regular Army and drastically altering its composition. Some
officers rose to the challenge, but many a grizzled veteran of the "Old Army,"
already weakened by the ravages of Cuba, proved incapable of adjusting to the
demands of war. William T. Sexton's description of Major General Loyd
Wheaton—"twenty-five years as a company commander had left him, mentally at least, a company officer"—could have been applied to many another
senior commander.[22] But the uneven performance of the upper command,
mired in decades of routine as junior officers, was not as disastrous as might be
expected. The Philippine War, perhaps more than any other, was a war of
company officers. It was the garrison commander who served as the most
tangible representative of American authority to the peasant; as one veteran
observed, "it is a fact that the disposition of nearly every town in the archipelago depends upon the officer or officers who have been commanding in
that town."[23] For the competent, the war offered fast promotion and recognition. Relatively junior officers who might otherwise have toiled for decades of
service as lieutenants and captains found themselves advanced to majors or
colonels or even generals. Having enjoyed battalion and regimental command at a comparatively early age, they had a far greater appreciation both of
their own capabilities and of their superiors' limitations. But the isolation and
the early assumption of responsibility that afforded so much opportunity were
also a threat to discipline. Both civil duties and small-unit combat required
initiative and pragmatism, and encouraged officers to act first and request
approval afterward. As might be expected, they often found themselves at odds
with the high command, to whom Major John H. Parker contemptuously
referred as fighting the war in "white suits and collars."[24] The strains and
animosities among officers created by service in the Philippines would con-
tribute greatly to factionalism and divisions within the new imperial army.

The war also harrowed the enlisted ranks. The Old Army Regular had been
a long-service soldier who found both a job and a permanent home in the
ranks. When James C. Barr joined the 4th Cavalry in 1898 he was treated as a

curiosity—the man he displaced as most junior had sixteen years of service.[25] The Volunteers and Regulars who enlisted for service in the Philippines were not only younger, they were self-sufficient, innovative, and intelligent as well. Colonel Robert L. Bullard remembered that in his regiment there were men who could build a waterworks, operate a telegraph, navigate a steamer, and administer the law.[26] Predictably, these new soldiers were impatient with paperwork and routine; they were quick to assert their independence, and rather too casual with army traditions. In the prewar army, a recruit would have been paired off with a veteran comrade to teach him the ropes; but by war's end, "the veteran soldier, wearing from four to six chevrons on his arm, each representing a term of enlistment, [was] so rare as to exert little influence upon the mass of new men."[27] For Old Army veterans, the sloppy drill and casual attitude of the new soldiers were intolerable. From Manila an officer huffed that to restore the army "requires heroic measures, and I hope the senior officers in the Philippines will give the subject of army discipline careful and constant consideration."[28]

Much of the army's demoralization was physical, for there is some merit to historian William Ganoe's hyperbole: "probably in the Philippine War more than any other in history did the military man shorten his life, if he survived at all."[29] In some respects it was one of the least costly the army ever fought: between 4 February 1899 and 4 July 1902, only 1,004 officers and enlisted men died in combat, 2,911 were wounded, and a total of 4,165 died of all causes.[30] But empire building exacted other tolls: in 1900, 416 of the 766 officers on the retired list had been placed there due to disabilities incurred in the line of service. Many of those who remained were barely fit for duty: Bradford G. Chynoweth's father, an officer in the 17th Infantry, left for Cuba "a stalwart. He returned a mere skeleton, riddled with malaria."[31] Sent to the Philippines less than a year later, he contracted the amoebic dysentery that killed him in 1909. Constant alerts, night patrols, heat, rain, fatigue, disease, and rugged terrain contributed to physical collapse; homesickness, frustration, and similar stress bred severe cases of psychological depression, euphemistically termed "nostalgia." Commanding officers learned they had to juggle the benefits of aggressive operations against their costs. One general, criticized for not keeping more of his soldiers in the field, responded that every time he kept his troops in the field for more than a few days, the "sick reports go up alarmingly, averaging over fifty percent, and a considerable proportion of this number are permanently incapacitated from further duty. I am forced to keep this fact prominent in all my operations in this section."[32]

After all these physical hardships, veterans had to endure vilification by domestic critics who charged the army with fighting an immoral war of conquest—and in a brutal and savage manner. There is no doubt that the American conquest of the Philippines was, as the French would later term such conflicts, a "dirty war" in which both sides inflicted atrocities upon each other and upon the helpless Filipino civilians. It should be noted, however, that many of the actions that outraged the war's opponents both then and now— the burning of houses and crops, the relocation of civilians, the taking of hostages, and the killing of "treacherous" guides—were procedures sanctioned by past practice and contemporary international law.[33] Far more serious were the charges of torture and summary executions that appeared in the antiimperialist press early in the war and reached a crescendo in 1902. American soldiers were reported to have made widespread use of the "water cure," in which water was forced down the victim's throat until he gave the required information. But despite the popular view, the available evidence suggests that torture was not common among line soldiers; it was largely the work of intelligence and reconnaissance units. Nevertheless, reports of such atrocities reinforced highly colored accounts of the Batangas and Samar campaigns and led many Americans, both then and now, to conclude that army conduct toward Filipinos had been uniformly brutal and atrocious.

To some soldiers, all such allegations were unjust and unfair. Lieutenant Charles G. Clifton listed the guerrillas' "inhuman tricks" with which he was personally acquainted—thrusting a sharpened stake through a captured soldier's tongue, for example—and wondered whether, if such treatment were applied to those censuring the army, "would they go around on the street corners or sit in their homes making remarks about us and [say] that we were abusing the little brown people?"[34] Speaking in the antiimperialist stronghold of Boston, General J. Franklin Bell produced an old woodcut of colonists forcing tea down the throat of a British tax collector and asked "who would believe that the water cure originated in Boston?"[35] The War Department's official explanation was that individual soldiers may have committed outrages but the overall behavior of the troops, especially given the illegal and uncivilized practices of their opponents, had been humane and restrained. Veterans pointed out, with cynical insight, that soldiers treated Filipinos no worse than they had treated their fellow Americans during the Civil War or than police currently treated criminals.[36]

Behind this outward show of defiance, the complicity of their colleagues in torture and murder divided the officer corps and left many disenchanted with imperial pacification. Major Edwin F. Glenn, who was court-martialed twice for war crimes, reflected bitterly: "I have but one regret through it all which is that our responsible commanders who were in a position to do so did not protect us in doing that which they sent us to do and which in fact they showed great anxiety that we should do in order that credit might come to them."[37] Others drew a different lesson. An anonymous correspondent protested that soldiers "fail to see that both our honor and our interest dictate that our treatment of the Filipinos must be strictly just and enlightened. I have been surprised to hear so many say, 'kill them off.' "[38] Major Cornelius Gardener wrote to the Philippine Commission complaining that troops were committing numerous inhumane and criminal actions and Lieutenant General Nelson A. Miles compiled a list of alleged war criminals and demanded they be punished.[39] Colonel Arthur Murray, who believed that the Filipinos "as a rule were treated with far more kindness and consideration than they deserved," believed that the actions of a few officers such as Glenn had provided the antiimperialists "with an admirable opportunity to throw mud at the army."[40] Luke Wright, a Civil War veteran now serving on the Philippine Commission, voiced similar sentiments. His own observations led him to conclude that throughout the Philippine War "the army and men of our army have generally conducted this war in a very humane manner." But he anticipated that all soldiers would be judged by a few cases of misbehavior: "The effect of grouping together a number of isolated instances of wrong-doing will be to produce in the public mind at home a very erroneous impression as to the manner in which military operations have been conducted in these islands and also do harm here by inflaming the minds of the natives themselves."[41] Wright's prediction proved correct: lurid accounts of the "howling wilderness" and "water cure" have dominated subsequent accounts of the Philippine War.

The army was also angered at the treatment accorded to it by political leaders in both the United States and the Philippines. In August 1898 McKinley had given the commander of ground forces in the archipelago full executive, legislative, and judicial authority, but almost immediately the War Department began preparing for the transition from military to civil rule. In June 1900 the Philippine Commission arrived, headed by governor-designate Taft, eager to turn the Philippines into a model of enlightened colonialism and the Filipinos into enthusiastic, patriotic little brown brothers. Instead they found a frustrating and apparently interminable guerrilla war, and a hostile and suspicious military governor, Arthur MacArthur. Some of the stress that characterized civil-military relations for the next few years may have been inevitable, but much of the acrimony reflected a clash between two egotists. The pontifical MacArthur alternated between lecturing and snubbing the commissioners. Taft's jovial exterior masked a political in-fighter who cultivated his own group of disaffected officers and continually undermined the general's authority in Washington. Beneath the personal animosity lay important philosophical differences as well. According to Taft, the majority of Filipinos were not hostile to the United States, and "but for the terrorism of the insurgents in arms, and the ladrones [brigands], they would be entirely willing to welcome American civil government." MacArthur, in turn, viewed "his task as one of conquering eight millions of recalcitrant, treacherous, and sullen people," and he confessed to "very little hope that the establishment of civil authority as distinguished from the strong hand of the military [would] do any good."[42] Convinced that MacArthur was delaying the transfer of pacified provinces to civilian control, Taft relied more and more on direct personal appeals to the secretary of war and the president. He masterminded MacArthur's recall in mid-1901, thereby sending a none too subtle message to future commanders that Washington would uphold civil over military authority in the colonies.[43]

At the core of this personal struggle lay the central issue: who was ultimately responsible for law, order, and government? Clearly the army must be in control so long as active military operations continued. However, once a province had been declared pacified and turned over to the Philippine Commission, responsibility devolved on the government, which had its own paramilitary colonial police, the Philippine Constabulary. This force had been created in July 1901; under Henry T. Allen, a Regular cavalry captain detached to the civil government, it mustered 2,000 men by January 1902. Although it was a boon to the overextended army, enabling Major General Adna R. Chaffee to vacate over a hundred posts and concentrate on the remaining recalcitrant provinces, it was also a source of friction, for, as one veteran remembered, "the army did not take the Constabulary very seriously in those days."[44] Predictably, matters worsened when both organizations served in the same province. The Constabulary was poorly armed and ill-drilled and its officers, many of them ex-Volunteers and former noncommissioned officers in the Regulars, were inferior in status and training to those of the Regular Army. Chief Allen did little to soothe relations; he sought to expand the Constabulary's prerogatives and responsibilities, often at the expense of the army. A final point of contention was the Constabulary's relation to the army's Native Scouts. The Filipinos in the Scouts had been invaluable during the war for their fieldcraft, their command of dialects, and their knowledge of local conditions. But now, with pacification so far advanced, should not these skills be placed at the service of the organization charged with maintaining internal peace? The Constabulary's efforts to incorporate all Filipino forces within its ranks precluded any real possibility of forming a Fil-American colonial army, and thus became a major source of civil-military tension.

The acquisition of a Pacific empire was thus a traumatic and perplexing experience, and those who analyzed it were cautious in their conclusions. On the one hand, the army had fought exceptionally well, overcoming a stubborn and courageous enemy with an efficiency that later efforts would render all the more impressive. But the satisfaction of the victory had been marred by antiimperialist attacks, civil-military disputes, and terrible physical stress, especially on the members of the Old Army. In some, McKinley's message of "benevolent assimilation" created a sense of mission, almost a crusading spirit. Veterans' letters and reports show great personal and professional satisfaction in bringing education, sanitation, law, and free trade to the Filipinos. Even officers who seriously doubted the ability of the inhabitants to benefit from these improvements nevertheless threw themselves into the task of building schools, encouraging agriculture, building roads and bridges, and reducing disease. Far from being antiexpansionist, some soldiers and civilians envisioned a new role for the army as a great civilizing institution in the colonies. A 1903 editorial "The American Army" in the popular journal *Outlook* proudly commented that whereas other armies trained for war, America's army "was inspired with the spirit of construction." Henceforth its mission was to act as the agent of progress in "destroying the barbarisms which ought to be destroyed, but no less in building on the ground, when cleared from the ruins of the past, the foundations of a new and better civilization."[45] Some, citing biblical text or social Darwinism, believed that the forcible acquisition of a new empire was the working out of Divine Will or scientific law. Others declared that the new empire allowed the nation to "fulfill our duty as a Great Power."[46]

Perhaps the most coherent and integrated argument for a Pacific empire was advanced by MacArthur in his testimony before the Senate Committee on the Philippines in 1902. Blending appeals to the pocketbook with national destiny, MacArthur presented an almost messianic vision of empire. The United States, like all great nations, was destined to expand, and "our permanent occupation [of the Philippines] was simply one of the necessary consequences of our great prosperity." Nevertheless, America's continued progress was endangered; only by free trade with the untouched and unlimited Asian market could it survive. Mere pecuniary concerns alone did not explain America's role in the islands. The Filipinos were the "chosen people," who would, after a suitable period of tuition, act as missionaries for American ideals, commerce, and republican institutions to the rest of the Far East. Finally, the Philippine Islands' "strategical position is unexcelled by that of any other position in the world." Their possession would protect United States interests and provide "a commanding position" against any Far Eastern enemy. Best of all, MacArthur was convinced their defense could be accomplished "with the least output of physical power" on the part of the United

States.[47] MacArthur's views—when expanded to include other Pacific territories—struck all of the principal themes that imperialist officers would continue to echo: overseas colonies were necessary to insure American economic, strategic, and political interests in the Pacific Rim; the United States had an obligation to improve the condition of the inhabitants; Pacific possessions were of vital strategic importance; and the Pacific territories could be protected with small expenditure of American blood and capital.

There were dissenters. Glenn believed that "many people intimate that we made a mistake in assuming control of the Philippine Islands and other foreign territory; this may be a fact, but that we have them is also a fact and we cannot let them go."[48] But Major John H. Parker, in a 1902 article in *Forum*, appropriately titled "What Shall We Do with the Philippines?" did provide a spirited and well-reasoned rebuttal to MacArthur's imperialism. The iconoclastic Parker, nicknamed "Gatling Gun," as much for his personality as for his advocacy of machine guns, asked a question that few officers were willing to consider: did the retention of the Philippines really accord with the national interest? To protect and maintain order there would cost the United States $67.5 million annually and require a permanent garrison of 45,000. Such sacrifice seemed excessive for possessions that did "not promise to be a source of national pride or aggrandizement even in time of peace." Not only did the Philippine Islands produce little of use to the United States, they had little strategic value, for their abandonment would in no way influence the United States's ability to maintain the "Open Door." Indeed, their possession was a positive threat to the nation's commercial and strategic interests, for by seizing territory in the western Pacific, the United States lost the moral right to enforce Monroe Doctrine on other imperialist powers seeking to expand into the Americas. Moreover, "in time of war the Philippines become a source of public danger and national weakness, absorbing our preparations and dividing our energies."[49] He concluded that the archipelago should be given to a European or Asian power and that the United States confine its interest to the Western Hemisphere. Although Parker's views would be refined and strengthened by later military writers, his 1902 article outlined what may be termed the basic arguments against the imperialist position: neither the nation's strategic nor economic interests were served by holding Far Eastern territory; the Philippines were fundamentally indefensible; the possession of the Philippines weakened the nation's diplomatic and military position and detracted from the defense of vital interests.

The development of two such detailed and attractive but mutually exclusive arguments might indicate how far the army had moved from its prewar focus on internal reform and continental defense. Now, swollen to three times the size of its prewar complement, it faced a new aggravation in an insular government both too weak to stand without military protection and too proud to admit its dependency. Other issues loomed equally large. How would it protect the overseas empire? How could the defense of the territories be integrated into its traditional duties? How best to balance overseas and continental defense? What type of military force was needed? What threats should this overseas force be designed to meet? These questions would dominate the early years of the army's experience in the Pacific.

CHAPTER 2

The Savage Wars of Peace

n 23 July 1902, a few weeks after President Theodore Roosevelt had formally proclaimed peace in the Philippines, the *Manila Times* addressed the misgivings of readers: "for years to come we must expect more or less disorder as a result of the war, but all general and recognized resistance has ended. . . . We have only a big job of policing on our hands."[1] A 23 August 1903 report from Lieutenant William E. W. McKinley showed that the job was big indeed. In that year alone, colonial military and police forces had suppressed an uprising on Cebu, brought an uneasy peace to Samar, and quelled outlawry on Misamis. Yet despite these achievements, from Northern Luzon to the tip of the Sulu archipelago the islands were still torn by strife; no sooner had the troops temporarily put down one outbreak than another flared up. And although the brunt of the pacification work fell to the civil government's police, the danger of a general insurrection kept the army constantly on the alert, as recalcitrant political, religious, and ethnic rebels continuously threatened the territory's peace. In the decade-long campaigns against bandits, sects, and Moros, the army would gain further experience in small wars, test the boundaries of civil-military relations, and create a Fil-American colonial army.[2]

Unfamiliar with the dynamics of Philippine politics or folk culture, Americans sought analogies to explain the continued resistance. The editor of the *Manila Times* dismissed all factions as "piping, puling, insignificant left-overs of the insurrection."[3] Philippine Governor William H. Taft looked to the Reconstruction, when former Confederates had "professed to be continuing the rebellion" by extortion and intimidation.[4] Others sought parallels with the experiences of other imperial powers: Archibald C. Coolidge noted that throughout Asia, Western invaders had overcome enemy governments—only to confront "half robbers, half patriots always apparently on the point of being suppressed or exterminated, [who] reappeared again and again to give the lie to official optimism and to weary public opinion at home."[5] Altogether too many attributed the source to an irrational and backward Asian society and a perverse and inferior people. Charles E. Woodruff, an army doctor, believed the Filipinos's physiognomy explained their penchant for crime and violence.[6] Leonard Wood blamed the continuing disturbances on the leaders of social protest, the "religious fakirs," who exploited the "poor Filipino of the country districts . . . [who is] tired of fighting revolutions, but being ignorant and very superstitious . . . is easily handled by religious leaders."[7] One prominent civil official, J. M. Sheriden, classified the dissidents into four groups: brigands, religious sects, pirates, and homicidal devotees of Islam—none of which represented legitimate political movements, but were lawless gangs whose very existence demonstrated the need for American control. Like many, Sheriden contrasted the common Filipinos—whom he denigrated as ignorant, emotional, and obedient—with the "shrewd outlaws" and religious charlatans who exploited these violent outbreaks.[8]

Racial prejudice aside, the very idealism and philanthropy of U.S. colonialism hindered any real understanding of Filipino opposition. Impelled by the progressive vision of order, homogeneity and scientific reform, colonial administrators set themselves to encourage trade, improve roads and communications, humanize and rationalize the archaic law codes, provide secular public education, and dispense health care. Firm in their commitment to Western science, civilization, and progress, they dismissed any opposition as further evidence of their charges' superstition, childishness, and irresponsibility. Such prejudices were reinforced by their Filipino colleagues, whose contempt for the common peasant, or *tao*, often exceeded even that of the Americans. The colonial administration and its supporters trod carelessly on hallowed social traditions and sought to overcome popular unrest by making criminals of all who opposed its supremacy. The Brigandage Act of 10 November 1902 and the Reconcentration Act of 1 June 1903, coupled with an almost threefold increase in the Philippine Constabulary to 7,500 members, demonstrated its determination to enforce its authority.[9]

The civil government's reluctance or inability to recognize the seriousness and depth of the disorder compounded the problem. Throughout the war, Taft had maintained that the islands were ready for civil government and accused the army of undue pessimism. As governor, he minimized reports of banditry and sect violence, stating in 1903 that "the suppression of this kind of disorder is necessarily the work of time; but it is evidently progressing as rapidly as can be expected."[10] Army and civil authorities agreed it was to their mutual interest to leave internal security—that is, pacification—to the colonial government. The U.S. Army, under the leadership of Secretary of War Elihu Root, was seeking to transform itself into a modern military organization. It resented the distractions of providing the government with intelligence, of detaching officers for administrative duties, and of supplying cadres for the Philippine Scouts. For their part, the insular authorities derived their legitimacy from the U.S. government's declaration that organized resistance had ended; to admit otherwise was to accept the possibility of a return to military rule. Accordingly, they misinterpreted and belittled the nature and severity of the opposition, and they compounded the deception by a quasi-legal appropriation of the Philippine Scouts, which by 1904 relegated half its strength to internal security duties.[11] Both Taft and his successor, Luke E. Wright, relied overmuch on Philippine Constabulary Chief Henry T. Allen's overoptimistic appraisal that malefactors were being "continually decimated."[12] The colonial government's perverse confidence led the bishop of Cebu in 1904 to complain to President Roosevelt that the Philippines were "in a state of war, though officially at peace."[13] Eventually, not even the most sanguine official could overlook the violence and lawlessness in the archipelago, and it fell once again to the military to impose American law and order on the provinces.

However much politicians and soldiers shared a desire to divorce the military from the civil, conditions in the Philippines required their constant integration. The United States had no trained corps of colonial civil servants and no institutional machinery to create one. With some exceptions—most notably teachers—educated Americans did not flock to the new territory to take up colonial service; and those who did arrive showed a marked preference for Manila. To govern the provinces the Philippine Commission was forced to rely on either the local elites who had led the resistance or the army officers who had subdued them. For several years after the end of the war, dozens of officers were detached from troop command to serve as provincial governors, treasurers, customs collectors, inspectors, auditors, and a host of other functionaries. Relatively junior officers might, by virtue of their civil status, outrank their military superiors. Even military personnel with no civil rank were deeply involved in civil affairs; soldiers built roads, schools, and marketplaces, and their wages constituted a vital part of many a town's economy. Further, the civil government was dependent on the army's intelligence service to supervise the mapping of the archipelago as well as for its excellent library on Asian and Pacific affairs.[14] Constant contact between civilian and military personnel exacerbated personal rivalries and deflected both agencies from major goals.

The first attempt to establish the Philippine army's status in civil disturbances appeared in General Orders 152 of 7 July 1902. This document declared a state of peace in the Philippines outside the Moro provinces, abolished the office of military governor, and turned responsibility for the enforcement of law and order over to civil officials and the Philippine Constabulary. But General Orders 152 also stated that "the military forces in the Division of the Philippines, shall be at all times subject, under the orders of the military commander, to the call of the civil authorities for maintenance of law and order, and the enforcement of their authority." Only a provincial governor or a higher official could request military support and then only to a brigade or department commander; the civil official's request had to be in writing, specify the service the troops were to perform, and acknowledge that the civil authorities were unable to cope with the situation. In all other cases, military personnel were forbidden to offer suggestions, to arrest lawbreakers, or to use their weapons "unless in response to an attack by fire-arms or assault by bolos [long knives] being made upon the troops."[15]

General Orders 152 left a number of legal issues unresolved, the most important of which were the rights and obligations of troops acting in civil disturbances. Brigadier General Tasker H. Bliss pointed out that most officers were "not fully acquainted with the niceties of the law and the legal relations of the military to the civil powers. Acting in good faith they may . . . perform an act which would be perfectly legal on the part of a member of the Constabulary, but which, committed by them, may cost them their liberty and even life."[16] Brigadier General William H. Carter described an incident in 1904 in which a Scout officer had sent a patrol out to recover the bodies of a massacred Constabulary detachment. Carter approved the lieutenant's action, but noted that it was in violation of General Orders 152, which restricted officers to informing the provincial governor that an attack had taken place.[17] The civil government took three-and-a-half years to clarify the issues; not until 18 December 1905 did its attorney general declare that troops maintaining law and order at the request of the civil authorities were accorded the status of peace officers and were therefore not liable for civil suits.

Neither General Orders 152 nor other legislation clarified whether soldiers were subject to constitutional and military law or to the Spanish-based Philippine law. This question became acute in 1905 as a result of two controversial legal cases. In the first, Major Frank Carrington, a Scout officer, was tried in a Philippine court without benefit of jury, found guilty of embezzling $1,500, and sentenced to forty years' imprisonment. Equally peculiar, under the vagaries of insular law, he retained his commission, pay, and benefits.[18] The second and more serious case inflamed civil-military relations for two years.

On 24 July 1904, Private Homer Grafton shot and killed two Filipinos who allegedly attacked him as he stood guard. Acquitted by court-martial, Grafton was tried again by a Philippine court and sentenced to twelve years' imprisonment. In 1907 the United States Supreme Court ruled that the court-martial had indeed been legal and set aside Grafton's later conviction. But the court did not rule on the far more important issue of whether soldiers overseas forfeited their rights as U.S. citizens. Although exulting in the acquittal, the *Army and Navy Journal* warned, "One of the simplest lessons of the Grafton case . . . is that there should be the broadest possible exercise of military authority by the Army in the Philippines. Every offender whose act falls within the scope of military jurisdiction should be tried by court-martial and never surrendered to a bastard civil tribunal like that which usurped the rights of Grafton."[19]

Not surprisingly, the institutional clashes occurred most often over the control of the troops most involved in pacification operations, the Philippine Scouts. To Governor Taft, "the political importance in the Islands of suppressing disturbances with native forces under civilian control" gave his office a proprietary right to all Filipino soldiers.[20] Aided by Chief Allen, Taft turned to congressional action, securing the passage of the "Act to Promote the Efficiency of the Philippine Constabulary" on 30 January 1903. This legislation left the army with the obligation to maintain, shelter, feed, clothe, transport, and pay Scout companies detached to the civil government, but turned their actual command in the field over to Regular Army officers assigned to the senior positions in the Constabulary. As one commanding general succinctly put it, this "in effect made the scout companies a reserve force of the Philippine Constabulary."[21] Within a few months, 60 percent of these companies were under civil control. In November 1905 the Department of Luzon's commander responded to the government's plea for reinforcements for the Visayas by pointing out that every one of his eighteen Scout companies had already been appropriated. Although they were supposed to be assigned for temporary duty, in June 1905 Allen admitted that he expected the "permanent assistance" of the Scouts.[22]

The split was most apparent in the long controversy over Scout battalions. Virtually all civil government tasks—antibanditry, quarantine, garrisoning, guarding prisoners—required that the Scouts be deployed as detachments in isolated little towns, often in the most primitive conditions. Both civil and military leaders urged that the Scouts be formed into four-company battalions, but for different reasons. The army envisioned the battalions as consolidated tactical units that would serve alongside the Regulars in conventional operations. By assigning its best captains to a tour of duty as majors in the Scouts, it could provide them with experience in large-unit command. In contrast, the civil government envisioned Scout battalions not as tactical, but as administrative units. Because a battalion was assigned extra officers, its companies could be broken up into even smaller detachments and its commanding officer could be appointed as supervisor to a Constabulary district. The hazards of satisfying these diverse expectations were illustrated by the case of battalion commander Major Robert W. Mearns, whose military superior ordered he bring his four companies to their "highest state of efficiency" but whose civil superiors insisted he deploy them across an area of 600 miles.[23] The word soon got out, and by 1905 the Philippines Division's commander noted that promising officers avoided battalion command because "they consider that, in all possibility, it means simply administrative work under the constabulary."[24]

By 1904 a curious situation existed in the Philippines. In one respect, the joint civil-military goal of removing the army from pacification duties had been achieved. Only in the Moro Province were American soldiers still clearly engaged in their historic mission of taming the frontier. Elsewhere, they were consolidating companies into battalions, building permanent barracks, and turning their attention toward training for modern warfare. But for one significant part of the army, the Philippine Scouts, conditions had become steadily worse. Armed with obsolete black-powder rifles and with scant drill in their use, scattered into dozens of little posts, constantly on the move against bandits and sectarians, the Scouts constituted little more than paramilitary police. Many companies, detached to civil service since the passage of the Constabulary Act, had not served with the army for two years. Indeed, one historian concludes that "by 1904, there was little difference between the Constabulary and the Scouts in regard to functions in the field."[25] Before a Fil-American colonial army could emerge, the civil government had to rely solely on the Constabulary and release the Scouts from service as auxiliaries. The most direct solution was to enforce colonial authority on any region that still opposed it, which in turn required the army once again to march to the boondocks and return to the task of pacification.

The army's resumption of counterinsurgency duty was in response to a particularly fierce outbreak of banditry and sect violence, which stretched the thin Constabulary and Scout forces to the breaking point. Indeed, by the end of 1904, it appeared that in some regions the civil government was struggling to maintain even a semblance of control. *Ladrones* (brigands) raided to the outskirts of Manila, imposed a reign of terror on Cavite Province, and proclaimed themselves the vanguard of a new army of independence. In the Visayas, sectarian rebels, known collectively as Pulahanes, gained a number of victories over outnumbered and poorly equipped government forces. To harried civil leaders, it seemed that no matter how many outlaws were killed or captured, there were dozens more to take their place. Within a year Taft conceded, "the time has come when the calls upon the Commanding General for the use of the Army for the suppression of disturbances should be made more frequently and with less reluctance than heretofore. For one cause or another, the Filipinos have become suspicious of the Constabulary and resent its use as a colonial army."[26]

In most locales, *ladrones* were little more than blackmailers and extortionists who ran a rural protection racket in which the peasants parted with a portion of their crops to secure the lives of their families. But in some areas, particularly in Cavite Province, General Bliss found that, to many peasants, "a friendly Ladron has come to represent all the protection of the law that they know of." Bliss described the symbiotic relationship thus: "Wherever a band of Ladrones exists it always has some village or group of villages the inhabitants of which are friendly to them. That is because this band agrees to protect them against all other thieving bands in return for a tribute at stated intervals of rice and cloth and a few other of the simple necessities of this climate . . . those which are outside of their 'sphere of influence,' they treat with the utmost cruelty, torturing them to death, burying them alive, carrying off their women and plundering their property."[27]

The army's pacification campaign in the Philippine War had failed to eradicate southwestern Luzon's brigands, and by 1904 they had coalesced around Macario Sakay, the self-proclaimed "Supreme President of the Tagalog Isles." With bands of several hundred men, Sakay's lieutenants robbed, kidnapped, and slaughtered throughout Cavite, Laguna, Rizal, and Batangas Provinces. In May 1904 the situation was sufficiently serious that the civil government, in an effort to cut the outlaws off from food and information, forcibly relocated the inhabitants of several barrios into protected zones. Unfortunately, the outbreak of the Pulahan troubles late in the year led to the withdrawal of Scout and Constabulary companies, whereupon the *ladrones* went on a rampage, marching into towns, disarming the police, looting, kidnapping for ransom, and sometimes murdering. On the evening of 24 January 1905, between 300 and 500 outlaws marched into San Francisco de Malabon in Cavite, overcame the Constabulary detachment, looted the town, and captured the wife and two children of a former provincial governor. The brazenness of the attack—not more than twenty miles from Manila—coupled with the Constabulary's halfhearted resistance, galvanized the civil government. Cavite's governor, David Shanks, declared this was no "mere raid of the ladrones" but rather "an incipient insurrection and if not suppressed at once may develop into something serious."[28] Within a week Governor-General Wright suspended habeas corpus in Cavite and Batangas Provinces. A few days earlier, three troops of the 2nd Cavalry and four companies of the 7th Infantry under Major Frederick W. Sibley crossed into Cavite to provide assistance.

The antibanditry campaign in southwestern Luzon was a joint civil-military project in which the lines of authority were conveniently blurred. Sibley rapidly developed an excellent relationship with Governor Shanks and the senior Constabulary officer, Colonel D. J. Baker, both of whom were army officers on detached duty with the civil government. The three coordinated field operations, targeting individual brigand chieftains and assigning combined civil-military forces to deal with them. While some soldiers garrisoned towns and rooted out the brigands' civilian supporters, others hunted them in the field. Confronted by well-armed soldiers, the bandits soon lost their combativeness. Some of their leaders were killed in sweeps, others faded into the hills. By 24 February Sibley could report, "the ladrones are now broken into smaller bands and it is expected this plan will render the provinces uninhabitable for them as they have to move to procure supplies and will be in constant fear of meeting troops."[29] So effective were army operations that in July the Regulars were withdrawn and the Constabulary again resumed control; henceforth the brigands were reduced to an annoyance.

A far more serious threat to the tenuous peace was the Pulahan campaign of 2 August 1904 to 30 June 1907, which began on Samar and spilled over to the neighboring island of Leyte. Samar is an impoverished island and one of the most uninhabitable wastelands in the world; with the exception of a few coastal plains and river valleys, it is a wilderness of jagged mountains, murky swamps, steaming jungles, and dense grasslands. Banditry and civil disobedience, which had long flourished, broke into open rebellion between 1884 and 1886 when mountain sectarians, called Dios Dios, attacked the coastal towns before retreating back to the mountains. During the Philippine War, the massacre of an infantry company at Balangiga in 1901 brought the vitriolic Jacob H. Smith to command, and the campaign on Samar was made infamous by civil-military squabbles, widespread property destruction, and summary executions. The imposition of civil government did little to heal these wounds; political factions flourished and mountain dwellers selling hemp in the coastal towns were routinely cheated, beaten, and jailed by the very officials who were supposed to protect them.

Out of this poverty and misery arose a religious movement that promised both salvation and revenge. Virtually nothing is known about the members of this fascinating sect. Even their name for themselves is a mystery; the term

"Pulahanes"—a reference to their practice of dressing in *pula* (red) uniforms—comes from their enemies, who quickly broadened the term to include brigands, smugglers, and assorted political opponents. One Constabulary officer discovered that many self-confessed Pulahanes had no connection whatever with the cult and believed the term meant "mountaineer."[30] The Pulahanes' political and religious views are equally obscure. Their designation of their religious leader as "pope," their pseudo-Latin blessings and scapulars, as well as the red and black crosses which adorned their hats, coat collars, breasts, and backs clearly show Christian influence. Other practices may owe more to Visayan folklore: their uncut hair, their belief in magic, and their conviction that all who died in battle would be reincarnated.[31] Their political views are also unclear. In some respects, such as in their appropriation of revolutionary regalia and their attacks on government officials, they appear to have viewed themselves as continuing the war for independence. But their leaders never claimed to serve a Philippine or Visayan state, and interviews with captured Pulahanes revealed no grievances against the United States. Certainly their beliefs confused contemporaries, who ascribed the Pulahan outbreak to decades-old feuds between towns or between families, to religious fanaticism, to the socioeconomic disruption of the Philippine War, to long-standing oppression, and to "no cause nor reason . . . except resistance to all control."[32]

However obscure their message, it had considerable popular appeal. At the height of the Pulahanes' strength, in 1904–5, whole villages joined the movement and crowds numbering in the hundreds participated in pitched battles with the colonial authorities. From their mountain communities they descended on coastal towns, taking food and plunder, kidnapping workers, and meting out savage punishment to individual merchants, officials, and policemen.

What made the Pulahanes such a threat was less their raiding—which was little more than brigandage on a grand scale—than their proficiency in irregular warfare. Led by priest-warlords such as Dagohob, the Pulahanes developed simple but effective tactics: "The attack will usually consist of firing into the column from front or rear immediately followed by a rush of bolomen who will jump through the column from one or both flanks from high grass or thick cover, sometimes with the idea of dividing the column into two sections. The bolomen usually do not stop but do damage by a quick rush and then get away."[33] As long as they retained their élan, and a large number of willing bolomen, Pulahan tactics were devastating, especially when applied against outnumbered and poorly armed Filipino troops.

Beset with civil unrest throughout the archipelago, the civil government pursued a disastrous policy on Samar, neither alleviating the population's distress nor providing sufficient forces for repression. In the fall of 1904 the Pulahanes delivered a series of smashing defeats to the government forces, virtually annihilating two Scout companies. Encouraged by this, dozens of new bands, many with only a tenuous connection to the religious devotees, joined the looting and pillaging. By the end of the year the colonial forces in North and East Samar were reduced to a few demoralized garrisons and the island verged on anarchy. At this rapid slide into disorder the civil government finally responded; by 2 January 1905 there were some 900 Constabulary, 700 Scouts, and 400 American soldiers on Samar.[34]

In the early months of 1905, Allen personally commanded the campaign, demonstrating that, whatever his faults, he was an imaginative and courageous combat officer. He deployed mixed Scout and Constabulary units to several interior towns where they could secure information, protect the population, and destroy Pulahan supplies. More important, on 20 February 1905, he issued an amnesty for all but the senior leadership and took practical steps to abate the injustices that fostered unrest, ordering the Constabulary "to investigate and correct abuses connected with trade in the interior. . . . This is equally as important as capturing leaders and getting their guns."[35] In January, with the assistance of George Curry, Samar's new governor, Allen conducted a purge of civic officials, removing those who had been either conspicuously corrupt or insufficiently aggressive.[36]

But despite his energy and resourcefulness, by May 1905 Allen faced growing pressure from General William H. Carter, commander of the Department of the Visayas, to turn Samar's eastern coast over to army control. Carter, nursing a personal vendetta that dated from Allen's successful effort to deny him a choice assignment, dispatched Lieutenant Albert W. Foreman to Samar, and Foreman's realistic reports undercut the Constabulary chief's consistently rosy ones. With a stunning military victory Allen still might have prevailed, but most of the engagements in early 1905 were indecisive at best, and his early boasts that he could withdraw troops from Samar sounded increasingly hollow. On 23 May Allen turned over responsibility for the east coast and much of the interior to Carter; little more than a week later, on 2 June, Governor-General Henry C. Ide formally requested army assistance "to put an end to the conditions of disorder in those portions of Samar which are now disaffected."[37]

For all the military's criticism of Allen, it is difficult to detect any drastic change in pacification procedures in the following months. For the most part, the army continued to rely upon large-unit expeditions against Pulahan strongholds and the maintenance of small garrisons in disaffected areas. Its most dramatic success was undoubtedly the killing of Dagohob and over a hundred of his followers on 4 June by a mixed force of soldiers and Scouts. With Dagohob's death, the ferocious horde that had wreaked such havoc on the colonial forces broke into smaller bands commanded by lesser figures.[38] Carter received a large influx of Regulars, and his nine Scout companies were completely equipped with modern magazine rifles. No longer dependent on antiquated single-shot black-powder weapons, the Scouts finally possessed sufficient firepower to transform the Pulahanes' one military advantage—the sudden bolo rush—to a suicidal slaughter. A small U.S. Navy flotilla of five gunboats and two steam launches transported soldiers along the coast and provided impressive firepower. The process of winning popular support was hastened by bringing refugees in from the mountains and depriving the Pula- hanes of supplies and manpower. A citizen's committee of former guerrilla leaders raised militia units to patrol the hills and hunt Pulahanes. Post officers distributed land to the returnees, encouraged crop cultivation, and tried to prevent officials from exploiting their new subjects. The army also engaged in a number of public works projects; soldiers helped rebuild the town of Oras where, in one month, they distributed 2,728 pounds of flour, 2,100 pounds of beans, and 15,260 pounds of rice to destitute Filipinos.[39]

The army's progress prompted Governor Curry, in a laudable attempt to end the suffering on Samar, to propose that peace negotiations be conducted at a neutral site. He selected Magtaon, a highland barrio so small and insig- nificant it did not appear on the army's maps. Accordingly, the army garrison was withdrawn and replaced by a Constabulary unit, and active operations ceased to allow the scattered Pulahan bands to concentrate. On 24 March 1905, the governor, along with a Constabulary honor guard and a host of visi- tors, prepared for the surrender ceremonies. The Pulahanes filed in, looked at the crowds, and then suddenly charged in a wave of flashing bolos; they cut down twenty-two Constabulary, captured fifty rifles, and then disappeared into the jungle. Curry, who had narrowly escaped the slaughter, made his way back to the coast—a convert to repression.[40]

Across the San Juanico Strait on Leyte increasing numbers of red-uni- formed mountain bands also were attacking villages. The term "Pulahan" was immediately applied to Leyte's dissidents, but contemporary and later sources agree there was no direct connection between the two uprisings. In June 1906 the civil government called on the army, and on 25 July a mixed force of Con- stabulary and the newly arrived 24th Infantry fought a pitched battle, beating off assaults by hundreds of bolomen. Like their colleagues across the straits in Samar, the troops garrisoned towns and patrolled the countryside, seeking to separate the dissidents from the population. There were few pitched battles, but Leyte's rebels, like Samar's, showed an impressive ability to congregate suddenly and maul unwary patrols before vanishing into the countryside.[41]

The events at Magtaon and Leyte did not provoke the blind fury and indiscriminate retaliation that had followed the Balangiga massacre in 1901. Nor was there a substantial shift in military operations, in part because the Pulahanes appeared to have shot their bolt at Magtaon. Most of the Pulahan chiefs involved in the attack were soon killed or captured. Despite intensive searches, patrols discovered only desolated farms, abandoned huts, and a countryside devoid of habitation. In May 1906 all but a few Regulars returned to garrisoning the coast; in June the Department of the Visayas declared northwestern Samar pacified. By the end of summer, all that remained were a few scattered gangs of twenty to fifty people, desperately seeking food and shelter, relentlessly pursued by troops and local volunteers. Although few Pulahanes were killed, the casualties included the top leadership; a futile hunt for one evasive Pulahan chief delayed the official close of the campaign until 30 June 1907, but by the end of 1906 it was all but finished.[42]

With the exception of the long pacification of the Moros, the Pulahan conflict was the longest and most costly postconquest campaign the army faced in the Philippines. Between 1904 and 1907 on Samar alone it required the 1st, 14th, and 21st Infantry, detached companies from the 6th, 12th, and 24th Infantry, and from six to eighteen Scout companies. Another four Regular companies were stationed on Leyte in 1906 and 1907. By the standards of Philippine campaigns, casualties were high: between 4 September 1904 and 25 October 1906, soldiers and Scouts suffered seventy-three combat casualties on Samar and another four on Leyte.[43] Other costs are harder to measure. Neither the military nor the civil government attempted to compile equivalent statistics on the total number of Pulahan or civilian casualties. The Pulahanes routinely burned towns and destroyed fields, impressing entire populations into forced labor in the mountains. In turn, the government forces burned houses and fields in an attempt to starve out the rebels and to drive the hill people into the coastal towns. But statistics, even if available, would be an inadequate measure of the widespread destruction and human misery. The army scattered the Pulahan bands, but the island continued to be a poverty-stricken backwater, torn by religious sects and violence, where government authority was largely unknown. During World War II a new Pulahan movement emerged, and to this day sects, political dissidents, and bandits continue to flourish on Samar.

In contrast to the virtually unknown antibanditry and Pulahan campaigns, the army's conflicts in "Moroland" against the Muslim Moros of the Sulu archipelago and Mindanao are legendary. In part this reflects the presence of such army luminaries as Wood, Bliss, Hugh L. Scott, John J. Pershing, Robert L. Bullard, Benjamin Foulois, and Hugh A. Drum. In part, it celebrates the color and romance of both the Moros and the American attempt to "civilize" them. In contrast to the Filipino Christians, the Moros were a truly romantic opponent, America's equivalent of the fierce Pathans of British India's Northwest Frontier. Their exotic dress, their firm adherence to Islam, their fierceness and courage, their love of fighting, particularly in hand-to-hand combat—all these made them as archaic and colorful as the army's former opponents, the American Indians. Indeed, to the Progressive Era Americans still coming to terms with the end of their own Wild West, Moroland resonated with the richness, mystery, and danger both of the lost continental frontier and the yet unexploited Pacific "New West." It is thus not surprising that some drew on this imagery in likening Moroland to a giant reservation inhabited by savage tribes ruled by warrior chieftains. Service against the Moros allowed the new imperial army to maintain, however symbolically, its tie to the old frontier army and to march with the ghosts of Custer, Mackenzie, and Crook.[44]

Nostalgia aside, there was little question among the Americans that the Moros were savages who needed to be "civilized." Their slavery, piracy, polygamy, autocratic clan government, blood feuds, endemic warfare, and the ritual of *juramentado*—in which a devotee sought to kill as many Christians as possible—were all self-evident barbarities to the new colonial administration. So too was the poverty, ignorance, and disease that pervaded Moroland. But most offensive to practical officers were the constant attacks on U.S. soldiers and coastal towns. Neither the sultans, nor the hereditary tribal chiefs (*datus*), nor the religious authorities seemed able to control their people or to prevent this provocation. Clearly to the army the first step in the civilizing mission was to impose U.S. standards of law and order on their recalcitrant subjects. This mission promised great difficulties. Moroland's boundaries stretched from Mindanao along the dozens of islands of the Sulu Archipelago almost 200 miles to Borneo. It included Mindanao's 36,500 square miles of mountains and jungles, the 345-square-mile volcanic island of Jolo, home of the sultan of Sulu, and tiny and picturesque Tawi-Tawi. For centuries the Moros had resisted the efforts of the Spanish, and their Christian Filipino allies, to convert them and few soldiers believed they would meekly accept U.S. authority. One sympathetic officer commented: the Moros "are a proud fierce stubborn ignorant fanatic superstitious and unstable people—who have the courage of their convictions and are willing to die when they think the [time?] comes; they freely acknowledge they cannot hope to successfully fight the Americans but they can die."[45] Foulois agreed: "the Moro question will eventually be settled in the same manner as the Indian question, that is by gradual extermination."[46] Even Bullard, one of the most cerebral of the officers faced with the "Moro question," believed they were savages and must cross a "great gulf" to reach civilization. In bridging this gap there was the possibility that, like the American Indian, the Moros might be "lost." Nevertheless, the risk must be taken: either Moroland "must be turned over to the savagery of aggressive Moros, or all be taken over to civilization. Because, finally, as savages the Moros stand in the way of our destiny, and we cannot permit that."[47]

Although commonly used, the term "Moro Wars" is a misnomer; the Americans were not opposed by a united Moro nation, nor even a tribal confederation, but rather by a fragmented array of clans and factions. The major campaigns—whether against rebel *datus* such as Ali and Jikiri, against defiant tribes such as those faced by the Taraca and Bacalod expeditions, or the pitched battles of Bud Dajo and Bud Bagsak—were all individual conflicts that bore little or no relationship to one another.

Contemporaries recognized that these were uneven contests and that superior discipline, equipment, and training gave Regulars an overwhelming advantage over individuals armed with knives, swords, and antiquated cannon. Officers quickly learned, in Pershing's words, that the Moros "cannot stand open fighting. Their losses are too great."[48] In the face of American expeditions, they retreated to their *cottas*—rock and earth forts surrounded by bamboo palisades and deep, obstacle-filled trenches—and from there they fired their few primitive cannon, brandished their swords, and maintained a cacophony of defiance. As early as 1902, Brigadier General George W. Davis had commented, "we know beforehand exactly where to find the enemy and what will be his general plan of operations. . . . There have been hundreds of favorable opportunities for a Moro force of a hundred or so to fall upon little parties of eight or ten and annihilate them, but there has been no such attack nor any that resembled it."[49]

The Moros' individualism and disunity also weakened their resistance. As Foulois noted, "we would have had a great deal more serious trouble with the Moros, if they had combined, or could combine under a common ruler, but each chief is always jealous of the power of his neighbor, and in this lies their weakness and our strength."[50] In all their campaigns, the Americans found a host of Moro allies eager to help subjugate one of their own. The revealing incident in which a panic-stricken *datu* sought Bullard's help against Pershing's expedition illustrates the Moros' persistence in viewing the army as little more than a particularly well armed clan. Islam alone had the power to bind the Moros, but any possibility of jihad was vitiated by religious divisions as well as by the army's success in convincing many of them that the United States did not seek conversions.[51]

In Cavite and Samar the army was the agent of colonial government, reestablishing peace in areas already turned over to civilian rule. But in the southern Philippines, the army ruled Moroland in a military proconsulship. On 1 June 1903 the Philippine Commission constituted the Muslim areas of Mindanao and Sulu as the Moro Province and established a curious form of civil-military government. Not only were the offices of the provincial government and much of the Legislative Council filled by military personnel, but the governor also served as commander of the army's Department of Mindanao. In the event of an uprising or lawlessness, he could request military support from himself.[52]

This governorship was clearly a task for an officer of the "New Army," a man who combined military skills with administrative, political, and managerial expertise. Both the Roosevelt administration and the Philippine Commission were convinced they had such an imperial viceroy when they appointed Leonard Wood in August 1903. Already a controversial figure, Wood had entered the army as a contract surgeon and owed much of his advancement to the personal connections he had made, first as presidential doctor and then as commander of the Rough Riders. His capable administration in Cuba had demonstrated both his skill and his ruthless intriguing, winning him promotion to brigadier general in 1902. Soon after taking office, Wood made a whirlwind tour of Mindanao and the Sulu archipelago and found the answer to what he termed the "Moro Problem": the sultans and high ranking *datus* would be pensioned off, the social institutions that kept the Moros savages— their clan governments, slavery, blood feuds, and their adherence to Islamic law—would be abolished, and the country itself thrown open to outside development. To Wood, the benefits of American law, medicine, education, government, and religion were so manifest that any who resisted were clearly perverse at best, evil at worst.[53]

Prior to Wood's arrival, most officers had tried to pursue a policy of conciliation, leaving local government to the *datus*, ignoring slavery, and striking only at those who physically attacked soldiers. Eli Helmick recalled that when stationed at Cotabato in 1902, the situation was tense and provocation constant, but "it was impressed on us, however, that we must at all times avoid any situation that might bring on a rupture or unfriendliness."[54] Military operations had been characterized by strict rules of engagement. Orders for troops marching against one *cotta* stressed that the soldiers were to punish only those known to be hostile, there was to be no destruction of crops or property except the *cotta* itself, and all persons were to be treated humanely. In short, officers and men were to keep in mind that "we are after effect, not revenge for wrongs done."[55]

The most prominent exemplar of the American's conciliatory policy was Captain Pershing, who commanded Camp Vicars on Mindanao's Lake Lanao, in the heart of one of the most troublesome districts in Moroland. Pershing sought to convince the Moros of the benefits of trade, but even more of the benefits of peace and toleration, assuring them that the United States would respect their religion and allow them to manage their own affairs. He resisted pressure to fight, from both the Moros and his superiors, writing that the United States "can well afford to wait and exhaust every effort to establish friendly relations."[56] When he did take to the field, as in his "explorations" around Lake Lanao in 1903, he made it clear that it was against individual clans, not the Moro people, and, having convinced other *datus* of his friendly intentions, his column passed through much of the area unmolested. When he was forced to fight, as at the *cotta* of Bacolod, Pershing displayed a shrewd grasp of small war tactics, bombarding the fortress with high explosive shells from his mountain guns and field mortars and withholding his infantry until many of the Moros had deserted.[57]

This slow and patient approach was alien to Wood. Bullard, a proponent of conciliation, noted that Wood "completely reversed [his predecessor's] policy of patient and mild treatment of Moros. We are going after Mr. Moro with a rough hand, we are holding him up to all the high ideals of civilization."[58] Perhaps seeking to surpass the reputation Pershing had won, Wood and a huge expedition of infantry, cavalry, and field artillery set off in November 1903 on a march around Lake Lanao. He soon revealed his inexperience in Philippine warfare, disregarding the advice of veterans and launching his expedition into the teeth of the monsoon. The heavily burdened troops thrashed through the mud and swamps, losing supplies and equipment, and finally made a frontal attack on a small *cotta*, which left one soldier dead and five wounded.[59] Fortunately for Wood, an outbreak on Jolo gave him an excuse to withdraw from Lanao and rush his troops to the new theater. From 7 to 12 November, he marched through that island, attacking recalcitrant *datus*. Before the expedition, Wood had explained to Roosevelt his strategy for pacifying the Moros: "one clean-cut lesson will be quite sufficient for them but it should be of such character as not to need a dozen frittering expeditions."[60] His summation of the Jolo campaign was characteristic: "They had been hunting for a fight for two or three years, and started this trouble by attacking our troops while they were engaged in making a survey, and of course they had to be spanked afterwards."[61] In his two-and-a-half years as governor, his troops fought perhaps a hundred engagements, none of which disturbed his conviction that just one more "spanking" would quell Moro resistance.[62]

The climax of Wood's confrontational policies occurred on Jolo at Bud Dajo. In 1905 this 2,000-foot volcanic crater became the beacon for hundreds of Moros fleeing American attempts to impose a head tax. One veteran of the area had warned, "I believe the people of this district will be friendly if left alone; I also believe that if stirred up, they will be the most formidable army of any in the Island."[63] Wood dispatched Colonel Joseph W. Duncan and a force of 800 soldiers and Constabulary to disperse the Bud Dajo Moros. The expedition arrived at the town of Jolo on 3 March, and Duncan and his officers mulled over the problem of assaulting a slope varying from forty to sixty degrees and with a single access of three narrow trails blocked by strong *cottas* at the summit. Duncan divided his force into four columns, and under cover of his field artillery, moved up the crater on 5 March. The columns halted some 1,000 feet up, where the troops spent an uneasy night subjected to chanting, gongs, drums, and sniper fire. The next day the American guns resumed their shelling and the troops resumed their advance, coming under sustained fire from Moro rifles and cannon and halting shortly before the summit. The main assault occurred on 7 March, a frenzied close-quarters melee that lasted much of the day. The final *cotta* was taken early the next morning; as one veteran remembered, "they turned that machine gun on them and they'd stand there, the Moros would, and just look like dominoes falling."[64] The crater resembled a slaughter house, with hundreds of bodies—of men, women, and children—carpeting the ground. Months later, even hardened soldiers were horrified at the "ghastly evidence of the fight."[65] The combined army and Constabulary losses of twenty-one dead and seventy-three wounded were the heaviest of any post–Philippine War engagement.

Bud Dajo provoked widespread publicity about Wood's aggressive Moro policy. He was castigated in the Senate; even proadministration newspapers questioned the necessity of the battle. The general defended himself with typical spirit and indignation, insisting that armed women and children had repeatedly joined the men in wild charges on the troops. Roosevelt upheld his friend, and Wood was promoted to command of the Philippines Division. Once freed from a personal stake in subduing the Moros, the most aggressive and provocative governor in the Moro Province's history became a spokesman for conciliation and tact.[66]

Wood's successor, Tasker H. Bliss, abandoned the practice of escalating minor skirmishes into full-fledged military campaigns. He ended the large punitive expeditions and treated Moro Province's incessant raiding, murders, and tribal feuds as criminal actions, not challenges to American sovereignty. He relied on the Constabulary to hunt down all but the most dangerous outlaws and kept his soldiers in reserve. Officers sought to avoid confrontation, for as Colonel Edgar Z. Steever noted, "If I understand the policy from above aright, it is to refrain from bringing on hostilities unless some vital principle is at stake or some of these headmen act in defiance of United States authority."[67] The provincial government—itself composed largely of officers—encouraged commercial development, holding fairs, issuing contracts for Moro labor and products, and developing native industries. Unlike Wood, Bliss was scrupulous in honoring Moro rights, remarking in one incident in which Moros were claiming land in the vicinity of Camp Vicars that, although they could not prove their case in court, "they cannot justly be ousted without proper compensation, otherwise the resulting enmity would undo the good results that have been accomplished in pacifying them in recent years."[68] In 1907 one Constabulary officer remarked that the Moros were "pretty well pacified and are becoming, strange to say, intensely American."[69]

Bliss's successor, Pershing, in 1909 became the last person to hold simultaneously both the offices of governor of the Moro Province and of commanding general of the Department of Mindanao. He maintained Bliss's benevolent policies, and it is unfortunate that he is remembered more for the bloody disarmament campaign on Jolo than for the benefits he sought to bring. Pershing had been an early advocate of conciliation, and he strengthened Moro Province's finances, improved the roads, held trade fairs, increased school attendance, and reformed sanitation and public health. He also maintained Bliss's policy of treating Moro violence as criminal behavior and using Constabulary for all but the most serious cases. The exception to this accommodation was his decision in 1911 to enforce the provisions of a 1908 order allowing the governor to disarm Moros throughout the province. He believed that only by taking away firearms could he end the constant blood feuds, raids, outlawry, and tribal skirmishes that kept the province in turmoil. However, disarmament prompted a rebellion in distant Jolo, where 1,300 Moros fortified the old battlefield at Bud Dajo. Sailing quickly, Pershing arrived in early December and through negotiations managed to convince the majority to leave. In his diary, he outlined his strategy: "Dajo will not mean the slaughter of women and children nor hasty assaults against strong entrenchments. I shall lose as few men and kill as few Moros as possible. I think I can take Dajo without a fight—Moros cannot stand a siege."[70] The remaining rebels he surrounded with 1,000 troops and lines of barbed wire. For over a week the Moros attacked the American defenses before finally surrendering on 26 December. The second Bud Dajo campaign left only twelve Moros killed and three Americans wounded.[71]

Pershing employed similar restraint in January 1913 when as many as 10,000 inhabitants fled to the mountain of Bud Bagsak crater on Jolo. Once again Pershing surrounded the stronghold and negotiated, relying on hunger instead of bullets; and in March the Bagsak Moros agreed to surrender their firearms at the request at the sultan of Sulu.[72] An uneasy peace followed, with the Moros growing steadily more defiant, firing into the town of Jolo, proclaiming their refusal to surrender their guns, and threatening to withdraw again to Bud Bagsak if the troops appeared. Again Pershing moved swiftly. Aware that there were at least 1,000 Moros already on Bagsak, he tried to prevent a further exodus to its slopes. On 11 June he left Zamboanga, ostensibly to visit his family, but then his transport changed course and arrived in Jolo with Scout companies picked up en route. Like Bud Dajo, Bud Bagsak was a steep volcanic cone, virtually perpendicular near the top, and the Moros had built *cottas* along the trails. Scrambling up its slopes, at times pulling themselves up on vines, the soldiers captured the two strongest *cottas*, outflanking the defenses and thus allowing the artillery to concentrate on the remainder. For the next two days the soldiers worked their way through the crater, shelling *cottas*, and beating off counterattacks that were pressed with fanatical determination. On 15 June the 51st and 52nd Philippine Scout companies, Moros themselves, assaulted the last *cotta*. As the defenders slashed at them with kris and sword, the Scouts tore down the barricades with their bare hands and poured fire into the packed interior. Throughout the battle, the Moros refused to surrender, hurling themselves against Pershing's massed rifle and artillery fire in a desperate attempt to close with the attackers. Over 500 were killed; as many as 10 percent of them women and children. Pershing's expedition lost fifteen dead and twenty-five wounded.[73]

The Battle of Bud Bagsak marked the end of the Moro campaigns. Pershing had urged that the Regulars be withdrawn in 1912 and had repeated this request in 1913, but Philippines Division commander Major General J. Franklin Bell dissuaded him until the Jolo Moros were pacified. After the battle, Pershing again recommended removing American soldiers. This time Bell agreed, noting that the Scouts had done the bulk of the pacification work, with the Regulars used largely for "moral effect."[74] Bell concentrated the Scouts at four battalion-strength posts, strategically placed to allow them to move rapidly throughout the Moro Province in case of further outbreaks. An uneasy peace existed in Mindanao and Sulu—broken by endemic piracy, homicides, and tribal wars—but these were now the problems of the Constabulary, and occasionally the Scouts. The army had established colonial authority and it was up to the civil government to prove itself worthy of Moro allegiance.

With the departure of the last American forces from Moroland, the U.S. Army's fourteen-year pacification of the Philippines came to a close. During this time Filipino and American soldiers had battled conventional infantry, guerrillas, *ladrones*, Pulahanes, Moros, and a host of other religious, political, and criminal adversaries. They triumphed not only over human opponents, but over tropical diseases, heat, monsoons, dust, inadequate food, and poisonous water. A steady stream of reports flowed from each company post— detailing patrols, skirmishes, tactics, casualties, local conditions—up to headquarters, where, stored by the thousands, they constitute a compendium of the practical day-to-day business of counterinsurgency. Some veterans kept diaries, contributed articles, or wrote their recollections down for their children. From this mass of material, it is possible to determine, in very broad outline, the fundamentals of U.S. Army pacification methods in the Philippines.

In general, army field operations consisted of two types: extended sweeps by columns and the establishment of outposts in areas of enemy influence. Composed of between fifty and several hundred soldiers, often broken into several detachments converging on a strategic area, sweeps sought to force the enemy to battle. They were most successful against opponents such as Aguinaldo's Republican Army or the Moros, who stood behind field fortifications and allowed the columns to approach unhindered. During the Philippine War, when the enemy lacked discipline and firepower, soldiers would deploy from their marching formation into a long open-order skirmish line, usually sending a detachment to launch a simultaneous flank attack. After a few volleys, the troops would rush forward, firing as they went, seeking to close before the enemy could escape. The Moros' strong fortifications and their willingness to defend them to the death required some modification of these headlong assault tactics. Pershing, probably the most skillful commander, softened up *cottas* with long-range field artillery and rifle fire, demoralizing the Moros, who had no means to retaliate. The final attack was directed at a preselected spot, the infantry advancing in waves and covered by overhead fire. Once inside the defenses, fighting quickly became hand to hand, with pistol, rifle butt, and bayonet against sword, spear, and knife.

Against opponents such as the revolutionaries or the *ladrones*, who adopted guerrilla tactics—hit-and-run attacks, constant movement, and hiding among the population—the army relied on the considerable fieldcraft and small-unit tactical ability of its officers and men. Officers modified existing tactics freely for, as one veteran noted, if the marching formation outlined in the army's

Field Regulations were followed in Philippine terrain, "the main body would be held down to a gait of about two miles a day, while the only connection with [flankers] would be by the obviously undesirable means of shouting."[75] Because a patrol might encounter anything from booby traps to long-range sniping to massed bolo charges, adaptability was crucial: "no fixed plan of attack can be made in advance—the officer must decide upon his plan of attack at the time."[76] In order to maintain control, officers had to develop simple formations that combined firepower and shock in such a way that with a few voice commands troops could go from marching formation to the defensive or attack. On the march soldiers went in a single file—the terrain made any other formation impossible—with their rifles at the ready, a round in a chamber, and bayonets fixed. A small advance guard looked for ambushes and supervised native porters cutting trail. Officers moved back and forth over the column, keeping their troops closed up and insuring their advance and rear guards were always in sight. When attacking, soldiers first assigned a guard for their porters, formed into a single closely packed skirmish line, and charged forward.[77]

Although both contemporaries and later historians have focused on the big-unit campaigns of 1899 or the spectacular battles at Bud Dajo and Bud Bag-sak, these were exceptions. Typical Philippine field operations consisted of a laborious hike through drenching jungle or choking dust, a search of some isolated village, and an equally arduous march back to the outpost. Colonel Baker noted that in such campaigns the traditional measures of military success, such as enemy casualties or weapons captured, were "defective in that they give no indication of the weary waits for information, the carefully planned but generally indecisive attacks, the tedious and often fruitless negotiations, and the patient but often disappointing efforts to induce the people to free themselves from the irresponsible bondage of ladronism."[78] Indeed, most of the conventional criteria for victory—the destruction of the enemy army, the capture of the enemy capital, and the surrender of the enemy government—were inapplicable. As in most unconventional wars, the government forces had to expend enormous energy for apparently meager results. During the Pulahan campaign between 13 June and 15 December 1906, soldiers and volunteers conducted 184 expeditions and spent a total of 786 days in the field, but killed only 49 Pulahanes.[79] Correspondingly, casualties, at least to gunfire and weapons, were quite light: in the small wars of 1903 to 1913 only 107 Regulars and 111 Scouts were killed in action.[80]

Ironically for an army that later committed itself to "search and destroy," U.S. pacification in the early 1900s was based as much on the occupation of hostile territory as upon active field operations. Placing garrisons in major towns began in 1900 with Otis's decision to break up the large tactical commands and continued in every subsequent campaign. Against rural insurgents such as the Moros and Pulahanes, who had few commercial centers to occupy, the army established outposts at the end of the logistical line, which served as supply points for sweeps, allowing columns to rest and refit before returning to the field. But the infantry companies who manned these outposts provided a more direct function by controlling the immediate vicinity. Since most Filipino irregulars had fixed areas of operations and survived only by maintaining strong contacts with a few villages, they were demoralized when these villages were occupied and their territory swept by small but fast-moving patrols.

Outposts also provided protection and support for refugees, sheltering the often sizable community that grew up outside their perimeters and thereby enabling soldiers to establish intelligence networks within the population, create village militias, and even organize local government. And to demonstrate the benefits of colonial rule, the garrison disbursed funds for the transportation of supplies, road building, and barracks construction, as well as outright gifts of food to the destitute. The outpost commander often became a temporary chieftain, providing the rudiments of stability in a society that depended so heavily upon traditional authority. Unfortunately, outposts also could serve as prisons for civilians caught up the fighting. In the Batangas campaign of the Philippine War and against *ladrones* in Cavite, the army forcibly relocated, or concentrated, the populations of some outlying barrios inside their municipalities. Concentration was a highly successful tactic, for it prevented the guerrillas from securing food, shelter, and recruits and allowed soldiers to fire with impunity on any people found outside the protected zones. Although only implemented in the most serious circumstances, the army's willingness to place civilians in concentration camps had disturbing implications for future conflicts.[81]

The paucity of battles and the small numbers of troops engaged should not obscure the prodigious efforts necessary to maintain combat forces in the archipelago's jungles, swamps, and mountains. In its own way, the army's ability to maintain a company of infantry at a desolate interior outpost on Samar or Mindanao was as impressive as its ability to put thousands of troops in the field for divisional maneuvers. On Mindanao the army had to build hundreds of miles of roads to allow troops and supplies to move from the coast into the troublesome interior. To sustain the forces in the Pulahan campaign, quartermasters established a rickety supply line of native dugouts, carabao, and human porters, or *cargadores*. The latter were so essential that the army established a special corps of *cargadores* and emphasized "they will be thoroughly trained and treated with kindness, in order to build up a willing and reliable service."[82] One incident is indicative that such orders were followed. In May 1907 during an extended patrol by twenty-seven soldiers of the 1st Infantry, one of the thirty-seven porters slashed his hand on a can of bacon. The patrol immediately turned back to its base and its lieutenant and four other soldiers then marched an additional twenty-five miles to bring back a medical orderly.[83] It was their ability to support military operations, as much as their combat ability, that distinguished the Americans from the Spanish and rendered them so effective against their opponents.

An essential factor in American pacification was to turn the population against the guerrillas. The army pitted ethnic, political, and religious factions against each other, for example, by recruiting its first Scouts from a municipality with a historic hatred of the Tagalogs who dominated the revolutionary leadership. Officers in Moroland, with the exception of Wood, excelled at breaking up tribal alliances and convincing *datus* to turn on each other. Recognizing that Filipino interpersonal relations were socially stratified and governed by deference, mutual obligation, and kinship ties, commanders brought pressure on the elites to demonstrate their allegiance by giving information, raising volunteers, making public displays of loyalty, and securing the surrender of guerrillas. The army employed loyal Filipinos in a variety of military and paramilitary organizations: Scouts, auxiliaries, local militia and self-defense forces, and as municipal police, guides, *cargadores*, and boatmen.

Army pacification supplemented intimidation with the policies associated with "benevolent assimilation." In the midst of often savage guerrilla wars, soldiers continued to teach school, build roads, provide medicine and treatment, insure religious toleration, uphold law and order, and in dozens of other ways demonstrate the benefits of American rule. This benevolence extended to most enemy leaders, who received liberal surrender terms and reaped immediate benefits. The experience of Pio del Pilar, one of the most notorious *insurrectos*, was not unusual: after his capture he turned on his former comrades and was given a lucrative contract to provide wood to army garrisons. The Americans' ability to reward collaborators—often with political office in the new colonial administration—tied the Filipino elite to the new regime. During the Pulahan campaign, the government forces received invaluable assistance from those who had led the resistance during the Philippine War. Similarly, many Moro *datus* became fervent supporters of U.S. authority and looked to the army for protection against other Filipinos.

Although this Filipino cooperation was invaluable, it was purchased at a price. Because both civil and military officials depended on local elites, they helped to perpetuate the same oppressive practices that had initially provoked popular resistance. At the end of the Pulahan campaign, Major George Bell pointed out that the revolt had been due largely to the widespread "corruption and oppression" of the American-appointed civil governments and that "the causes which many of the pulajanes claimed drove them into the field have not been removed and while pulajanism has received its death blow here . . . there will be another insurrection within a year unless these causes are removed."[84]

As part of its efforts to minimize opposition, the army sought to avoid actions that would alienate either Americans or Filipinos. Reports of the atrocities in the Philippine War had aroused a storm of public indignation at home and soldiers recognized that blind repression was counterproductive. Field Orders No. 3, issued on 28 March 1903 to the Surigao expedition—the first major commitment of American field forces after the declaration of peace—reveals this newfound sensitivity. Soldiers were ordered to pay careful attention to local customs and sensibilities and expressly prohibited from indiscriminate arrests, property destruction, or looting. Although officers were enjoined to "use every possible facility in strict accordance with the rule of civilized war in obtaining information," they were warned, "let there be no water curing or severity that is not plainly authorized without straining inter-pretations of [the] law of war. . . . Any one who disgraces our uniform by engaging in such barbarous practices will be punished on the spot. . . . Success will not be marred by any well founded complaints of undue severity and flagrant misconduct."[85]

From operational records it is clear that, despite good intentions, the usual excesses of war occurred. On occasion, prisoners were shot, crops and homes destroyed, women and children killed in cross fire, and provocation met by violence. The U.S. Army had its share of vindictive racists, such as Major George T. Langhorne, who pressed for war on the grounds that "every conces-sion to an Asiatic, as a general rule, is a mistake. It is only when they beg for mercy that they should get, not more than they beg for, if anything, less."[86] Yet balanced against such sentiments were those of officers such as Colonel Steever, who protested when authorities urged prompt action against a Moro chief, "Of course I could undoubtedly force him into hostilities by adopting harsh and perhaps unnecessary measures . . . but I do not desire to do this unless higher authority insists upon me pushing affairs further than appears to me necessary or advisable."[87] Even Wood was somewhat chastened by the bloodshed he had earlier provoked, and urged an aggressive subordinate to "give [the Moros] a chance to do the square thing themselves, and after that to resort to active measures."[88] Aware of both public opinion in the United States and the need to govern with Filipino consent, American officers—ethnocentric, culturally insensitive, and arrogant though they were—nevertheless tried to direct pacification efforts so that the hard hand of war fell only on those in violent rebellion, and then only for as long as they continued to fight.

Despite the success of the U.S. Army in the Philippines—a success all the more impressive when contrasted both with contemporary imperial conquests and the army's own later experience with Asian guerrilla war—the army as an institution retained very little of its hard-won knowledge. This was not for lack of information, for in the decade following the Spanish-American War there was a great deal of correspondence on tactics, logistics, and field craft. Officers deploying against the Pulahanes were issued "Circular No. 1" outlining simple bush warfare tactics and providing such practical advice as to be "constantly on watch for ambushes, pitfalls and traps especially in the mountains. At night when camping positions will always be selected which can not be rushed by the enemy."[89] The Military Information Division circulated articles written by Spanish officers on fighting the Moros, and in 1906 a pamphlet based on notes from field service in Mindanao was provided to soldiers in Samar and Leyte. In an effort to retain the lessons of the Pulahan campaign, on 20 October 1906 the Department of the Visayas sent a detailed questionnaire to field officers requesting their views on tactics, weapons, equipment, marching and combat formations, porters, and other crucial details.[90] The most ambitious project—John R. M. Taylor's official history of the Philippine War—might have provided a complete and coherent military survey. Unfortunately, the author's diligence and talent lay more in the collection of Filipino and American documents than in their analysis. The result is a fragmented, often contradictory compendium, which oscillates from incisive comment to unsubstantiated conjecture. Nor were others allowed to study the documents and draw their own conclusions: Taylor's criticism of civil government in the islands so offended Taft that he suppressed the manuscript. Relegated to the archives, Taylor's work was virtually unknown within the army.[91]

What was lacking in the American military was any systematic attempt to distill accepted tactical principles and practices into a coherent small-wars doctrine. In contrast to the British, whose 1902 regulations included a section on "Savage Warfare" and who modified their tactics after the experience of the Boer War, the postwar U.S. Army's infantry drill manuals and field service regulations all but ignored the Philippines. Some officers questioned the army's fascination with conventional warfare and, like Charles G. Morton, believed the "future operations of United States forces are more likely to follow the nature of the colonial wars of Great Britain, rather than those fought on the continent of Europe, in other words are more apt to be carried on by small forces, acting more or less independently."[92] Bullard believed that the army's experiences since 1898 showed "if army officers and the army have had to know something of the art of war, they have had to know and use far more the art of pacification. In the Philippines the work was four-fifths peace and one fifth war making. . . . by the study of war alone we shall be but little prepared for by far the greater burdens which are to fall upon us, which are the making of peace."[93] Guerrilla warfare in the Philippines was a shared experience of most of the top commanders of World War I: Pershing, Bullard, Bliss, Hunter Liggett, James G. Harbord, Henry T. Allen, Peyton C. March. It was also the baptism of fire for a the generation that would guide the U.S. Army, and the nation's Pacific policy, through the interwar period: Charles P. Summerall, William Lassiter, Briant H. Wells, Malin Craig, Charles E. Kilbourne, William Mitchell. Unfortunately, it was all too easy for officers oriented toward conventional, European-style modern warfare to argue, as did Wood, that in the Philippine conflicts "we were opposed by a very inferior enemy and moved as it suited us, conditions which do not exist when confronted by troops trained for war and well-handled. Lessons taught in schools of this sort (service against an inferior enemy) are of little value and usually result in false deductions and a confidence which spells disaster when called upon to play the real game."[94]

Yet in one important aspect the Philippine conflicts forever changed the U.S. Army, creating a unique and distinct Fil-American "Carabao Army." In service against bandits, sectarians, and Moros, the Philippine Scouts demonstrated both loyalty and ability, and gained a firm place in the army establishment. The Scouts improved dramatically from a nondescript and poorly armed band of irregulars to a well-armed, well-trained, and well-disciplined light infantry force. Those who served with the Scouts in the boondocks were enthusiastic. In an essay on soldiering in the tropics, Lieutenant Jesse Cullison emphasized that "Scouts and constabulary know more about the people and country than regular troops, and they can often show you some new wrinkles in getting information, scouting, etc."[95] Scout Major William H. Johnston reported that the "Scouts fill an important role and in that role are without equal. For service in the islands they can frequently be of more service than American troops."[96] By 1907 the U.S. Army had largely turned over pacification duties to its Filipino soldiers. For example, at the beginning of the Pulahan uprising in 1904 there were six Scout and twelve American companies on Samar; by the end of the campaign in 1907 there were two American and eighteen Scout companies. Similarly, the first campaigns against the Moros were fought largely by American units, but at the final battle of Bud Bagsak, there were two American and seven Scout companies, including two

Moro units.[97] By that time only the most racist officers disputed the skill and ability of Filipino troops or denied them a place in the army.

By 1907 the danger of a local outbreak's igniting an archipelago-wide uprising had receded. Although opponents such as the Pulahanes and Moros had fought with fanaticism and vigor, they had remained isolated and unable to secure widespread support. With a well-armed and experienced force of counterinsurgency troops in the Philippine Scouts and the logistical ability to support extensive military operations in the most forbidding terrain, the army was able to suppress its poorly armed and undisciplined opponents. Ironically, just when internal opposition was diminishing to a police matter, a new threat—invasion from Japan—emerged with unsettling rapidity. The guardians of empire now had to turn their attention to external dangers, and in the process transform themselves from an imperial constabulary into a modern military force.

CHAPTER 3

The Pacific Army

The Pacific Army that existed between the Philippine War and World War II was a unique institution. The unplanned child of America's rush to empire, it was born from President McKinley's opportunistic decision to send an expedition to Manila via Honolulu. From the first "Days of Empire" it was both an integral part of the U.S. Army and separate from it. For most of its existence the War Department treated it as a special force, assigning the Pacific Army and the Panama garrison their own administrative and tactical organizations. But more than that, the Pacific Army was a distinct social milieu. It was an army with its own customs, its own taboos and privileges, its own internal dynamics. Its character, language, and social environment have been captured by James Jones in *From Here to Eternity*. But perhaps the best short description of its soldiers is that of another veteran, Charles F. Ivins: "they were a lean sharp lot—their canvas gaiters scrubbed white, fitted over brilliantly shined shoes without a wrinkle, their uniforms made by Chinese tailors, at their expense, fitted their trim athletic bodies and bore no relation to the ill-shaped travesties of uniforms then issued to stateside garrisons. They could shoot well. Their drill was precise. . . . They talked of jungle marches, of the Igorrote head-hunters of Luzon, of the bloody treacherous Moros of Mindanao and Sulu. . . . These men were not intellectuals, probably a sixth grade education was their limit, but they were tough and they were loyal and they loved soldiering."[1]

The war that gave rise to the Pacific Army also marked the twilight of the old Western frontier army. The jingoistic celebrations that greeted Dewey's victory, the frenzied rush to the colors which led to a tenfold increase in the army, the stirring descriptions of the campaigning in Cuba and the Philippines—these ceased as abruptly as did the war. Muckraking journalists fell upon examples of apparent corruption and mismanagement in the War Department: the chaotic manpower mobilization, the poorly run camps where hundreds fell sick, the logistical nightmare at Tampa, the disorganized battles outside Santiago, the "embalmed beef" scandal. Overlooked were the deeper but less sensational structural problems. Years of inadequate budgets, stagnant promotion, cumbersome procedures, isolated service, poor planning, and public neglect had combined to render the nation's land forces ill-equipped for the challenges of modern war. In fact, as has been said about the British Army, the pre-1898 U.S. Army might be likened to a tribal confederation, united in its allegiance to the government but divided along regimental, branch, and personal lines. In a telling comment, Chief of Staff Hugh L. Scott called it "little more than a national constabulary," which achieved "tolerable results in time of peace" but "could not be made to work in war, as the events of 1898 abundantly proved."[2]

That the "Old Army" no longer served the nation's purposes and must be replaced by a new modern army was accepted by civilian and military officials alike. The catalyst for much of this transition, Elihu Root, secretary of war from August 1899 to January 1904, was appointed by McKinley in part because his background in corporate law fitted him well for creating the legal and administrative machinery for the government of America's new territories. He justified the president's trust by drawing up the basic policies that led to the establishment of governments in Cuba, Puerto Rico, and the Philippines. But Root's achievements as a colonial administrator were surpassed by his creation of a new model army. In his four-year tenure he implemented many of the changes that had been advocated by military progressives for two decades: a permanent increase in the Regular Army, reorganization of the artillery, the creation of a chief of staff and a General Staff, rotation between line and staff officers, an expanded education system culminating in the Army War College, a reserve manpower program, and the beginning of joint service planning.

It is tempting to speculate that the impetus for the "Root Reforms" stemmed from the secretary's vision of an army for the new empire, but there is insufficient evidence either in support or refutation. Root outlined his views on the nation's military and colonial policies on numerous occasions, but he never specifically explained his vision of a military organization for the Pacific territories, although certain of his actions clearly were instrumental in structuring the overseas army. His transfer of governing power to the Philippine Commission insured that the army would not be charged with permanent service in imperial administration. His sponsorship of the Army Reorganization Act of 2 February 1901 increased the Regulars' strength to a maximum of 100,000, including as many as 12,000 Philippine Scouts. His efforts, and those of his successors, to free the army from garrisoning numerous tiny and isolated Western posts was, in part, justified by the need to provide men for the Philippines and Hawaii. But beyond this, it is difficult to see Root's hand in the creation of a unique Pacific Army. He did not advocate, or apparently even consider, a distinct imperial organization such as Great Britain's Indian Army. Nor, once provided with the assistance of agencies charged with long-range planning, did Root direct the General Staff or the Army War College to pursue the matter.

Rather than devising a new military organization for the empire, Root may have believed that such a force would evolve naturally out of the improvement of the army as a whole. Certainly he argued his case for such reform in terms of the national rather than colonial interests. In his 1899 report he commented that federal parsimony, the absence of a foreign threat, and the demand that the army be ready for immediate use had resulted in "an elaborate system admirably adapted to secure pecuniary accountability and economy of expenditure in time of peace; a large number of small and separate commands, well officered and well disciplined, very efficient for police duty against Indians. . . . [But] the result did not include the effective organization and training of the army as a whole for the purposes of war." For Root, it was obvious that reorganization should be based on two "fundamental" propositions: "that the real object of having an army is to provide for war" and "that the regular establishment of the United States will probably never be by itself the whole machine with which any war will be fought."[3] At the heart of his reforms lay a realization that developments in technology, administration, and organization had transformed warfare: the nation whose army was better armed, trained, and administered would defeat a potentially more powerful, but less well prepared opponent. With possible enemies now able to transport forces in the hundreds of thousands, the United States could no longer rely on its minuscule Regular contingent and its coastal defenses to gain time for the mobilization of its manpower and industries. It required a force sufficient for immediate defense and for providing the cadre for a citizen army.[4] From the perspective of both the War Department and the entire army Root's emphasis on national rather than colonial concerns was the proper view, but it insured that the building of a foreign service army would become one of many competing projects. It also meant that building the Pacific Army would occur at a pace to suit the entire army, irrespective of the specific needs of the overseas forces.

According to one of Root's subordinates, General William H. Carter, the secretary left the army in a "state of preparedness for war on the part of the United States which had hitherto been unknown."[5] Reflecting the Progressive Era's interest in efficiency, order, and competence, Root sought a streamlined bureaucracy, responsible administration, and professional development. He hoped that his educational reforms would teach officers to comprehend modern warfare; at schools and review boards, they would henceforth be called upon to demonstrate their knowledge of international law, sanitation, tactics, map reading, military history, and the maneuver of large forces. Under J. Franklin Bell's direction, the schools at Leavenworth began training a new type of staff officer who could transform policy into action. The General Staff Act of 1903 created an agency to prepare the army in peace for future war; in the process, it was to monitor the army's efficiency, plan for national defense, and advise the secretary of war and field commanders. The Army War College, also founded in 1903, was charged with war planning, staff studies, and research. It promptly detailed military attachés to scour Europe for recent works on administration, logistics, medicine, equipment, tactics, and engineering. At the same time, the formation of the Joint Army and Navy Board in July 1903 provided the army chief of staff and his naval counterpart a forum "for the purposes of conferring upon, discussing, and reaching common conclusions regarding all matters calling for the cooperation of the two services."[6] Within a year, the Joint Board began the study of selected practical problems which became the basis of army-navy war plans. Root established the Artillery Corps and transferred coastal defenses from post commanders to its central command. He sponsored a committee to draft field regulations to provide a common combat doctrine for all soldiers; these new tactics emphasized large formations, firepower, and combined arms. New weaponry, most notably the famous 1903 Springfield rifle and the three-inch field artillery piece, provided American soldiers with armaments as good as, or better than, those of European forces. Such changes moved the continental U.S. Army permanently away from a coast defense and frontier constabulary and toward a modern fighting force prepared for large-unit warfare against a comparable nation-state.

The extent of the post-1898 military reforms, their apparent vindication in World War I, and the army's continued emphasis on conventional warfare, have combined to give Root's reforms an aura of historical inevitability. But contemporary evidence indicates that they were controversial, traumatic, and, in the short term, often detrimental. Root added to the turmoil in a variety of ways. His failure to clarify the duties and responsibilities of the General Staff, for example, contributed to a decades-long turf battle between the chief of staff and the administrative bureaus. Neither Root nor his successors were able to convince Congress that the nation's new military commitments required much larger forces. Between 1902 and 1914 manpower hovered between 64,000 and 100,000 soldiers, a force that Secretary of War Taft aptly termed "nothing but a skeleton army."[7] Nor could they persuade Congress to close down small posts and concentrate troops into the tactical commands they would fight in during wartime. Over a decade after the Root reforms began, Secretary of War Henry L. Stimson complained "we have scattered our Army over the country as if it were merely groups of local constabulary instead of a national organization. The result is an Army which is extraordinarily expensive to maintain, and one whose efficiency for the main purpose of its existence has been nullified as far as geographical location can nullify it."[8] Thus, as was to happen again in 1920, the army endured major structural changes without the necessary manpower, finances, or political support.

Within the army itself there was far from universal approval of Root's plans. Conservative officers such as Nelson A. Miles and Fred C. Ainsworth supported minor reforms, but believed it wrong to overturn a system tested and proven in the Civil War. James Parker serves as an example of a moderate reformer who supported improvements in reserve policy and education. Despite believing Root to be "the greatest man and patriot of the present time," Parker had doubts about the General Staff—which he found slow and fond of excessive paperwork—and the replacement of the commanding general by a chief of staff, which he believed deprived the army of a highly respected senior officer whose stewardship and "courageous opposition" had protected the army from interference by spiteful or ignorant civilians.[9] Harsher critics claimed that Root imposed European practices on military institutions that had painfully evolved to deal with uniquely American conditions. They charged that the emphasis on military education and the constant demands of overseas service were weakening efficiency, with no demonstrable benefits. A correspondent signing himself "Right Oblique" complained in 1907 that "it will be many a day before we have as good an army as we had in '98'" and that "we would do well to look back a few years and stop attempting to conduct our volunteer Army as the European machines are run."[10] Still others, disciples of Emory Upton, believed Root's reforms were insufficient; they advocated universal military training, a dramatic increase in personnel, and promotion by selection. Thus to many officers—conservative, moderate, and radical—the nation had thrown aside the protection afforded by its time-tested military system in exchange for one of dubious strength and utility.

The dissension deepened the army's pessimistic appraisal of the nation's defense; whatever their leanings, officers agreed that the military forces were dangerously weak. Ainsworth predicted it would require "national disaster and humiliation" for the American people to learn "that the effective maintenance of an army of professional soldiers is absolutely essential to the preservation of the national honor and life, and that the trained and disciplined troops of a modern enemy can not be withstood by hastily organized armies of untrained or half-trained civilians."[11] Wood, a prominent reformer whose feud with Ainsworth almost paralyzed the War Department, agreed with his rival's assessment: "Our present condition, so far as the land force is concerned, is one of unpreparedness for war with any first-class power."[12] Lower-ranking officers shared their superiors' foreboding. In one prize-winning essay in 1906, Lieutenant Colonel James L. Pettit contrasted the efficiency and aggressiveness of the armed forces of the European monarchies with the individualism, lack of discipline, and inefficiency of those of democracies. Lieutenant Hugh Johnson pointed out that Americans were no longer woodsmen and could not march or shoot, and that even if the nation had sufficient time to raise volunteers, there were insufficient weapons to arm them and too few soldiers to train them. Captain Paul B. Malone assured the readers of Century magazine that in nineteen days a "first class power" could land 100,000 troops at Long Island, against which the United States could deploy only 75,000 partially trained men. With the Hudson River cut, half-a-million New Yorkers would be thrown out of work and soon reduced to starvation. The city's minuscule military forces "would not be able to control, without great bloodshed, the blind, unreasoning fury of this hunger-stricken mob, thirty-seven per cent of which would be composed of foreigners, many of whom know no such thing as patriotism, and hate all form of government."[13]

As contemporaries noted, many of the difficulties were the result of demobilization and the shift from wartime to peacetime military needs. Yet the post–Philippine War transition seems to have been especially rocky. Officers claimed that in contrast to the excellent soldiers they had commanded in 1898, their recruits were a sorry lot. The quality of the army's manpower appears to have reached its nadir between 1903 and 1904 when, with the end of their three-year enlistment, nearly 30,000 veterans left the service. In Jolo, an officer in the 14th Cavalry wrote that the regiment's "Old Men" had departed; the new recruits were lazy, drunken, and insubordinate, an all-around "hard bunch."[14] Chief of Staff Adna R. Chaffee returned from an inspection of forty-nine continental posts distressed to find so many recruits were young, poorly nourished "weaklings" and remarked that "evidently the minimums of the standards for admission to the army had been closely observed, if not trespassed on in the enlistment of these unsatisfactory men."[15] Discipline problems rose at times to shocking levels: some commands averaged one court-martial for every soldier. Desertion, which had been negligible in the 1890s, climbed alarmingly from less than 2 percent in 1898 to 7 percent in 1903 to 11 percent in 1905, before returning to an acceptable 2 percent in 1911. The Old Army had been filled with long-service veterans, but between 1900 and 1908 there were roughly three first-timers for every reenlistment. A 1907 army survey found that "the great majority" of soldiers "when their time is out, leave the service, and the result is that organizations are so reduced in numbers that in many of them drills and practical instruction have become a farce."[16]

If Secretary of War Taft professed himself mystified that "for some reason or other the life of a soldier as at present constituted is not one to attract the most desirable class of enlisted men," the causes were clear to any number of critics.[17] Virtually everyone agreed that wages were pitiful: in 1907 a private earned thirteen dollars a month, whereas an unskilled laborer made as much as two-and-a-half dollars a day. The discrepancies were even greater for the electricians and mechanics of the Coast Artillery, Engineers, and Signal Corps, who as civilians could have earned from four to ten times as much. Small wonder that in 1906 the Coast Artillery could man only 390 of the nation's 1,199 coast defense guns. The War Department's emphasis on realistic training, or "hardening"—and especially Roosevelt's 1906 requirement that troops conduct weekly field marches in full gear—was a source of much discontent. General Frederick Funston claimed that "Nothing makes men curse and damn the service like a peace-time practice march in snow and mud, merely to carry out somebody's theory about hardening them. To work out this theory fully we should line the soldiers up and shoot at them once a week to get them used to the sound of bullets."[18]

Many argued that the poor quality and worse morale reflected the low esteem in which the military services were held. As long as states refused soldiers the franchise or denied them access to public places, the army would continue to attract marginal types. The highly publicized atrocities of the Philippine War may have contributed to an unsavory reputation, but at the heart of it were age-old stereotypes of soldiers as idlers, immigrants, and criminals; officers in turn were regarded as ballroom popinjays and petty tyrants. The United States produced no author of the stature of Britain's G. A. Henty to stir the nation's youth with the glory of military service and imperial conquest. In *Under MacArthur in Luzon,* one of the few juvenile novels to come out of the war, Edward Stratemeyer demonstrated the rewards of pluck and virtue by having his hero inherit a fortune and return home to civilian life.[19] His works, and those by such friends of the army as Charles King, perpetuated the view of a service peopled with rough, intemperate foreigners and hillbillies. In 1907 journalist Will Adams depicted Trooper Brown as a typical young recruit, an illiterate "child of the people, sheltered in a tenement, brought up in a gutter, and in desperation shunted into the army by a family that had grown tired of his inexhaustible capacity for intoxicating liquor."[20] Very rarely was the service portrayed as a place to learn skills, receive an education, develop character, or even to find adventure. Soldiers claimed they received scant military training, but instead were used as menial laborers to wash dishes, clean spittoons, and empty garbage, leading *Cosmopolitan* to warn its readers "to the average recruit life in the Army is one studied round of monotonous and uncongenial tasks."[21]

In many respects, the turmoil and demoralization of the enlisted ranks was paralleled in the officer corps, where resignations increased fivefold between 1900 and 1907, and where, according to one veteran of three decades' service, "the unrest, discontent and dissatisfaction now existing . . . are more pronounced than at any period in my entire experience."[22] Paradoxically, the very period which historians now see as marking the emergence of a professional officer corps was perceived by contemporaries as plagued by favoritism and political meddling. Roosevelt was so incensed by military politicking that he publicly warned both services in 1905 that he would punish any further attempts by officers to secure promotions, decorations, and assignments. The irony of this was not lost upon Stephen C. Mills: "the intolerable personal interference of Mr. Roosevelt in the details of the service, and more particularly his absolute disregard of everything save his own personal favorites when he did take a hand in Army administration, have resulted in a demoralizing condition."[23]

Perhaps even more than the enlisted ranks, the officer corps revealed the demise of the Old Army. Root's new model army was new indeed: of the 2,900 line officers in 1902, 1,818 had been commissioned since the beginning of the Spanish-American War. The best had proved themselves competent in small-unit command and colonial warfare; the worst, according to Charles D. Rhodes, suffered from "limited military experience and more or less instability of character."[24] The education and professionalization of these junior officers was, in the words of Chief of Staff Samuel B. M. Young, "the most important duty of the Army."[25] However, such schooling conflicted with other essential duties such as instructing their recruits, staffing the new positions in the colonial administration, and training the reserve forces. Not Root, or his successors, or the army bureaucracy managed to assign priorities to these conflicting mandates, and the result was a chaotic level of officer absenteeism, transfer, and detached service. By 1909, 27 percent of the army's line officers were absent from their units; as the inspector general reported, "There is a general complaint from all directions that the service is more or less crippled, especially in general instruction, discipline, and efficiency . . . by reason of the large percentage of officers constantly absent from their commands, by detail or otherwise."[26] That same year, the *Army and Navy Journal* reported that the 23rd Infantry regiment, scheduled to leave for the Philippines at full war strength, lacked its lieutenant colonel, all its majors, half its captains, and a third of its lieutenants. Some of these officers had never joined the regiment since their assignment to it, and others had been on detached duty for years.[27]

The problems of overseas service exacerbated these tensions and stretched the nation's military to the breaking point. The new possessions were voracious in their demand for manpower. In the decade and a half between the end of the Philippine War and America's entry into World War I, 20 to 30 percent of the small postwar army was serving outside the continental United States.

That Washington felt it necessary to station so many Americans abroad illustrates its general unwillingness to place the security of the new possessions in the hands of their inhabitants. Despite much correspondence and a number of articles in military periodicals, neither the Republican administration nor the War Department appears to have given serious thought to a separate native army. The United States had experimented with colonial troops in the spring of 1899 when it raised a Puerto Rican Provisional Regiment and some companies of Filipino irregulars. The latter proved so effective that by 1901 the Americans had fifty companies of Native Scouts. The success of these units, marred somewhat by allegations of brutality, led some officers to advocate the creation of a Filipino colonial army. Perhaps aware of a War Department survey of colonial armies of other Western powers, they stressed the desirability of recruiting from the "martial races," of keeping units divided by language and locale, and of creating a separate American colonial officer corps. They argued that native troops were cheaper than American soldiers, knew the terrain and language, were more resistant to tropical disease, and would serve as agents of Americanization. In the words of army surgeon Louis Livingstone Seaman, the "liberal utilization of native troops" would "save the flower of our army for service at home, and preserve it from degrading conditions that, alas! too often, are brought to this country by returning troops."[28] Although most of the discussion of a Filipino army centered on internal security and pacification operations, some advocates raised the possibility of its serving in wars against other imperial powers.[29] However, Root, who strongly supported the incorporation of the Philippine Scouts into the Regular Army establishment, made little effort to recruit them even to their statutory limit of 12,000 soldiers. The Hawaiian Republic's 600-man force, largely native Hawaiian but with white officers, quickly became the Hawaii National

Guard, but the War Department showed no interest in a plan by its commander to create a 5,000-man volunteer contingent.[30]

The War Department initially attempted to distribute the burdens of empire by rotating regiments overseas for two years and then returning them to continental service, but this system foundered on a number of obstacles. Foreign service was borne primarily by the mobile forces in the infantry, cavalry, and field artillery, which at times expended half their strength on it. Moreover, the army moved slowly to develop an equitable division of overseas assignments. As in the pre-1898 army, newly enlisted soldiers were attached to regiments in such a way that each unit was composed of a mixture of recruits, experienced troops with a year or two of service, and short-timers scheduled for discharge. The absurdity of shipping the latter several thousands of miles was immediately apparent; so, in September 1904 the War Department ordered that regiments sent to the Philippines could be composed only of soldiers owing more than two years of service. This proved to be no cure at all. The majority of soldiers refused to reenlist for overseas duty, forcing Pacific-bound regiments to leave behind their experienced men and fill up with new recruits. The process was repeated when the regiments returned after their two-year tours and immediately had to discharge most of their personnel. For example, in 1907 Company H, 7th Infantry, recently returned from the Philippines, could muster but one officer and thirteen soldiers at a grand review. Scheduled to return to the Philippines in 1908, its captain reported that less than a quarter of the remaining soldiers intended to reenlist, "so the company will doubtless go to the islands filled up with recruits."[31]

Further complicating the War Department's rotation policy was its decision to exclude black Americans from service in the Philippines. Soldiers from all four "colored" regiments—the 9th and 10th Cavalry and the 24th and 25th Infantry—had served with distinction in Cuba or the Philippines, and the U.S. Volunteers had included two excellent "colored" regiments. Nevertheless, after the war black troops were barred from the Philippines "at the demand of the Civil Governor of the Islands [Taft]. No charge of misconduct was made against them; from a military point of view their service had been perfectly satisfactory."[32] Taft maintained that Negroes and Malays were incompatible; during his tenure the Philippine Civil Service Board refused to hire qualified African Americans. His views were not shared by many officers, who believed, quite as sweepingly, that "there was a natural bond between the rural Filipinos and the American Negro."[33] Indeed, this "natural bond" may have been the real motive behind Taft's decision, for in 1902, when the black regiments were withdrawn from the Philippines, there were several highly publicized cases of abandoned wives and children. African American soldiers responded with justifiable heat that they were "held responsible for all the bastard children in the archipelago" and pointed to the number of white soldiers who had illegitimate children by local women.[34]

The manpower demands of Pacific service eventually forced Taft, now secretary of war, to reconsider his decision. A General Staff report on 26 November 1906 had noted the unfairness of throwing "the burden of Philippine service" exclusively on white troops.[35] As a result, on 4 January 1907 the War Department announced that the "colored" regiments would be placed on the foreign duty roster. Ignoring Taft's instructions that they be used only in Moroland, Wood committed them against Pulahanes on Leyte, where, according to one witness, they proved superior to white units. Thereafter, they performed so well overseas that when they were assigned to Hawaii in 1912, Stimson responded to one local critic: "I cannot for a moment consider the question of discriminating in the use of the regiment because of its color. The adoption of such a policy would be most unfortunate to the service, and unjust to the colored regiments. The 25th Infantry is a good regiment, and I feel sure that during its period of service in the Hawaiian Islands you will have no occasion for complaint."[36]

The manpower problems created by overseas service were magnified in the officer corps, where they were complicated by promotion and transfer. In a hypothetical case, an infantry lieutenant upon arrival in the Philippines might receive notice of his promotion to captain in a metropolitan regiment, requiring him to take the same transport back. Even worse, a lieutenant who had served with his regiment in the archipelago for its two-year tour could be promoted into a regiment detailed for Philippine service; he would then have to serve another two years in the tropics. Moreover, regiments were frequently stripped of officers for administrative and staff duties. Detached duty was eagerly sought, for there was a wide difference between a Manila posting— with its opportunity for family quarters, cheap servants, and glittering social life—and service in the field, summed up by General Bliss as "the hardest kind of roughing it."[37] In 1908 the Philippines Division commander reported an average absentee rate of 42 percent in his line units, with at least three regiments missing 60 percent of their officers.[38] Those who remained with their regiments were so overburdened with administrative duties that they had little chance to master the responsibilities of troop command. Second Lieutenant Campbell B. Hodges wrote that in addition to substituting for his absent captain as company commander, he was expected to spend four hours daily on schoolwork, function as both his battalion's quartermaster and its commissary officer, supervise post construction, serve as assistant intelligence officer, and, in the time remaining, coach athletics.[39]

All of these problems placed a crippling burden on a military organization already traumatized by Root's organizational changes. The continental army was shifting from small-company tactics to training for war under a command system based on corporate management. Such a structural overhaul was virtually impossible when every year one soldier in three was assigned to foreign service. The problem was exacerbated in the Pacific territories, whose own needs were often hostage to the immediate concerns of the metropolitan army. Although the numbers of American soldiers in the Philippines had declined from 16,346 in 1903 to 12,282 in 1910, the demands for overseas manpower were actually increasing. The Panama Canal Zone was to gain its first permanent garrison of 800 in 1911 and Hawaii, already reinforced by 1,300 men, was scheduled to receive several thousand more. Small wonder that in 1910 General Carter told Congress that overseas commitments were the primary source of the army's problems: "the trouble is that we have grown from a little frontier army to one spread all over the world—in America, Porto Rico, Hawaii, Alaska, the Philippines, and sometimes in Cuba—and we have not got the officers and men to do it."[40]

In order to avoid both the disruption of constant troop rotation and insure that continental and overseas forces were ready for their individual missions, "the only practical solution would be to assign certain regiments permanently to the several foreign stations."[41] That, at least, was the conclusion of a General Staff study by Captain John McAuley Palmer. In his sweeping 1911 "Report on a Scheme for a Well Balanced Army," Palmer urged the divorce of the overseas forces from the continental army and their separation into distinct tactical commands whose organization, equipment, and training could reflect their unique military situation. He suggested that the Philippine's current mobile garrison—eight infantry and four cavalry regiments, each at half their wartime strength—be consolidated into four infantry and two cavalry regiments, each at full strength. This would release six regiments, exactly the number required for Hawaii. Officers and men would rotate into overseas regiments every three years and would then be replaced by entirely new personnel. According to Palmer, his plan would result in no significant change in the overall strength of the garrison and would save over $1 million in transportation costs.[42] Secretary of War Stimson saw another reason for separation: "the foreign garrison should be prepared to defend itself at an instant's notice against a foe who may command the sea. Unlike the troops in the United States it can not count upon reinforcement or recruitment. It is an outpost on which will fall the brunt of the first attack in case of war."[43]

The War Department recommended the creation of a distinct overseas force in its 1912 "Report of the Land Forces of the United States." This Colonial Army would be kept at permanent war strength, would cost less, would simplify training and administration, and would allow the establishment of tactical commands in the continental United States.[44] Moving rapidly, on 30 March 1912 the department issued General Orders 8 designating the 8th, 13th, 15th, and 24th Infantry, the 7th and 8th Cavalry, and the 2nd Field Artillery regiments—a total of 9,800 soldiers—as the permanent American garrison in the Philippines. A year later, the Colonial Army system was extended to Hawaii and the Canal Zone.[45]

From its inception the Colonial Army was controversial. The commander of the District of Luzon noted the effect of bringing units up to war strength: "for the first time in years I have seen every company with a captain and nearly all subalterns present for duty."[46] However, the great majority of those on foreign duty detested Palmer's creation. It struck at the hallowed tradition of a soldier's permanent affiliation with one regiment, it imposed a three-year tour overseas, and it permanently exiled some of the most famous units in the army. By abolishing extra pay, allowances, and double time toward retirement, it not only removed the chief incentives to foreign service but made it a financial burden. Even more serious, the legislation made no provision for infantry and cavalry noncommissioned officers—career soldiers who, unlike their Coast Artillery peers, held their rank only within their regiment. In the Colonial Army they had the unhappy choice of either spending their entire military service abroad or returning to the United States as privates. Additional problems developed in 1915 when Congress limited the Philippine tour to two years, and again when critics noted that the War Department had somehow managed to station both African American infantry units abroad. A year later the department blundered further when it took advantage of a temporary suspension of the two-year limit and transferred many of the departing 8th Cavalry's troopers into the newly arrived 15th Cavalry. The men justifiably felt their enlistment contracts had been violated and began refusing duty in order to be court-martialed and discharged. One officer commented that the soldiers "prefer the certainty of a few months at Alcatraz to the prospect of a longer term out here. The offenses are committed deliberately, and are carefully calculated to bring a prison sentence shorter than the remaining period of their enlistment."[47] The most controversial practice, however, was that of rotating individuals rather than units, and criticism of this challenge to troop cohesion, discipline, and efficiency continued throughout the Pacific Army's existence.[48]

The Colonial Army system also failed to keep the overseas units at full strength. The War Department's accounting practices robbed the overseas garrisons of manpower and created a marked difference between their paper strength and their actuality. Washington counted men as serving in the Pacific garrisons who were on leave, in transit, convalescing in mainland hospitals, or already in the United States awaiting discharge. One Philippine Department commander complained in 1921 that he could "never tell what strength to count upon, since vacancies are not filled until the men returning, either for discharge or on expiration of foreign service, have been disposed of and notification received here. Even then, there is no assurance that recruits will arrive to fill vacancies. There is no arrangement existing so that this headquarters is regularly supplied with men."[49] High turnover continued to be a problem to the eve of World War II. In 1926 Hawaii's commander reported that in the preceding twelve months 38 percent of his officers and 46 percent of his enlisted men had completed their tour of duty and left Oahu.[50] In 1931 the Hawaiian Division replaced 27 percent of its overall enlisted strength, 44 percent of its infantry officers, 56 percent of its field artillery officers, and 85 percent of its Air Corps contingent.[51] That same year the lone American infantry regiment in the Philippines, the 31st Infantry, lost 587 of its 1,336 men to the expiration of their tours.[52] Throughout its entire existence, the Pacific Army was composed of units in constant flux of new recruits, men halfway through their enlistment, and short-timers.

Despite its unpopularity, the Colonial Army system survived until World War II—not necessarily for its military efficiency, for, as Palmer himself pointed out in his proposal, the forces he allocated to the Philippines were insufficient to perform their mission. Rather, it continued because it proved far more advantageous to the army as a whole. Unwilling and unable to make the local populations responsible for their own defense, the army had to rely on its Regulars to guard the empire. Stationing regiments permanently overseas cut the expenses of the Philippine garrison by almost a third in the first two years of its adoption. Moreover, as a 1915 General Staff survey admitted, despite its many drawbacks there appeared no better alternative. Finally, and perhaps most important, the Colonial Army system had substantial benefits, not for the overseas territories but for the continental army. With the rotation of officers and men finally stable, the War Department could now assign officers and men in the United States to permanent divisions, staff schools, and other institutions necessary to insure a modern military force. Ironically, much of the modernization after the Spanish-American War had been motivated by the need to create an army for the new empire, but all too soon the continental forces had to divorce the imperial forces to modernize themselves.[53]

Despite all these difficulties, and despite the continuation of almost perverse disincentives for overseas service, there nevertheless developed, from the very outset, an esprit de corps among the Pacific forces. Out of the two-year transients, there emerged a cadre of semipermanent colonials, to whom the Pacific Army was both home and career. To some it was the shared experience of service in exotic tropical locales tinged with danger. Douglas MacArthur, assigned to the Philippines in 1908, predicted with characteristic histrionics, "this means for me the whirling swing of the old life unless some day out there in the jungle a Moro bolo or a snub-nosed forty-five change it all—into still waters and silence."[54] Others remained overseas because they could not leave. Charles Willeford remembered an Air Corps sergeant who had married a Filipino woman and fathered six children. The Asian Exclusion Act and his state's laws against interracial marriage kept his family out of the United States, so "he was doomed by his marriage to stay in the Philippines until he died."[55] Still others enjoyed the relaxed tempo of tropical soldiering and the vibrant social life: during the 1920s, when the Philippines were exempt from Prohibition, 80 percent of the officers on the foreign service roster selected it as their first or second preference. Others wanted to stay with their unit, either to keep their rank and privileges or because the "outfit" had become their home.

Whatever their motives for remaining, the Pacific soldiers recognized their distinctiveness in their references: they belonged to the Bamboo or Carabao or Pineapple armies; they served in places like "Wahoo" or "the Rock" or simply the "boonies," and prided themselves as "sunshiners" or "homesteaders," superior to those from the "mainland." They spoke pidgin or "bamboo" English, went "hiking" in the "boondocks," their sergeants urging them to "wiki wiki" (hurry), the men complaining about unnecessary "hila hila" (work) and plotting how to obtain "jawbone" (credit) to last until payday. They had their own marching songs, most of which, such as "Damn the Insurrectos," "I Won't Come Back to Wahoo Anymore," and "The Monkeys Have No Tails in Zamboanga," expressed their amused contempt for the people they protected.

With few exceptions, the enlisted men who filled the ranks of the Pacific Army were volunteers who had signed up for either two years in the Philippines or three years in Hawaii. In the peacetime army, they enlisted to fill a vacancy in a particular branch, such as the Air Corps or Infantry, and quite often to fill a specific slot. A recruit could thus select, from a limited number of choices, the regiment or battery or squadron he would serve in and where he would be stationed. Once he joined his "outfit," he usually remained there for the rest of his service. If he had a good character, he could reenlist to fill his own position; some soldiers remained with a single company for over a decade. That the army rarely had problems meeting its enlistment quotas says much about the harshness of social conditions back home, for beyond bed and board there were few incentives to military service prior to World War II. In 1907 the monthly wage of a private was $13, in the interwar period it ranged between $17 and $21; and even this was subject to a number of deductions. Advancement was glacial; it was not unusual for a soldier to serve ten years in one company before making corporal. Thus, in many respects the habits and practices of the "Old Army" of the Western frontier continued in the "New Army" on the Pacific frontier.

The quality of these enlisted man varied greatly. In the first few years after both the Philippine War and World War I there were complaints about the low physical, intellectual, and moral standards of the troops; for most of the interwar period, however, the army attracted long-term recruits—referred to as "thirty-year men"—who made soldiering a life occupation. Prior to World War I, there was a substantial number of foreign-born soldiers in the ranks; a survey of the 14,000 American troops in the Philippines in June 1917 revealed 1,529 immigrants, of whom the largest minorities were Austro-Hungarians (358), Russians (321), Germans (272), and British (260). The most totally "American" unit was the "colored" 9th Cavalry, whereas almost a third of the 31st Infantry was foreign born.[56] After the war, domestic recruitment increased, but the army continued to be a haven for men who could not make a living in the civilian world. Stanley G. Larsen, an officer in Hawaii in the 1930s, recalled his illiterate company sergeant and soldiers who "joined the Army for three square meals a day and a bed."[57] Sergeant Russell A. Eberhardt, who served in Hawaii at the same time, believed a man joined the army "in order to live like a human instead of being in jail, or crime, or hoboing."[58] It was from such material that the Pacific Army produced the "lean sharp lot" so admired by young Lieutenant Ivins in 1931.

Officers were assigned a two-year overseas duty by a complicated rotation system based on their rank and branch. As vacancies appeared overseas, the War Department selected replacements from the foreign service list, who were notified they would soon be sent abroad for two years. At the end of his tour an officer could volunteer for an additional year of foreign service. The two-year term was mandated by Congress and greatly resented by the War Department. According to Chief of Staff Scott: "[it was] very disrupting to the efficiency of the service, expensive to the public funds in the carrying out, and it is involving many of our young officers with families in serious financial problems. Every officer in the Philippines must change station at least once every two years, and he may be detailed to staff and other duty while there, and then return to a camp station on the border, with the only provisions for their family in rented rooms in houses in a near-by town. For the young married officers of limited income this frequent change of station is a veritable curse."[59]

The trip over the Pacific to Hawaii or the Philippines could be a memorable experience. Prior to the institution of the Colonial Army system, a regiment moved like a circus troupe, packing and shipping all its equipment, its records, and virtually everything else. After 1912 the discomfort was mostly individual, but still considerable. Military families arrived in the tropics with steamer trunks filled with the furs and woolens they had needed during garrison life in Montana. Officers with families had either to sell their possessions or entrust them, at their own expense, to the mercies of the Quartermaster Corps, which even in the 1920s still damaged 10 percent of the household goods entrusted to it.[60]

During the Philippine War the Quartermaster Corps had established its own Transport Service, refitting several steamers with mattresses, showers, cold-storage rooms, and hospitals, and, according to one senior officer, had "spared no expense in making them comfortable and sanitary."[61] Here was the perspective of one who enjoyed the privileges of rank: the palatial suites, excellent food, and the power over shipboard society.[62] It was far different for everyone else. Junior officers could be separated from their families, find their reserved cabins abruptly commandeered, and be crowded so many to a room as to have to sleep in shifts. The Transport Service commonly overbooked first-class cabins, and worse, forced officers out of them in order to make room for civil servants and junketing politicians. One officer, "ranked out" of his room, referred to his transport as the "Congressional Limited,"[63] and "An Army Wife" complained that "the War Department seems to consider the Philippines a burden of expense and that money must be saved on the misery of the unfortunates who have to do duty in those islands and the families who support them."[64] For their part, single officers resented the social pressure that forced them to give up their cabins to married colleagues and then to find "a thousand squalling brats under foot."[65] When Lieutenant Matthew K. Deichelmann sailed on the *Grant* in 1930 he shared a tiny stateroom with six other officers; on deck they all had to wear full uniform, including boots and spurs. Douglas MacArthur won the young lieutenant's admiration when he vowed on leaving the Philippines that one of his first priorities as chief of staff would be to allow officers to wear civilian clothes on transports.[66] Although officers contributed the bulk of written complaints, it is clear that enlisted man suffered far more. One correspondent related an incident in which a sergeant's wife was denied permission to accompany her husband until she agreed to serve as an officer's servant.[67]

Transports crossed the Pacific every three months, and their arrival overseas prompted a major celebration. Troops en route to the Philippines made a short stop in Hawaii, and for three decades Honolulu was renowned for its hospitality. On docking, the ship would be serenaded by a regimental band and, for the officers, a host of service friends would descend with flower leis. The clannish Air Corps welcomed its new arrivals by flying out to meet them as they approached the harbor. The Moana Hotel staged transport dances where wives and daughters could show off mainland fashions. Resident units would host those in transit; in 1916 members of the 9th Cavalry en route to the Philippines were treated to a dinner and a dance by comrades in the 25th Infantry. Enlisted men were offered a variety of entertainment ranging from athletic competitions, passes for movies or theaters, or simply the leisure to visit the fleshpots of Honolulu. Thirsty soldiers could obtain the liquor denied them on board, and many took full advantage in the short time allowed before journeying on to the Philippines. The 1916 dance for the 9th Cavalry, for example, ended in a drunken riot when the soldiers decided to avenge the insulting treatment they had received from local prostitutes. Deichlmann's vague memories of Honolulu consisted of a three-day binge and crawling up the gangplank on his hands and knees. Lieutenant Joseph H. Nazarro remembered one intoxicated officer whose insistence on taking pictures of the farewell festivities left him stranded on the dock.[68]

After the advent of the Colonial Army in 1912, all soldiers except senior noncommissioned officers arrived as privates. In the Philippines, the troops received a cursory inspection and then traveled up the Pasig River to Fort McKinley where they were assigned to special recruit companies. In Hawaii, they were lined up on the dock while officers walked through the ranks and detailed soldiers to the infantry, artillery, or staff units. Usually the Hawaiian Department Military Police had first pick, and selected men at least six-foot tall with a high school diploma. For infantry, field artillerymen, and other members of the mobile army, the next experience was a ride on the pineapple train to Schofield, while soldiers assigned to the coast defenses went to Fort Kamehameha. After three days in quarantine, the new soldiers joined recruit squads for their basic training. Once this was complete, they joined their "outfit" and remained with it for the rest of their tour unless they went to school, secured a specialist's rating, or were transferred.[69]

For officers the assimilation period was somewhat different. In the first decades of overseas occupation, there was little effort to assist military families; new arrivals had to shift for themselves. By the 1920s an informal social support system had developed; if newcomers did not already have friends to meet them, they would be assigned a sponsor to smooth the transition to Pacific duty. Officers assigned to Oahu, a posting notoriously short of quarters, would assume the rental lease, and sometimes a car, from a departing officer. When Arthur L. Koch arrived at Fort Stotsenburg his sponsor not only took care of introductions but had already prepared his quarters, purchased food, and hired servants for him.[70] Lieutenant Ivins and his wife, arriving in Manila in 1931, were quartered with one captain's family and another captain was charged with showing them Manila. Ivins recalled that the system had both good and bad features. An evening might consist of their being taken to a party, a dinner, then dancing at the Santa Anna Cabaret, followed by late-night entertainment at the Poodle Dog bistro, an early morning breakfast at Dixie Dick's, and then finally returning to their residence, where their sponsors welcomed everyone in and insisted they all have a round of drinks. As their residential hosts had arranged an equally strenuous round of daytime activities, the young couple were glad to ship out for Zamboanga.[71]

In the first decade of the Pacific Army, living conditions varied greatly. In Hawaii the small garrison of infantry and artillerymen was stationed at Camp McKinley, at the time an unhealthy Waikiki swamp. They had a miserable time in rotting lean-tos and torn tents; worse, they served as menial laborers— in army parlance they drew fatigue duty—clearing away trees and coral, draining swamps, and building roads.[72] For anyone lucky enough to be stationed in Manila and rich enough to afford decent housing, life could be very pleasant indeed. For those with meager incomes, quarters in Manila were cramped, expensive, and unhealthy. Outside the capital, for years the conditions ranged from very comfortable to extremely primitive. Prior to their commitment in the Pulahan campaign, many of the American troops were stationed at Camp Jossman, a healthy post with newly built wood barracks, large porches, and modern facilities. One of those fortunate enough to be deployed to Camp Connell, Samar, described it as much "like a modern health resort" located in a coconut grove near a sandy beach, with comfortable quarters, distilled water, and an ice plant.[73] Although isolated, Connell had band concerts, a ladies card club, regimental dinners, dances, and a library of several hundred books. Such amenities could seldom be found in the more isolated camps in the interior, especially in posts held by the Scouts. At Mutiong, the officers lived in shacks in the middle of a swamp and waited for the weekly steamer to leave them their ice ration—enough for three highballs each. Another described his camp in Mindanao, as "a most desirable post for mosquitoes, mud, rain and lizards. The post has blown down two or three times in the last twelve months."[74]

In both possessions, the army established its main posts with similar strategic concerns. The location of the coast defense forces was simple—by definition, next to their guns. Planning for the mobile forces—infantry, cavalry, and field artillery—was a far more complicated task. These had to be stationed where they could immediately deploy to protect the capital city from riot or a surprise attack, could guard the main invasion routes, and could find sufficient room to train.

In the Philippines the dispersal caused by pacification operations prevented the immediate consolidation of troops into permanent garrisons. By the first decade the coast defenders were stationed at Fort Wint at Subic Bay—a post that was later held by no more than a caretaker detachment—and the Manila Bay complex of Fort Mills on Corregidor, as well as forts Frank, Drum, and Hughes on the smaller islands. During his tenure as commanding general, Leonard Wood consolidated the bulk of the scattered American forces either at Fort William McKinley, an 8,000-acre infantry post six miles outside Manila in Rizal Province (which both protected Manila and guarded against an invasion from the south) or at Fort Stotsenburg in the Central Luzon Valley, sixty-five miles from the capital (allowing the troops to move either against a landing at Lingayen Gulf or into the Bataan Peninsula).[75] In addition, there was a small infantry force at two old Spanish barracks in Manila, the Cuartel de Espana and the Cuartel de Infanteria; Fort Santiago served as the departmental headquarters. After World War I, the Americans occupied only the harbor fortifications, the 31st Infantry's quarters in Manila proper, and a 15th Infantry battalion at Fort William McKinley. Stotsenburg became virtually all Filipino, with the exception of a small Air Corps base at Clark Field. By the 1920s the only troops outside these were two Scout battalions, one at Pettit Barracks in Zamboanga and the other at Camp John Hay in Baguio.

As in the Philippines, the Hawaiian garrison was divided into coast defense and mobile forces. In Hawaii the Coast Artillery occupied three major posts—Fort Ruger on Diamond Head, Fort DeRussy on Waikiki Beach, and Fort Kamehameha at Pearl Harbor—and a smaller battery-size post, Fort Armstrong, at Honolulu Harbor. In 1923 the army completed Fort Weaver across the main channel of Pearl Harbor from Fort Kamehameha and, a decade later, Fort Barrette in the hills overlooking the bay. The location of Hawaii's mobile garrison required almost a decade to decide because of numerous constraints. The need to protect both Honolulu and Pearl, the rugged Koolau and Waianae Mountains, the prevalence of sugarcane and pineapple agriculture in the Leilehua Plateau, and the necessity to insure title to all land restricted the army's choices to two locations: a 1,344-acre lot at Kahauki between Honolulu and Pearl Harbor and a 14,400-acre area on the Leilehua Plateau, some twenty miles from Honolulu and eight miles from Pearl Harbor. For both financial and political reasons, locals supported the Kahauki location. Honolulu's merchants looked hungrily to free-spending soldiers, while the territorial government sought to reserve the immense Leilehua tract for American homesteaders. As long as the major threat to Hawaii was a small raiding party with no ability to mount a siege, Kahauki's location between Honolulu and Pearl made it ideal. Accordingly, the building of Fort Shafter began in 1905. However, the fear of an actual invasion soon made a more centrally located reservation necessary, and in 1908 the first workmen boarded trains for Leilehua to begin construction of what was to become Schofield Barracks. Situated amid pineapple and sugarcane fields some five miles north of Pearl Harbor, Schofield covered the vulnerable western and northern approaches to Honolulu and the naval base. After World War I, Hawaii's posts also included Wheeler Field at Schofield and Luke Field on Ford Island in Pearl Harbor, the latter eventually replaced by Hickam Field next to the naval base.[76]

Living conditions on Hawaii varied greatly. Officers at Fort Kamehameha resided in comfortable three-bedroom houses with a servant's quarters but the barracks were so abysmal that in 1927 one outraged officer sent photographs of them to the inspector general with the comment that it was "not reasonable to expect men to have pride in their service when they are required to live in such a hovel in a permanent post in peace time."[77] Fort Weaver, described by one veteran as "a hodgepodge of buildings," had barracks made of galvanized tin.[78] In contrast, Forts Ruger and DeRussy in Honolulu—which boasted good quarters, recreational facilities, and close proximity to beaches and the city—were considered excellent assignments.[79] Shafter's reputation was somewhat mixed. In 1913, when soldiers were living in tents, one officer boasted of killing 300 centipedes in a year; fifteen years later, Mrs. Fox Conner, wife of the Hawaiian Department commander, declared that Shafter was "not an attractive place. The house itself was hideous."[80] But others remembered its majestic tree-lined Palm Circle, its large and spacious frame houses, and its cool climate, and argued that Shafter's main drawback was its size; 90 percent of the department's officers were forced to live off post.[81]

Schofield Barracks, the home of the Hawaiian Division, had some of the most impressive, and some of the worst, facilities in the army. Construction had barely begun in 1909 when the 5th Cavalry arrived in response to fears of Japanese invasion. The troopers found a barren expanse of red dirt, surrounded by pineapple and sugarcane fields, on which a few rough barracks had been placed. Within three years, the garrison had grown to four regiments, still housed in shacks and tents. In many respects, Schofield never recovered from this initial shock. For decades, inspections reported the post was still unfinished, and one commanding general bluntly told his troops that conditions "not only were a great injustice but rotten wrong."[82] In 1915 many of the buildings still had dirt floors, and much of the garrison was under canvas; there were few sewers and even fewer roads—a crucial weakness given the garrison's mission of deploying anywhere in the island. Schofield also suffered a serious water shortage, occasionally forcing troops to move to other camps; the problem persisted until a reservoir system was completed in the mid-1920s.

Following World War I, Schofield, like posts throughout the United States, was cursed with dozens of wartime structures of the flimsiest construction. The 19th Infantry, for example, had to live in collapsing barracks with leaking roofs, no water, and malfunctioning sewers for over a decade. In 1928 over half the posts' enlisted men lived in "dilapidated shacks" that were "practically uninhabitable."[83] As late as 1932, General Drum informed a congressional committee that Schofield's junior officers lived in conditions that "compare unfavorably with those of laborers on the adjoining sugar plantations."[84] The post's miserable living conditions were apparent only to those who looked inside the quarters, for successive commanding officers devoted their attention to beautification projects such as planting trees, laying out fields and roads, and painting exteriors. Not until the late 1930s were most of the old temporary barracks finally replaced by brand new concrete structures with modern plumbing. One veteran who served there in 1940 recalled barracks in which the 200 members of his company slept in single cots, head to toe: "Living conditions were the best while I was at Schofield. . . . We kept the building in A-1 condition—clean and neat—you could eat off the floor."[85]

In the Philippines, during the first decade of occupation the troops were so peripatetic that it made little sense to build permanent quarters. Congress showed a marked reluctance to allocate funds for buildings, and the War Department often displayed a poor understanding of tropical conditions: it spent over $2 million constructing barracks out of American wood, which the climate and termites soon rendered uninhabitable. As the Regulars were concentrated into permanent camps, living conditions improved, albeit very slowly. When Arthur Koch was stationed at Fort Mills in 1913, the quarters were still under construction; there were "no fit places for living and the poor bachelor was out of luck completely. No one wanted to go there and after I saw the place I could not blame them."[86] In contrast, ten years later it was considered one of the best postings in the army, with comfortable quarters, riding, movies, and a vibrant social life.[87]

A similar transformation occurred at Fort Stotsenburg. Caroline Shunk, a colonel's wife who arrived in 1909 shortly after a typhoon had destroyed most of the buildings, claimed conditions were worse than when she had lived in a tent in the Dakotas. The wooden houses had no windows, there were numerous cracks and holes, snakes and rats abounded, and the thatched roofs leaked so badly that babies had to be placed under umbrellas.[88] Between 1910 and 1913, these shoddy accommodations were replaced by concrete and steel housing, and the barren countryside gave way to shaded avenues and rows of hibiscus. Officers' quarters were built along a tree-lined boulevard. Nicknamed "barns" because of their high roofs and broad porches, they featured a raised floor, which allowed the cool breeze to pass through; they were prized as quarters for the next seventy years. After World War I, both Stotsenburg and Fort McKinley were primarily Scout posts with large civilian communities, called barrios, where military families lived.[89]

To the American soldiers of the 31st Infantry unfortunate enough to be assigned to the old Spanish barracks in Manila, conditions remained consistently bad. Inspectors described the two cuartels as crumbling stone hovels, dank, hot, airless, comfortless, and unsanitary. Private Michael J. Campbell, stationed there in 1941, remembered windowless rooms crawling with vermin where soldiers amused themselves by burning the voracious bedbugs out of their bed frames with blowtorches.[90]

Once in their quarters, soldiers found they had to make a considerable outlay for tropical clothing. The Pacific Army was a spit-and-polish outfit whose officers and men prided themselves on their snappy appearance. An officer at Schofield in the interwar period would be expected to wear his khakis during drill, his white uniform at all post functions before retreat, his white mess uniform at formal evening events, and either a tuxedo or his white dress uniform off duty after retreat.[91] In both Hawaii and the Philippines, social conventions required officers' wives to bring or purchase a good number of dresses and evening gowns for the numerous teas, dinners, and dances. Enlisted men also had high clothing expenses: during the interwar period, when a buck private made less than twenty dollars a month—some of it in the form of canteen scrip—he would pay from ten to twelve dollars for a tailor-made khaki "Class A" uniform, and as much again for such accessories as off-duty cap, leggings, and black cravat. The blocked felt campaign hat in which long-term soldiers took such pride might represent a year of financial scrimping. Army inspectors brooded about nonregulation uniforms, but they realized that the army's standard issue—the "O.D." uniform—was so bad that "no commander would be caught dead letting his troops wear government issue khaki uniforms at review, parades, and inspections."[92] Colonel C. H. Conrad concluded a litany of grievances against O.D. clothing "scarcely entitled to the name uniform" with the comment "the wearing of such uniforms (?) is humiliating and cannot be expected to command the respect with which the uniform of the Country is entitled."[93] Such complaints were answered by the Office of the Quartermaster General in 1925: "The unsatisfactory condition of the present O.D. uniform is known to the War Department and to this office. However, the War Department is faced with the proposition of having on hand from the World War 3,184,00 pairs of breeches, O.D., and 2,683,000 coats, cotton, O.D. and these uniforms must be used before funds for the purchase of new cotton uniforms can be requested from Congress."[94] Accordingly, throughout the interwar years soldiers bought their own clothes, and the tailored uniform and accessories distinguished the Pacific soldier from his continental comrades.[95]

The dangers of prolonged overseas service created considerable worry. Army doctor Charles E. Woodruff argued that Caucasians were susceptible to solar "actinic rays" which overstimulated their nervous system, caused disease, and resulted in physical and mental breakdown.[96] In 1906, surgeon James S. Taylor charged that many of the military personnel were being misdiagnosed as having beriberi when they were actually suffering from alcoholism brought on by the "depression of spirits" resulting from "prolonged residence in the Philippines."[97] One correspondent warned in 1907 that "our retired list is being loaded up with lieutenants and young captains broken down by continuous service under tropical suns"; soon there would be nothing but an army of "neurasthenic wrecks."[98] Psychological problems were common, and the advice to officers in the tropics was to "keep men off their bunks except in the middle of the day and at night, as many get sick from homesickness as from any other cause, do not work them to death but keep their minds and bodies exercised."[99] Veterans referred to "Philippinitis," described by the *Army and Navy Journal* as "a lay term for what medical men call tropical neurasthenia" in which the sufferer was overcome with apathy, inertia, fatigue, and depression.[100] As a young officer on Corregidor observed, "It seems to me I can see in the faces of most of the officers the expression of tropical lassitude and indifference that gets hold of one here. It is a constant fight to keep out of the slough."[101] On Hawaii, soldiers coined the term "rock happy" or "gone pineapple" to refer to comrades' depressed, moody, or erratic behavior. One private wrote of two suicides in his company: "It happens quite often here as it is a tough post to pull. The time drags away if you don't have anything to do."[102]

Next to venereal diseases, to be discussed later, the most formidable enemy in the wars in Cuba and the Philippines proved to be tropical microbes. These so devastated the first contingents that some medical authorities doubted whether the United States could maintain troops in the tropics. Indeed, health concerns underlay much of the argument for a Filipino colonial army. Experienced field officers writing on the lessons of pacification campaigns devoted as much attention to field sanitation and preventive medicine as to tactics and march formation. The end of open warfare did not reduce disease: in 1903 the army in the Philippines had a malarial rate of 45 percent against 6 percent for the continental forces and a diarrheal disease rate of 32 percent against 8 percent. Junior officers on pacification duties soon recognized that human enemies were less dangerous than cholera and dysentery. During the Pulahan campaign, for example, the commander at Camp Avery found over a third of the garrison on sick report, another third feverish, and "the majority of the command . . . physically unable to perform more hard service."[103]

The army devoted intensive effort to keeping soldiers in the tropics healthy. In Hawaii between 1910 and 1912, a joint civil-military board supervised a vigorous campaign to rid Honolulu of malaria, bubonic plague, cholera, and yellow fever. The city was divided into forty sections, in each of which ten laborers under a noncommissioned officer were detailed to clear up refuse. The construction of Tripler Hospital, rapid advances in tropical medicine, and strict sanitation and quarantine laws enforced by both civil and military authorities combined to cut the disease rate drastically and made Hawaii one of the healthiest postings in the service.[104] Between 1900 and 1903 it sent three medical boards to investigate Philippine diseases; their findings resulted in treatments for dengue fever, beriberi, and dysentery. Malaria was greatly reduced through a concerted campaign: post officers collected mosquitoes for the Medical Museum laboratory; the army drained swamps; and soldiers were forced to take quinine. Officers were proud of the indirect effects of their activities on the local population. Chaplain J. M. Sutherland boasted in 1908 that he had "seen the Army, with the aid of its rifles and cannon, doing more in five years to take a race out of the clutches of disease and epidemics by enforcing sanitary regulations than could be effected by peaceful means of education in probably ten times that number of years."[105] Despite these precautions, the Philippines remained an unhealthy place with a disease rate higher than average. Oscar Reeder who served there in the 1930s, remembered that soldiers were forbidden to eat food or drink water anywhere except at a military facility and were advised to remain indoors at night to avoid malaria.[106]

The army also devoted much attention to insuring that its troops were well fed. The issue of a special tropical ration was vigorously debated in the first decade of occupation. Some officers believed soldiers should eat even more beef and pork; others argued for a lighter, lower-protein diet. The army eventually decided to feed its overseas troops the same rations they would get on the mainland, but including local fruit and rice. During the interwar period, the availability of fresh vegetables and meat ebbed and flowed with the arrival of shipping. Howard C. Fields remembered that because the army issued mess sergeants their funds at the beginning of each month, "we usually ate very good the first 10 days or so. Then it could get pretty bad at times."[107] In the 1920s the persistence of huge wartime stocks led to frequent forced issues of canned foods. One officer enclosed a can of decade-old potatoes in a letter to his superiors with the comment that to provide such food was an "outrageous breach of faith with our enlisted men."[108] Although this problem had largely disappeared by the 1930s, many soldiers shared the sentiments of the private who complained that being ordered to wear his Class A uniform in the mess hall was the equivalent of being required to wear a tuxedo to shovel manure.[109] But Schofield's kitchens elicited praise from the inspector general himself, who in 1921 reported "I have never seen cleaner kitchens, kitchen tables and dining room tables or neater and more orderly store rooms than I found in these regiments."[110] The post's famous Cooks and Bakers School served as a model for army cooking, and each new company and field officer had to take its month-long course on food preparation. One soldier who served at Schofield in 1940 remembered that "the food in the Army was first class" and praised his mess sergeant, who managed to save enough money to feed his company steak each month, a delicacy he had never tasted until he joined the army.[111]

Underlying the problem of adequate sustenance was the far greater matter of logistics. Virtually everything that soldiers wore, lived in, fought with, and ate had to be brought thousands of miles across the Pacific. The army's needs were prodigious and its appetites voracious. In 1912, for example, the 19,000 soldiers in the Philippines consumed 400,000 pounds of beef each month. Such demand stretched the capacity of the overcrowded harbors at Honolulu and Manila, and congressional parsimony prevented the construction of adequate warehouse space. The need for storage became critical after World War I, when, in a misconceived effort to free shipping space for expeditionary personnel, the War Department decided to ship sufficient equipment for 50,000 soldiers to Hawaii and the Philippines. The result was an appalling waste of equipment and manpower: not only were thousands of tons of supplies ruined by exposure to tropical weather, but training virtually ceased as soldiers pulled duty as stevedores and warehouse guards. For years afterward, Pacific troops were expected to eat war surplus food, drive war surplus vehicles, train with war surplus weapons, and live in wartime temporary buildings.[112]

Such problems, created by Washington's mistakes and about which local officers could do little, should not detract from the commendable efforts of the overseas commissaries. Koch, a sergeant with the Subsistence Department in Manila in 1912, recalled with some awe the Army Depot Commissary. His own duties with the Cold Storage Division required that he maintain a reserve of 1,000,000 pounds of beef. When the beef arrived from Australia, he had to insure its immediate transfer to cold storage, for even a few hours' exposure to the Philippine climate would cause it to decay.[113] In Hawaii, local officers made recurrent efforts to encourage the local production of food and live-stock, so as to secure sustenance in case of war; but the high prices gained by sugarcane and pineapple inhibited the growth of domestic staples, and cattle raising was confined largely to the island of Hawaii, certain to be cut off from Oahu by invasion.[114]

In retrospect, the creation of the Pacific Army was the result of a long series of compromises. Unlike some imperial powers, the United States did not form two distinct establishments for its colonial and metropolitan garrisons. Rather it chose to maintain the integrity of its existing army and treat overseas service as a temporary duty. Like most compromises, the system contained many shortcomings, the most serious of which were the sacrifice of regimental spirit and a poorly administered replacement system. But the essential weaknesses of the Pacific Army stemmed from the fact that it remained secondary to continental defense. It never received the resources, either in matériel or personnel, to fulfill the missions that Washington gave it. There were periods of great interest in Pacific defense and eras when money and men were available, but, on the whole, the problems of the overseas forces remained distinctly subordinate to the broader interests of the U.S. Army.

CHAPTER 4

The Dilemmas of Pacific Defense

Until the advent of the airplane, American land defense against overseas threats rested on two deterrents: fortifications to protect vital coastal areas from seaward bombardment, and mobile supporting forces to repel land attack. The heavy guns in the citadels would discourage direct assault on cities and harbors, forcing enemies to land at less favorable locations where they could be defeated by Regulars and militia. Despite the fact that much of the Regular Army was stationed on the western frontier and few citizen soldiers were sufficiently trained to offer any but the most perfunctory resistance, this strategy proved sufficient throughout the nineteenth century. The organization of combat troops into coastal or fortress units (virtually identical to the later Coast Artillery Corps) and mobile troops (infantry, cavalry, field artillery) reflected this conceptual framework. It might be argued that the post-1898 reforms were intended to provide an effective means to implement this strategy, as exemplified by the artillery reorganization, the 1903 Militia Act, the National Coast Defense Board, and the effort to concentrate the mobile troops into tactical divisions capable of repelling foreign invasion.[1]

In the Pacific possessions, as in the continental United States, the army's mission was to fortify and defend strategic harbors; but beyond this similarity, continental and overseas defense displayed numerous differences. Continental land defense was largely independent of the navy. Moreover, only the more pessimistic military planners could find any potential opponent with the military or naval capacity to mount a successful invasion; the nation's greatest peril lay in a foreign navy's seizing a vital city and holding it for ransom. In contrast, the Pacific possessions, with no reservoir of American manpower and with populations neutral at best and perhaps actively hostile, might be entirely conquered in a matter of weeks. The overseas garrison's primary task was to protect naval bases and thus insure the U.S. Navy's ability to move its fleet throughout the Pacific, a subsidiary role quite the opposite of its independence in continental coast defense. Finally, army officers were predisposed to think in terms of positional defense—to see Hawaii and the Philippines as two discrete entities, not as interconnected points in a larger scheme of Pacific defense. Thus for the army the defense of the overseas possessions required a substantial recasting of traditional military ideas, a change that was long in coming.

The first military studies in the Pacific occurred in Hawaii, for in the Philippines the army was fully occupied with pacification. With the annexation of Hawaii in 1898, the War Department assigned Major William C. Langfitt to report on the fortification of Oahu's harbors, the current plans to defend them, and the cost of maintaining these defenses. Langfitt's response was brief: "at the present time, there are no defenses whatever constructed for the defense of the cities of these Islands."[2] This laconic summary spurred the chief of engineers to request an appropriation of $8.4 million for fortifications at Pearl Harbor and San Juan, Puerto Rico. For two years, this request circulated through Washington's corridors, a victim of the turmoil of the Philippine War, Root's reforms, and the navy's indifference.

In 1901 the War Department dispatched a board headed by Lieutenant Colonel William H. Heuer to make a military survey of Oahu. The committee recognized Pearl Harbor's dual role as a "rendezvous and base for naval defensive and offensive purposes." Without it, the defense of the Philippines was impossible: "An enemy once in possession of this harbor would command the whole Hawaiian Group and place our base of operations at least 2,000 miles from our Oriental possessions, interposing squarely across our lines of communication therewith."[3] In accord with the established pattern of American defensive thinking, the board anticipated threats from seaward bombardment and from naval landing forces. To deal with the first contingency, it recommended linking the defense of Pearl and Honolulu harbors with interlocking fields of fire. Honolulu would be shielded by great guns mounted near Diamond Head, Waikiki Beach, and the port entrance, with smaller batteries providing flanking fire. Pearl Harbor would be guarded by guns placed along the sea-swept coral banks at the harbor mouth and on the Waipio Peninsula inside the harbor. The board endorsed a main armament of twelve twelve-inch rifled cannon capable of throwing a half-ton projectile 13,500 yards and thirty-two twelve-inch mortars which could drop 700-pound armor-piercing shells through the vulnerable decks of enemy warships. Forty-one smaller guns, ranging in size from three to six inches, would protect the great guns against enemy landing parties. Seven minefields would close passages and channel enemy warships into fire-swept killing zones. The board estimated such defenses would cost $4 million, of which half would go for the guns and half for the land and the emplacements. To man these defenses, it called for a permanent garrison of ten coast artillery companies, to be expanded to thirty companies in wartime.

The members of the Heuer Board were engineers and artillery officers, and perhaps for that reason their plans for defense against land attack were far less developed. Nevertheless, they recognized the danger posed by an enemy's landing on an unguarded beach and attacking Pearl Harbor and Honolulu from the flank or rear. The most obvious route, the long northeastern coast, was blocked by the daunting Koolau Mountains, a rugged, almost perpendicular volcanic chain ranging from 1,200 to 3,000 feet. Only one narrow, easily defensible pass at the Nuuanu Pali allowed access from what locals call the "Windward Side" to Honolulu. A more serious threat to the city lay to the southeast in the long expanse of Maunalua Bay between Diamond Head and Hanauma Bay. To forestall this danger, the board recommended stationing a mobile garrison near the coast defense guns on the crest of the 760-foot crater at Diamond Head. The board devoted little attention to the western or Waianae coast. Hemmed in by the Waianae Mountains, the only approach from these beaches to Pearl Harbor lay through a narrow gap between Makakilo and Barber's Point, which would be well within range of the harbor's heavy guns. By far the most serious danger was from the North Shore: an enemy which landed on one of the numerous beaches between Mokuleia and Kahuku Point could march down the wide Leilehua Plateau, between the Koolau and the Waianae Mountains, to the valley's southern terminus at Pearl Harbor. To counter this threat, the board suggested field works and entrenchments around Pearl Harbor. These, and a wartime army of 10,000 men, would suffice to defend Oahu's vital positions from land attack.[4]

In the next few years, the defense of Hawaii remained largely an army concern. The Navy Department, eager to acquire advanced bases in the Philippines, Cuba, and Asia, evinced little interest and the Joint Army and Navy Board, under Admiral Dewey's control, barely discussed Hawaii between 1902 and 1905. The National Coast Defense Board, or Taft Board, echoing the navy, concluded in January 1907 that Pearl was of "secondary importance" behind the development of a Philippines base.[5] Despite this lack of support, the army pressed ahead with fortifying Oahu: in 1903 alone there were three separate studies. Colonel Alexander Mackenzie led a committee that determined the locations for two military reservations and confirmed the Heuer

Board's defensive scheme. The General Staff's Colonel Enoch Crowder urged the immediate dispatch of an infantry regiment to protect the harbors from "a dash by the enemy" and "as representative of the government and in readiness to support its civil authority."[6] Arthur MacArthur, who visited Oahu in December, predicted "the Pacific will be the theater of future commercial and military struggles between Nations, and . . . these Islands will be the center of all such future contests for supremacy."[7] His inspection convinced him that until considerably more progress had been made in the construction of both the naval base and the fortifications, two regiments of infantry, bolstered by a third regiment of National Guardsmen—"a force sufficient to display the flag with becoming dignity, and give more support to the local authorities"—was all that was needed. MacArthur, who had earlier argued that the Philippines could be defended with minimal American effort, was confident that Hawaii's "remoteness from the shores of either side of the ocean is a perfect defense against an unexpected raid."[8] What is perhaps most interesting, especially in the context both of later developments and the Philippine example, is the complete absence of any perceived internal threat from the Hawaiian or Oriental populations.[9]

Like Hawaii, the defense of the Philippines was inextricably tied to the protection of a safe harbor. The War Department's blueprint, the 1916 "Report of the Proper Military Policy of the United States," admitted that "unless our Navy has undisputed control of the sea, we can not reinforce the peace garrison after a declaration of war or while war is imminent"[10] and, as one secretary of the navy pointed out, "without a sufficient naval base of our own in Asiatic waters, the position of our fleet would be untenable."[11] From the beginning there were many, such as Tasker H. Bliss, who believed that the Philippines was "more likely to be a vulnerable object of the enemy's attack rather than a base for aggressive movements of ours upon the Asiatic mainland."[12] But this pessimistic realism was balanced by an appreciation of the advantages a Philippine base offered. Major Munroe McFarlane accepted that "we may expect to have a losing fight to make in the Philippines" and that the garrison's "only hope" lay in immediate relief by the fleet. However, if "by good management and vigorous measures we can secure, delay and maintain a single foothold" until the fleet arrived, the enemy invasion force would have to withdraw.[13] Moreover, having relieved the garrison, the fleet could then use this Philippine base "for offensive operations against the Oriental colonies and trade routes of European nations, and secondly against Oriental powers as a base for blockading and expeditionary forces."[14] With a Philippine base, the United States might be able to fight a short and victorious war; without one it would have to mount a long and costly campaign across the Pacific. Leonard

Wood summarized the dilemma of archipelago defense: "If we have a strong fleet, a base in the Philippines would be extremely useful for operations in Asiatic waters or for controlling the sea communications of an Asiatic power. The Philippine Islands would be a source of military weakness to the extent that we might lose a garrison stationed there unless we had a strong or adequate Navy able to clear the sea and relieve the pressure on our forces."[15] To Wood, and to many other strategists, the enormous benefits that might result from possessing a Far Eastern base in wartime were far more important than the dangers of holding an exposed position with a minimal force.

Unlike Hawaii, the site of the proposed naval base was not obvious: between 1899 and 1903 naval officers debated the merits of Iloilo, Guimaras, Basilan, Cavite, and Dumanquilas Bay. The army contributed little to the discussion, for as the secretary of war reported, the navy maintained, and army officers accepted, "the selection of the site for the naval base was a matter which concerned the Navy alone."[16] Moreover, it was not until 1906 that army engineers began extensive surveys of the archipelago's harbors and environs. The navy's choice of Olongapo on Subic (Subig) Bay appears to have been due to the influence of Admiral Dewey, president of the navy's General Board, and not to officers in the Philippines. Dewey had strong reasons for advocating Subic, thirty miles northwest of Manila on the Bataan Peninsula. Its configuration was almost ideal for seaward defense: deep, wide, and surrounded on three sides by steep hills which would prevent enemy warships from firing into it. At its mouth Grande Island commanded both the channels and the surrounding sea. Protected by one or two batteries of heavy artillery and a few lighter guns and minefields, the entire American fleet could lie in the bay in complete safety from seaward attack. Accordingly, Subic was selected by an all-navy board in 1900 and accepted by the War Department in 1902. By 1903, its importance had become a point of dogma: as the Dewey-dominated General Board declared categorically, "whoever holds Luzon, holds and controls the Philippines; whoever holds Subig Bay, controls Manila and consequently the Island of Luzon."[17] As chairman of the Joint Board, the admiral imposed a consensus that was more apparent than real, and reported that the services were "united in demanding the fortification of Subig bay as essential to any plans of defense."[18] Taft's National Coast Defense Board concurred with Dewey and made fortifying Subic Bay the top priority in the Pacific.

Although unchallenged in Washington, the selection of Subic grew steadily more unpopular among officers in the Philippines. Local objections were both strategic and tactical. As capital city, communications center, and psychological heart, Manila had to be held if the United States were to continue to claim political sovereignty. There was also a tactical problem: unlike Oahu, where the coastal defenses of Pearl and Honolulu were symbiotic, those of Subic and Manila were too far apart for mutual support, and troops assigned to defend Subic would be isolated on the Bataan Peninsula and unable to influence the battle for Manila. Even more disturbing, Subic was vulnerable to land attack. The high hills which rendered it impregnable from the sea could be climbed by enemy soldiers, who would then command both the coastal defenses and any warships in the harbor. Moreover, Manila Bay seemed as well endowed as Subic for the deployment of coast defenses. At the bay's entrance, between the tip of the Bataan Peninsula and the Cavite shore, were several small islands—Corregidor, Caballo, Carabao, and El Fraile—that could provide excellent artillery platforms to sweep the channels and prevent any seaborne approach. Clearly the whole question of the defense of the Philippines demanded further attention.[19]

The outbreak of the Russo-Japanese War in February 1904 catapulted Pacific defense to the forefront of strategic priorities. Several aspects of Japanese war making held special relevance for the overseas territories. Even conceding the legality of Japan's decision to initiate hostilities with a sudden attack on the Russian fleet, the implication was clear that it could deal similarly with America's Pacific possessions. Japan's naval blockade of the Russian fleet in Port Arthur had effectively prevented interference in its overseas deployments, leading Admiral William M. Folger to question the locating of a naval base at the similarly situated "rat trap" of Subic Bay.[20] Japan's aptitude for joint operations was also disturbing: a 1908 General Staff report noted that it had transported and disembarked a force of 100,000 soldiers in complete secrecy, and postulated that a similar force could invade Hawaii before reinforcements could arrive from the West Coast. And finally, the Japanese army's destruction of the fleet at Port Arthur by heavy artillery mounted on the surrounding heights raised the possibility that the overseas bases might fall to a similar attack. Subic Bay, so completely surrounded by mountains it was described by one officer as "the bottom of a soup plate," bore an uncanny resemblance to Port Arthur.[21] After the Russo-Japanese War, Americans could no longer assume that the greatest external threat to the insular possessions was a small raiding force that lacked manpower, artillery, or the logistics for a sustained campaign.

The rapid success of the Japanese provoked alarms in Hawaii and the Philippines, where local issues became projected increasingly through a screen of presumed Japanese intrigue. In the Philippines the Constabulary tracked down rumors of Japanese espionage and the army and naval commanders met to discuss contingency planning in case the war expanded. In Hawaii, a minor crisis over the Territorial Legislature's refusal to fund its militia escalated to accusations that "Japanese and other foreign agitators are inciting the workingmen to riot."[22]

The depth of suspicion became all too apparent during the War Scare of 1907. The San Francisco school board's decision in October 1906 to segregate Asian pupils touched off a strong response in both countries and near panic in the Pacific territories. Convinced that Japan would soon invade, Hawaii's political leaders demanded the completion of the fortifications and the immediate dispatch of a large garrison. Their pleas were supported by a General Staff report of 21 January 1907, which declared Hawaii to be "in a deplorably defenseless position."[23] Indeed, according to one correspondent, "the islands in case of war with Japan would be the key to the situation" but currently were "without a fort, in fact without a decent saluting battery."[24] War alarms swept the Philippines, prompting Wood to comment that "through the Islands there is a very extensive and well-developed unrest" and a "most curious and widespread impression among the people that we are on the verge of war with Japan. . . . I should not be surprised to see trouble at any time."[25] Lieutenant Colonel T. W. Jones of the Military Information Division assembled a pastiche of rumors, innuendo, unsubstantiated reports, and conspiracy theories going back for a decade, and thereby discerned clear threats of invasion and domestic rebellion. Letters to the War Department from the West Coast reported Japanese spies, secret meetings, arsenals, and similar dangers. European observers waited anxiously for the outbreak of war and one French correspondent bravely took up residence in a San Francisco hotel to watch for the arrival of the Japanese fleet.[26]

On 9 January 1907 Chief of Staff J. Franklin Bell requested the Army War College to draw up plans for war. Its report, delivered on 12 June, concluded that Japan held the initiative throughout the western Pacific and predicted an attack on the Philippines, with the possibility of attacks on Hawaii and the West Coast. Lacking both naval bases and adequate garrisons, the option for the United States was to leave the Pacific garrisons to their fate.[27] The War College's pessimism was echoed in the Joint Board's three-page war plan, transmitted to the commanding general of the Philippines Division on 6 July. The plan reflected the General Staff's estimate that the Japanese could land between 70,000 and 100,000 men at Lingayen Gulf in fifteen days and reach Manila less than two months later. It also revealed the navy's admission of its helplessness against "an Asiatic power whose fleet is superior to any which the United States can habitually keep in Asiatic waters, and which would, therefore, in the absence of a practically invulnerable American base, have the Philippines at its mercy during the three months required to bring over the

Atlantic fleet."[28] At a meeting on 16 June 1907, the Joint Board agreed that in the event of war the navy would withdraw all but the weakest of its warships to the West Coast while the Philippine garrison deployed to Subic Bay to protect the naval facilities, giving secondary consideration to the defense of Manila. The 200 soldiers on Oahu would attempt to protect Pearl Harbor. Neither garrison should, or could, be reinforced.[29] Brigadier General William W. Wotherspoon later commented on the illogic of this plan: the navy insisted that the army subordinate everything to the protection of Subic Bay in order to allow the fleet to operate, "yet when it comes to a question of war, their very first act is to withdraw everything they have from Philippines waters. . . . In other words, we are to hold the bag until they get out."[30]

Wotherspoon's reaction indicates the growing disagreement between army and navy planners over the role of naval bases in Pacific defense. Spurred by the Russo-Japanese War, Congress appropriated $862,395 for the fortifications at Subic Bay and $700,000 for other bases in the Philippines. The appearance of such bounty ignited the smoldering conflict between Philippine military personnel and Washington's departments over Subic's suitability. The navy's General Board may have deliberately misinterpreted the army's acquiescence in the 1907 war plan as signifying its commitment that all forces would protect Subic in any future crisis. If so, they were soon undeceived; on 5 September 1907, Bell telegraphed Secretary of War Taft requesting a "full and complete reconsideration" of the entire project. The chief of staff's own sentiments were made clear in a follow-up letter of the same day, in which he stated it was "absurd" to defend Subic against Japan.[31] In response, on 3 October the General Board reemphasized the importance of fortifying the naval stations at Subic and Pearl Harbor and declared that in case of war Subic was the "sole place" where ships could be docked and repaired.[32] Thereupon the navy's outmoded staff organization encountered the full force of Root's managerial reforms. The Army War College and the General Staff turned their newly acquired administrative talents to collating dozens of documents detailing the case against Subic. From the Philippines, Wood forwarded his engineers' topographical maps to demonstrate that the capture of any one of the surrounding hills would render the bay untenable. He estimated that Subic's land defenses required between 80,000 and 125,000 soldiers spread over a defensive perimeter of up to thirty-six miles, complete with field fortifications, roads, and a separate water supply. The hyperactive general buttonholed the visiting Taft and persuaded him of the impossibility of defending Subic.[33]

These efforts won a partial victory at the Joint Board meetings in January 1908, after Bell had stated that the army members were convinced that no future garrison would ever suffice to defend Subic's fortifications against a land attack. The board reaffirmed the importance of a naval base in the Philippines and reemphasized Subic's desirability as an anchorage but acknowledged its unsuitability as a potential fortress, and suggested fortifying both Subic and Manila Bay. This compromise was not good enough for Theodore Roosevelt, who delivered a blistering reprimand on 11 February, pointing out the "grave harm done the army and navy by such vacillation and one-sided consideration as has been shown in the treatment by the army and navy experts of the Philippine problem."[34] Much of the president's anger was no doubt personal; he had ignored the warnings of his close friend Wood and accepted Dewey's assurances. But whatever the source, Roosevelt was on the mark in noting that both services' sloppy staff work, parochialism, and poor communications had embarrassed him in front of Congress and rendered all future funding for a Philippine base problematical.

Roosevelt's reprimand proved to be the death knell for the navy's plan to make the Philippines the bastion of its Pacific defense, and in that sense the army may have won a Pyrrhic victory. Following Roosevelt's directives, the navy turned its attention to Pearl Harbor, and in 1908 Congress appropriated $900,000 for its fortification, apparently designating it as the primary Pacific base. For the next decade, Dewey presided over both the Joint Board and the General Board, and used his considerable influence against a naval base in Manila. Dewey's obstructionism, whatever its motives, was strategically sound, for the army's conviction of Manila's suitability was as mistaken as his faith in Subic. The city's harbors were needed for commercial use, or were too exposed, or were so undeveloped as to require enormous expense. Nor could the Americans build a base under the harbor defenses at the mouth of Manila Bay; Corregidor could offer neither shelter from tropical storms nor adequate space on shore. During the debate over Subic, the General Staff had cited Corregidor's impregnability to attack from the land and maintained that with proper fortifications the army could defend Manila Bay for the three to four months required for the American fleet to arrive in the Pacific.[35] But Manila's own vulnerability to both sea and land attack had been made manifest in 1898, and would become even more obvious when army officers approached the problem of its fortification.

The Russo-Japanese War and the 1907 War Scare also led to a major revision in Hawaiian defense planning. During the 1907–8 academic year, a joint army-navy War College committee headed by Commander W. L. Rodgers composed a report on "The Value of the Hawaiian Islands . . ." that represents one of the few attempts to place the defense of Hawaii in a larger Pacific strategic context. Declaring that the "principal military value of the Hawaiian Islands lies in their advanced position as a point of mobilization for all military and naval operations of the United States in Oriental waters," it anticipated by two years a similar navy declaration that with a fortified naval base at Pearl the battle fleet could protect the Philippines from there. The committee also broke with the army's earlier focus on harbor defense: the siege of Port Arthur had shown that "if the enemy is permitted to land and organize for attack, the fall of the place becomes only a question of time" and that therefore Oahu's shore line must be "the principal line of defense."[36]

The emergence of Japan as the major threat in the Pacific brought on a spate of pessimistic studies by civilian and military authorities. The year 1909 saw the publication of three books that predicted a Japanese victory in a war with the United States: Homer Lea's *The Valor of Ignorance*; Ernest Fitzpatrick's *The Coming Conflict of Nations or the Japanese-American War*; and Thomas F. Millard's *America and the Far Eastern Question*. These dark visions were shared by military officers: in his introduction to Lea's work, Major General J. P. Storey stated Japan could disembark 400,000 troops anywhere on the West Coast in three months.[37]

Nowhere was this trepidation more apparent than in the Army War College's annual Orange (Japan) versus Blue (U.S.) war games. The first of these, played by the class of 1907–8, featured an Orange army of 50,000 assaulting the entrance of Manila Bay and defeating Blue's 15,000-man defenders at Subic in less than a month. A second expedition landed on Oahu's North Shore and, after a bloody battle around Pearl, captured the island in three weeks. Replenishing its combat losses from the local Japanese population, the expedition then embarked for San Francisco. By the time the American battle fleet arrived off the California shoreline—four months after the war began— much of the West Coast was in Japanese hands.[38] Subsequent games were equally grim. Inevitably, the United States lost Hawaii and the Philippines and often much of the West Coast. The students compared their nation's diverse population and national contempt for military service unfavorably with the Japanese, whose typical soldier, one 1910 study concluded, "probably has no superior. The qualities noted in him are fine physique, agility, initiative, pertinacity, valor and intense patriotism, with contempt of death."[39] Students noted that in 1913 Japan could immediately mobilize twenty-five fully equipped divisions, and reflected on their own nation's abortive effort to create one field division on the Mexican border. For the War College's Lieutenant Colonel Benjamin A. Poore, the irony was clear—in a war with Japan, the United States was "in much the same situation as Spain in 1898, being involved in the defense of a dependency, fairly well garrisoned but distant, against attack by a nearby strong power."[40]

As Poore discerned, the core of the army's dilemma was that its defense of the overseas possessions, and the Pacific itself, required the cooperation of a rival institution with separate, often incompatible views. The solution was also obvious: "distant overseas possessions can be defended effectively only on the high seas; seapower, and not local armies, will determine the ultimate fate of such possessions."[41] The navy, following the seapower doctrine of Alfred Thayer Mahan, championed a deep-ocean fleet which would meet the enemy far from the nation's shores and, in a decisive naval battle, gain control of the sea. Mahan argued that the fleet must be kept concentrated; any diversion of precious warships for local defense or convoying would weaken its power, perhaps fatally, in the climactic battle with the enemy. He was emphatic that the U.S. battle fleet must never be tied to the defense of geographical positions. Paradoxically, he also maintained that without overseas naval stations "the ships of war of the United States, in war, will be like land birds, unable to fly far from their shores."[42]

The interrelationship of bases to oceanic mobility lay at the heart of the navy-supported Joint Board declaration in 1909 that a fleet superior to Japan's, based at Pearl Harbor, "would control the Pacific and provide a strategic defense against the invasion of the Philippines by land. *The final solution of the question is the maintenance of an adequate naval force in the Pacific.*"[43] The navy's argument thus hinged on the assumption that it could offer "strategic protection" to the Philippines and control the western Pacific from Pearl Harbor, a position consonant with Mahan's principles but at odds both with the realities of Pearl's limited facilities and the fleet's usual station in the Atlantic. The navy further weakened its case by simultaneously supporting alternative bases to Pearl—Guam, the Philippines, and those seized by the Marine Corps's advanced base force—all of which implied both that a fleet stationed in Hawaii could not extend "strategic protection" and that the navy was still uncertain of its commitment to Pearl Harbor.[44]

Recognizing that the overseas garrisons were unable to defend themselves against the Japanese threat, Pacific Army officers concurred that protection of naval bases was their mission. Their reasons for doing so were quite pragmatic and self-serving. When lauding the freedom that overseas bases provided the fleet, they also stressed the importance of protecting them against land attack. In short, a quid pro quo was expected: the army would commit money, resources, and manpower to defend the Pacific harbors, and in return the navy would hazard the fleet to prevent their conquest. The symbiotic relationship was given its most sardonic form by Brigadier General Frederick Funston during one war scare: "I hope that it will not be improper for me to say that as the Army under the plans outlined is to stake all on the defense of the Naval Station and the Pearl Harbor channel it would seem only right and proper that the Navy Department should be prepared to lend all possible aid."[45] Because the services were officially partners in overseas defenses, local commanders such as Funston were confused by the navy's airy indifference to the protection of its bases. Hawaii's commander, William H. Carter noted that the army was spending millions on fortifications, guns, and emplacements to defend the Pearl Harbor naval base, but it still had no idea of the navy's plans: "This all leads to the question as to why the army and the navy do not get together and coordinate action on this problem," for if the two services continued to "work entirely apart" the result could only be waste and weakness.[46] A simpler comment came from Bell, who in the midst of preparing to defend Corregidor against imminent attack wired his superiors that "no orders [of] any kind contemplate cooperation. [The army] does not know Navy orders. Navy does not know ours."[47] The confusion and anger were shared in Washington, where Chief of Staff Wood complained that despite the obvious necessity for the services to "speak the same language" in planning the defense of the overseas naval bases, the navy consistently refused to follow through on its commitments.[48]

Underlying the service's differences were strategic views that brooked little compromise. Army officers, concerned with positional defense, saw the overseas possessions as frontier outposts anchored by the bastions of Pearl Harbor–Honolulu and Manila Bay. Rather than developing a Pacific outlook, they blended military views reminiscent of their long service on the western border and the Atlantic coast. In some respects they conceived of the Pacific both as a watery frontier and as the site of two vital port cities. Their outlook was defensive: the army's task was to protect terrain, and especially Pearl Harbor and Manila, until the navy could arrive to take over the task. In contrast, naval officers viewed territorial defense as anathema. That would tie down the fleet and force it to become little more than a long range coast defense force. The navy outlook encompassed the entire Pacific, with Manila Bay and Pearl serving as protected resting places from which to embark upon an offensive campaign. Imbued with Mahan's vision of the fleet as a strategic weapon, ranging far across oceanic highways to smash the enemy fleet and secure command of the sea, the navy had no intention of binding its battle fleet to the defense of territory. The two services thus maintained separate visions of a correct Pacific military policy: the army seeing it as land-based, defensive, and tactical, and the navy as sea-based, offensive, and strategic. Both services continued to make plans and even to speak the same language of bases and fleets, but to misunderstand the other's priorities. Despite Roosevelt's demand that joint projects be jointly studied, army and navy planners went their separate ways.

Frustrating as army-navy disharmony was, it was also liberating, for it freed army commanders from having to face circumstances in all their depressing reality. Dissenters such as Major DeRosey C. Cabell, safe in Washington, could argue that in the Pacific, and especially the Philippines, "the apparent hopelessness of an obstinate and prolonged defense is unmistakable," but this was unacceptable to the officers stationed there.[49] Their faith in the battle fleet's arrival allowed officers both in Washington and overseas to reject the inevitability of humiliating defeat and focus on questions that had some hope of solution. Army officers, essentially practical men, could immerse themselves in the engineering problems of fortifications and heavy artillery or in such tactical issues as meeting the enemy on the beaches or from within a citadel. They could calculate the size of the garrison, the number of guns, and the enemy's potential and then determine how and for how long the defense could hold until the fleet arrived. Grappling with these questions was not only psychologically more comforting than pondering a futile sacrifice, but supported the development of the professional priorities of the post-Root army—large unit maneuvers, combined arms, the integration of a citizen army with the Regulars, war planning, officer education, and so on. In short, the expectation of naval relief allowed military planners to concentrate on the trees and ignore the forest.

The army's interest in positional defense and tactical matters can be witnessed in local plans for the Philippines. Commanding generals Leonard Wood (1906–8), William P. Duvall (1909–10), and J. Franklin Bell (1911–14) shared a common fixation with the Manila Bay fortifications. Wood accompanied the members of the National Coast Defense Board during their inspection of Manila Bay in 1906 and lectured them on the best locations for guns and entrenchments.[50] Duvall presided over a board that subordinated archipelago defense to the protection of a secure fleet anchorage in Manila Bay. Predicting that Luzon would be invaded immediately, the board determined that the proper strategy was to abandon Manila and retreat to Corregidor. Duvall threw himself into improving the Manila Bay defenses, berating the War Department and the navy for their lack of interest and support. Bell shared Duvall's strategic priorities, confessing that no other issue "has given me so much trouble and monopolized so much of my time as the Corregidor project—the making of the 'keep' of this island."[51] Washington too accepted the fact that the defense of Manila Bay had become the top priority of the archipelago's garrison. In 1911, Leonard Wood, now chief of staff, ordered that all subsequent Philippine defense plans be "founded and based" on the "holding and defense of Corregidor, Carabao, Caballo and El Fraile Islands . . . until the arrival of a relieving fleet" and "that no plan of general defense be contemplated for a moment that would jeopardize, in the slightest degree, the defense of Corregidor or the other islands named, in any effort to delay the advance of an enemy on Manila."[52]

The army's preoccupation with the Manila Bay fortifications produced impressive results. By 1916 Fort Mills, Fort Hughes on Caballo Island, and Fort Frank on Carabao Island together boasted a devastating complement of twelve-inch and ten-inch cannon, twelve-inch mortars, and lighter rapid fire artillery. Although Fort Mills was the most powerful, the showpiece was Fort Drum, a small island in the bay that was leveled in an enormous explosion. Upon the flattened surface emerged what one officer termed a "stupendous piece of work—staggering," a "concrete battleship" with four fourteen-inch guns mounted in two turrets.[53] In 1916 a permanent Coast Artillery garrison of 1,842 officers and men was stationed inside the Manila Bay fortifications. In wartime, these defenses would be augmented by extensive minefields across the channels and the promised stationing by the navy of a permanent floating defense of obsolete warships—two monitors, six cruisers, two gunboats, six destroyers, and six submarines—in the harbor.

On Oahu the Japanese threat prompted an equal outburst of activity. The first gun emplacement on Diamond Head—Fort Ruger's Battery Harlow—was completed in 1910 and the entire fortification largely finished by 1916. At Fort DeRussy, an engineer battalion filled in the Waikiki swamp and blasted a quarter-mile channel through the reef to permit dredging. Fort Kamehameha, built on a small strip of coral surrounded by marsh and ocean, was created with material dredged up from Pearl Harbor. Virtually invisible from the sea, shielded from enemy fire by concrete and sand, equipped with the most modern range-finding systems, and directed and manned by the most technically expert branch of the army, Oahu's forts were a potent counter to any attack on the harbors.[54]

Unfortunately, even as the army was pushing forward with their construction, military technology rendered many of the Pacific defenses obsolete. In 1914 Colonel John W. Ruckman, one of the officers most involved in the Manila Bay project, confessed the fortifications had been built on "conditions and methods which long ago passed off the stage."[55] The reports that served as the basis for the defense of both the Philippines and Oahu had been completed before their authors had grasped the full implications of the revolution in capital ship construction symbolized by H.M.S. *Dreadnought*. The massive batteries of these new warships outranged many of the recently installed coast artillery cannon. No sooner had Oahu's guns been mounted than the twelve-inch cannon and mortars were superseded by demands for more and heavier guns; ultimately the army would mount sixteen-inch cannon at Pearl. In a telling memo, the chief of ordnance pointed out that the army had committed itself to a coast defense program in the Pacific governed by the same conceptions with which it had fortified the nation's own seacoast: "to protect important places [so] that an enemy would be forced to make a landing in order to accomplish anything; the fortifications themselves have not been designed to increase the difficulty of such landing, it having been supposed that we would have ample resources on shore."[56] But in Hawaii and the Philippines these military resources were absent, and he himself had grave doubts that a coast defense system designed to protect a few vital locations could expand to become the basis of an entire island's protection.

As early as 1910 suspicions had arisen that the islands in Manila Bay were vulnerable to fire both from Cavite and Mariveles Heights on the Bataan Peninsula. During the 1914 maneuvers, within twenty hours a light mountain battery moved into position on Mariveles Heights and opened fire, preventing the defenders from mining the North Channel. It was followed by Captain Harrison Hall's coast artillery company, which in one week's time landed four seven-inch howitzers on the Bataan Peninsula, built a road to Mariveles, and fired twenty rounds on a target battery on Fort Mills, scoring seven hits and effectively destroying the position. Corregidor's gunners had no means of replying; they could not see Hall's battery, nor did they have artillery suitable for land targets. Such experiments convinced the president of the Army War College that "if an enemy gains a foothold in the vicinity of Mariveles, the fortifications of Corregidor will be exposed to mortar fire and their reduction must follow."[57] Two years later, Brigadier General C. J. Bailey concluded his tour as Corregidor's commander with the blunt statement that "the only defense against hostile guns on Mariveles is to occupy the latter with sufficient force to keep them out."[58] Concern over Corregidor's weaknesses led its commander to demand a full reexamination of the Manila Bay defenses in 1915. In denying the request, Brigadier General Hugh Scott conceded that the fortifications might indeed be obsolete, but pointed out that they had already cost $15 million, more than all continental coast defenses combined.[59]

The growing recognition that the coastal defenses might not suffice raised anew the question of whether it would be better to meet the enemy behind fortifications or on the beaches. In 1908 the Rodgers Committee had urged that Oahu's "defense should be planned with the idea of denying the enemy any foothold on the shore. That is, to make the shore line the principal line of defense." This aggressive stance would not only be in the national character, but was good tactics, for "if the enemy is permitted to land and organize for attack, the fall of the place becomes only a question of time, no matter how elaborate the disposition for defense may be."[60] This view gained increased support with the arrival of the first infantry and cavalry units in 1909. Beginning in 1910, the Officers School at Schofield Barracks assigned students to reconnoiter, map Oahu, and prepare plans for holding the island. Most proved to be limited tactical studies of the relative merits of beach or inland defense, and of artillery support, force composition, and possible defense sites; but in the process they added a great deal to the army's growing knowledge of Oahu's trails, beaches, and mountains. They called into question the assumptions of the Heuer and other defense boards that this was solely a coastal defense problem by revealing that many beaches were suitable for landing, and that the Koolau and Waianae ranges could be crossed.[61]

To some officers, the solution lay in expanding the harbor defenses to the entire island. In 1910 a committee of infantry officers stationed at Schofield outlined an ambitious proposal for the "Land Defense of Oahu" based on mounting heavy coast defense guns along the North Shore. An even more ambitious plan was put forth by Arthur Murray, Hawaii's department commander and a former chief of Coast Artillery. Murray argued that the existing plans to transport the bulk of Hawaii's wartime garrison from San Francisco at the first sign of war were based on a strategic misconception. Although San Francisco was indeed 1,200 miles closer to Honolulu than was Yokohama, the fleet to guard the army's transports would have to transit the Panama Canal, 1,400 miles further from Honolulu than Yokohama. Murray argued that given the likelihood that the battle fleet would be stationed in the Atlantic when Japan attacked, Oahu's defenders must hold off a major invasion for at least a month. To do this it was necessary that the full wartime complement of twelve infantry regiments be garrisoned permanently on the island. Even more crucial than manpower, however, was technology and firepower. Rejecting traditional views that the purpose of coast defenses was to defend harbors and force the enemy to land at less attractive beaches, Murray argued that heavy mortar batteries be built throughout Oahu, allowing the defenders to rain devastation on any warship approaching within 10,000 yards of the island.[62]

Murray's proposal had two immediate effects. The first was a reexamination of plans to reinforce Oahu by sea, which resulted in the General Staff's urging the immediate deployment of an additional infantry regiment and the stationing of the entire peacetime garrison on Oahu by the end of the year. The second was the creation in 1911 of a joint army-navy committee to inspect Oahu's coastline. The committee confirmed that "landings can be made from torpedo boats, launches and row boats at a number of places at any side of the island at practically all times of the year."[63] Once ashore, the invaders could easily avoid the existing coastal defenses and approach Pearl Harbor and Honolulu via the Leilehua Plateau. The committee seconded Murray's recommendations for reinforcing the garrison and placing twelve-inch mortar batteries along Oahu's coasts.

The joint committee's report was duly forwarded to the Army War College, which studied it at some length and recommended the creation of yet another committee to investigate further the entire subject of the mobile and the fixed defenses of Oahu. The resultant board, chaired by Brigadier General Montgomery M. Macomb, was given a broad mandate to study the military problem of Oahu, the proper system of mobile defense, the ideal size of the garrison, and the nature and location of fixed defenses. Meeting in Honolulu in early 1912, the Macomb Board reflected the army's appreciation of Japan's military power. Whereas the Rodgers Committee of 1908 had seen Oahu as a "point of mobilization for all military and naval operations of the United States in Oriental waters," the Macomb Board emphasized its value as a point of "first defense" in a war with Japan: "So long as Japan has no base nearer our coast than her home country, and Oahu is firmly on the flank of her line of advance to either the California coast or Panama, we have little to fear; her line of advance is too long and too vulnerable." From this, the board drew a clear implication: "the Japanese in case of war will undoubtedly try to seize Oahu by a sudden rush, and make it secure for further operations against our coast and Panama."[64] If Oahu were taken, the Japanese could arm the local population for defense, forcing the United States to take unacceptable losses to recapture it.

The Macomb Board concluded that all plans of Oahu's defense should be based on holding it against an attack by up to 100,000 Japanese for the month it would take the U.S. fleet to arrive from the Atlantic once the Panama Canal was available. To defend every beach would require too many men; even if the Americans abandoned the east and west coasts and defended only the north and south, they would still need 60,000 soldiers. Exiguous manpower precluded even a limited fortified line across the central valley north of Schofield Barracks; so the Macomb Board determined that the best the garrison could do was to construct two short east-west lines. The first would consist of a 650-foot trench stretching along the high ground from Diamond Head through the suburb of Kaimuki to the mountains, flanked by machine guns and fixed guns and anchored by an impregnable fortress at Diamond Head. The second line's location was a long trench from Pearl Harbor to the Koolau Mountains, anchored by a citadel at Red Hill. As one reviewing committee noted, the board's suggestions were "very different from any previously proposed. No elaborate defenses were to be prepared to prevent a landing, but a defensive line designed to cover Pearl Harbor and Honolulu was made of great strength and not too long to be adequately manned by the garrison allotted."[65]

Reaction to the Macomb Board of 1912 was mixed. The War College urged that its conclusions become the basis of Oahu's defenses; others were far less supportive. One member privately complained that the board's instructions were so narrow that no other findings were possible. Chief of Coast Artillery Erasmus M. Wheeler not only disagreed with the Macomb Board's requests for additional guns, but pointed out that Congress had approved recent expenditures on the condition that these moneys would complete Oahu's fortifications. With a Washington bureaucrat's barometer for the political climate, Wheeler argued that a request for additional funds to revise the existing defenses would provoke a political storm.[66] From Hawaii, Macomb's successor protested that the Diamond Head line could be outflanked by troops attacking through the mountains. In response to this criticism, Macomb chaired a second board in April 1913 which reaffirmed the importance of the Diamond Head–Red Hill line and suggested even more field fortifications and firepower. Macomb's subsequent return to Hawaiian Department command seemed to insure the triumph of his defensive scheme.[67]

But, as in the Subic Bay controversy, local officers displayed a remarkable ability to delay and obstruct policy. Objections to the Macomb Board's findings persisted, especially after the general's transfer to head the Army War College in mid-1914. Captain Warren Hannum submitted a fifty-five-page paper claiming the proposed lines could not prevent enemy artillery from shelling Pearl Harbor and that "the more one studies the problem the more desirable does it seem to use every means available to break up his landing parties and prevent them reaching shore."[68] In the 1915 exercises, Oahu's mobile troops practiced a two-part defense against an attack from the North Shore, first retreating down the Leilehua Plateau to Red Hill and then entrenching the proposed line against attack. The exercises demonstrated that, after landing, an enemy could rapidly advance to Red Hill, bring up siege artillery, and destroy most of the navy base.[69] The Oahu Defense Board, charged with examining the entire defense of the island, concluded it was impossible to "prevent serious damage to the naval establishment by artillery fire in land attack, even though the lines be held intact."[70] Even the officer in charge of building the Red Hill line soon became convinced that "the project upon which we are working today is confessedly a project for defeat."[71]

In April 1916 Captain John McAuley Palmer, a early supporter of the Macomb Board, submitted a report to a Joint Army-Navy War College committee on Oahu's defense advocating tactics he had developed to protect Corregidor from enemy landings and from studying the fighting on the western front in Europe. Palmer argued that mobile forces, properly organized into beach and support troops and provided with firepower and transportation, were far more effective in repelling invaders than fixed fortifications. As at Corregidor, Oahu's defenders had the advantage: they would be on known terrain, they had ample time to prepare, and they could use motorized transport to shift troops to key points. These advantages allowed the defenders to "invite an enemy when he is at his weakest to enter a battlefield deliberately prepared by us. No matter what his numerical preponderance may be, we may hope to have a superiority at the actual place of contact."[72] Palmer's own studies had convinced him that of Oahu's 146 miles of coast, only 30 miles offered suitable landing sites; these, of course, should be defended in depth. At sea, a picket line of destroyers and submarines would harass the enemy invasion fleet. The existing coast defenses would repel enemy warships from the harbors while lighter fixed batteries could do the same for the north and west shores, dampening supporting fire and forcing the transports to unload troops into their landing boats miles offshore. As the invaders approached, beach obstacles would channel them into killing zones swept by light artillery and machine guns. The mobile forces would be held back, out of range, and then, at the crucial moment, they could be committed to a counterattack via motorized transport.

Perhaps convinced by these critiques, and by his own reading of the lessons of European trench warfare, Macomb retreated. He now argued his proposed lines were intended only as "an inner keep," which should not be occupied "until every reasonable effort is made to defeat the enemy before his arrival in front of the final defensive position."[73] Thus in a few years Hawaiian defense had shifted from the protection of two harbors to the defense of fortified lines and thence to meeting the enemy on Oahu's beaches.

In the Philippines the issue of land defense was perhaps even more important than on Oahu. Army officers had based their objection to Subic Bay in part on the necessity to defend Manila as the political capital of the islands. Following the 1907 War Scare, American plans called for a mobile defense throughout Luzon, delaying the enemy at rivers and passes, destroying the railroad, and only in the last extremity taking up positions behind a fifteen-mile entrenchment around Manila. Local plans continued to call for mobile defense, culminating in March 1911 when Bell's fortification board declared that in the event of war "our forces should assume the offensive against the enemy at the water's edge and oppose his advance as long as it is possible to do so without being invested in the city of Manila or driven into a restricted area where they could be captured."[74] Only in the last extreme would the Americans hole up in the almost completed fortresses in Manila Bay. But such a scheme was anathema in Washington. Palmer's influential 1911 "Report on a Scheme for a Well Balanced Army," in which he outlined the Colonial Army system, declared that "the primary function of the army in the Philippines is to hold the defenses at the mouth of Manila Bay until such time as our fleet can be expected to arrive in Philippine waters"; it must "never be employed in any enterprise that might jeopardize its immediate withdrawal to Corregidor."[75] Chief of Staff Wood, who had earlier argued that holding Manila was essential to U.S. sovereignty, agreed with Palmer. His long service in the Philippines had convinced him that the garrison could not defend both Corregidor and Manila; to attempt to do so would insure the loss of both. On 26 December 1911 he had a strong message sent to Bell that henceforth all war plans must be based on "holding the Manila Bay fortifications until the arrival of the fleet" and "that no plan of general defense be contemplated for a moment that would jeopardize, in the slightest degree, the defense of Corregidor . . . in any effort to delay the advance of an enemy on Manila."[76]

This "Corregidor first" strategy may have been the best possible, but it failed to account for either the force composition in the Philippines or the independence of Pacific Army commanders. Both before and after the Colonial Army system, the majority of the archipelago's garrison comprised the infantry and cavalry intended for pacification; in 1914 there were but ten understrength coast defense companies stationed at Corregidor. Bell's 1912 attempt to increase Manila Bay's wartime garrison to 7,500 men by adding two infantry regiments still left a mobile force of 6,000 outside the protection of the forts. For these troops, the War Department's 1911 directive offered the bleak task of abandoning Luzon and Manila without contest, digging in on the Mariveles Heights of Bataan, and fighting a defensive battle until they were relieved by the fleet or forced to surrender. This operational plan was neither appealing nor did it make strategic sense. Luzon's beaches offered numerous locations where an enemy could land, and once the enemy was ashore in strength, it was only a matter of time before the mobile forces on Bataan succumbed.

The drumbeat of criticism against the "Corregidor first" strategy led Barry to create a special Philippine Defense Board in 1915, one of the most important in the history of Philippine defense. Headed by Brigadier General Hunter Liggett, it soon determined that to examine the defense of Manila Bay properly it was "necessary for the Board to consider every phase of the Philippines Islands" and to "submit its report in the form of a general analysis of the military problems in the Philippines." Given the new realities of Woodrow Wilson's election, the government's cutback in funding for Manila Bay's defenses, and congressional debate over immediate Philippine independence, the Liggett Board no longer regarded America's possession of the archipelago as a fixed proposition, but instead attempted to determine the mission of the military forces in the islands within the context of the nation's defense needs in the Pacific. Although it concluded that "it is the War Mission of the American forces in the Philippines to defend the territory, authority and sovereignty of the United States within the Archipelago to the utmost limit of our available military resources therein," it clearly viewed the defense of the Philippines themselves as strategically irrelevant: the "ultimate control" of the islands would be decided, irrespective of local defenses, by the naval struggle for command of the Pacific.

The Liggett Board sought to balance both tactical and psychological factors, and thus was led to abandon Manila Bay as the focus of defense efforts. Perhaps drawing on 1914 maneuvers, it concluded that Corregidor's defenses themselves were vulnerable to land-based artillery. Moreover, even if the defenders managed to hold out, they could not secure the harbor for the U.S. fleet: an enemy in possession of Bataan or Cavite could mount artillery and close Manila Bay to American battleships. Choosing from a number of unsatisfactory options, the board rejected citadel defense and advocated counterattacking an enemy on the beaches. If defeated, the Philippine garrison could withdraw to prepared fortifications in front of Manila, since possession of the capital had a symbolic importance to the international community and would "giv[e] assurance to the Filipino people that their interests are being safeguarded." At the same time, the defense plans should not be based on the illusion of "holding Manila or Corregidor [as] delaying actions of primary strategic importance. In holding them we are simply defending American sovereignty and dignity to the utmost limit of our resources, but we are not holding anything of fundamental strategic importance from the standpoint of the main naval campaign."[77]

Not content merely to question the possibility of the defense of the Philippines, the Liggett Board challenged even its desirability. Whereas Wood and others had argued for defending the Philippines on the optimistic grounds that, should the garrison defy odds and hold out, it would give the United States a base for offensive operations, the Liggett Board suggested that such prolonged resistance was undesirable. Having concluded that holding the entrance to Manila Bay conferred no strategic benefit, the board stressed that "it should, however, be well recognized by those concerned with directing our military policies that the existing reasons for the defense of Manila Bay do not furnish sufficient grounds for sending our battle fleet to their relief in the event of war and that such a procedure would be prejudicial to national interests."[78] The navy's Commander E. S. Kellog, a member of the Liggett Board, made this point strongly in a separate report: "Corregidor is a drain on the Naval strategy and consequently a drag on the general strategy of a war of this nature." He predicted that a prolonged resistance by Manila Bay's defenders would lead the American public to take up the cry of "On to Corregidor" and cause the premature commitment of the fleet. The relieving force would have to pass through submarine-infested waters for hundreds of miles and perhaps even to fight a fleet action: "When the relief is accomplished much time has been lost, a very large percentage of the force has been lost, the force has no base, and the enemy *can* have control of the main line of communication." Kellog believed the solution was for the United States to remove most of its military forces from the Philippines, thus obviating any need for the nation to hasten its advance and allowing the navy to pick its point of attack and retain the initiative.[79]

An even stronger argument for withdrawal came from Brigadier General John F. Morrison, one of the most respected tactical minds in the army. Morrison recognized the contradiction between the Liggett Board's assertion that the archipelago was "strategically irrelevant" and its support of an operational plan that entailed meeting the enemy at the beaches and retreating across Luzon to Manila. He argued that this was militarily unsound: "We have in no way aided the Navy in the real decision of the war, but on the contrary, it is liable to cause through the public clamor a premature advance of the fleet." Moreover, he foretold with grim accuracy the consequences of a similar policy in 1941: "our forces will destroy millions of dollars worth of property, set back the progress and advancement of these people for many years, cause great suffering to the people of the islands due to our armed resistance, and result in the death of a very large part of our own force. The result to be accomplished is to 'save our face.' "[80]

In Washington a board of review which included the chief of staff, several bureau chiefs, and the head of the Army War College debated the Liggett Board's findings at some length. The most thorough critique was by the War College's Macomb, who agreed that control of Manila Bay could not preserve a base for the fleet but maintained the fortifications did serve a purpose: they denied the Manila Bay to an enemy fleet and protected Manila from naval attack, thus forcing an enemy to conduct "major operations" to supplant the United States in the Philippines.[81] After much discussion, the board of review rejected the recommendations of the Liggett Board and reaffirmed the 1911 mission of the forces as the defense of the entrance of Manila Bay. This decision was further confirmed in the Army War College's "Statement of a Proper Military Policy for the United States" on 11 September 1915, which declared that "to keep the American flag flying in the Philippines in war as in peace it becomes essential to hold Manila Bay," and this in turn required that the army "securely hold the Bataan Peninsula."[82]

Manila Bay's designation as the centerpoint of defense was temporary, however, for within a year the Philippine garrison would be given a larger and more inclusive mission. Part of this reassessment was the result of Liggett's elevation to the command of the Philippine Department. Convinced that both the mission of guarding Manila Bay and the plan for immediate retreat to Bataan were mistaken, he conducted a number of staff rides to show that meeting the enemy on the beaches would be more effective. Liggett maintained that Congress's passage of the Jones Act in 1916, which guaranteed independence to the Philippines, would allow the United States to secure sufficient Filipino manpower to defend all of Luzon. His criticism of the "Corregidor first" strategy was echoed by the a joint army-navy committee in the Philippines, which in June 1916 urged that the mission of the armed forces be changed from "to hold Manila Bay" to "hold Manila and Manila Bay as long as practicable, and to keep up a semblance of resistance on Luzon until the final decision of the war."[83] This expanded mission received further support on 17 August 1916 when the secretary of the navy urged that the two services agree on the joint wartime mission as "to defend Manila and Manila Bay."[84]

The proposal to expand the garrison's tasks to include Manila was sent to the Army War College, where it was vigorously debated. Colonel William H. Johnston pointed out that the navy's efforts to broaden the mission were not the result of strategic insight, but rather an attempt to transfer naval stores and equipment from Subic to Manila Bay for administrative convenience. The War College's own "Statement of a Proper Military Policy" of the preceding year had estimated that a force of 50,000 was required to defend Manila Bay. Now, with a Philippine garrison of less than half that number, the college proposed to increase this mission. To Johnston, the consequences of expanding the garrison's mission were clear: "After placing the few troops on Corregidor which constitute the artillery supports, a commander in the Philippines will be justified in stationing the remainder of his mobile force so as to cover the city of Manila. His force will be so small that the fall of the city will follow, and if an attack be made simultaneously from Bataan, he will have no troops with which to delay occupation of that position. If Manila be defended in its immediate vicinity, many buildings will be destroyed by an enemy, which in civilized warfare would be spared the results of war if no defense be made in that vicinity."[85]

Despite Johnston's forecast, the War College committee recommended that the services defend Manila and Manila Bay jointly. In effect the committee threw up its hands; it accepted the enlarged mission primarily on the grounds that this change was favored by both local commanders and was "one on which agreement can be had at present. The adoption of some definite present mission is extremely important."[86] Macomb approved its recommendations, although his penciled comments indicate that he too sought to reconcile the 1911 "Corregidor first" policy with the new expanded task: "My policy is to 'hold Manila Bay.' To do this requires the 'joint forces' to 'Defend Manila and Manila Bay' to the best of their ability. Corregidor will naturally be the citadel or 'keep' to be held until the last."[87] In passing the report on to the chief of staff, he gave further reasons for his support: "it is important to note the distinction between the *ultimate capacity to hold* and the *duty or mission to defend*. While it is true that our forces are insufficient to *hold* Manila against the superior forces that our enemy may employ on Luzon, it is certainly our duty and our interest to maintain possession of the Capital of the Philippines as long as the actual military situation permits." Returning to an earlier theme, Macomb stressed that if the United States abandoned Manila immediately, the city could be taken by a small expedition, but if it were defended, the enemy would be forced to deploy much of his army: "in so far as we make the invasion of central Luzon a major military operation, we invoke the ultimate deterrent power of our fleet."[88] Macomb thus returned to his earlier argument that the purpose of the Philippine garrison was not so much to hold the islands as to force the enemy to undertake a large and costly invasion, and thereby to give the American fleet more time to deploy.

The shift in the army's mission from the limited responsibility of safeguarding the entrance to Manila Bay outlined in 1911 to the larger challenge of defending both Manila and Manila Bay in 1916 deserves some study. The majority of the troops in the Philippines were infantry and cavalry, mobile forces who were well suited to suppress insurrection. But such troops were of limited utility in fortress defense; they were far too small a force to protect Manila but too large to be housed in the Manila Bay forts. Moreover, few in the mobile forces were pleased with war plans based on immediate withdrawal to Bataan or with a static defense. At best they would be protecting Corregidor's shoreline from assault, at worst they would be condemned to trench warfare in the malaria-ridden jungles of Bataan. Most important, by 1916 some planners in both Washington and the Philippines agreed that the archipelago was doomed regardless of tactics and that a prolonged defense might force the precipitous commitment of the fleet. General Macomb offered a new mission for the Philippine army—to impel the enemy to commit a large force to the invasion—but even he avoided the logical implication that, once the enemy commitment had been made, the garrison's mission would have been accomplished; he returned instead to the possibility of fighting a successful mobile defense. Ultimately, the problem of the garrison was not that it was too weak, but that both Manila and Washington clung to the illusion of a satisfactory solution to this dilemma. They could see, but could not quite face, the bleak fact that the Philippine garrison would be sacrificed. Instead of questioning the need for such immolation, or finding an adequate justification for it, they sought to convince themselves that there was some chance of victory.

Although they might be pessimistic about the outcome, overseas commanders sought to insure that their military forces were prepared for invasion. Convinced that the Philippines were "the best field for the training of troops of any we have," Wood wanted the archipelago's garrison to serve as a laboratory for the organizational and tactical reforms he anticipated imposing on the entire army.[89] He pried the Scouts away from the civil government, upgraded their equipment, professionalized their officer corps, and fully integrated them into the U.S. Army.[90] Under his sponsorship, Pershing established a brigade tactical school at Fort William McKinley which incorporated a "thorough and progressive system of military training" that moved troops steadily from the development of individual skills through maneuvers as part of a field army. During the rainy season, officers studied military science, history, law, and tactical problems, while enlisted men attended classes on cooking, animal care, signaling, carpentry, drill and military exercises. In the dry season, they applied these lessons in exercises that stressed combined arms, staff rides, and logistical planning, culminating in brigade maneuvers.[91]

Unlike their counterparts in the United States, the commanders in Hawaii and the Philippines were not constrained by a lack of maneuver room, by the need to include National Guard, or by public expectations of a sham battle. Summing up one joint army-navy exercise in 1907, Wood stressed it had "called for the performance of pretty much everything which a soldier may be called upon to do in time of war—construction of hasty entrenchments, passing unfordable bodies of water, marches, passing obstacles, taking positions, close-order formations, etc."[92] The Philippine maneuvers between 1910 and 1914 drew high praise from observers and participants for their realism and rigor. Those of 1914 featured two scenarios: the first was a field exercise to defend Manila from an attack from the south; the second, to test the Manila Bay fortifications, was an amphibious landing on the Bataan Peninsula. Both phases were initially a joint army-navy exercise, but at the last moment the navy commander canceled his participation, allegedly because of Washington's fear of offending Japan. Disappointed but unwilling to stop, staff officers managed to scrape together enough boats both to exercise Corregidor's guns and to land an expeditionary force at Bataan.[93]

The Pacific Army's maneuvers were significant for a variety of reasons. At a time when the metropolitan army took three months to concentrate a barely functioning division, the Philippine garrison routinely put a combat-ready force of 6,000 into the field with virtually no prior notice. The maneuvers gave the army an opportunity to exercise combined forces, to use new technology such as the airplane, and to practice on the actual ground it would have to defend. They contributed to the already strong tendency among military planners to focus on tactics and troop performance and to avoid the much larger strategic and operational issues. Officers took commendable pride in overcoming the difficulties of deploying cavalry in the jungle or maneuvering in the mountains, but their very efficiency revealed the tremendous problems of defending the overseas territories. The 1914 Hawaiian maneuvers demonstrated the weaknesses of the Red Hill line and highlighted the vulnerability of Pearl Harbor to land attack. The Philippine maneuvers were even more disheartening, and, at one point in 1912, the umpires stopped the final attack "to increase the morale of the defenders, for whose instruction this maneuver was really held."[94] The vulnerability of the Manila Bay defenses was especially disturbing. In the 1914 exercises, a coast artillery company took only seven days to land, transport, and mount four siege howitzers on the Bataan Peninsula and completely destroy a dummy battery on Corregidor. According to Johnson Hagood, "the Corregidor maneuvers of 1914 showed up every difficulty that was developed twenty-eight years later in the final capitulation of the fortress. But nobody ever paid any attention to it then or later."[95]

As Pacific Army officers grappled with the problems of external defense, they also devoted increasing attention to the danger from within. Lieutenant C. H. Mason spoke for most officers when he claimed that war plans must be based on the premise that invasion would "inevitably be complicated by an insurrection probably instigated and assuredly assisted by the foreign enemy."[96] A major factor in the decision to locate Manila Bay's defenses entirely on islands was that both Leonard Wood and General Storey of the Taft Board believed that "the defense of the bay differs from that of harbors in the United States in that, while designed against a foe from without, sight must not be lost of the possibility of enemies from within. A defense made by utilizing the existing islands will reduce very materially the chance of capture by an uprising of the natives, or by a land attack assisted by natives."[97]

Nowhere was the connection between external threat and internal security more apparent than in Hawaii. After the 1907 War Scare, the Rodgers Committee asserted that the Japanese population was the "principal factor to be considered." According to army statistics, in 1908 Hawaii's population of 160,000 contained 65,000 Japanese, 47,000 of whom were males over 18 years of age. Although not all officers shared the committee's nightmare that thousands of Japanese cane workers would rise to support an invasion, they were concerned with the prospect of sabotage, espionage, or guerrilla attacks on troops as they rushed to the beaches. Although repeated investigations failed to reveal any proof of espionage by Hawaii's Japanese community, many officers shared Lieutenant Consuelo Seone's conviction that "wherever there are Japanese it is taken as an assured fact that many of their number are spies or have some connection with their country's intelligence department."[98] Only a few were as practical as Colonel Walter S. Schuyler, who confided: "Personally I take little stock in this idea of the Japs ever making an attack upon us, but that is not the question at all. The question is whether it is the policy of the government to be prepared for an attack. If so, Japan is undoubtedly the most likely source. In the event of such an attack the first thing to be done would be to take care of [Hawaii's] . . . Japanese."[99]

The solution to this internal security problem advocated by most officers was later manifested in the forced relocation of Japanese Americans in World War II. Palmer summed it up in cold logic: "it is obvious that the defense of the island must provide for some disposition of these aliens at the outbreak of trouble. There are apparently two solutions to the problem—deportation or reconcentration. On account of lack of shipping, deportation to another island is impracticable, and reconcentration must be the only practicable solution of the problem." Reconcentration, the forced resettlement of civilians to deny the enemy access to their help, was a measure supported both by international law and historical precedent. A strong suggestion of it appears in the Army War College's 1907 war plan, which urged that the Japanese population be "made, so far as possible, hostages to secure immunity from attack." A year later, the Rodgers Committee was explicit: "some form of reconcentration will be necessary" but "fortunately the topography of Oahu is such that for this island, the situation may be quickly met by removing all Japanese across the mountains to the eastern coast of the island." Students at the War College were virtually unanimous in advocating reconcentration and a committee at Schofield drew up detailed plans for two stockades complete with barbed wire and guard towers.[100]

Both humanitarian and pragmatic concerns caused reconcentration—initially perceived as a simple solution—to become a thorny issue. The War College students insisted that it "should involve the minimum of hardships towards such individuals and the care and maintenance of both them and their dependent families." This raised the practical problems of where to put this population and how to feed it. A variety of sites were considered—the outer islands, the north coast of Oahu, Pearl Harbor, Schofield Barracks—but none met the twin requirements of military security for the Americans and protection and subsistence for the Japanese. The 1912 defense board chaired by Macomb wrestled with the problem: "To collect and deport the 80,000 [Japanese in Hawaii] is practically impossible. To have any large number of them inside our defensive lines is out of the question. The Board recommends the following solution of the problem. When war is certain, promptly draw an outpost line well beyond our defense lines and permit no Japanese to cross it. Round up all Japanese inside the line, and if possible to get transportation, deport them; if not, put them outside our lines. . . . Forcing the enemy to feed this population, or sending it home, will be no small embarrassment to him. On the other hand, turning over so many able bodied men has its drawbacks, but it is the lesser of evils."[101]

Repugnant as it appears in retrospect, the willingness of army officers to place civilians, including American citizens, in concentration camps must be viewed in the context of military thought at the time. People today are accustomed to the principle of civilian participation in warfare and the role of guerrillas as lawful combatants, but such views were quite alien in the pre–World War II army, whose rules and regulations excluded civilians both as participants and as targets. They rejected the concept of total war as practiced by Sherman and Sheridan, and shared with John M. Schofield a belief that "civilized nations" should fight only limited wars in which the ultimate goal was "peace and profitable friendship."[102] The desirability of limited warfare—and the corollary that such warfare should be passionless, pragmatic, and restricted to professional soldiers—was deduced from their selective study of recent European warfare and the Civil War and confirmed by their experiences in the "savage" warfare in the West and the Philippines. Major James Chester saw civilian participation as part of an increasing "drift towards barbarism," and observed with distress that in recent conflicts wherein civilians had resisted invasion, military forces had reverted to "old methods" such as crop destruction, driving off women and children, and the military occupation of territory. Inevitably, the blurring of soldier-civilian roles would again "arouse the savage which sleeps in the beast of every man and retaliation will seem to be a duty, and the end will be barbarism."[103] Accordingly, the army's early discussions of relocating the population may be judged as an attempt, however misguided, to maintain clear lines between civilians and soldiers and between civilized war and chaos.

The internal danger led some officers into behavior that approached the paranoid. In 1909, the army intelligence service in the Philippines helped convince Duvall "there exists here a system of Japanese espionage that is minute and exhaustive, coupled with political agitation having for its apparent object the destruction of American sovereignty in these Islands."[104] One army intelligence officer in Hong Kong claimed to have uncovered a Japanese conspiracy to corner the rice crop, thus undermining U.S. prestige through-out Asia.[105] The Constabulary's Secret Service sent the secretary of war a forty-three-page report detailing Japanese activities. Not to be outdone, Philippines Division headquarters compiled "Secret Service File, 1909" on Japanese-Filipino connections that dated back to 1898: three boxes of newspaper clippings, military reports, interviews, and unsubstantiated gossip.[106] In point of fact, the military and civil authorities uncovered only one real conspiracy, an attempt by two Japanese civilians to purchase photographs of Corregidor from an army photographer. Duvall, however, remained haunted by the specter of invasion and attributed its absence to his constant vigilance. By the time he left, there had been so many crises that one officer complained that "irreverent and cynical youngsters at the Army and Navy Club spend their time classifying various rumors as 'the old man's fourth war' or 'the General's fifth war.'"[107]

Bell, who succeeded Duvall, was given strict instructions to end Manila's propensity for alarms, but in May 1913 a sudden crisis in Japanese-American relations prompted the War Department to warn him of surprise attack. Bell immediately reinforced Corregidor's garrison to war strength, mined the harbor, and ordered coast artillerymen to sleep by their guns. Although W. Cameron Forbes later dismissed it as a "flutter of war scare . . . mostly encouraged by army ladies who viewed the movements of their husbands with a rather unnecessary alarm," Hawaii's General Funston regarded the 1913 war scare as more serious than that of 1907.[108] The emergency passed, but it confirmed Pacific commanders in their fear of imminent and sudden attack.

The war scares heightened the often strained relations between Washington and its overseas commanders. Duvall was bitter in denouncing the lack of support his superiors extended him during the 1909–10 crisis. Bell sardonically observed that, although staff officers in Washington could "discuss with equanimity theoretical possibilities of weakness," those who actually had to face their consequences found it "more difficult to maintain composure."[109] Brigadier General A. L. Mills complained that the constant parade of inspections, surveys, and urgent messages from Washington resulted in "annoyance and irritation to department commanders" and, more important, widespread "confusion" both overseas and in Washington as to "what precisely was . . . the general policy in regard to the defenses of the United States and overseas possessions at large."[110] In a stinging criticism of a General Staff review of Manila Bay's defense plans, Macomb protested the degree to which "such subjects as the extent to which the jungle should be cleared and the kind, caliber, number and locations of guns for defense, etc., etc., are being discussed in an academic way in Washington—12,000 miles from Corregidor."[111] Bell became so exasperated by the War Department's capriciousness—at the same time one bureau was demanding he implement the plans for the Manila Bay defenses, another was changing those plans—that he demanded an impartial investigation. He pointed out that since he was held responsible for defending Manila Bay, he deserved the right to make suggestions for its protection.[112]

Frustration with Washington contributed to a conviction among some Pacific Army officers that they knew more than did their far distant superiors, a view that often revealed itself in an almost insubordinate independence. Not surprisingly, this view was most pronounced in the Philippines, where not only was the danger of invasion greater but where there was a growing conviction that the garrison could not rely on Washington's commitment to its relief. Distrusting both their superiors and the navy, overseas commanders often went their own way, considering Washington's policies as subject to wide interpretation. There is considerable evidence that during the 1907 War Scare Wood intended to disobey the Joint Board's instructions to defend Subic Bay and instead fight a delaying action across Luzon before retreating on Manila.[113] Bell was equally audacious. According to Hagood, if Japan invaded he planned to ignore the 1911 directive, turn Corregidor's defense over to a Coast Artillery officer, march his remaining troops to northern Luzon, and harass the Japanese rear: "the mobile forces were doomed anyway, and this play would save the devastation of Manila."[114] Bell's successor, Major General Thomas H. Barry, was openly contemptuous of the 1911 directive, informing Washington "so far as I am concerned, I shall never tie myself up in Corregidor and practically invite the enemy to come and take me."[115] Such pronounced independence of thought demonstrated commendable self-reliance and initiative, but it also established a dangerous tendency among Pacific Army commanders to overlook or overrule national policy when it conflicted with their local interests—to be the tail that wagged the dog.

As the Great Powers drifted toward war in Europe, the Pacific Army remained in a quandary. The heavy guns and concrete fortifications at Honolulu, Pearl Harbor, and Manila Bay were impressive barriers, but they guarded against a threat that appeared increasingly unlikely. As one skeptic commented, no enemy would "pay the price they would probably have to pay to force open the sea gate . . . when the land gate stands wide open."[116] Plans to fall back to prepared defenses at Manila or Bataan or Diamond Head–Red Hill clashed with alternative schemes to meet the enemy on the beaches. The onrush of new weapons technology rendered the most painstaking and expensive fortifications obsolete and created new threats. To compound this peril was the internal threat that, if not nearly as great as some officers supposed, was still sufficiently real to insure that no responsible commander could focus exclusively on external defense. Against these myriad dangers, American officers could find no workable safeguards. The Colonial Army system proved manifestly inadequate to supply sufficient manpower. Ultimately, frustration forced some officers to question whether the defense of the Philippines was not only tactically impossible, but strategically unwise. Oahu must be defended, but the Philippines, in Roosevelt's memorable phrase, were the nation's Achilles heel. They welcomed the passage of the Jones Act to grant the Philippines independence, and looked forward to the day when the army would no longer serve as imperial guardians.

The United States entry into World War I postponed further discussion of Pacific defense. The Hawaiian garrison, which in May 1917 numbered some 12,000 officers and men, shrank by two-thirds by October 1918. After assurance by the chief of the Bureau of Insular Affairs that "conditions in the Philippines are such now as not to require, for the maintenance of law and order therein, Regular troops. The Scouts and Constabulary will be ample for any emergency within the Islands," the number of American soldiers dropped from 14,400 in 1917 to 9,300 a year later, and then shrunk to 5,200 with the dispatch of the expedition to Siberia.[117] The actual turnover among personnel was even greater. Officers transferred to the mainland or to the American Expeditionary Forces; and more than a few of those who replaced them had proved unsatisfactory in other commands. The frequent departures, and scarcer arrivals, precluded any coherence in leadership; between July and September 1917, six different officers commanded the Hawaiian Department.[118] Field training and exercises were suspended; soldiers pulled interminable guard duty at navy yards, pipelines, railroads, water stations, and other utilities. With erratic leadership at the top and neither the inclination nor the ability to train, the troops could do little more than await their own departure orders.[119]

The withdrawal of the American garrisons again raised the issue of a separate colonial army composed of native troops. Previous proposals had always foundered on the widespread belief that the Philippine or Hawaiian populations were unreliable and lacked military ability; and the army had created instead either a small military elite, the Philippine Scouts, or had supervised an even smaller militia, the Hawaii National Guard. Prior to World War I high wages, good rations, and great prestige had made the Scouts attractive: most companies kept waiting lists. Both in Manila and Washington, planners worried that expansion would weaken the esprit de corps of the Scouts. The war did indeed lead to a major reorganization: between June 1917 and July 1918 the Scouts grew from 182 officers and 5,567 men in thirteen battalions stationed in six posts to 292 officers and 8,230 men in four infantry regiments, a field artillery regiment, and three independent battalions in six posts, most of which were in Manila. The war thus sped their transformation from irregulars to conventional forces. Socially, they were changed by an influx of Filipinos in the officer corps and by the recruitment of younger enlisted men unwilling to accept the traditional paternalistic relationship.[120]

The Hawaii National Guard, like the Scouts, had been officered by white Americans and loosely segregated into companies of Hawaiians, Chinese, and Caucasians. In the first decade and a half after annexation, the guard's strength grew from 416 in 1906 to 1,879 in 1914, a considerable increase but still a far cry from the 5,000-man force envisioned by Arthur MacArthur in 1904. Although defense plans had often referred vaguely to "local volunteers," the guard itself was largely discounted as a war reserve and regarded with much suspicion.[121] After the outbreak of war in 1914, Governor Lucius Pinkham launched a preparedness campaign, which doubled the Hawaii National Guard to 3,693 by November 1915 and to 5,150 in August 1916. The new recruits were primarily Hawaiians, since the two haole (white) companies could barely maintain their current strength and only fifteen Japanese were permitted in the entire guard. Pinkham saw its purpose as threefold: it would police the islands and prevent disorder (a euphemism for strikebreaking); it would provide trained infantry for the army in time of war; and it would "Americanize" Hawaii's diverse population. In the tradition of territorial politics, the governor sought to have the federal government pick up much of its cost; he requested a yearly stipend of fifty dollars for each soldier, and more for officers. Pinkham recognized that it was unprecedented for the national government to maintain a paid militia, but justified it by Hawaii's position as "the apex, the exposed point far out in the Pacific, looking toward trouble should it ever come."[122] He also believed that Hawaii's defenders must look inward as well: he included a chart showing the predominance of the Japanese population. Neither Washington nor Hawaii's military commanders were impressed; indeed, in 1916 the Hawaiian Department commander suggested circumventing the entire scheme by establishing two federal regiments of "colonial troops"—one Hawaiian and one Filipino—enlisted for service in Hawaii only. He believed such regiments would not only provide trained soldiers familiar with local conditions, but might prevent the gradual extinction of the Hawaiian race by teaching proper sanitation.[123]

By temporizing over the proper structure for the native forces, the army surrendered the initiative in manpower mobilization to civil governments that moved—all too often—with reckless haste. Early in 1917, Manuel Quezon urged that Filipinos be allowed to fight in Europe, and although neither the War Department nor Wilson had any intention of allowing them even to train in the continental United States, the president was eager to withdraw American troops from the Pacific. With Governor-General Francis B. Harrison's strong encouragement, the Philippine Senate passed the Militia Act of 17 March 1917 to create a Philippine National Guard and impose compulsory military service on all males. Enthusiastically supported by the Filipino populace, the guard was organized into a division of nine infantry regiments, one field artillery regiment, and coast artillery and cavalry components. Harrison was its commander in chief and the Philippine Assembly its constitutional authority. He soon mobilized it and demanded it be armed for immediate deployment to France. As a face-saving measure the guard, numbering 14,000 soldiers, many unarmed and none trained, was called into federal service in 1918 for three months. To Regular officers, the charade had demonstrated little more than Quezon's ambition and Harrison's fantasy of troop command in France. The governor's complaints that the army delayed equipping and training the division further exacerbated the antagonism. One officer reflected upon the affair thus: "the political machinations of the leaders, the appointment of officers to high command without the slightest degree of training, the favoritism and nepotism shown in the past, especially during the war, were such as to exclude consideration of using the Philippine National Guard as a reserve force in time of peace or war."[124] Overall, the experience confirmed the army in its prejudice against local troops—with the result that no foundations were laid for an organization that would prove crucial when the long foreseen invasion finally occurred.

Hawaii underwent its own politically inspired mobilization. Despite the protests of local planters, who feared the disruption of their work force, the departure of the Regulars forced the calling up of the Hawaii National Guard on 27 May 1918 as the 1st and 2nd Hawaiian Infantry Regiments. Both territorial and federal authorities agreed that the units would remain in Hawaii: a steady flow of sugar was more important than bodies in the trenches. Because so many guardsmen failed the physical, the regiments conscripted recruits from the ethnic groups that were felt to be most reliable: 4,000 Filipinos, 1,200 Hawaiians; 750 Japanese; 500 Portuguese; 140 Koreans; and 140 Puerto Ricans. The disproportionate number of Filipinos caused Secretary of War Newton D. Baker some embarrassment, for many had been banned from service by the National Defense Act of 1916, and their enlistment required congressional approval.[125] Hawaii's Japanese were angry for another reason. They were not accepted into the territorial armed forces until very late in the war, and most of those who eventually served were assigned to two detached companies that drew the worst details. Despite prewar concerns, army intelligence reported "there was practically no evidence of disloyalty in these organizations of foreign speaking soldiers."[126] Fidelity aside, however, both the draft and the prewar expansion appear to have diluted the quality of Hawaii's local forces considerably: a study of August 1918 found an illiteracy rate of 87 percent in the 1st Hawaiian Infantry and 60 percent in the 2nd. In the latter, 30 percent of the soldiers could not speak, read, or write English, and the unit devoted a quarter of its training to language instruction.[127]

Japan's association with the Allies insured the security of the American territorial possessions from outside attack and allowed the army to strip them of their garrisons for service in France and Siberia. Since the Pacific territories suffered neither foreign invasion nor internal rebellion, the War Department's decision to turn their protection over to the native populations proved justified. But beyond this, it is difficult to avoid the conclusion that neither Washington nor the overseas commanders gave sufficient time or energy to the problems of manning the Pacific outposts should the United States become involved in the war in Europe. As a result, as the United States moved inexorably toward intervention, the initiative was seized by the territorial political figures, who mobilized the population without regard either to military sensibilities or realities. In both Hawaii and the Philippines, governors appealed over the head of the local commanders for equipment, training, and manpower increases. The commanders responded with passive resistance, complying with direct orders but giving little encouragement. Neither the Philippine National Guard nor the Hawaiian Infantry was a notable military organization, in its training, officers, or equipment. Yet the army officers who damned both organizations, perhaps accurately, as political tools failed to appreciate the potential manpower pool they had uncovered. A year after the declaration of war, native forces equaled the size of the prewar American garrisons, and this despite the exclusion of much of Hawaii's Japanese population and restricting the Philippine National Guard to 14,000. Moreover, they proved loyal and enthusiastic, even when it became clear that their units were not destined for overseas service. The World War I mobilization presented the army with a challenge: should it seize upon the potential offered by native forces or focus on their weaknesses?

In the period between 1898 and 1918 the U.S. Army moved haltingly toward a practical scheme of defense for the Pacific possessions. Through the Colonial Army system it created a distinct Pacific Army and, in the case of the Scouts, a small but capable local force. It completed the most costly and efficient coast defenses in the nation's history and effectively removed the threat of foreign warships steaming into Manila or Pearl to destroy the naval facilities or the U.S. fleet at harbor. It moved more quickly than the continental army to concentrate forces, form tactical commands, and stage realistic maneuvers. But despite these accomplishments, the army failed to devise a plausible and consistent plan for the Pacific territories' protection or to adjust to changing circumstances. The completion of the coastal fortifications focused attention on land defense, exposing glaring weaknesses, while developments in military technology posed new challenges even as they provided potential solutions. The garrisons were too small to defend against invasion but, in the case of the Philippines, too large to be used exclusively for fortress defense. As Wotherspoon pungently noted, the army's failure to secure the navy's firm promise that the fleet would be committed to relieving the garrisons left them "holding the bag." Despite Roosevelt's 1907 scolding and his demand that henceforth both services cooperate in resolving joint problems, the army and the navy went their own ways. Instead of insisting that the navy make clear its intentions, and thus obtaining a realistic foundation for planning, the army operated as if there were a contract between the two services: in return for the garrisons holding the Pacific bases the navy would agree to relieve them. Only quite late did the Liggett Board challenge this assumption and pose the difficult question: was the defense of the Pacific territories worth the cost? In a sense, World War I offered an opportunity for the army to revise and restructure the Pacific defenses: the withdrawal of the troops wiped the slate clean.

CHAPTER 5

The Pacific Army and the Community

T he Pacific Army was both a part of Hawaiian and Philippine societies and a distinct entity—its ranks primarily filled with men who served a two-year hitch and then returned stateside, and with others who "went Asiatic" and reenlisted for overseas duty. In some respects, the army was segregated in its enclaves, which civilians were seldom invited to visit. The officers dined and danced at the palatial Army and Navy Club in Manila and rode or played golf at private army courses; the soldiers spent much of their time out of sight on post, and even on leave were isolated, by common consent, in places like Angeles Town or Santa Anna on Luzon, in the Iwilei and Hotel Street sections of Honolulu, in the "Blood Town" area of Wahiawa. But the Pacific Army was also very much part of the local community and left a permanent mark on the local cultures. Officers played polo with local businessmen and politicians, served as everything from health inspectors to governors, supervised public fetes like the Philippines Carnival or Hawaii's Army Day, courted and married the daughters of the local elite, and retired to positions in overseas businesses. The soldiers, forbidden to marry, had equally intimate contacts with "wahines" or "queridas" with whom they "shacked up" and with the "American meztizos" or "half-Schofield" children they fathered. The host of local men and women who worked in the brothels, saloons, tattoo parlors, cafés, and tailor shops relied on the army for their livelihood. Many others were actually employed by the military, either on the reservations or on construction projects. Other locals, although not directly associated with the military community, were affected by it daily; they jammed the seats at athletic events, attended concerts and theatricals, watched the military maneuvers and grumbled during blackout exercises and defense alerts. The Pacific Army affected overseas culture as well, leaving its mark on Philippine and Hawaiian language, customs, cuisine, and music.

From the beginning, the army recognized that overseas service could be traumatic and destructive to morale; as one officer noted in 1905, soldiers were "far away from home and home influences, and dependent for their amusements and recreation on the offerings of a semi-hostile and half-civilized country."[1] This was especially true in the early years, when the army's adjutant general referred to the "burden of Philippine service"[2] and the *Army and Navy Journal* reported "[t]he officers and men of the Army are by no means infatuated with the Philippines. Service in the islands is monotonous and enervating, involving a heavy increase in personal expenses" and "the average member of the military service would view the withdrawal of the forces from the Philippines with serene content, if not with positive delight."[3] In 1907 Hawaii's acting governor, E. A. Mott-Smith, commented that morale among soldiers was very poor and that virtually no one reenlisted, an observation repeated in 1911 by the islands' commanding general.[4]

The army's answer to morale problems was activity, most notably in its emphasis on sports. No sooner had troops arrived in their overseas stations, whether the Waikiki swamp at Camp McKinley or the isolated villages in the Philippines, than their officers sought to organize baseball games. In 1903, general orders in the Department of Mindanao prescribed an intensive training program that included one day each month devoted entirely to athletics. Under General Wood's sponsorship, the department held its first field day; by 1907 this had evolved into the Military Tournament, in which every regiment in the islands competed. Athletics soon attained almost as high a priority as fighting: during the height of the Moro Wars, it was not considered unusual for the 15th Infantry's baseball team to leave Mindanao for an interisland tour. Following World War I, overseas soldiers participated in some athletic activity at least twice a week, and the service and local newspapers carried reports of the games between regimental and battery teams, posted army league rankings and speculated on new prospects. Victories on the playing field became a primary source of esprit de corps: soldiers kept track of their regiment's standings in every competitive sport and boasted of their trophies and awards. When Hawaii's 27th Infantry published a regimental history, it gave almost as much prominence to its athletic championships as to its combat service.[5]

The army's sports programs attracted thousands of spectators; in the Philippines the annual military tournament was the islands' most popular athletic event, and Schofield Barracks was widely known as the biggest "jock strap post" in the army. In the 1930s, Schofield boasted some of the finest boxers in

the world and "smokers" at the post's "Boxing Bowl" regularly attracted between 8,000 and 12,000 spectators. Orders required each of Schofield's regiments to field a team for boxing, football, baseball, track, and basketball, and
to pay $100 a month in dues to support league competition. They also warned
enlisted men against engaging in taunting, rowdy behavior, or other un-
sportsmanlike activities. Officers, being gentlemen, were excluded from these
provisions, but at one game tempers grew so hot that the wives of the two
participating regiments refused to speak to each other for weeks. In the Philippines, the Scout units were famous for their athletic program, and their stars
were archipelago-wide heroes. They dominated the Philippine teams that
competed in the Far Eastern Games, and included athletes who held or
matched world records in swimming and running.[6]

Although ostensibly begun as a way of encouraging both unit morale and
physical fitness, competitive sports soon became the province of a special class
of soldier-athletes. In 1922 the Hawaiian Department's Morale Officer formed
an elite squad at Schofield Barracks with a training table, coaches, and medical supervision. For a few years these teams dominated interpost and interservice boxing, routinely humiliating the navy contingent from Pearl Harbor.[7]
Other commands were quick to respond, fielding their own semiprofessional
boxing, baseball, football, and basketball teams, so that by 1926 the commanding general of the Hawaiian Department reported, "all competitors in these
sports are carefully trained and selected so they attain remarkably high efficiency, while the enthusiasm aroused in their competition is unbounded."[8]

The fictional Captain "Dynamite" Holmes's ruthless pursuit of the cham-
pionship boxing team he believed would advance his career may have had
more than a few real-life counterparts. Certainly one Hawaii veteran was not
alone in believing an officer's rank and reputation depended on his "having
good jocks."[9] Stanley G. Larsen remembered that between 1931 and 1941 every
officer in the 35th Infantry was required to attend the regimental sporting
events. When the colonel found Larsen had been on West Point's track team,
he appointed him coach; during the track season the lieutenant's afternoons
were spent with the team.[10] Veteran Robert W. Keeney recalled in detail the
vigor with which officers pursued athletes:

Sports was a "big" thing at Schofield. In fact, so big that any enlisted man
who was one of the top in his sport was recruited to and by Schofield outfits
prior to his arriving. Let's say, a Commander had a West Point Friend at Fort
Benning, Georgia—an outfit in Benning had a first class running back or
quarterback who was going to re-enlist but wanted to leave Benning and go
to Hawaii. The friend at Benning would let the friend at Schofield know

that this "hot shot" was coming to Hawaii. The Commander or Coach of the Schofield outfit would be at the dock when the "hot shot" arrived and promise him another stripe if he came to their outfit. . . . First class athletes were not given any special food but were given special privileges, such as very easy assignments. Most of their time was spent in practice of their sport.[11]

As veteran Walter Maciejowski recalled, an athlete was a member of a "privileged class. He would be excused from any K.P., fatigue duty, etc. He would be likely to advance in rank more rapidly. Have more liberty to visit Honolulu, etc."[12] When Major General Hugh A. Drum took command a decade later, he found it necessary to issue orders stressing that military training would have a higher priority than competitive athletics and that enlisted men would no longer be excused from duty to prepare for sports.[13]

In addition to athletics, the army increasingly sought to provide both officers and enlisted men with numerous on-post recreational opportunities. In the Philippines, Fort Mills comprised a complete community with tailors, dressmakers, a photo studio, several stores, and a 12,000-volume library. At Fort McKinley, Major Edward Almond, president of the dramatic club, staged four plays for 1,500 soldiers. The Air Corps personnel at isolated Clark Field had tennis, swimming, golf, and nightly movies. But the antiquated and crowded barracks of the 31st Infantry featured few such opportunities. The regiment's colonel complained in 1928 that the "Y.M.C.A. is practically the sole place in Manila for wholesome recreation of the men, where they feel welcome because they are soldiers and not because they have money to spend."[14] He complained that virtually every other entertainment—movies, a swimming pool, athletic events, dances, and team sports—had to be paid for by the regiment. Hawaii's Fort Kamehameha had a movie theater, bowling alley, basketball and tennis courts, baseball diamonds, and a swimming area. Even tiny Luke Field prided itself on its vaudeville society, three baseball teams, polo team, post exchange, several specialty stores, barber shop, restaurant, tailors, and clothing store.[15] Honolulu's Service Club, located in the old Royal Barracks, provided a variety of entertainment, including dances in which "carefully supervised and suitable partners" were provided for the enlisted men.[16]

Schofield Barracks, the second largest city on Oahu, had better entertainment facilities than those provided to the citizens of many contemporary cities. In February 1920, for example, Schofield offered 27 movies to 4,330 attendees, hosted informal athletics for 5,265 soldiers, conducted 270 education classes for 3,780 students, and held 13 religious meetings of 2,325 attendees which resulted in 4 "Christian decisions" and 34 "Christian interviews."[17] The Kaala Club, completed in 1921, was reputed to be the best enlisted men's club in the army, with six movie theaters, weekly dances, pool tables, roller skating, a library, and a large recreation room. Schofield boasted a post exchange, which in 1929 conducted $1 million in business and provided meat, dairy and vegetable markets, a filling station, a beauty parlor, a jeweler, and a dozen restaurants. In 1930, Schofield expanded its recreation center to include a gymnasium, a 1,700-seat theater, a 10,000 seat "Boxing Bowl," a swimming pool, athletic fields, and a library.[18] After the repeal of the Eighteenth Amendment, soldiers could go to their regimental beer garden or walk off post to Hasebes or Kemoo Farms for food and drink.

With an eye to keeping soldiers out of the brothels and bars, the army provided healthy and wholesome off-duty entertainment. In the 1920s Schofield leased Haleiwa Beach on Oahu's North Shore; any soldier who could scrape up the twenty-cent round-trip bus fare could spend the weekend swimming, hiking, playing sports, or sleeping. The army also established mountain resorts, similar to the hill stations of the British India Army, to provide rest and recreation, allow soldiers to recover from the tropical climate, and create an environment similar to that of home. The most famous of these was Camp John Hay in Baguio, which was built as a joint civil-military effort and reached by the breathtaking "Zig Zag" road. In the first decades of American rule, virtually the entire political and military leadership left Manila for Baguio during the worst of the hot season. Each officer in the Philippine Department was allowed to spend a month at the resort without its counting against his leave.[19] On the island of Hawaii in 1916, the army established Kilauea Camp, which had shelter for 300 enlisted men and twenty-two cottages which officers could rent for $1.50 a day. Like Baguio, Kilauea's mountain location, cool nights, and low humidity gave visitors a welcome relief from tropical weather. During the interwar period, soldiers could travel to Kilauea on army transports for a few dollars, and hike around the active volcano or enjoy the camp's post exchange, library, and restaurant.[20]

The Pacific Army hosted a variety of entertainment that attracted large military and civilian audiences. The "Wild West Show" staged by the black troopers of the 10th Cavalry in 1907 to raise funds for the Fourth of July festival featured daredevil riding and breathtaking horsemanship; it was reported to have been witnessed by the largest number of Americans ever gathered under one roof in the Orient.[21] Perhaps the greatest undertaking was the Philippine Carnival, a huge gala organized by Governor Forbes and several army officers in 1908, and held annually thereafter. The army supplied tents, labor, and entertainers; officers' daughters often served as part of the Queen of the Occident's entourage; and as many as 8,000 soldiers participated in drills, exercises, and athletics. In Hawaii, the army was equally active, holding an annual military tournament, a transportation and horse show, and providing the bulk of the organization and entertainment for the Armistice Day Pageant.[22]

Officers and their families enjoyed a wide variety of privileges, amenities, and entertainment. In Hawaii, they could participate in Schofield's extensive club activities—which featured riding, golf, music, and drama—and they could join Honolulu's active civilian social life. Lieutenant Floyd L. Parks's 1926 diary details luaus, swimming, fishing, golf, and hikes: military duties intrude only rarely.[23] In 1930 Corregidor's commander boasted that the needs of every officer and his family could be supplied on post. Domestic help was cheap and plentiful—the monthly wages of a cook were fixed at fifteen dollars and those of a laundress at ten—and left officers and their families free to enjoy the Corregidor Club's golf, tennis, and dances.[24] Colonel Joseph R. Darnell remembered life in Zamboanga in 1926 as a "tiny colony of white men and women from all parts of the world who danced in spotless mess jackets and evening gowns at the Overseas Club."[25] But these paled beside Manila's fabulous Army and Navy Club. Founded in 1898, it "combined the qualities of a hotel, casino, library, and assembly hall, [and might] be regarded as the center of Manila's social life."[26] In 1906 it improved its facilities for women, and included a special ladies café with tables, writing desk, and refreshments to which men were allowed only when accompanied by a female member. The Army and Navy Club was heartily disliked by governors Taft and Harrison; the former founded the rival University Club, while the latter labeled it a hotbed of rumors and anti-Filipino sentiment. By the 1920s, the club admitted civilian members and included a bowling alley, billiards, seventy furnished rooms, and three acres of grounds. Its luxurious furnishings, food, entertainment, and bar were famous throughout the Orient, and throughout the U.S. Army.[27]

Among overseas officers, polo appears to have assumed the status of a distinct subculture, equal to that of boxing among enlisted men. Critics complained that officers received an extra ten dollars a month subsistence for each horse but nothing for their wives until after five years' service. An inspection of Schofield Barracks in 1916 revealed a stable staffed by six enlisted men who drilled only once a week; the rest of the time they cared for eight government horses which were used exclusively for polo. In the 1920s Schofield boasted the best polo field in the army; officers, mounted on locally raised ponies, played year around. Even the mavericks in the Air Service participated: the commanding officer at Luke Field boasted that the game had "taken hold in fine shape" and that one officer was considering extending his tour in the islands in order to continue on the post team.[28] In the Philippines, polo arrived with the founding of the Manila Polo Club in 1909; by the 1920s the army boasted eight polo teams and participated in a six-month season in which matches often were played three times a week. McKinley and Stotsenburg each had its own field and stable; officers brought their polo ponies with them and there was keen interest in breeding with European and Australian stock. The sport so dominated social life that in 1927, when the *Infantry Journal* devoted an issue to the Philippine army, Major G. H. Paine contributed an article on "Polo in the Philippines."[29]

Officers' wives in the Pacific Army were obligated to provide a respectable, domestic American environment for their husbands and children. Some wives helped their husband's careers more directly: when an inspector discovered that the lieutenant in charge of Manila's post exchange employed his wife, his commander defended the appointment thus: "Lt. White accepted the detail under protest and with fear and trembling. It was thought that Mrs. White would more conscientiously and efficiently guard the interests of the Exchange Officer and the Exchange than any other employee."[30] Army society expected wives to participate in a near-endless round of card games, teas, golf, charity functions, and other social activities. Women's clubs sprang up almost with the arrival of a unit to the post. No sooner had the 21st Infantry taken station at Camp Connell to campaign against the Pulahanes than a ladies club arose; so too with the deployment of the 25th Infantry in Mindanao in 1907 came its ladies bridge club. Two decades later, the Ladies Reading Club of Schofield Barracks held weekly meetings which discussed works on Hawaii, art, and famous women. The continual visiting, card games, and entertaining were detested by some. Mrs. Fox Conner, wife of the commanding general of the Hawaiian Department, complained that "neither Fox nor I had ever cared much for society, and we had an endless round of it when we lived on the outskirts of Honolulu."[31] Her great pleasures were her Monday afternoon classical music recitals and her beach house, where she and her husband could relax. At one point, when it appeared that prohibition agents would discover the five-gallon jug of homemade liquor she was smuggling to a party, she reflected that prison would not be a bad life: "No more enforced entertaining; just my fiddle and I. I don't think I ever felt so calm."[32]

Among civilian writers, the general perception has been that relations between soldiers and civilians were poor. In 1909 Thomas F. Millard's *America and the Far Eastern Question* blamed the army in the Philippines for "dividing the community into two classes, foreign and native, each feeling that its interests were somewhat antagonistic to those of the other."[33] One highly regarded history of Hawaii concludes its one-page summation of the prewar army by declaring that civil-military relations were characterized by "estrangement."[34]

Another recent work excoriates the service's racism, particularly against Hawaii's Japanese.[35] That there was racism in the army and resentment among the locals, that some posts were segregated enclaves (as were some Hawaiian and Philippine neighborhoods), and that the gap between officers and enlisted men found a ready parallel within the civilian caste system of the day—all this is indisputable. But those who castigate past generations for failing to share current social attitudes ignore both historical context and the changing web of relationships that escape simple categories.

Certainly the army made great efforts to insure good public relations with the overseas communities, and there is much to Lieutenant Colonel H. L. Landers's enthusiastic declaration: "I have never known in the past of any situation where the Army and the civilian community lived more pleasantly in their inter-relationship than do the two groups in Hawaii. The people are friendly to the man in uniform, the Press regards the Army as part of a great national organization and not as something to write hypercritical or salacious articles about; the Territory of Hawaii is our friend."[36] The islands' civil and military elite were closely tied, so much so that one veteran recalled that his fellow penniless lieutenants were virtually the only ones who remained at Schofield Barracks during weekends.[37] The army and the civil government cooperated on roads, lending each other equipment, supplies, and expertise. The army assisted territorial agencies in their efforts to eradicate disease, increase agricultural productivity, and improve communications. Between 1922 and 1937 army airmen dropped ten tons of seed throughout the Hawaiian Islands and were credited with preventing erosion; they took pictures of lava flows for the tourist bureau; and they tested pesticides on the sugar and pineapple crops.[38] A 1924 article in the *Honolulu Advertiser* noted the army's leading role in charity drives and contributions, and praised Hawaiian Department commander Charles P. Summerall for working "tirelessly to make the army an integral part of the civil life here." It also commended Lieutenant Colonel Stephen O. Fuqua, the public relations officer, for providing articles and pictures to the local papers, for encouraging officers to write letters about Hawaii to their hometown papers, and for ensuring that the April 1924 issue of the *Infantry Journal* issue featured army life in Hawaii.[39]

Perhaps the greatest exemplar of the close ties between army and civil officials was Major General Briant H. Wells, commander of the Hawaiian Division in 1930 and 1931 and of the Hawaiian Department between 1931 and 1934, who was, in the words of the *Honolulu Advertiser,* "unquestionably the most popular commanding officer the department has ever had."[40] Together with Charles Judd, the governor's brother, Wells founded the Piko Club—after the Hawaiian word for navel, the locus of courage—whose hundred members hiked through the islands' mountains and rediscovered Hawaiian trails. During the notorious Massie affair of 1931 and 1932, when local naval officers urged the imposition of military government on Hawaii, Governor Judd praised Wells for his "splendid attitude of cooperation"; and, while the admiral commanding Pearl Harbor was claiming that Honolulu was dangerous for white women, Wells let it be known he considered it as safe as any American city.[41] Indeed, he reportedly told his officers that he would hold them responsible if their wives echoed the navy spouses in criticizing Hawaii or its people. Not surprisingly, when he was reappointed as department commander in 1933, the *Advertiser* hailed him as "a foremost citizen of Hawaii" and "well beloved in the Islands. Civilian and military relations and understanding have never been better or more sympathetic."[42] Upon his retirement, he remained in Hawaii as secretary of the Hawaii Sugar Planters Association and continued to play an active role in social affairs, founding a still-extant dramatic society and serving as a forceful advocate for Hawaii's Japanese Americans.

Although often uncomfortable with Hawaii's diverse population, the army sought to avoid racial conflicts: one general order explicitly stated "such delicate subjects as . . . the race question, etc., will not be discussed at all except among ourselves and officially."[43] Army wife and author Nancy Shea cautioned other military dependents, "the social implications of the mixture of races in Hawaii are packed with dynamite, and waiting to explode in the face of the careless or unsophisticated newcomer. Be very tactful in your conversation, because you seldom know the background of the person you are addressing. Uncomplimentary remarks about the residents of the 'Paradise of the Pacific' are better left unsaid."[44] Behind a surface of toleration, army officers drew rigid invisible lines to protect themselves and their families from unwanted contact. Their "aversion . . . to the co-mingling of their children (particularly of girls) with the Oriental races" led most to place their children in private schools.[45] The extensive entertainment facilities on each post and Oahu's segregated social clubs allowed them to spend most of their off-duty time among people of similar racial and class background. In this respect, army attitudes and mores mirrored that of the local community where, as Captain S. A. Wood noted, there was "comparatively little racial animosity and prejudice except socially."[46]

In the Philippines, the army cooperated with the American overseas community in the maintenance of a color line between Filipinos and whites. Throughout the archipelago, posts were segregated; even the Scout camp at Zamboanga had a separate club, golf course, and movie theater section for its white officers. As commander of Fort Stotsenburg, Hagood argued that his post's segregation was "not because of any race prejudice but as a matter of convenience, to conform to law, regulations, the standards of living [and] the customs of the people themselves."[47] Some Americans, perhaps borrowing from English authors critical of the "memsahib," blamed officers' wives for this racism. John R. White, who served in the archipelago as a soldier and Constabulary officer for fifteen years, claimed that "in the Philippines wherever an American woman has had her say—and she has had it almost everywhere—a massive dam of social prejudice was built across the stream of that mutual intercourse which was necessary to a complete and proper understanding."[48] But army wives cannot be blamed for such proposals as Major John C. H. Lee's: that white soldiers be forbidden to perform menial labor on the grounds that it lowered the status of all whites.[49] Major Vicente Lim, a Philippine Scout officer and a West Point graduate, confessed that he and other Filipino officers had several times considered resigning their commissions because of prejudice.[50] Filipinos commented that Americans treated them far better in the United States than they did in their native land. That the racism of the civil and military communities was not only self-defeating but dangerous did not go unnoticed. A 1924 analysis of the Philippine political situation observed that even upper-class Filipinos might join a rebellion despite their economic interest in preserving American rule: "The great stumbling block for this group is the race question. In the United States they count themselves received by white people, and in some cases sought by whites. Some have married white women and brought them to the Philippines. Their unfortunate position in the social scheme has added to the conservative element's desires to see the Philippines independent."[51]

Enlisted men's relations with the population were somewhat more restricted. Soldiers at Ruger or DeRussy could be in the heart of the Waikiki district within a few minutes' walk, while men stationed at Schofield or Fort Kamehameha could reach Honolulu relatively cheaply by bus or by sharing taxis. The result was that soldiers were in continual contact with civilians. But whereas officers could mingle with a social class as sophisticated as their own, as General Wells noted "there is practically no stratum of society corresponding to that from which the average enlisted man is drawn, or, more accurately, that stratum in the Hawaiian Islands is Oriental."[52]

Perhaps in recognition of the potential for civil-military conflict, one departmental commander stressed that the necessity to "interlock our personnel with the civilian population" meant the War Department must send only the best troops to Hawaii.[53] In 1913 Brigadier General Frederick Funston, seeking to motivate the "limited number of enlisted men whose slovenly appearance in uniform, failure to salute officers, and drunkenness and disorderly conduct in the city of Honolulu" disgraced the army, instituted a system in which passes were freely granted except to soldiers who misbehaved.[54] This policy continued during the interwar period; soldiers at Schofield could obtain a pass by going to the company day room. In return for their freedom, they were expected simply to maintain a clean and orderly appearance and stay out of trouble, although now and then they were subjected to such bizarre orders as those of 1921, which maintained "that walking or standing in a slouching manner, with hands in their pockets, leaning up against walls or telegraph poles or eating ice cream cones or other similar things cannot be permitted."[55] Within a few years, off duty soldiers were encouraged to wear "civvies" and, clad in brightly patterned "Aloha shirts," they flocked to Honolulu for entertainment.

From the arrival of American troops in 1898, the reaction of the local population to this khaki invasion varied greatly. In Hawaii the first transports had been met with flowers and music, but enthusiasm waned as sporadic clashes between soldiers and civilians even brought threats of martial law. In the Philippines contact with the population was complicated by some soldiers behaving as members of an occupying army, referring to the inhabitants as "gugus" and "niggers." For the 31st Infantry in Manila, the local community was a walk across the street, and those at Fort McKinley had almost equally easy access, but most contact was limited to servants, waiters, and prostitutes. Soldiers like Michael J. Campbell, who sought to meet Filipinos, were often shocked by their poverty, religious practices, and poor sanitation. On one occasion, Campbell was invited to the village rice festival, where a dog was fed until bloated, then whipped to death, roasted on a fire, torn into pieces, and eaten by the villagers.[56]

Relations between the guardians of the Pacific empire and their wards could turn violent. According to one army report in 1922, Honolulu's "School Street gang, composed of about 500 Kanakas and Portuguese, wait for soldiers who they believe have money, pick an argument, beat up the soldier and take his money. . . . Any solider, drunk or sober, is a mark for this gang."[57] One commander of the Military Police justified its alacrity to make arrests on the grounds that local "gangsters" in Honolulu "do not hesitate to beat up a soldier for his money."[58] Soldiers were often equally ready to resort to violence, and between 1916 and early 1923 there were several riots and street fights among soldiers, sailors, and civilians.[59]

Much of the ill feeling between locals and servicemen was due to competition for eligible females. Russell A. Eberhardt, who remembered Hawaii's civil-military social relations as "cordial but not familiar" recalled that "we knew that all the locals thought we were after their daughters or wives if we showed any attention."[60] As one Hawaiian Department report noted, the lack of a sizable white community "makes it difficult and often impossible for soldiers to find congenial associates, particularly girls, with whom to dance and amuse themselves, and they are frequently forced to go without congenial human association or else to consort with the vicious element present in cities."[61] Although poorly paid by mainland standards, the American service-man was relatively well off when compared with many civilians in Hawaii and the Philippines. Younger workers, who also were overwhelmingly male, found themselves in competition with soldiers for women at dancehalls and clubs while older, married workers worried about their daughters' "shacking up." Howard Fields recalled that in prewar Hawaii, "Many GIs had 'shack jobs' (local girls the servicemen lived with). This caused a lot of resentment from the local men. . . . However, the locals usually got the worse of these con-frontations since the troops were bigger and better trained."[62] A Hawaiian beach boy remembered several fights with servicemen who were "cocky peo-ple" and "sometimes got nasty with our girls. So we always protected our girls."[63] One near riot in Waikiki began when locals and soldiers exchanged words over a female companion; within a short time two mobs armed with rocks, sticks, and bottles had formed.[64]

The army did its very best to discourage marriage between enlisted men and local women. In 1905 a self-styled "Friend of the Army Girl" worried that "however indiscreet he may have been in the tropics, I trust the day may never come when an American officer may be induced by fear of a court-martial to escort as a wife into one of our Army posts, a diminutive, brown-skinned, ill-odored rice eater."[65] Nearly two decades later, the Philippine Department's plan against insurrection—the Brown Plan—urged "all legal means to prevent intermarriage and other intimate social relations."[66] Some officers proposed limiting the term that soldiers could serve overseas in order to prevent them, as one Hawaiian Department commander delicately put it, from making "ties" that would not fit into their home community.[67] The number of Ameri-can Scout officers who married Filipinas led one officer to complain that "many of the present and former officers of the Philippine Scouts have forgot-ten that they were white men, presumably white gentlemen."[68] Soldiers who admitted to marriage or paternity with native women were discharged over-seas, though this informal policy was not put into a formal law until 1925, when it was ordered that "white Americans married to natives will not be reenlisted without approval of the department commander."[69]

Despite legal and social prohibitions, an informal "shack up" system in which enlisted men cohabited with permanent companions began almost at once. In 1901 Captain Willard A. Holbrook reported that many officers were living openly with Filipina mistresses, warning that the forthcoming arrival of

American schoolteachers would bring this scandal to the American public.[70] In 1905 Colonel Constant Williams chastised a court-martial that acquitted a sergeant who lived with a Filipina of "notorious character." Williams warned that the acquittal sanctioned "the propriety of American troops adopting the above practices which would result in the destruction of the social fabric by reason of their immorality."[71] Nevertheless, and despite several orders against the practice of keeping "queridas," a 1907 survey in Manila found 351 soldiers married to or cohabiting with Filipinas, and another 862 living with Filipino families.[72] In 1921 an officer reported that among the troopers of the 9th Cavalry "there are about 200 married to Filipino wives and approximately 187 (last count) living with Filipino women in common law marriage relationship, we are not setting the natives a very high standard of living."[73] Three years later an inspection of the 31st Infantry revealed that of the regiment's 1,123 soldiers, at least 71 were married to or living with Filipinas. The inspector was not sure that this was all to the bad: the 31st's overall venereal disease rate was 14 percent, but among married men with wives present or men living with native women it was only 3 percent.[74] According to one veteran, "the Philippines had a liberal 'shack up' system. . . . It was to provide a G.I. with $5.00 rent. A bag of rice purchased by him would last a long time. The girl would be clean and honest and the army was happy because V.D. was down, AWOL's were down. Although I never gave it a thought, I'm sure that's why so many men stayed in [the] P.I. and China."[75]

Besides "shack jobs," most of the enlisted man's sexual contact was with prostitutes. Respectable women would not date poorly paid army enlisted men; one private found that even Hawaii's famous "wicky wacky girls" were "just like the girls back home. If you have money to take them out they are all smiles [but] if you don't they don't want to be bothered with you."[76] The result was that soldiers found a more sympathetic and perhaps more economical environment in the brothels that sprang up around army posts. As early as the Philippine War reports of soldiers' licentiousness created a minor scandal in the United States and prompted army denials that Manila was an immoral city. Prostitution was illegal in Manila, but this did little but encourage graft; prostitutes were readily available to soldiers for two pesos or one dollar. Despite periodic reform campaigns, one inspector complained in 1931 that Manila remained an "oriental city. There is little, if any, opportunity for [soldiers] to associate with men or women. They patronize cheap gin shops and low priced native prostitutes."[77] Hardened regulars from the metropolitan army were shocked at the depravity among its garrison; one recalled "there seemed to be no limits, no dampers, no matter what the excess."[78]

For most of the first half of the century, Honolulu offered legal houses of prostitution; the women were registered and ostensibly inspected by government doctors. In 1914, the Honolulu Social Survey reported that "in proportion to their numbers, the increase of disorder and sexual vice has been less than might be expected" but that "in the community it is a matter of common observation that prostitution has greatly increased since the coming of the army."[79] Prior to World War I, it was confined largely to the Iwilei district, a rough dockside area long frequented by sailors. One prewar visitor counted 100 prostitutes and about 100 men, most of whom were in uniform.[80] After 1918, the vice district moved to the Hotel and River Street area, where brothels now were disguised as hotels and clubs. In the 1930s, Honolulu had a dozen army-approved and inspected brothels like the New Senator and Ritz where a soldier paid three dollars for sex with a white prostitute. At an off-limits brothel such as the Honolulu Rooms' famous Big Virginia he would pay two dollars for the services of a local girl or an erotic massage known as a "buzz job." According to one 1925 army report, soldiers in Hawaii were encouraged to visit the "better class" of "white American women" who took precautions against disease. Military Police warned them away from brothels that employed a "lower class of professional prostitute other than white. These places are filthy and are considered very dangerous as a venereal menace." The worst hazard, however, came from "clandestine" prostitutes who used cars and public parks, and varied "from white women of the 'Gold Digger type' to the lower class of natives."[81]

Although several commanding generals fulminated against brothels and vice, the army's main concern was to insure that sexual contact did not harm the soldier. There was good reason for this, for the enlisted man's ability to contract venereal diseases was, in the words of one doctor "most deplorable in extent and apparently uncontrollable."[82] In Hawaii between 1908 and 1914 one soldier in four was infected, and in the Philippines the venereal rate averaged 17 percent of the command from 1902 to 1917. Initially the War Department viewed the problem as a moral one that could be treated by exhortation. Typical was Theodore Roosevelt's 18 March 1902 general order warning soldiers in the tropics of "the inevitable misery and disaster which follow upon intemperance and upon moral uncleanliness and vicious living."[83] The president's message had so little effect in the Philippines that in 1905 it was reissued, along with orders that chaplains and medical officers encourage men to avoid temptation. In a similar moral appeal, one army doctor called for the nation to fund "innocent, wholesome, decent recreation to our exiles" in the Philippines, warning of "the climatic tendency of the tropics to lower the moral and intellectual standards of men and women" and to render them prey to the "vino joints, gambling houses, brothels who throw open doors and welcome lonely Americans."[84] In 1904, Episcopalian Bishop Charles H. Brent, a close friend of Wood and Pershing, helped fund Manila's Columbia Club, where soldiers could relax in a virtuous, sober environment. But appeals to morality, or docking soldiers' pay for time spent on sick call, or even holding officers accountable for their men's health—none of these were successful. The venereal disease rate remained high.[85]

As appeals to chastity clearly did not work, the army began to concentrate on education, prevention, and treatment. In the Philippines one chief surgeon argued in 1911, "we can not upset natural habits of thousands of years by any means short of chaining men up when off duty. Indeed, the evils of continence, now undergoing scientific investigation, may show that success in the crusade may be worse in its moral results than the present condition. Until then it is wise to invite men to use the preventative measures, but not punish them for neglect."[86] The surgeon general reported that in July 1909 the soldiers at Fort Shafter had been given a combination of physical inspection, education, and prophylaxis, thereby reducing the venereal disease rate by over 50 percent.[87] The army also pressed the city government to inspect prostitutes and certify they were disease-free. By 1914 the Honolulu Social Survey noted that, "the attitude of military authorities towards the question is one mainly of solicitude for physical efficiency in the army. The sole object of the regulations seems to be to guard their men from disease."[88] The first overseas prophylaxis clinic, or "pro shop," was established in Honolulu's Iwilei district in 1914; soldiers on pass could go for immediate treatment without punishment. In one three-month period in 1917, the clinic gave 3,513 prophylactic treatments and was widely credited with bringing the venereal disease rate down to 8 per 1,000 soldiers, a record low.[89] One veteran recalled, "If you caught a venereal disease (which I didn't) as long as you had that pro-station shop showing you had recent treatment to avert 'V.D.' you were clear. Otherwise, you had to spend the time you used to treat your V.D. plus time lost from duty, plus a summary court martial."[90]

In general, the army's measures proved effective; between 1922 and 1926, Hawaii's venereal disease rate averaged 3 to 5 percent of the command, a ratio that appears to have been constant throughout the interwar period. It was no mean achievement; as Colonel Darnell boasted, "opportunities for obtaining alcoholics [sic] in the city of Honolulu and the island of Oahu as a whole are practically unlimited and, as there is absolutely no local control over prostitution, it is believed that the results of this anti-venereal campaign are most remarkable."[91] The Philippines launched a similar campaign, though with less conspicuous success: in 1924 the 31st Infantry's venereal disease rate was 20 percent, the highest in the army. Persistent effort led to successive declines: to 17 percent in 1926, to 10 percent in 1931 and to 9 percent two years later.[92]

The treatment of gays in the military has recently become a subject of much controversy. The extent of homosexuality in the service is almost impossible to determine, but arrests for such activity constituted a very small percentage of those recorded for all crimes. In 1925, for example, out of 1,450 arrests by the Hawaiian Department's Military Police, only 1 was for sodomy. Similarly, the number of courts-martial is very small: between May 1917 and June 1941 the entire U.S. Army court-martialed only 1,010 soldiers for sodomy, of whom 273 were acquitted. Of that number, 211 trials (43 acquittals) occurred in the Hawaiian Department and 55 trials (23 acquittals) in the Philippines.[93] Despite these small numbers, most officers believed the army must employ both social as well as legal sanctions against a promiscuous homosexual who was a danger to his unit and who could both "corrupt his fellows" and find "willing participants in his crimes."[94]

Military attitudes toward gay activity reflect a great deal of ambiguity, as much based on the alleged life-style and behavior that accompanied homosexuality as on the issue of sexual preference. Given their lower-class backgrounds and limited education, it is not surprising that many soldiers had vague notions of what constituted homosexuality and what did not. Within the barracks, a soldier suspected of being a "punk," "fruit," or "fairy" was subject to constant hazing, and violence was not unusual: one soldier beat up an alleged homosexual on the grounds that "the guy is sloppy, he doesn't take any pride in himself and I don't like to be in the same company with queers. I don't like queers."[95] In some cases, suspected gays were victimized by other, predatory homosexuals.[96] Yet from James Jones's *From Here to Eternity* and official records, it appears that some soldiers saw nothing deviant in hustling drinks and money from openly gay men. One private dismissed such behavior in his outfit: "These soldiers are not queer, they just go out with them."[97] Even those who engaged in homosexual actions did not necessarily consider themselves gay; an investigator reported that several soldiers in Honolulu "emphatically deny doing anything more than submitting their privates to the wishes of others. They do not fully comprehend the equal seriousness of their own offense."[98] Because of this distinction between active and passive participant, some denounced their sexual partners without recognizing that they too could be tried for sodomy. One soldier, later convicted of homosexual relations with eleven members of his battery, was arrested after three of his sexual partners complained to a noncommissioned officer about "that cocksucker hanging around our outfit."[99]

The soldiers' ignorance was shared by many of their officers. Even allowing for the limited state of psychological knowledge at the time, some of the scientific testimony was bizarre. One Medical Corps officer, whose experience was limited to one year's internship at the State Lunatic Asylum in Austin, Texas, declared that a soldier's homosexuality was manifest in his "effeminate disposition which is almost a constant finding in cases of sexual perverts." To clinch his case, the doctor declared "(e)very man in the court here probably sized this same man up when he came in. I formed my opinion the first time I saw him."[100] Not all doctors were so casual or so ignorant. At the court-martial of a private who had sexual relations with seven soldiers in less than a month, one specialist in psychiatry testified that "no medicine can cure the accused, but that a psychiatrist may be of some help and that in his opinion the case is incurable and that a long period of confinement would be of no benefit in so far as it would be helpful in changing accused in connection with his sexual deficiency."[101]

There is abundant evidence that in their efforts to stamp out homosexuality, both the Military Police and the courts were guilty of procedures that were arbitrary and unfair, and that would now be considered gross violations of civil liberties. Some authorities sought to track down and entrap gays. In Manila in 1931 the Military Police employed plainclothesmen, one of whom described himself as "detailed for special duty to go out and hunt men that take other men out and suck their penis."[102] Soldiers were convicted on clearly specious or contradictory evidence, and on the testimony of known enemies or confessed criminals. Commanding officers used threats and even beatings to extort confessions.[103] In one of the most blatantly unjust incidents, a nineteen-year-old private was fondled by a civilian while drunk and unconscious. His fellow soldiers testified that he was an outstanding soldier, his commanding officer stated he would welcome him back in his company, and the court-martial recommended clemency. Nevertheless, the judge advocate maintained that "the situation here demands that adequate punishment be awarded and administered, not only to deter others with like motives but to keep the service wholesome and clear for the individuals who compose it."[104] He gave the soldier a dishonorable discharge and one year of hard labor at a federal penitentiary.

Such outrages become somewhat more understandable in the context of the army's efforts to prevent homosexual rape. In the entire U.S. Army between July 1918 and June 1941 only 86 soldiers were court-martialed for raping women, but there were a total of 250 general courts-martial for assault with intent to commit sodomy. Of these, Hawaii had 34 convictions and 20 acquittals and the Philippines 10 convictions and 7 acquittals.[105] Included were multiple rapes involving either known or suspected gay soldiers. Some victims were too terrified to report the abuse or, worse, found their complaints ignored. Others were raped during alcoholic sprees or even as public entertainment. In 1921 while quartered in the tunnel on Carabao Island, one soldier had anal intercourse with a drunken companion in front of a large crowd: one witness testified that "every night in the tunnel we would always have a few little recreations."[106] A more brutal case involved an assault on a military policeman by two inmates in Corregidor's hospital on 4 June 1931. After beating their victim nearly unconscious, they took turns sodomizing him while the other patients cheered them on.[107] Sergeant Ivory Oakes battered and then raped a teenage recruit in the barracks. The soldier was found bleeding and in a state of shock, mumbling "Sergeant Oakes you are hurting me" and "Mother, it was not my fault, he made me do it."[108] Small wonder that prosecutor found the maximum five-year sentence Oakes received inadequate: "Five years for the reputation, the self respect and manhood of a boy. . . . Something must be done to stamp this crime out of the service. The being, I cannot say human because that term does not apply, who stoops to this type of crime, recognizes but one thing, and that is fear of punishment."[109] The predatory savagery in such rape cases may go far to explain the army's own ruthlessness in seeking to rid the service of all homosexuals.

Court-martial records deal, of course, chiefly with gay liaisons between soldiers; but there is some evidence of civil-military contacts and of soldiers' participation in the wider gay community. One Military Police officer testified in 1933, "it is known that there are schools of perversion in Honolulu. It is also known that soldiers and sailors are members and act both as the principal and subject of these acts."[110] In 1931 an inspector reported, "Native perverts abound in Manila, I understand that many of the recent General Court Martial cases are the result of enlisted men's association with these people."[111] One veteran remembered some of his fellow soldiers enjoyed liaisons with Manila's transvestites, or "binnie boys," despite their being strictly off limits.[112] The local authorities cooperated enthusiastically with the military authorities in suppressing gay contacts between soldiers and civilians. During a major antihomosexual operation in Honolulu in 1933, soldiers were given immunity if they testified against a "well known pervert."[113] The references both to homosexuality and to the army's efforts to suppress it are numerous enough to show that it was a consistent, if minor, aspect of the Pacific Army's relations with the civilian community.

Along with sexual and racial relations, the army also faced the explosive issue of substance abuse. During the Philippine War, soldiers were reputed to take opium to control dysentery and other stomach diseases. Rumors of drug abuse continued to circulate. In 1914, the first year of the Harrison Anti-Narcotic Act, a former noncommissioned officer charged that boredom and mistreatment by officers led "a good many men" at Schofield Barracks to use cocaine to escape a "disagreeable station."[114] Three years later, the commander of the Hawaiian Department vowed to "protect young soldiers from the insidious ravages of the opium habit" and warned that all convicted addicts would receive three years in jail and a dishonorable discharge.[115] However, narcotic abuse seems to have been a small problem in the overseas army, even though drugs—chiefly opium and cocaine—were readily available in Honolulu and Manila. The legal record is relatively free: between July 1917 and June 1941 there were a total of 242 general courts-martial convictions for use and possession of narcotics in the entire U.S. Army, of which Hawaii had 20 and the Philippines 14. In the same period, there were a total of 70 convictions for introducing drugs into camp, of which 4 occurred in Hawaii and 6 in the Philippines.[116] The Hawaiian Anti-Narcotic Commission found little evidence among servicemen, reporting that between 1923 and 1925 there were only eight cases of narcotic use in the entire Hawaiian Department.[117] In 1925 the officer in charge of the department's Military Police reported "the use of drugs by soldiers is limited, there are very few real addicts"; in fact, he was aware of only three.[118]

A far more serious problem was alcohol. Drinking was socially accepted among officers and enlisted ranks; a comic poem circulating during the Philippines War listed the chief U.S. exports to the islands as firearms, beer, and Cyrus Noble whiskey.[119] Temperance workers citing both America's civilizing mission and the dangers to young soldiers secured the abolition of beer sales on army posts in 1901.[120] Troops who previously could purchase beer and wines at the post canteen, and consume them under the watchful eyes of their noncommissioned officers, were now forced to go off post. The results, as virtually every officer agreed, were disastrous, and nowhere was this more apparent than overseas. Within a year of the prohibition of beer at canteens there was a 100 percent increase in trials for drunkenness and a 220 percent increase in desertions in Oahu's garrison. From the Philippines, commanders reported in 1909 that between 50 and 80 percent of their courts-martial were alcohol related, chiefly the result of drinking native liquors. In 1914, among the 8,000 soldiers on Oahu there were 2,230 arrests for drunkenness on duty, 2,797 arrests for drunkenness in quarters, 2,297 arrests for drunk and disorderly behavior, 254 arrests for possession of liquor, 829 arrests for introducing liquor in camp, and 262 arrests for public drunkenness in Honolulu.[121] The loss of liquor sales drastically reduced the revenue from the post exchange, rendering it impossible to finance diet supplements, books, and athletic equipment for the regiment. Private enterprise burgeoned; saloons and brothels sprang up around garrisons, so that a survey in 1903 found 5,586 liquor establishments operating within a one-mile radius of the 139 army posts in the Philippines.[122] Moreover, the soldiers, denied access to cheap beer, spurned the expensive imported liquors and turned to local spirits—such as vino, a Philippine native gin made from the palm tree, or, in Hawaii, okolehao, distilled from the ti plant—and homemade fermented fruit-based brews known as "swipes." One officer blamed swipes for a "great deal of trouble and [it] occasionally causes an epidemic of drunkenness" because economy-minded soldiers discovered they could drink it until intoxicated, pass out and apparently sleep it off, then drink water and become drunk again: "the liquor is cheap and with two drunks for one drink is quite popular with some of the men."[123]

The Pacific Army was thus in the awkward position of enforcing civilian-mandated prohibition laws that many officers regarded as harmful to discipline and health. This became an even greater problem in the 1920s, when the Eighteenth Amendment was in effect in Hawaii. Predictably, the production of cheap domestic liquors markedly increased; one officer foresaw in 1921 that "the okolehao menace, due to bootleggers in civil life, is one that will have to be fought for some time to come."[124] Federal investigations revealed that most on-base bootlegging was a small-scale business in which such entrepreneurs as the "broken leg Chinaman" sold okolehao to soldiers.[125] In periodic raids, hundreds of quarts were seized at Schofield Barracks—thereby encouraging soldiers to go to Honolulu or Haleiwa, where alcohol was readily available and where the civil authorities, according to one department commander, "have never accomplished anything in checking the sales of intoxicants."[126] With the end of prohibition, alcohol consumption became far less of a problem. On-post beer gardens appeared, where soldiers could purchase beer for a nickel a can. Many preferred to go off base to a local saloon or to drive to Honolulu and drink at their "outfit's" bar.[127]

For local people, the major problems caused by alcohol were its by-products—fighting, public drunkenness, rowdy behavior, and driving while intoxicated—which made up the bulk of off-post discipline problems. The headline of one Honolulu newspaper story—"Okolehao Blamed for Soldier and Civilian Brawls"—could have been applied to many such incidents.[128] Drunkenness also contributed to tension with hotel owners. Groups of soldiers would rent a hotel room and then engage in prolonged debauch, leading the manager of Honolulu's prestigious Alexander Young Hotel to complain that "the nuisances committed in the bath rooms cannot be repeated on paper."[129]

In Hawaii, such actions led to so much friction with the authorities that one officer claimed "the principal contact between [the Hawaiian] Department and officials of the City and County of Honolulu centers in the Police Department under the Sheriff."[130] Relations between the two were sometimes strained; soldiers complained, and much of the primary material corroborates, that the police were all too ready to harass or mistreat servicemen. One Military Police commander believed "the ordinary Honolulu Police officer is as a rule an extremely ignorant and unintelligent man who is not capable of performing his duties in any sort of intelligent manner, and is more a hindrance than a help."[131] According to Colonel D. L. Howell, "There is no doubt in my mind that while the soldiers are sometimes a little disorderly they are treated with undue severity by the native police and sometimes with unprovoked brutality."[132] In one notorious case, police repeatedly clubbed two soldiers despite their pleas for mercy, then dragged them into a paddy wagon and beat them unconscious before taking them to jail. The incident prompted the Hawaiian Division commander to demand that the "extraordinary brutality" of the Honolulu Police cease at once.[133] An officer who investigated a later affair in which police violence touched off a minor riot concluded that "the underlying cause of all the trouble is the race question. All civil police in Honolulu are Hawaiian, and are regarded by the soldiers as negroes. The soldiers therefore resent being handled by them. The civil police on the other hand are fully conscious of the racial differences and are afraid of the soldiers. The opinion prevails that the civil police never give a soldier a chance, but generally hit him first and arrest him afterward . . . [and that] he is always at a disadvantage in any altercation with a Jap, Chinaman, or any of the colored races. . . . Any time a soldier is arrested they start beating up on him. Intense hatred is caused by this."[134]

To prevent such confrontations, in 1914 the army and navy established a joint Military Police–shore patrol unit to keep servicemen "out of the hands of the civil police."[135] This evolved into the famous Hawaiian Department Military Police, an elite unit of brawny six-footers. Considering the hundreds of soldiers in Honolulu, the number of MPs on duty was surprisingly small. In the 1930s the unit maintained an officer and two enlisted men at the Honolulu Police headquarters, a similar squad in an automobile, and two two-man beat-walking squads patrolling downtown and Waikiki. With the exception of pay-day nights, which could get quite wild, the MPs and the navy's shore patrol had little trouble maintaining order. By 1925 the Honolulu city government granted the MPs the right to arrest soldiers for civil offenses, a concession that owed something to the army's threat to prosecute policemen who treated soldiers with excessive severity. Behind the physically intimidating Military Police was the even more fearsome specter of the Schofield Stockade, a prison whose harshness was captured graphically in *From Here to Eternity*. Walter Maciejowski, who served in Hawaii shortly before the war, remembered, "I found the Honolulu Police to be *very friendly*. The M.P.s were the ones to avoid providing you were unruly or drunk. I never heard or saw the local police 'push' the service personnel around."[136] However, Howard Fields recalled the Honolulu Police "liked to impose indignations on us by making us give up our belts and shoelaces, knowing full well we would be turned out to the MPs pretty soon. Most of the servicemen would rather be picked up by the MPs."[137]

The Pacific Army's relations with the local community covered almost forty years of shifting social mores—the Days of Empire, World War I, the Jazz Age, the Depression, and the approach of World War II. It is difficult for current readers, with views on race and class shaped by the experience of World War II and the civil rights movement, not to resist blanket condemnation of the behavior and attitudes of earlier soldiers out of hand. But imposing our morality on the past precludes any understanding of the nuances of civil-military relations. In many respects, the army in the Philippine and Hawaiian communities was an alien entity that was never absorbed, but in many other ways it was an integral part of the continental American contingent overseas. This military presence grew increasingly comforting as expansionist Japan emerged as a threat. In Hawaii, General Fox Conner reported in 1929: "In general the civilian community appreciates the importance of the military establishment here and is usually ready to give sympathetic consideration to the solution of problems affecting both the Army and the local community."[138] In the Philippines, civilians reacted to the presence of the army with more ambivalence. The American expatriates viewed it as a foundation of public order and security, but some Filipinos regarded it as an intrusive and perhaps dangerous presence. Despite the claims of postwar revisionists, there is little evidence that off-duty soldiers were a serious public nuisance or that they conducted themselves as—or were generally viewed as—members of a foreign army of occupation. And, as has been well documented, the services formed a major segment of the economic base of both outposts—a fact that doubtless helped to temper some of the resentment. In both Pacific outposts, social relations between soldiers and the overseas' populations were multilayered, defying simplistic generalizations or easy classification.

U.S. soldiers in mess line at Waikiki, with Diamond Head in the background (1898).
Courtesy U.S. Army Museum of Hawaii.

U.S. troops destroying Moro cotta, Mindanao, P.I. (1901). Courtesy U.S. Army
Military History Institute.

Soldiers in the Philippines (c. 1900). Courtesy U.S. Army Military History Institute.

Parade of 25th Infantry Regiment in Honolulu (1913–15). Courtesy U.S. Army Museum of Hawaii.

U.S. soldiers in Hawaii, 1913–15. Courtesy U.S. Army Museum of Hawaii.

Firing of 14-inch coast artillery gun at Fort DeRussy, Oahu (1920s). Courtesy U.S. Army Museum of Hawaii.

Fort Drum, Manila Bay, "the concrete battleship." Courtesy U.S. Army Air Defense Museum.

Firing of 12-inch coast defense gun at Fort Mills, Corregidor (1930s). Courtesy U.S. Army Air Defense Museum.

Firing of 16-inch coast artillery gun at Pearl Harbor (1940). Courtesy U.S. Army
Museum of Hawaii.

Troops with 155-millimeter gun in Oahu Mountains (1930s). Courtesy U.S. Army
Museum of Hawaii.

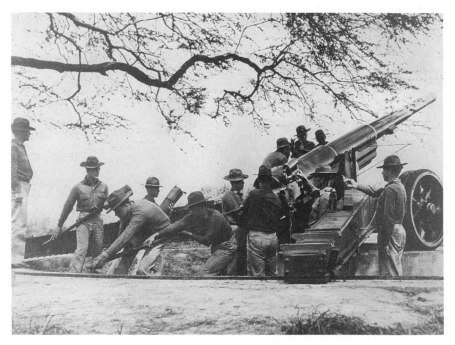

Beach defense troops preparing to fire 155-millimeter gun (1930s). Courtesy U.S.
Army Museum of Hawaii.

Antiaircraft gun camouflaged with sugarcane, Hawaii (1933). Courtesy U.S. Army Museum of Hawaii.

P-12C pursuit planes over Oahu (early 1930s). Courtesy U.S. Army Museum of Hawaii.

Fort Kamehameha's champion boxing team, Oahu (1940). Courtesy Howard C. Fields, 15th C.A.

Soldier on guard in front of Diamond Head (1938). Courtesy U.S. Army Museum of Hawaii.

CHAPTER 6

Manpower and Internal Security

y the Armistice, the U.S. Army had all but vanished from Hawaii and the Philippines. The Hawaiian garrison was on the mainland or in France, its place taken by two locally raised infantry regiments; except for a few coast artillerymen, the Philippines garrison was composed entirely of Scouts and the despised Philippine National Guard. Tensions among the erstwhile allies and unsettled conditions in the Far East mandated the immediate buildup of troop strength on the Pacific frontier because the most likely contingency—a war against an Anglo-Japanese coalition—meant they could not be reinforced for months. At the same time, internal problems were coming to a head. In the Philippines the Jones Act of 1916 and the Filipinization policies of Governor Francis B. Harrison had created the widespread expectation of immediate independence. Officers reported an undercurrent of political unrest, encouraged by the Japanese, that could turn violent. In Hawaii, a local defense board identified the Japanese inhabitants as the greatest menace to the safety of the islands. These apprehensions were somewhat balanced by a cautious optimism. The withdrawal of the Regulars had not triggered an immediate rebellion; indeed, the native populations remained loyal and provided manpower in sufficient quantity to hold the territories. For planners in Washington, Honolulu, and Manila, the questions were many. What balance of local and Regular forces would provide optimum combat strength? What should the army's role be if, as appeared likely, the Philippine Islands were given their independence? And, most important, could the army incorporate local forces for external defense without jeopardizing its ability to deal with internal threats?

The size and composition of the postwar Pacific forces became subsumed in the general debate over the U.S. Army that occurred between 1919 and 1920. On the advice of his own General Staff, Chief of Staff Peyton C. March advocated a peacetime complement of 509,000 men, in which the Philippine and Hawaiian departments would each be separate tactical commands of some 22,000 divided into a mobile division and a coast defense force. Congress rejected March's plan and, after testimony by John McAuley Palmer, passed the 1920 Defense Act, which made the Regular Army one part of the Army of the United States. The Regular's mission was to garrison the overseas possessions, to provide a field force which could protect the nation, and to serve as a training cadre for the rest of the Army of the United States—the National Guard and Organized Reserves—which would be mobilized in the event of war. It also slashed March's peacetime army by 45 percent, to a maximum of 280,000. In 1922, Congress cut it further to 147,000 and in 1925 to 135,000, where it remained until 1936. Funding plummeted. In 1924 the army calculated it needed $380 million annually; it received $250 million, or 65 percent of its request.[1]

The most obvious effect of the 1920 Defense Act was that the Regular forces in the Pacific never approached the peacetime strength envisioned by March. In 1921 the Philippines had a garrison of 13,251 and Hawaii one of 15,368; three years later their forces totaled 11,808 and 13,096 respectively. Throughout the interwar period, the Philippine Department's troop strength hovered between 11,000 and 12,000, about 40 percent of it American. The Hawaiian Department's manpower remained between 14,000 and 15,000 until 1936, when it was increased first to 19,000, and then, in 1939, to 21,500. Moreover, the overseas forces would always be considerably weaker than their continental counterparts, because they lacked supporting reserves. At least theoretically, a mainland peacetime corps consisted of a few tactical units and a small Regular cadre serving in "skeletonized" divisions which in wartime would be rapidly fleshed out by trained Organized Reserves. But in the Pacific commands such reserves did not exist, and to create them required the resolution of three issues. The first was simply one of numbers: to defend the territories against Japan would require anywhere from a twofold to a tenfold increase in the peacetime garrison. Second, unlike the continental United States, the Pacific possessions faced the prospect of sudden invasion; consequently, their forces had to be ready for immediate deployment. The third issue was whether local forces would prove loyal. Throughout the interwar period, the Pacific Army had to balance these three factors, seeking to achieve some mixture of manpower and security that would allow it to guard against both domestic and foreign enemies.

March's successor as chief of staff, John J. Pershing, aware of the maxim that he who tries to protect everything protects nothing, soon decided that the primary function of the Regulars was to serve as a cadre for the mass army, which in turn meant that the plans to station some 42,000 Regulars in Hawaii and the Philippines must be abandoned. In July 1922 he cut the authorized Regular garrisons in Hawaii and the Philippines almost in half. The War Plans Division's director, Colonel John L. DeWitt, protested that the nation's small Regular contingent should not be dispersed into training camps, but concentrated in the Pacific garrisons and in a 66,352-man rapid deployment force.[2] In a strong rejoinder, Brigadier General Hugh A. Drum argued that World War I had demonstrated the fallacy of relying on Regulars and neglecting to provide a strong reserve component. Disputing DeWitt's assertion that Pacific naval bases were essential to U.S. security, Drum claimed that "both the Philippines and Hawaii might be lost to us without materially affecting the safety of the continental United States provided we had an adequate force on land available for its protection."[3]

The DeWitt-Drum exchange highlighted yet another unanswered question of the 1920 legislation: was the U.S. Army to be a small, highly trained, technologically sophisticated, mobile elite or would it serve as the cadre for a large mass army such as the American Expeditionary Force in World War I? This controversy had repercussions on virtually all aspects of the interwar army—weapons development, doctrine, training, industrial mobilization—but especially on manpower and war planning. Most planners in the 1920s envisioned a return to trench warfare and set-piece battles which would be fought by a mass army equipped with simple weapons and copious firepower. As a result, much of their work dealt with industrial mobilization, transportation, and the creation of manpower reserves. Implicit in their viewpoint was that the nation would have ample time to recruit and train the millions of soldiers necessary for such a conflict. In the 1930s, after years of debate, the War Department shifted toward a view of the next war as highly mobile, waged by military technicians employing sophisticated weapons who would strike rapidly, paralyzing a more powerful opponent before he could complete his cumbersome mobilization. Planners now emphasized the army's immediate readiness, as witnessed by the Four Army Plan and the Initial Protective Force.[4]

Like their continental colleagues, Pacific Army officers were split between those who saw war in terms of crushing an enemy with mass and those who envisioned war as unhinging the enemy, and winning victory by mobility, skill, and equipment. But on the frontier, the debate took on even more significance: unlike the skeletonized mainland organizations, the overseas departments were supposed to be fully operational commands ready to fight at an instant's notice. The question thus became whether the Pacific Army's well-equipped, tactically proficient, but undermanned Regulars be broken up to train poorly equipped, made-from-scratch local units filled with people of dubious loyalty.

This issue had particular importance for the Philippines, where the Scouts provided a highly skilled native military force. But the Scouts, too few to supply sufficient manpower, were also politically suspect; dissatisfaction had increased during the wartime boom as their wages, once relatively high, now lagged behind both inflation and those in comparable civilian occupations. Many were angered that the 1920 Defense Act incorporating them into the Regular Army had not mandated the same pay as for American troops. Although aware of the discontent, and of contacts between individual Scouts and political secret societies, Philippine Department headquarters failed to pass this information on to field commanders. Many Scout officers, like their British counterparts before the Sepoy Mutiny, refused to believe that their own troops might rebel. According to one Scout officer: "they had been out in the Far East too long and had deteriorated both physically and mentally. Their life was not competitive, their duties were not complex, and their future was very limited. A number of them became fat and lazy and went to seed."[5]

Trouble broke out at Fort William McKinley on 7 July 1924, when 380 members of the 57th Infantry refused to fall in for routine drill. They were joined the next day by members of the 12th Medical Regiment, bringing the total number of mutineers to 602. Only the quick action of their superiors—one officer drove his troops out of their quarters with a baseball bat—prevented many more from refusing to drill. After having been warned of the seriousness of their offense, 393 Scouts rejoined their units without punishment; the remaining 209 were tried before a court-martial headed by Douglas MacArthur and given sentences of between five and twenty years.

American officers were divided over the implications of the mutiny, some maintaining it had been little more than a "peaceful strike" over pay, and others claiming it showed the loyalty of the Scouts was compromised.[6] William E. Carraway, a Scout officer who interviewed many of the participants, concluded that the soldiers' grievances were primarily a result of their inequitable pay, but he was disturbed to find other signs of deep dissatisfaction. Significantly, the protesters included members of different linguistic and geographical backgrounds and ranged from new recruits to veterans with two decades of service.[7] Clearly the army's traditional methods of securing loyalty—subdividing formations into "tribal" units and encouraging multiple reenlistments—were no longer effective. Although the 1924 mutiny had no successors, commanders continued to fear the influence of nationalist secret societies and maintained a strict watch on the political sentiments expressed by their Filipino troops.[8]

The major problem with the Scouts, however, was not loyalty but a lack of sufficient troops to defend the archipelago. Although troop levels of the post-war Scouts increased to between 6,500 and 7,000 soldiers, roughly 3,000 of these were assigned to the coast defenses and the departmental staff. The number of rifles the Scouts could put in the field actually declined; in some exercises, the entire Philippine Division deployed fewer than 1,000 troops and companies were commonly assigned areas that a brigade would have been strained to defend. Reenlisting the same men led to exceptionally well disciplined and well drilled soldiers, but it prevented the creation of a trained manpower reserve in the civilian population, and it led to declining effectiveness: by 1934, one inspector concluded "a large percentage of the Philippine Scout soldiers have reached an age where they no longer have a desired physical condition."[9] Composed of lifelong soldiers, each an excellent infantryman or gunner, the Scouts remained too small to provide more than a token defense. The only solution was to raise, equip, and train suitable forces from the Philippine population.

Turning to the second source of manpower authorized by the 1920 Defense Act, the citizen-soldier, the army weighed the equally unpleasant choices of a National Guard or the Organized Reserves. In the continental United States the National Guard constituted a well established and powerful political lobby at both the state and federal level. In the Pacific territories its influence was negligible. Filipino politicians supported a guard, but army officers were convinced that any native organization "would be political in character, and a waste of effort and time."[10] Their position was reinforced by Congress's refusal to include the archipelago in militia appropriations. In contrast, Hawaii had a guard, but it found little popular or political support. Indeed, the territorial legislature saw little reason to fund a local militia when thousands of Regular soldiers were near, and often debated its abolition. Organized into two two-battalion regiments, the 298th Infantry on Oahu and the 299th Infantry split among Kauai, Maui, and Hawaii, the Hawaii National Guard grew slowly between 1922 and 1940 from 1,300 to 1,800 officers and men. It reflected the islands' diverse population, with the conspicuous underrepresentation of Japanese and Filipinos; and as one commander noted, "the inability of many members to speak English was a serious handicap to some units."[11] In 1928 the guard was judged sufficiently capable to be assimilated into the primary tactical plan and an Army War College student called it "an excellent force."[12] But however effective its individual members, the guard was incapable of furnishing the numbers required for Hawaiian defense. With fewer than 2,000 officers and men, and with one of its regiments a long boat ride from Oahu, it could at best provide a small beach guard for the outer islands and an internal security force for Honolulu.

The third source of manpower authorized by the 1920 Defense Act, the Organized Reserves, presented a potentially explosive option. The act created an Enlisted Reserve Corps, composed of former soldiers or volunteers trained by Regular cadres at Citizens Military Training Camps, and officered by Reserved Officers Training Corps (ROTC) graduates. But could the non-white populations in the Pacific meet the requirements? In the Philippines the issue was further confused by the question of whether the reserve provisions of the 1920 act extended to the archipelago. In 1921, the army's judge advocate ruled they applied only to actual and potential American citizens, and therefore did not include Filipinos. In what now appears extraordinary negligence, and despite repeated demands from the Philippine Department, the War Department failed to challenge this ruling until October 1928, when it was quickly overturned.[13] The War Department's lethargy was symptomatic of Washington's inertia. Congress showed no enthusiasm for spending the money necessary even to establish the rudiments of a Filipino reserve system—an estimated $3 million over ten years for training camps alone—and the War Department did not press. Even the General Staff was lukewarm, though it continued to demand that the Philippine Department include Filipino reserve forces in its war plans.[14]

For Philippine officers, the reserve manpower question was frustrating in the extreme, in part because of the bitter feud between the Philippine Assembly and Governor-General Leonard Wood that virtually paralyzed the archipelago's government in the 1920s. Wood, deeply concerned with defensive issues, had introduced a comprehensive bill for a Filipino reserve. But the Assembly understandably took the position that since the United States had refused to follow through on the promise of independence, and since Filipinos were to be allowed no voice in their military organization, the Americans should be solely responsible for the archipelago's defense. Unfortunately, they accompanied these quite logical arguments with a great deal of inflammatory rhetoric that, at least to many, sounded seditious.[15] Army officers, who revered Wood, shared his conviction that the islands' politicians were dishonest, bombastic, and incapable of placing the greater good above their own selfishness. They noted that under Governor Harrison the Constabulary had become a tool for local bosses. The only way to avert a similar fate for the militia was to have the army in sole command.

The army's distrust of Filipino political leaders created an impossible dilemma. Most planners agreed with Colonel Duncan Major's 1924 assessment that "it is obvious that our main dependence in the beginning, if not ultimately, would rest on the Filipino, who to be of use in such an emergency should be trained for his role in war."[16] But they could not reconcile their need for Filipino manpower with the prospect of Filipino participation in decision making. As a result, mobilization planning either ignored the problem or posited improbable scenarios. In 1921 Major Robert C. Richardson determined that Luzon alone could provide 98,000 loyal and courageous soldiers, a force sufficient to repel any invader. In order to avoid Filipino political influence, the U.S. government would fund this reserve and the Regulars would provide its training cadre and field commanders.[17] The Annex of the 1924 Basic Project for the Defense of the Philippine Islands estimated that the defense of Luzon would require a garrison of 118,496 and an additional 27,000 replacements after six months. This meant the U.S. Army needed to recruit 93,000 officers and men, or roughly 10 percent of Luzon's male population between eighteen and forty-five. However, having determined these specific requirements, it made no provision to meet them. Conscription was rejected: if handled by the U.S. Army, it would be unpopular; and if controlled by Filipino civil authorities, it would be "characterized by corruption, ignorance of requirements, and careless administration to such an extent as to defeat the primary purposes of the measure."[18] A National Guard was similarly impossible, because, as the G-2 (Intelligence) Annex concluded, "such a force would be subject to the pernicious influence of native politicians." Thus, "our main reliance for adequate defense must be native reserve forces" raised and trained by "loyal American officers" and "disassociated entirely from the influence of native politicians."[19] Unable to reconcile their need for troops with their distrust of Filipino participation, the department's planners accomplished little; in 1923 the Organized Reserve forces in the Philippines numbered but 156 officers, of whom 122 were Americans.[20]

The end of the decade witnessed a new effort to breathe life into the moribund manpower issue. In 1928 Philippine Department commander William Lassiter outlined a defensive plan combining air power with a large Filipino army.[21] His successor, Douglas MacArthur, argued that since it was "evident that upon the loyalty and response of the Filipino people depends the success of our mission, it is of primary importance that every effort be made in times of peace to insure their loyalty and to inculcate in them the basic understanding that the defense of their country rests upon them." Then, with a MacArthurian flourish he dismissed the army's long debate on the subject and declared "it is the well digested belief of all who have made a careful study of the subject, that the adhesion of the Filipino people to the United States as against Orange can easily be assured."[22]

MacArthur's 1929 Basic War Plan Orange called for 76,000 soldiers in three divisions (North, Central, South), a Departmental Artillery and Machine Gun Brigade for beach defense, and the fortress command. This manpower would be obtained through a ten-year program that would train 9,000 officers in ROTC and 30,000 enlisted men in Citizens Military Training Camps (CMTC). If Japan attacked after 1939, the Philippine forces could muster 60,000 qualified enlisted men within fifteen days.[23] The plan not only ignored the legal question of whether Filipino reserve organizations qualified under the 1920 Defense Act, but further assumed they would be funded at a time when Congress showed little inclination to allocate enough money to keep the American reserve system going. As the adjutant general informed MacArthur in December 1929, the War Department could not even request the funds to implement the plan until the 1931 appropriation, and then only for 3,000 CMTC students: "such an ambitious undertaking" should be approached "step by step."[24] Not until 1935, when MacArthur became military advisor to the Commonwealth government's Philippine Army, would the prospect of a mass Filipino militia again be raised.

The Organized Reserve provisions of the 1920 National Defense Act clearly applied to Hawaii, but the army failed to implement them. As in the Philippines, the dilatory behavior of both Washington and local commanders is indicative of their deep ambivalence. The War Department failed to authorize an Organized Reserve unit for Hawaii and stalled until 1923 before assigning the territory's reserves to the Hawaiian Department's Regular formations in wartime. Even then, because of financial cutbacks, lethargy, and the absence of opportunities, few people received sufficient duty time with the Regulars even to qualify to remain in the reserves, much less achieve promotion.

The Hawaiian Department showed little enthusiasm for citizen soldiers, in part because of racial bias. In 1924 Commanding General Charles P. Summerall offered a summary of the shortcomings of Hawaii's ethnic groups: the Chinese were "cautious, secretive, patient, slow to anger, peaceful and sober"; the Koreans "somewhat easily excited, superstitious and inclined to timidity"; the Filipinos too saturated with anti-American independence rhetoric and "rather easily influenced by any smooth-tongued charlatan"; the Hawaiians "light hearted, easy-going, fond of music, dancing and singing"; and the Portuguese, "both adults and children, are of inferior intelligence." Only the Caucasians and the "energetic and ambitious, aggressive, shrewd, cunning, secretive, persistent, clannish, and astute" Japanese possessed the qualities that made good soldiers. In sum, Hawaii's manpower pool "is of very low quality, lacks homogeneity, community interests and unity of purpose, speaks no common language, and its loyalty is questionable."[25]

Unwilling to trust the nonwhite population, Summerall found himself drawing up a defensive scheme, which he himself recognized was "tactically correct in principle, though based upon a fallacy regarding manpower."[26] The 1924 Basic Project for the Defense of Oahu outlined a defensive scheme that required 94,000 soldiers, despite the fact that the Hawaiian Department was barely two-thirds of its authorized component of 14,780. Moreover, the project also declared that "local man-power will only be used for labor purposes" because "from a military viewpoint, the civil population in general is below average in intelligence and is materially deficient in usable occupational specialists. There is a seriously large proportion which is unfriendly."[27] Summerall's concurrent Basic Defense Plan Red-Orange, the blueprint for repelling an immediate invasion, was even more flawed. Not only did it assume a garrison of 48,000 troops, but it required that "all available males, fit for military duty, are to be enlisted or inducted into military service and assigned to *combat units*."[28] In both cases, Summerall's staff resolved the discrepancy between needed and actual manpower by predicating their plans on immediate reinforcement from the mainland—in clear disregard of the War Department's Red-Orange plan, in which Hawaii would be cut off for one to four months.

To Summerall, and to some succeeding commanders, Hawaii's racial diversity meant that the bulwark of continental defense—the cadre army supported by local reserves envisioned by the National Defense Act of 1920—was inapplicable. Instead, Oahu needed a permanent Regular garrison sufficient to handle the defense virtually unaided: "the situation here requires that the *standing* force be sufficient in strength and training to be able to exert the necessary power immediately and to meet the enemy initially with a fair chance of success in denying him beachheads behind which he could develop forces sufficiently large for invasion."[29] Summerall made no effort to establish the Citizens Military Training Camps which the 1920 act intended as the major source of trained reserves. His successor, Major General Edward M. Lewis, opposed the camps on the grounds that it was impossible to insure either the "loyalty of the Hawaiian born Japanese; or the possibility of debarring Hawaiian born Japanese from prospective camps without adding to local racial prejudices."[30] Perhaps reciprocating army distrust, Hawaii's population, which had come to look on the Regulars as the sole source of military defense, avoided service in the reserves. A year after the passage of the Defense Act there were only 121 reserve officers, and in 1924 the Organized Reserves numbered but 1,500 members. A decade later there was no Enlisted Reserve organization and only 532 reserve officers. Few could obtain sufficient duty time for promotion, with the result that the best of them soon resigned.[31]

One solution that maintained the integrity of the Regulars while providing a local reserve force was offered by department commander Hugh A. Drum in 1934. Drum wanted to form a service command, composed of guardsmen and reserve officers, which would relieve combat troops by guarding utilities, mobilizing local manpower for defense projects, maintaining communications, public health, police, and transport. He also sought to create a Home Guard composed of trustworthy citizens who would maintain order and guard enemy aliens. When the War Department subjected these proposals to its customary delays, Drum formed the Hawaiian Service Command on his own. By 1937 the Service Command's army officers and civilian volunteers had produced detailed plans for maintaining Honolulu's essential social services during the transition from peace to war. But these initiatives were soon thwarted by Washington. The executive for Reserve Affairs noted that many of those designated for reserve commissions were plantation managers and argued the whole proposal smelled of special privilege. The War Department refused to promote 250 reserve officers or to commission the civilian specialists designated by Drum as essential, and in 1937 it disapproved the entire project. Composed as it was of a small group of the haole elite, the Hawaiian Service Command neither conformed to the 1920 act nor provided sufficient manpower for the department's needs.[32]

Looming over the entire manpower issue was the question of loyalty, and especially the allegiance of Hawaii's large Japanese community. No sooner had the 1920 act been passed than the Territorial Government and army had quarreled over who could and could not join the Organized Reserves. Hawaii's governor, Wallace R. Farrington, had supported the inclusion of Japanese as a means to increase numbers, to inculcate patriotism in the nisei—second-generation Japanese Americans—and to counteract the influence of Japanese nationalist organizations.[33] The army, and especially department commander Major General Charles G. Morton, had opposed giving either training or responsibility to a people that might join the invaders. When attempting to establish the reserve system mandated by the Defense Act, Morton was shocked to discover that among those recommended for commissions were three nisei. He admitted that, despite extensive surveillance by military intelligence and federal agencies, there was "nothing definite" to indicate these three were disloyal or unfit, but he maintained that "no individuals of Japanese blood should be permitted under any circumstances to obtain [a] commission or to enlist in any organization or branch of the Army of the United States."[34] Nevertheless, the territorial government, although restricting the number of Japanese Americans in the Hawaii National Guard, continued to admit them. In 1932 Japanese composed about 45 percent of the population, but only 10 percent of the guard.[35]

Somewhat ironically, one of the most successful programs for tapping Japanese manpower was established by Summerall, whose prejudice against Hawaii's population has already been described. His creation of an ROTC unit at McKinley High School—nicknamed "Little Tokyo" for its predominantly Japanese student body—was, in his words, "eminently successful and the Japanese students showed themselves to be capable of becoming very efficient military students. There is no better way of securing the loyalty of such people than to incorporate them in our military forces with the environment of obligation to duty that cannot fail to win their allegiance in most, if not all cases. Such a course would also tend to remove the resentment the Japanese citizens now feel at the discrimination that is made against them."[36] The program was very popular; one officer reported there was "no city in the United States where the R.O.T.C. is given more enthusiastic support by the school authorities and the general public than it receives in Honolulu."[37] The result was that Hawaii's reserve organizations continued to be unbalanced, with far more officers—including a growing number of Japanese American ROTC graduates—than enlisted men.

In 1931 a board of officers convened by Hawaiian Department commander Lassiter examined the entire issue of Orientals in the Organized Reserves. The board recommended that Asian Americans be encouraged to join the Enlisted Reserve Corps as a means of "Americanizing" them and ensuring their loyalty. The War Plans Division rejected this proposal on the preposterous grounds that because Hawaii's reserve organizations were in such terrible condition, any Asian officer who remained must be either concerned with social prestige or a traitor.[38]

Lassiter's successor, Major General Briant H. Wells, took up the struggle in 1934, urging not that Japanese Americans be recruited into the Organized Reserves, but that a few selected nisei officers be slotted for wartime duty with Regular units. Wells advocated this radical suggestion after successive maneuvers demonstrated his forces were insufficient to guard Oahu's beaches. Since the War Department refused either to send more Regulars or authorize a special force of irregulars, the only source of manpower left were the nisei: "What is to be done with these thousands of American citizens of military age? Should mere suspicion of them lead us to forego the opportunity—to shirk the duty—of employing them if they prove loyal?" To Wells, the problem was two-dimensional: "The course of Americanization has not progressed to positive belief in undivided loyalty of the group, nor has the American Caucasian soldier reached the stage of willingness to be commanded by or associated in the ranks with individuals of this group with confidence and without discrimination."[39] He suggested the formation of a special Japanese American force of six battalions, commanded, in part, by nisei reserve officers. Brigadier General Stanley D. Embick, the War Plans Division director, rejected this plan and instead urged a reduction of Japanese officers. Both Washington and Honolulu accepted Embick's suggestion, and during Drum's tenure, department war plans called for the exclusion of Japanese from any duties but labor. Drum also purged the National Guard; between 1932 and 1935 the number of Japanese Guardsmen fell from 188 to 72.[40]

Wells's views were revived in 1938 by a new division commander, Major General Charles D. Herron, after Wells, now secretary of the Hawaii Sugar Planters Association, introduced him to a number of the territory's civil and political leaders. They convinced Herron that the army's policy, based on Washington's complete unfamiliarity with changing local conditions, was outdated and counterproductive. It treated Hawaii's Japanese as a solid bloc, when in fact they were deeply divided between younger American-born leaders, many of them educated at the University of Hawaii and participants in its ROTC program, and their Japan-born parents whose loyalty was to their homeland. The army's policy was a standing insult to the former and hampered them in winning over the Japanese community. Herron believed the Hawaii-born Japanese "can do nothing but adhere to the United States in war. Some will adhere through conviction and some because their children, their property, their business and all of their future prospects are here." Local Japanese visiting Japan had been treated with such "suspicion and discrimination" that they had happily come home. Noting that "the Japanese population, by its attitude and actions, may well decide the fate of these islands in the next war," he urged his superiors to consider that "until fully trusted, they will never become trustworthy."[41] He proposed assigning selected nisei reservist officers to Regular combat units in wartime and establishing a multiethnic reserve infantry regiment. This would both demonstrate American faith in its citizens and allow for complete army supervision and control. If the experiment was successful, further steps could be taken to integrate locals, and especially Japanese, into the Organized Reserves.

Reflecting the increased importance attached to Hawaii in the late 1930s, Herron's proposal drew a far more thoughtful and reasoned response than had Wells's. The paper was circulated to all the divisions of the General Staff, and extensive critiques were obtained. By a slight majority, officers opposed assigning nisei reserve lieutenants to Regular infantry and field artillery units for the present, but all supported a multiethnic reserve infantry regiment. Most agreed with Herron's view of the Japanese community as divided and the majority of Japanese as loyal; their primary objection to Japanese reservists in Regular units was that white soldiers would not accept them. The General Staff concurred with the majority opinion, but Chief of Staff Malin Craig disapproved the proposal without explanation.[42]

Despite Craig's veto, Hawaiian officers seemed to have reached a consensus by the late 1930s that the nisei could be trusted. Although in August 1940 the War Department ordered that no commission be given to "descendants of races whose characteristics are such as make them unadaptable,"[43] when Hawaii's reserves were called up in February 1941, department commander Lieutenant General Walter C. Short, declared "if we expect loyalty from a second generation citizen we must show the same loyalty to him," and announced there would be no racial quotas and Japanese Americans would serve with everyone else.[44]

In assessing the army's attempts to develop local forces of sufficient size and ability to bolster the insufficient Regular garrisons, it is difficult not to conclude that here, as in so many matters, both Washington and the overseas departments found it far easier to procrastinate than to make a strong, and perhaps irrevocable commitment. There were always reasons for such delays: the army was financially strapped, the reserves were expensive, and their performance was erratic. But the major problem was suspicion. It was difficult, perhaps impossible, for the same officers engaged in contingency planning against revolt and sabotage to discuss objectively the arming and training of citizen-soldiers. The contradiction was inherent in the overseas army's mission. Throughout its existence, the Pacific Army was charged with guarding against two threats—the internal one of revolt and the external one of invasion.

In the Philippines, the internal security requirement was avouched in the War Department's 1922 reaffirmation that the Philippine army's secondary mission was to uphold the civil government. The Philippine Department needed little encouragement to embrace this duty. Indeed, throughout the interwar period there was a minority who held that the garrison should abandon its pretensions to defend Manila Bay and trim to the minimum necessary to uphold public order.[45] From its inception the army's Philippine intelligence office had served as a clearinghouse; producing monographs of economic, political, and psychological information on Asian and Philippine affairs. Army intelligence officers collaborated with the Constabulary and the Manila police to keep track of Filipino nationalists: in 1924, Wood dispatched an army officer to Hawaii to investigate Filipino labor movements and radical politics. After the Philippine Scout mutiny in 1924, the army's Secret Service

Section inserted agents in the Scout companies. Throughout the interwar period a steady stream of reports on Filipino political developments and putative conspiracies continued to flow from Manila to Washington, all of which provided support for army suspicions of Filipino disloyalty. Conservative in their outlook, officers tended to ignore that much of this Filipino discontent was generated by a patriotic longing for independence or a desire to rectify the archipelago's social and economic inequalities.[46]

Army interest in internal security led to a series of plans to combat insurrection, code-named the Brown Plans. These were variations of the White contingency plans that the War Department ordered all continental and overseas commanders to develop to deal with labor or radical unrest in the immediate postwar years. Because of the "embarrassment and evil consequences that would ensure if even a suspicion of the preparation of such a Plan become public," secrecy was essential. Only a few senior staff officers worked on it; "no mention of it will be made to any native whatsoever" and all notes were to be burned, and only six copies kept.[47]

The first Brown Plan was written in 1923 and outlined the characteristic tenets of such plans through their last major revision in 1933. After a lengthy, and largely unfavorable, view of archipelago politics and the current situation, it discussed a number of possible contingencies ranging from the disturbances requiring the protection of U.S. property, to the deployment of military forces in support of the civil government, and thence to a full rebellion, with the Scouts and Constabulary either unreliable or mutinous. For the present, the army would work to improve relations with the Filipino people and secure the loyalty of the Scouts. If the intermediate situations developed, the army would deploy and, if necessary, suppress unrest. In the final, and most serious contingency, the Americans would disarm the Scouts, secure the Manila Bay forts, and maintain an enclave in the Walled City and port area until reinforcements could arrive from Hawaii.[48]

Successive revisions included contingency plans for individual commands, aviation and chemical warfare, and additional data on the Hawaii garrison's plans for rescue. The major difference was that after the Scout mutiny, there was fuller recognition that "if the native troops remain loyal there is little prospect of a successful insurrection. If they join the insurrection, either in part or in whole, a very serious situation may develop requiring drastic action and large reinforcements."[49] With the creation of the Philippine Commonwealth in 1936, the Brown Plan was rendered obsolete; the last one, that of 1933, was ordered destroyed in 1937. Although never activated, the plans reveal the anxiety of both Washington and Manila at the prospect of revolt.

Preventive measures against internal unrest were stringent in Hawaii; in

1919 one Hawaii commander claimed that the Japanese community was "the greatest menace to the military safety of this island."[50] The outbreak of labor unrest, particularly the 1920 strike by sugarcane workers in which Filipino and Japanese laborers united, raised fears of domestic violence even higher. During the strike, troops at Schofield were twice deployed to Shafter in case of serious disorder in Honolulu.[51] In 1921 General Morton told a Justice Department investigator: "Our ignorance of the machinations, intrigues, and activities of the Japanese population in Hawaii, is abysmal. The Japanese would endeavor to take the Islands tomorrow if they dared."[52] His fears were deepened by his intelligence officer, George M. Brooke, a former attaché in Tokyo, who recruited a network of plantation owners and supervisors known as the Voluntary Aids for Information. Not surprisingly, Brooke's reports were strongly antilabor and filled with putative conspiracies. Reporting on a peaceful demonstration of Japanese and Filipinos in support of the cane workers, Brooke seized on the playing of a popular folk song as "convincing proof that this strike has behind it strong forces connected with the Japanese government." "How long," he declaimed, "is our country to be made 'the spoil' of designing aliens under the plea of human liberty and brotherly love—a glorious plea, but one which does not fit the case?"[53]

But racism and class interests aside, there was abundant circumstantial evidence to justify the worries that the Japanese minority—43 percent of Hawaii's population in 1921—owed their loyalty to their homeland. As Summerall pointed out in a speech to a Japanese congregation in 1922, "no nation can view with ease the presence of an overwhelming group who choose to remain foreign citizens," especially citizens of a nation often estranged from the United States.[54] Officers noted that in contrast with other immigrants, "there is no evidence of the Japanese having become Americanized. They do not associate with the white people to any extent and the white people show no disposition to associate with them."[55] Perhaps worse, the Japanese were far more assertive of their rights than earlier immigrants. Their culture was based on assumptions of racial superiority and military prowess at least as arrogant and parochial as any American officer's; and the immigrants had been imbued with these assumptions. Local Japanese did not abandon their culture for American ways, but rather maintained it through language schools, temples, and a widely read and confrontational press. The cultural connections of other ethnic groups were not nearly as strong: in 1933 there were 174 Japanese language schools with 39,724 pupils; the Chinese and Koreans together had only 24 language schools with 3,003 students.[56] With the encouragement of the Japanese government, teachers and priests came to the islands to instruct the local population in traditional duties. Saluting the emperor and other displays of allegiance were common in the language schools, and in 1940 Hawaii sent one of the largest delegations to festivities marking the empire's birth and the declaration of the Greater East Asian Co-Prosperity Sphere. Japanese warships routinely visited the islands, their arrival serving as an occasion for immigrants to demonstrate support for their homeland's military power. Despite some discouragement from the Japanese government and consulate, parents continued to register their children as Japanese citizens. The issue was complicated by the fact that the alternative—that Hawaii's Japanese would take on the duties and responsibilities of Americans—was equally frightening.[57]

Because most radical and labor activity was tied to specific ethnic groups, particularly the Japanese and Filipinos, army intelligence officers tended to assume that ethnic and class consciousness were indistinguishable. Since the Brown Plan called for the dispatch of a relief force from Hawaii to the Philippines, the army investigated the possibility of Filipino labor groups and secret societies sabotaging Honolulu's docks or transport. These investigations, in common with those into similar Japanese organizations, rarely revealed anything more than overblown rhetoric and shady confidence tricksters, but the army continued its surveillance.[58]

Like the Philippine Department, the Hawaiian command developed a number of contingency plans to deal with local unrest. Essentially concerned with civil defense, they provided practical instruction on securing utilities, guarding U.S. property, and protecting the territorial government. The White contingency plans made little attempt at impartiality: the 1924 version, for example, attributed labor unrest not to the fact that agricultural workers were paid $1.63 a day, but to "unscrupulous Filipino Labor leaders" and the sympathy of the Asian community.[59] But trouble could come from those Caucasians, who "through idealism, internationalism, and religious fervor . . . are pacifists in every sense of the word and are a potential source of trouble due to their misguided efforts often based on misinformation."[60] However, the analysis was often shrewd: the 1928 plan noted that Hawaii's diverse population generated considerable animosity, and that "what might originally start as a situation without any racial aspects could, easily and without warning, develop into one along very definite racial lines"[61] and the 1932 plan recognized that the islands' haoles, because of their inordinate economic and political power "are naturally considered an oppressive race, especially by the Orientals."[62]

Separate from the White plans, which dealt with radical activity and labor unrest, the Hawaiian Department developed an extensive series of plans to deal with insurrection by local Japanese during an invasion. Placing the Japanese population in concentration camps, so appealing to earlier officers, was never seriously considered by any postwar department commander or his staff. The first postwar plan, and the harshest, restricted the Japanese to their four major residential areas on Oahu and would have put only suspected enemy agents in special camps.[63] However, Morton appears to have disregarded this suggestion and instead planned to use Japanese males as paid labor to build trenches and defenses and to deport all who refused such employment.[64] Summerall's 1924 Basic Defense Plan contained five "E-Plans" to deal with enemy sympathizers, ranging from E-1, with habeas corpus still in effect, civilians in charge, cooperation with the leaders of enemy aliens, and no martial law, to E-5, in which martial law was declared, the military took over key functions, and all male enemy sympathizers of military age were interned. Reacting to the brutalization of German Americans during World War I, the 1924 E-Plans maintained that in all cases, enemy aliens were to be "protected from unlawful violence on the part of the loyal population."[65] But as officers grew more familiar with Hawaiian society, army internal security plans became more moderate. Wells's 1933 Joint Defense Plan–Hawaiian Theater stressed that "in the absence of concrete evidence to the contrary, a citizen of the United States must be treated as loyal."[66] Drum declared internment was impossible for both moral and practical grounds and his successor commented in 1935 that "neither the segregation of the Orange nor the positive guarding of all facilities is practicable."[67] The 1936 Joint Defense Plan–Hawaiian Theater stated: "to attempt to segregate or intern this whole group or even the enemy portion . . . would require more troops and facilities than are available and should not be undertaken except as a last resort. To intern this group would seriously affect the economic system and facilities of the Territory."[68]

The most famous of the army's internal security plans, more because its author was George S. Patton than for its originality, was the 1935 "Plan for Initial Seizure of Orange Nationals." Patton would have interned those "who are considered most inimical to American interests, or those whom, due to their position and influence in the Orange community, it is desirable to retain as hostages." These suspects—a total of 97—included 14 American citizens, 2 of them identified as "haoles." The troops detailed to make the arrests were enjoined to "use no more force than is necessary. Reassure the relatives that no immediate harm will befall those whom you take."[69] In addition, all weapons and radios would be seized, all Japanese with the exception of servants would be barred from military installations, the Japanese language schools would be closed, press and mail would be censored, and martial law declared. If one considers that in 1935 Hawaii had a population of 150,000 Japanese—

40,000 of whom were Japanese citizens—a plan that interned but 97 people was notably moderate. It is thus curious that Patton's biographer has termed this a "brutal scheme" which demonstrates that officer's racial prejudices.[70] Even more suspect is Michael Slackman's supposition that Patton regarded the internees as "bargaining chips" whose lives could be forfeited—a conjecture that places the worst possible interpretation on the evidence.[71]

The internal security plans make it clear that by the late 1920s, Hawaii's officers viewed the possibility of an armed uprising as remote. Many recognized, as the Hawaiian Department's 1927 Orange plan declared, that "alien-born Japanese will be loyal to Japan. . . . The Hawaiian-born Japanese, however, have assimilated Occidental ideas to some extent and there is a tendency to break away."[72] A 1929 study by a former department staff officer mixes old suspicions and a new awareness that the nisei were different from their parents: "It may be generally assumed that all Japanese born in Japan will be hostile, but it is generally believed that Hawaiian-born Japanese will not have the same intense feelings for Japan. In any case, it is believed that the Japanese will not declare themselves hostile to the United States until they are reasonably sure of the success of Japan. They would stand to lose too much if they joined the attackers and the attack should fail. Their attitude probably will be one of *watchful waiting* until the outcome of the attack is foreseen."[73] This view was reiterated in 1935: a war would cause an "adverse reaction" among Hawaii's Japanese sympathizers, but it was "unlikely that mass action, either armed or unarmed . . . will develop."[74] But should the population revolt, the army would be ready. Hawaii's residents became accustomed to troop convoys barreling down the roads, to soldiers guarding roads and utilities, and to blackout exercises, drills, and alerts. Whether this activity averted sabotage or rebellion or merely antagonized people is an open question.[75]

To the end of its existence, the Pacific Army retained something of the character of imperial forces occupying a potentially hostile territory. Much of its clannishness was due to its self-imposed separation, a separation forced by its refusal to trust the native population to defend itself. For four decades, military planners toyed with the idea of creating sizable local forces in Hawaii and the Philippines, but failed to produce anything resembling a viable native militia in either territory. The causes were many, but perhaps the most important was that, ultimately, the army could not overcome its distrust of Filipino or Hawaiian or, especially, Japanese American citizen-soldiers. Military intelligence reports provided ample documentation for this mistrust. But it is also true that the suspicion tended to become self-fulfilling. The army's refusal to establish the groundwork for a local reserve contributed greatly to the poor combat performance of the Philippine Army. Besides encouraging those who championed Japanese nationalism, the army's persistent discrimination deprived it of the services of the ethnic group that in World War II would furnish its most highly decorated combat regiment. Like so many of the Pacific Army's efforts, the attempt to exploit local manpower was hampered by an absence of clear vision and determination. Individual officers proposed numerous solutions, but nowhere in Honolulu, Manila, or Washington was there the drive to carry them forward. Ultimately, the guardians of empire were unable to answer the basic question: whom were they guarding—and against whom?

CHAPTER 7

Orange to Rainbow, 1919–1940

T he "War to End All Wars" caused a pronounced shift in the balance of power in the Pacific. Japan seized German territories, bullied China, dominated Manchuria, and pushed into Siberia with 120,000 troops, demonstrating an ability to project military force into Asia that far exceeded that of any Western power. Even more alarming, the League of Nations gave Japan the mandate over much of the Marianas, Marshalls, and Carolines, placing it astride the American oceanic lifeline extending from Pearl Harbor to Manila Bay. To make matters worse, Japan's government smarted from interference in what it viewed as legitimate and necessary interests on the Asian mainland and resented American attempts to break the Anglo-Japanese alliance of 1902, to enforce the Open Door in China, to station a battle fleet in the Pacific, and to fortify Guam. Throughout the war, U.S. Navy planners had barely restrained their suspicion of their putative ally, and continued to press for a battle fleet equal to Japan's in the Pacific. Service alongside Japanese troops in Russia convinced some that Japan intended the conquest of East Asia and that its military was eagerly anticipating war with the United States. To make matters worse, the Anglo-Japanese alliance and British resentment over America's open challenge to the Royal Navy's supremacy prompted fears that the United States might have to fight a "Red-Orange" combination. Thus, even as soldiers came home from Europe, American strategists returned to the task that had preoccupied them since 1907, planning for a Pacific war with Japan.[1]

Within the army, the impact of the world war was felt on many levels. Chief of Staff Peyton C. March reorganized the General Staff, streamlined its procedures, eliminated redundant agencies, and consolidated bureaucratic power.

Responding to numerous complaints, March sought to eliminate the duplication and contradictory policies that had stemmed from myriad defense boards and committees circulating their ideas through the War Department's bureaucracy. In 1921 the War Plans Division (WPD) was upgraded from a branch to become the fifth section of the General Staff. In addition to its obvious duties to prepare war plans, WPD was charged with monitoring defense projects in the overseas departments. Henceforth there was to be only one agency responsible for strategic planning and for insuring harmony between Manila, Honolulu, and Washington. The war also demonstrated the nation's ability to harness its manpower and industry. In less than two years the U.S. had put nearly 5 million men into uniform, a quarter of whom served on the western front. The War Department built thirty-six camps, each capable of housing and training a 30,000-man division, and American industry produced thousands of rifles, artillery shells, engines, and other war supplies. To some, the very creation, training, transport, and deployment of this army demonstrated the nation's military prowess in any future conflict. But others pointed to waste, delays, mismanagement, excessive casualties, weapons and equipment shortages, poor training, erratic doctrine, and to a hundred other problems; they paled at the thought of having to fight an opponent twice as far away as Germany. To both optimists and pessimists, World War I demonstrated the totality of modern conflict. Planners could no longer just think in terms of generals and armies; peacetime planning had to incorporate not only grand strategy, but economic and manpower mobilization, technological developments, and tactical doctrine.[2]

Finally, the war left ambivalent military lessons. To some, it vindicated the imperialist vision of Arthur MacArthur and Leonard Wood. Noting that the Royal Navy's network of naval stations had allowed it to operate throughout the world's oceans, Matthew F. Steele declared that "nothing in our scheme of preparedness is more important than to hold onto these [overseas] bases, and especially the one nearest Japan and the mainland of the Orient."[3] Philippine Department chief of staff, Colonel Charles D. Rhodes, tied a strong military policy in the Pacific to a perverted form of Wilsonian morality: only by retaining the Philippines, insisting on free trade throughout Asia, and confronting Japan would "the Anglo-Saxon race . . . continue as in the World War to stand together for decent standards of national conduct."[4] In the related field of tactics, the lessons of the war offered a number of alternatives. John McAuley Palmer's 1916 plans to defend Hawaii with a defense in depth of beach obstacles, artillery, machine guns, and a light cordon of troops, while the bulk of the mobile forces waited in reserve to counterattack, were based in part on his study of trench warfare. Similarly, Macomb's study of the Galliopoli campaign led him to revise his earlier views of the Red Hill lines. Their war experiences gave most veterans a healthy awareness that victory went to the side with more manpower and matériel, but also that a few heavily armed and disciplined defenders, fighting behind entrenchments, could impose crippling losses on any aggressor.

When planners turned their attention back to the Pacific, they quickly found that what passed for military policy was a morass of contradictory and mutually incompatible projects, many uncompleted, others outdated, and still others desperately needed. In particular, the perennial issue of balancing War Department policies with Pacific realities needed to be resolved. Local commanders complained that Washington presented them with a barrage of contradictory demands, all requiring immediate compliance, and that it interfered in such minutiae as how far a particular area of jungle should be cleared back. For their part, local commanders often tabled or ignored policies they believed unwise; their protracted delaying campaigns against Subic Bay and the Red Hill lines illustrate their considerable autonomy. Such disorganization and independence were intolerable now that the Joint Army and Navy Board was engaged in drawing up detailed Orange plans for a Pacific war with Japan. War planning had to be systematized, bureaucratic procedures for collecting and disseminating information must be developed, and the defense of the overseas garrisons needed to be brought into the orbit of national security.

In an effort to restore order, on 26 November 1919 Chief of Staff March divided future strategic planning into "defense projects" and "plans." Under these guidelines, revised in 1925, defense projects outlined the object to be accomplished and the program for doing this. When approved by the War Department, the defense project became the basis for the plan, defined as the means to accomplish the object.[5] From now on, commanding generals in the three overseas departments—Hawaii, Panama, and the Philippines—were to devote their attention to drawing up basic defense projects, which would clearly state their mission and an estimate of the troops and equipment required to fulfill it. The projects were sent to WPD, where they were first examined to insure compliance with the national strategy and current war plans, and then passed to the various General Staff agencies for comment.

These defense projects soon became formidable compilations, each numbering hundreds of pages and including an overview of the military situation, appendixes covering aviation, coast defense, infantry, intelligence, and so on, but they failed to resolve the perennial discrepancy between missions and resources. The chief problem was that within three years of March's directive, the limitations imposed by the treaties from the 1921 Washington Conference on the Limitation of Naval Armaments and by the financial dearth of the interwar army reduced the projects to little more than an overseas staff's wish list. If WPD supported one part of a defense project, such as new ordnance or more troops, it had to battle the other divisions of the General Staff for priority allocations. Even then, a chief of staff or secretary of war with his own agenda could overturn or table the recommendation. Bare bones budgets imposed such scrutiny over funds that by the time a specific request had finally worked its way through the General Staff and the War Department bureaucracy to become a "project as approved," and receive funding, too often it proved either technologically obsolete or low in the priorities of a new departmental commander. Overseas officers soon learned that their carefully crafted defense projects would be pigeonholed at best, or worse, returned for extensive revision. In either case, little would be done to transform paperwork into tangible military assets. A WPD officer who visited the departmental staffs in Hawaii and the Philippines 1924 reported widespread cynicism with the entire process: "On the one hand those charged with preparing such plans are faced with the full realization of what might happen in case of emergency and their orders which require them to produce effective projects and plans. On the other hand is the feeling that on account of the uncertainty of the situation and financial considerations, no project or plan which really would be adequate has any chance of approval by the War Department at the present time or of securing the necessary funds for its execution from Congress. The result is a tendency to ask for something which is felt to be inadequate, but which is believed to be all that can be submitted with any hope of approval."[6]

One especially significant problem that eluded numerous efforts at clarification was the confusion between defense projects and plans. According to WPD's instructions, a Pacific command's "plan of defense" was to be based on its "project as approved."[7] But the long delays between a defense project's submission, its approval, and its funding meant that the department commanders in Hawaii and the Philippines were never sure whether their war plans were to be based on existent conditions, or on those conditions predicted when the project might be approved, or on conditions when the project had been completed. Some war plans—as will be seen—were actually projects, based not on how the commander would actually deal with an immediate challenge, but on a hypothetical, and doubtless overoptimistic, appraisal of his strength in the future. But even the integrated defense proposals based on a careful balancing of men, weapons, and matériel were vitiated as Washington altered or reduced them, ignoring the effect of each adjustment on the entire defense. Even more deleterious, Washington refused to rein in overseas commanders whose plans were clearly at variance with those enunciated by the nation's military and civil leaders. Rather than monitor and mentor these plans, WPD took the equivocating stance that whatever changes it forced on "projects," it never amended a "plan." Ambitious generals in Hawaii or the Philippines were thus free to create an Orange plan for their specific command which might be based on premises that were irreconcilable with the joint army-navy Orange plan in Washington. Despite the postwar attempt to clarify the planning procedure, and to insure harmony between Washington and its commanders in Honolulu and Manila, the actual result was perplexity, discord, and frustration. Confusion and misunderstandings continued, with consequences that would become appallingly clear in December 1941.[8]

The ambiguity and indecision that too often characterized Washington–Pacific Army relationships were mirrored in the uneasy relationship between army and navy strategists at the highest levels of strategic planning. Ignored by the Wilson administration after 1916, the Joint Army and Navy Board was reconstituted in April 1919 and strengthened by the Joint Army and Navy Planning Committee (JANPC), consisting of officers selected from each service's war plans agency to examine and propose policies and to coordinate such army and navy joint responsibilities as base and coast defense.[9] When the JANPC turned its attention to Pacific defense planning, it soon found itself unable to decide whether the national interest required Japan's decisive defeat or merely success in a relatively inexpensive war, with the loss of the Philippines and Far Eastern influence among the costs. A further complication appeared on 25 April 1919, when navy Captain Harry E. Yarnell informally notified fellow JANPC member Colonel John McAuley Palmer that the navy's strategic views had changed greatly in the decade since 1909; it no longer claimed it could defend the Philippines from its base on Hawaii. According to Yarnell, "at one time it was the plan of the Navy Department to send a fleet to the Philippines at the outbreak of war. I am quite sure this would not be done at the present time." Therefore "it would seem advisable for the Army to maintain their personnel and materiel at as low [sic] as possible to avoid their falling into the hands of the enemy."[10] Despite Yarnell's revelation, the JANPC's blueprint "Strategy of the Pacific" of October 1919 postulated that Japan and the U.S. were on a collision course in the Far East: Japan's fragile economy would force it to seek Asian markets; America's Far Eastern policies could not be reconciled with those ambitions. It outlined an ambitious plan to build a fortified base on Guam from which the navy could protect Hawaii, the Philippines, and the continental United States.[11]

On 18 December the Joint Board approved a revised version of "Strategy of the Pacific," the first timid attempt to develop a rational set of guidelines in the postwar Pacific. In his accompanying letter, the board's president offered three reasons for the United States to "dominate the Western Pacific": the Open Door, the nation's obligation to protect the Philippines, and the maintenance of friendly relations with Australia. To do this would necessitate building a base on Guam and stationing the Pacific fleet at Pearl Harbor. It reaffirmed the broad 1916 mission of the Philippine forces: "to defend Manila and Manila Bay." In so doing, it acknowledged that control of the Philippines was "entirely dependent upon our command of the sea," but maintained that the defenders could "force the Japanese to make the capture of this bay a major operation, and might offer sufficient prospect of resistance to deter an enemy from undertaking the capture of Manila and Manila Bay while a superior fleet was based at Oahu."[12] Based on the mistaken hope that the United States would continue its wartime shipbuilding program, add new naval bases, and deploy fleets in the Atlantic and Pacific, the Joint Board's strategic plan was soon rendered obsolete by financial cutbacks and the Washington Naval Treaties.

Planners in the immediate postwar era envisioned two possible scenarios for a Japanese-American war. The first was a limited conflict in which the United States would defend Hawaii and the West Coast and accept the loss of both the Philippines and its Far Eastern interests. The second was a full-scale war in which the United States would take the offensive, send the fleet into Asian waters, blockade Japan, and dictate a peace. The first contingency was never seriously considered: both "Strategy of the Pacific" and the 1920 Orange plan were based on an aggressive war. The former postulated a joint advance across the Pacific, using bases at Hawaii, Guam, and the Philippines, and culminating in a naval blockade of Japan with possible operations against the outlying islands. The Orange plan called for the army to furnish an expeditionary force of as many as 300,000 soldiers for a variety of theaters, including land operations in China. Recognizing the primacy of naval needs in either scenario, much of army planning consisted less of strategic discussion than of drawing up mobilization tables to move masses of men and supplies across the continent and over the ocean.[13]

This early discussion of strategy was eclipsed by the Washington Conference, called by the Harding administration in 1921 in an effort to defuse Far Eastern tensions and halt an escalating arms race among Japan, Great Britain, and the United States. The army brought no coherent agenda to the conference and asked only for a strong navy and fortified Pacific bases. The result was a variety of interrelated treaties, which, among other objectives, sought to calm the Pacific. In the Four-Power Treaty, the signatories reaffirmed each other's current possessions—providing reassurance to Japan for its Central Pacific acquisitions and to the United States for the Philippines. Its ratification was contingent on the signing of the Five-Power Pact, which set tonnage and ordnance limits on capital warships. Most important for the army, Article XIX maintained the status quo on fortifications in the Pacific, prohibiting the United States from establishing a fortified naval base further west than Oahu or strengthening those in Manila Bay. The Nine-Power Pact committed the signatories to recognizing the Open Door and Chinese territorial integrity. Thus, the conference essentially confirmed Japan as the dominant regional power in the western Pacific, but it temporarily checked Japanese activity in China. For the United States it provided a strong Alaska-Hawaii-Panama defensive perimeter at the minimal cost of conceding the nation's military weakness in the Philippines and Asia. Until the Washington treaties, planners had been most concerned with the prospect of war against an Anglo-Japanese coalition, a war that would have required the fleet to concentrate in the Atlantic and imposed a strictly defensive strategy in the Pacific. After the treaties, the only threat the United States faced to the west was Japan, and U.S. Pacific defense policy was thus often synonymous with war planning against Japan.[14]

Although the Washington Conference may have headed off a Far Eastern crisis, it did little to clarify the vision of American strategists. The JANPC's first evaluation of Pacific policy after the treaties mirrored the planners' uncertainty. On the one hand, the JANPC maintained an imperialist position, declaring that Asian markets were so necessary to the nation's economy that they must be protected by military force. Since Article XIX forbade a fortified naval base at Guam, "the Philippines are therefore, under the limitation imposed by the Treaty, our most valuable strategic possession in the Western Pacific." Yet at the same time, it reiterated the earlier argument that the Philippine garrison was essentially a deterrent: "It seems probable that a Japanese major effort could succeed in taking both the Philippines and Guam before our Fleet could arrive in the Western Pacific, but it is believed that the sacrifice of all our forces, both naval and military, would be justified by the damage done to the enemy."[15]

The Joint Board's problem throughout the interwar period, as Henry Gole has noted, was the cost of gambling on a faint opportunity: "the retention of the base at Manila would allow at least serious consideration of a swift projection of American power to the Western Pacific. The early loss of the Philippines to the Japanese, on the other hand, would rule out the possibility of a short war even if the United States and Japan were the sole belligerents."[16] Thus the dilemma: should American planners assume the best case or the worst? In 1923, the Joint Board was unequivocal in asserting the former. The Philippines was "of great strategic and economic value to the United States . . .

[as] a potential commercial center upon which the success of future American trade relations with the Asiatic continent depends to a very large extent." Moreover, Manila Bay was the best available base in western Pacific and must be defended to the utmost.[17] A year later, however, the board concluded that from a military viewpoint the United States should withdraw completely from the Philippines but from a naval perspective it should retain the Cavite station.[18] In a similar example of contradictory reasoning, the JANPC in one 1924 document declared both that the defense of the Philippines was of the "utmost importance" to insure a suitable naval base and that "the existing naval base facilities in the Philippines are limited and inadequately defended. In the event of war in the Pacific, we can and doubtless will seize such bases as may be necessary in connection with the operations of the Fleet."[19]

The confusion at the top was indicative of a strong division among military planners. A small number of pessimists argued that the nation's strategy must be based on defending its own coasts and the Alaska-Hawaii-Panama perimeter. To the War Plans Division's Stanley D. Embick and Briant H. Wells, the Philippines were clearly indefensible; they "cannot be accorded a definite role in our defensive plans."[20] Brigadier General Hugh A. Drum maintained that in any war with Japan "the Philippines would in all probability be lost." But since the islands' "ultimate fate" would depend on what happened in "the primary field of operations which would under no conceivable circumstances be the Philippines," their loss would be of little strategic significance.[21] In contrast, a larger body of optimists insisted that the benefits of holding the islands, or at least Manila Bay, mandated the strongest commitment to their defense. The WPD's Lieutenant Colonel John W. Gulick claimed a Philippine base was essential, "the time lost in capturing and developing such a base would greatly endanger the success of our efforts. In addition, the holding of such a base with an ample American force is essential to the execution of our Asiatic policy. The very presence of such a force will do much to prevent war between the United States and Japan."[22] Captain Robert Henderson told students at the War College that "the Philippines or at least Manila Bay will probably be the objective for both Blue and Orange—a race in both cases; hence speed is of primary consideration."[23] The Joint Board's 1923 Orange plan called for an immediate advance for the relief or retaking of Manila Bay by the fleet; a 50,000-man expeditionary force would embark for Hawaii within ten days of the national mobilization, and thence to the Philippines four days later. Equipment and supplies would be stockpiled in War Reserves in Hawaii and the Philippines, thereby preserving the limited transport space for personnel.[24] The Joint Army and Navy Basic War Plan Orange of 1924 repeated this scenario and further emphasized the need for an aggressive strategy; the "first and governing concern of the Army and Navy in such a war will be: To establish, at the earliest date, United States sea power in the Western Pacific in strength superior to that of Japan."[25] Ignoring its own 1924 study, which concluded that the Philippine fortifications were indefensible and that the United States could seize fleet bases where needed, the JANPC declared the armed forces' initial mission was "an immediate naval advance with land reinforcements for Manila" and "the promptest possible reinforcement of Manila Bay."[26]

But the "On to Manila" strategy ran into increasing resistance. By 1926 the JANPC had determined that henceforth war plans should be "based upon the probable necessity to seize a main outlying base for the fleet other than Manila Bay."[27] This was, in part, a recognition that the Washington Naval Treaties and postwar cutbacks had rendered the American fleet inferior to Japan's in the western Pacific. It also reflected the numerous caveats that specific branches had registered against the aggressive 1924 Orange plan. Marine officers argued that amphibious assaults could seize central Pacific islands, which could then be turned into bases, thus freeing the navy from dependence on Manila's facilities. Aviation officers revealed that the plan's estimates for aviation procurement were 30 percent higher than those of the Air Corps, which even so would require at least seventy-five days after mobilization.[28]

The Army Strategical Plan Orange of 1928, based on the Joint Army and Navy Basic War Plan Orange of that year, outlined a far more cautious strategy. Instead of military control in the western Pacific, it emphasized the destruction of Japan's military forces and economic system with the limited objective of forcing "Orange to accept terms of peace favorable to the United States."[29] Most significant, the 1928 plan reflected the retreat of both services from an open-ended commitment to the immediate rescue of the Philippines, and a shift toward a Hawaii-Panama defense perimeter. Whereas earlier versions had called for a large expeditionary force to the Philippines, that of 1928 emphasized that when war threatened, Oahu would be immediately reinforced by 90,000 soldiers and the Panama Canal by 40,000. Army representatives at a Joint Board meeting on 9 February 1928 stated that the "present garrison of Hawaii cannot secure Oahu against capture by a strong expeditionary force"; the new plan should "give consideration to the measures to be taken in case hostilities are initiated by a sudden raid and capture of Pearl Harbor, with consequent destruction of that base."[30] Instead of the immediate departure of a large expedition for Manila Bay, the army committed itself to a 16,000-man division thirty days after mobilization, which, with 20,000 Marines, would be used to seize and hold an unspecified base west of Hawaii. Moreover, the combined army-navy offensive into the western Pacific—the first task in the 1924 plan—was now ranked fourteenth. The forces in the Philippines were still expected to defend Manila Bay, but with a revised mission: "to deny this area to Orange as a naval base in case we cannot use it ourselves"—a revealing, if somewhat negative goal.[31]

This dramatic scaling back was due to several factors, the most important of which was a recognition that, as the pessimists contended, in all probability the Philippines would have fallen by the time the fleet arrived. An analysis of Japan's available forces implied it could land 300,000 soldiers on Luzon within a month, whereas most continental U.S. Army tactical units were "skeletonized": many lacked most of their enlisted manpower and some consisted of but a small administrative staff. Almost every soldier in the projected army of 1.2 million would have to be recruited, trained, and equipped and "would not be available for offensive operations, especially outside the continental limits of the United States, for a considerable period of time."[32]

The 1928 army Orange plan represented a substantial withdrawal from the "On to Manila" assumptions of its predecessors. It was based on the same premise as that outlined by the authors of the 1929 Joint Army-Navy Orange Plan: "we must plan on conditions as they are in reality and not as we would wish them to be."[33] But even this realism could not still the hope that somehow the garrison would hold out and allow the fleet to use Manila Bay. The 1929 Orange plan's "Estimate of the Situation" was indicative of this ambivalence. On the one hand, it recognized that, "[a]t present, Manila Bay is inadequately defended, especially against air attacks, and unless speedily reinforced by us it could not hold out against a major Japanese attack, while many of the facilities mentioned would be destroyed by attacks from the air before the arrival of our Fleet. If Manila is seriously invested by the Japanese our Fleet cannot use Manila Bay as a base."[34] Nevertheless, should the garrison hold out, Manila Bay could provide a staging point for a campaign on Japan's lines of communications; its naval facilities were the best available in the Far East; and it had excellent coastal defenses.

The arrival of Douglas MacArthur as chief of staff in 1930 brought to power a man to whom the defense of the Philippines and the nation's military policy in the Pacific were virtually identical. When asked by Secretary of War Patrick Hurley whether the Philippines were an asset or a liability, MacArthur responded with arguments that might have been used by his father: they provided an essential naval base in the western Pacific; their possession allowed the U.S. Navy to protect the nation's Far Eastern interests; and, most important, "the Philippines can be successfully defended by the employment of native manpower against any probable attack."[35] MacArthur's term as president of the Joint Board witnessed a revival of both imperialist views and a more optimistic appraisal of Philippine defense. Typical was a 1934 JANPC paper that claimed that "in granting complete independence to the Philippine Islands, we have relinquished our opportunities and our responsibilities. This action represents a surrender of a national policy." The islands were "an islet of growing Western development and thought surrounded by an ocean of Orientalism. They are the interpreters of American idealism to the Far East" and "constitute[d] a potential commercial center upon which depend, to a large extent, the development and success of future American trade relations with the Asiatic continent and Australasia." Withdrawal "would upset the balance of power in the Far East. . . . The attending unrest in the possessions of the white races and the economic and political encroachments of Japan may make the region of the East Indies and southeastern Asia such a menace to the peace of the world as the Balkan area was in Europe in the days preceding the World War." By retaining a naval base and a strong garrison, the United States could guarantee the security of U.S. interests against Japanese encroachments, but without one this would be "impossible."[36]

According to MacArthur, he arrived in Washington in 1930 already in "complete disagreement" with the 1928 Orange plan. Realizing he would be "wasting [his] time" convincing his subordinates in the General Staff, he "short-circuited" the process and went directly to President Herbert Hoover to inform him that, in the event of military mobilization, he would immediately dispatch two divisions to Panama, two more to Hawaii, and another two divisions to the Philippines via the Suez Canal. He told Hoover that he "intended to defend every inch of these possessions and defend them successfully. This being the case, the Orange Plan was a completely useless document."[37] The WPD director Brigadier General Charles E. Kilbourne provided a different version of this incident, one in which Hoover, MacArthur, and Chief of Naval Operations William V. Pratt discussed the Philippine situation in 1932 and "agreed to the prompt dispatch from the east coast of a force of two divisions with auxiliary supporting units via the Suez Canal."[38]

Kilbourne's account, although far less flamboyant, appears more accurate, for far from short-circuiting the General Staff, MacArthur's employed it extensively to insure the prompt relief of the Philippines. In 1930, at MacArthur's direction, the WPD conducted a study of U.S. policy toward the Philippines based on the following strategic premises: that the Philippines were the best available base in the western Pacific; that they were a potential center for U.S. trade with the Far East; that any radical change in their status would disrupt the Asian balance of power; that their loss would detract from American prestige and hamper national efforts to defend its Far Eastern interests; that the military effort to defend them was less than the effort to recapture them;

and, interestingly enough considering MacArthur's 1929 Philippine defense plan, that it was "not practicable" to build up a local defense force that could hold them without relief from the United States.[39] Given these intellectual suppositions, it is not surprising that the WPD concluded that in the event of war it was necessary to relieve the Philippines immediately. The General Staff also helped revise the Orange plan mobilization tables to conform to the resurgent "On to Manila" policy. In conformance with the 1928 Orange plan and its revisions, army mobilization schedules had distinguished between the "immediate" relief of Hawaii and Panama and the "ultimate" relief of the Philippines. But by November 1933 army plans contained an immediate commitment of two infantry divisions, some 63,000 men, to the Philippines by way of the Suez Canal.[40] According to unidentified marginalia discussing this augmentation of the Orange plan, "Genl MacA" stated his belief that such reinforcement was possible because the Japanese would not seek to capture the Philippines as long as the U.S. fleet in the Pacific was stronger. MacArthur then went on to predict "that war would be declared (if at all) by the enemy and initiated by a surprise attack on our fleet if surprise was possible."[41] Both predictions proved correct, but unfortunately MacArthur's clairvoyance failed to show him that, should Japan successfully attack the U.S. fleet, his plan to reinforce the Philippines was doomed.

In retrospect, MacArthur's overturning of the 1928 Orange plan displayed questionable military judgment. Having just commanded the Philippine Department, MacArthur knew better than most how appallingly weak the archipelago's defenses were. Moreover, in his five-year tenure as chief of staff he did almost nothing to improve them. Not only did he fail to push his 1929 plan for a Filipino reserve, he approved, perhaps even initiated a policy which forbade improvements on existing Philippine construction projects unless they saved money. This, in effect, sabotaged the other key element of his 1929 plan: the roads, beach defenses, airfields, weapons, motorized equipment, and the like that would allow the defenders to meet and defeat the enemy at the beaches.[42] MacArthur's policies were no less questionable when looked at from the perspective of the nation's own security. As numerous planners had pointed out, the Army of the United States created by the 1920 Defense Act required time to mobilize the Organized Reserves and flesh out its skeletal combat units. No one knew better than MacArthur that outside of Hawaii there was not a single combat division in the country and that the reserves were in desperate condition, their funding slashed to the bone in 1931. Yet his plan called for the immediate dispatch of six divisions—a force roughly equivalent to the entire Regular Army in the continental United States—at the very time these experienced troops would be most needed to train the reserves and conscripts. Even more incomprehensible, two of these divisions would be sent across thousands of miles of open ocean without protection to a destination that would, in all probability, be blockaded by an enemy fleet and under attack, if not actually occupied, by an invading army.

As the loyal Kilbourne noted in 1932, MacArthur's plan for the immediate relief of the Philippines grew "increasingly hazardous and difficult" with Japan's rearmament and the relative decline of U.S. power in the western Pacific.[43] In September 1931 Japan launched attacks into Manchuria, prompting a crisis in Japanese-American relations, which led, among other things, to the concentration of the U.S. fleet in the Pacific and the dispatch of the 31st Infantry from the Philippines to Shanghai. By 1937, the Japanese government had renounced the Washington Treaties, committed itself to a massive rearmament program, and begun the conquest of China. In contrast, the military power of the United States spiraled downward. The year 1934 may have marked the nadir of its military strength, with an army under 135,000, thousands of officers forced to take furloughs, and President Franklin D. Roosevelt determined to cut $144 million from the War Department budget. The Depression, the Bonus Army incident, pacifism, isolationism, and highly publicized charges against militarists and arms merchants all contributed to a profound distrust of both the military and international involvement. At the same time, the decades-long dream of a Philippine naval base was dealt a mortal blow. Roosevelt's defeat of Hoover in 1932 removed one of the last obstructions to the archipelago's independence. The 1934 Tydings-McDuffie Act created a Filipino government, the Philippine Commonwealth, to supervise the transition to full independence in 1946. More important, the act eliminated the provisions for permanent military bases in the archipelago contained in the earlier Hare-Hawes-Cutting Act of 1932. Thus by the mid-1930s American strategists confronted a new problem: should they plan for the future withdrawal from the western Pacific, or should they continue to plan for the nation's current commitment to protecting the Philippines?

Contrary to a popular belief—and one that is currently fashionable among some scholars—American planners respected their future opponent and had few illusions that a Japanese-American war would be anything but costly. According to one analysis, "from a military point of view the Japanese are courageous, loyal, self-sacrificing for their Emperor, and obedient to authority. It is an ideal psychology of a nation at war."[44] Such sentiments were common at the War College, where one 1931 committee warned that Japan would seek to employ its regional military superiority to seize the Philippines and Guam, causing the American public to insist on an immediate offensive into the western Pacific under conditions that would lead to a U.S. defeat and a negotiated settlement. Students in the class of 1932–33 studied a prescient scenario in which the United States was driven from the western Pacific and did not return until after it had built up overwhelming military and industrial strength and had established bases across the island chains of the Pacific, a process that would take two-and-a-half years. The outline of a delayed offensive from Hawaii became part of the Western Pacific Area scenario in the College's War Plans Division course in 1934. Students continued to study the immediate relief of the Philippines and tactical plans for defending Luzon, but an overview of student papers on Orange planning in the 1930s indicates a consensus that Japan was a formidable and dangerous opponent, and that war would require the nation to mobilize fully its military resources before embarking on a long, slow drive across the Pacific.[45]

The strategic outlook of the students, their acceptance of the fall of the Philippines—and the suggestion that prolonged defense of the archipelago was undesirable—and their predictions of a lengthy cross-Pacific offensive are all in sharp contrast to the optimism in Washington during MacArthur's tenure as chief of staff. As Henry Gole has convincingly argued, students at the War College were given considerable freedom to draw up realistic and original scenarios.[46] Although evidence is scanty, it is probable that their realistic pessimism was far more representative of army attitudes than the "On to Manila" enthusiasm of the MacArthur-dominated General Staff.

By the mid-1930s the Orange plan clearly needed revision; it conformed to neither domestic nor international realities, nor the views of a new generation of American Pacific strategists. The navy, although still committed to an offensive war against Japan, now anticipated an Orange plan that would incorporate a cautious, slow progression across the Pacific. The departure of MacArthur as chief of staff in October 1935 removed the army's primary impetus for the headlong relief of the Philippines and altered the strategic focus of the Joint Board. His successor, Malin Craig, was determined to prepare the nation's long-neglected military for instant readiness, and focused on threats to the Western Hemisphere rather than on distant Asian wars.[47] Craig's goals were shared by the new director of War Plans Division, the highly respected Brigadier General Stanley D. Embick, whose views on Pacific defense, and especially the Philippines, were a matter of record. On 19 April 1933, as commanding general of the Harbor Defenses of Manila and Subic Bays, Embick had written that "to carry out the present Orange Plan . . . would be literally an act of madness" and argued that the nation should "arrange for the neutralization of the Philippines, withdraw our military garrisons and naval shore establishments from the Philippines and China, and adopt the line, Alaska-Oahu-Panama, as our strategic peace-time frontier in the Pacific."

Such a policy would "be non-provocative, reduce the drain on the national budget, and, in the event of war, leave us free to take the offensive at our own volition" instead of "having our peace-time establishment forced to undertake premature military operations for the relief of outposts in enemy territory."[48]

One of Embick's first efforts after he assumed the directorship of the WPD was to negotiate an agreement with the navy that vitiated MacArthur's plan for the immediate relief of the Philippines. In the new Orange plan "an entirely new line of action was proposed for the advance of the United States Joint Asiatic Force towards the Western Pacific" which required that the Western advance "will be a progressive movement through the mandates."[49] Revealing either a complete lack of strategic consistency or total misunderstanding, MacArthur approved what he termed these "minor revisions."[50] Embick then began a complete overhaul of the existing war plans with Japan. In the resultant 2 December 1935 report, he expressed his concern the United States might be "maneuvered by interested European nations into a situation in which we would bear the first, perhaps the full, brunt of armed resistance to Japan." He repeated his criticisms of the current Orange plan, emphasized the necessity of withdrawing to an Alaska-Hawaii-Panama frontier, and rejected the idea of a direct thrust across the Pacific. Unless the United States was willing to jeopardize its own vital interests, it could meet Japan with decisive forces in the Far East only after it had conquered the Mandated Islands, and this in turn meant it could neither protect the Philippines from invasion nor move to the early relief of a Philippine base.[51]

Embick's proposals elicited strong support from two able WPD colonels, Sherman Miles and Walter Krueger. Miles, well aware of the isolationist mood in the country, argued "there can be little doubt that the nation now feels that we have no interests in the Far East, except the lives of our people, worth a war, and that we have no intention of bringing on such a war. . . . [This] means we must plan for such a war only on the basis of its being forced upon us, and not of our choosing."[52] In October 1935 Krueger wrote a harsh critique of past Pacific policy, the Orange plan, and the navy's continued efforts to retain a base in the Philippines after independence. He argued that military views of the Pacific, and particularly the Philippines were shaped by outdated imperialist concepts: "such phrases as 'the open door,' 'American interests,' 'trade expansion,' and so on, became, by mere repetition, dogma incontrovertible by force of reason, and it is by this dogma that our policy has been guided." Equally illogical was the navy's effort to retain a Philippine base, where its central function was the protection of the nation's merchant marine—a task that could be performed by a smaller navy untied to Asian territory. Why then did the navy continue to press for a base in the Philippines? "[T]here can be but one answer: namely, an offensive mission is visualized for our fleet, notwithstanding the fact that greater navy advocates point out that the fleet is maintained primarily as our first line of defense." In fact, Krueger noted, the United States's "strategic position is exceedingly strong," as the dominant power in the Western Hemisphere with "potential hegemony over it whenever we choose to avail ourselves thereof." The nation was economically self-supporting and "granted reasonable naval and military preparedness on our part, it is virtually invulnerable."[53]

The navy members of the JANPC vigorously opposed such a defensive strategy. They interpreted the granting of Philippine independence and the Alaska-Hawaii-Panama defensive perimeter as the start of a national retreat from overseas involvement—with obvious implications for the navy's status and size. Commander A. S. Carpender claimed the consequences of the army's position would be to "yield our nation's geographical barrier against the usurpation by the yellow race of the place of the white man in the Far East." The United States had vital interests in China and a "feeling of moral responsibility for the Philippines . . . our people will not throw the Philippines to the lions."[54] His colleagues argued that under the Tydings-McDuffie Act, the United States had the option to retain military and naval bases in the islands and they urged that a suitable one be identified, fortified, and held.[55] Not only would this ease supplying the Asiatic Fleet during peacetime; it was possible, if unlikely, that in wartime the base might hold out long enough for the battle fleet to arrive and launch an immediate offensive in the western Pacific. This was anaethma to the army members of the JANPC, who regarded the Philippines as "untenable" and believed that any effort to strengthen the islands' defenses was not only "impracticable" but would provoke war with Japan.[56] Unable to resolve their differences, the two services submitted different reports.[57]

The army's new thinking may be seen in the 1936 Army Strategical Plan Orange, which reflected efforts to come to terms with both the changing international situation and the ongoing dispute with the navy. Conspicuously absent was MacArthur's two-division Philippine relief force. The 1936 plan made no mention of an immediate relief of the Philippines, nor did it declare they were the ultimate destination of the U.S. joint expedition. Rather, a detailed study foresaw one million well-trained, well-equipped, and highly motivated Japanese soldiers mobilized within a month and rapidly occupying the Philippines, Guam, Saipan, the Palaus, the Carolines, and the Marshalls. These conquests would serve as "naturally built aircraft carriers" from which airplanes and warships could attack American communications. Although the planners thought it unlikely the Japanese would invade Hawaii, they would certainly raid it, and if Oahu could be taken by an uprising it would certainly be occupied. Japan would also seek to block the Panama Canal by sabotage, bombing or shelling, and raid the Pacific Coast. Once these goals were accomplished, Japan would go on the defensive, refusing a major battle but attempting to subject the U.S. fleet to heavy losses from warship, air, and submarine attacks. The United States would have to fight a slow, deliberate campaign, first evicting the Japanese from the Marshall and Caroline Islands, then capturing or neutralizing other "carriers," then seizing and defending a main advance base, and ultimately advancing west for the final battle. Perhaps to forestall the navy from a direct assault across the Pacific, the plan made provision for the immediate reinforcement of Hawaii and Panama but kept the U.S. Army Asiatic Expeditionary Force quite weak for the first four months.[58]

Despite the revisions of 1936, army planners remained dissatisfied with the Orange plan, believing that the navy had made an offensive war against Japan an end in itself and no longer considered its relevance to national interests. The WPD wanted to insure the security of the Alaska-Hawaii-Panama defensive perimeter before going on the attack. Embick felt the Orange plan to be "unsound in general and specifically to be wholly inapplicable to present conditions."[59] Under the plan's provisions, "the defense of the West Coast is to be wholly subordinate to an offensive movement" into the western Pacific.[60] Krueger also criticized the plan as inflexible and poorly conceived, involving great risk without consideration of international or domestic realities. It promoted a single strategy, an offensive unlimited war across 7,000 miles of ocean via the central Pacific, seizing defended islands on the way. He favored not one Orange plan but a series of them, each based on a different scenario, so as to allow the military to select the one most relevant to the current realities and the national strategy.[61] To Krueger, the army's insistence on placing the Alaska-Hawaii-Panama perimeter in a "position in readiness" was not "passive defense posture" but rather one based on U.S. political needs and the nation's desire "that we make no war plans that go beyond the necessity of defense and provision for contingencies."[62] Determined to force the navy to abandon its thrust into the western Pacific, Embick authored a memo for Craig that warned that in all previous hearings before Congressional committees, the War Department representatives had testified that the army's war plans concerned only the defense of the United States. Unless the Joint Board revised the existing Orange plan, at the next hearings they would "have to testify that the primary objective of the planning is to meet offensive needs."[63]

The army's objections to the navy's offensive plan required lengthy debate before a compromise—the Joint Army and Navy Basic War Plan Orange of 1938—was hammered out. In contrast to the 1920s plans, which had stressed offensive warfare and the destruction of Japan's military and economic power, the 1938 plan defined the joint mission: "to defeat Orange by operations against Orange armed forces, while conserving the resources of the United States and protecting United States territory, sea communications, and interests." Designed to deal with "any probable situation between the United States and Orange which requires action by the armed forces," the plan incorporated the Craig-Embick-Krueger view that in the earliest stages, the armed forces should take a "position in readiness" to protect the continental United States, Alaska, Oahu, and Panama. Hawaii would be immediately reinforced by 25,000 troops from the continent but the defense of the Philippines would be left to the garrison and whatever local forces could be raised.[64]

The 1938 version was the last true Orange plan. American strategists were already turning toward a two-ocean war in which the United States would fight a hostile coalition, and the Orange plans would soon become incorporated into the famous "Rainbow" plans. At the Army War College, the shift in emphasis was clear. For decades the G-2 (Intelligence) courses had focused on either the Orange or Red-Orange scenarios: the 1939–40 class had six committees working on the Americas and hemispheric defense and only one on Japan.[65]

It is tempting to assume that between 1935 and 1938 the course of army strategic planning solidified into its final position. Embick and Krueger, in particular, struck heavily at the cardinal tenets of Pacific strategic planning. The long-held dogma that a Philippine base was a naval necessity was now rejected, leaving the door open to a full withdrawal. The garrison's mission was restricted "to defend Luzon to the extent practicable with the existing garrison, augmented only by such personnel and facilities as are available locally."[66] It also led to the acceptance, at least in principle, of an Alaska-Hawaii-Panama defensive perimeter and the abandonment of an immediate naval offensive into the western Pacific. But such an elegant finale would hardly accord with the thirty-five-year tradition of American Pacific planning. The decision to abandon the Philippines, suggested in the 1928 plan and implicit in those of 1936 and 1938, and, most clearly in the 1940 revision, was revoked in mid-1941. On 17 July Craig's successor, George C. Marshall, approved a WPD directive that advocated MacArthur's appointment as commander of all U.S. military forces in the Far East, and the mobilization of the Commonwealth's Philippine Army. A few days later, Secretary of War Henry L. Stimson assured Roosevelt that these forces, augmented by new B-17 bombers, could defend the Philippines and prevent Japanese expansion. On 26 July Roosevelt mobilized the Philippine Army into U.S. service and simultaneously named MacArthur commander of the newly formed U.S. Army

Forces in the Far East. The War Department allocated 130 of its newest fighters and 272 bombers to the archipelago; thousands of soldiers, many of them recent draftees, embarked for Manila Bay. Buoyed by MacArthur's optimistic reports, Washington rushed precious men and resources to the Philippines, in a desperate attempt to do what generations of experienced soldiers had reluctantly, but realistically, come to see as impossible.[67]

In the years between the end of the first and the outbreak of the second world war, army planners proved unable to resolve the twin, and indivisible, dilemmas of Pacific defense and the Japanese threat. Sometimes in conjunction with, and sometimes in opposition to, their navy colleagues, they devised plans that ranged from a hurtling offensive to a defensive perimeter. Over these two decades Orange plans became more cautious, more concerned with protecting a limited Pacific defense perimeter, more determined to cut military ties to the Philippines. But such an overview does not convey the numerous backings and fillings, the reversals and epicycles that characterized American Pacific planning. The acquiescence of the General Staff to MacArthur's abrogation of the Orange plan indicates the absence of both any sustained consensus among army strategists or even the simple acceptance of their responsibility to enforce compliance. Too many were willing to see their task in narrowly practical terms, addressing specific problems but seldom questioning the underlying premise. The few who did have a vision and could address the problem in its entirety—Embick, Krueger, and even MacArthur— thus exerted exceptional influence, both for good and bad. Moreover, it is essential to remember that the ability of Washington planners to impose their views, to force either the continental army or the overseas commanders to comply with them, was rarely put to the test. As will be seen, those who guarded the Pacific frontier had their own ideas, their own views, their own strategic vision; whether they chose to obey Washington's directives was very much up to them.

CHAPTER 8

The Pacific Army in the 1920s

T he Orange plans drawn up in Washington offered a blueprint for how a Japanese-American war would be fought, and it was the task of the Pacific Army to parry the first blows. On the shoulders of those charged with holding the beaches and coast defenses, flying the airplanes, firing the artillery, and hurling their bodies into the counterattack fell the main burden. The "Pineapple Army" in Hawaii and the "Carabao Army" in the Philippines were outwardly identical. Each had similar administrative and tactical organizations: at the top was the commanding general of the department, controlling a coastal defense command and an infantry division, as well as air, staff, and support services.[1] Similar too were their missions and their tactical problem—to protect a naval base and to hold the harbors and beaches against attack by a common enemy, Japan. Beyond noting that much of the Carabao Army was Filipino and that the Pineapple Army was all white, in 1930 an observer might have been hard put to distinguish between them: the infantry in the Hawaiian Division and the Philippine Division carried the same Springfield rifles, the fortress troops manned similar cannon, the airmen flew the same obsolete DH-4 and Keystone airplanes. The 1920s would prove to be a decade of considerable intellectual ferment, as new defense plans were developed, new weapons explored, and new tactics invented. But it was also a decade in which numerous opportunities were missed and in which the gap between the Pacific Army's ambitious mission and its limited means remained large.

In the Philippines, the promise of the Jones Act of 1916 and Governor Harrison's regime had raised Filipino hopes of immediate independence. But for a variety of reasons most army officers, in both Washington and the archipelago, shared the Republican administrations' view that possession should be continued. The postwar decline of the nation's military strength and the Washington Treaties might have made the defense of the Philippines far more difficult, but it did not shake the Joint Board's conviction that the islands were "of great strategic and economic value to the United States," that they "constitute a potential commercial center upon which the success of future American trade relations with the Asiatic continent depends to a very large extent," and were necessary for the "defense of American Asiatic interests."[2] The 1921 Wood-Forbes Mission to the archipelago gathered local military commentaries that reiterated the imperialist position: the Philippines provided a valuable center for U.S.-Asian trade; U.S. withdrawal would be followed by a Japanese takeover; and, as Philippine Department commander Francis J. Kernan argued, "it would manifestly be a crime against humanity to withdraw our protecting supervision and leave these simple people a prey to a small oligarchy now in power and certain to perpetuate its power indefinitely."[3]

The independence issue was given an emotional edge by the prolonged battle between Governor-General Leonard Wood and the Philippine legislature, led by Manuel Quezon, which culminated in the resignation of the Council of State in 1923. Wood's contempt for the archipelago's politicians was of long-standing and his actions as governor showed that, if anything, he had grown even less tolerant. Far more flexible and astute than the self-righteous Wood, Quezon skillfully made opposition to the governor a litmus test for Filipino patriotism. Local officers were correct in recognizing that by leading the resistance Quezon had consolidated his own position, but, as Scout Major Vicente Lim pointed out, their inference that "the cry for independence is raised only by a few politicians is entirely erroneous," for the Filipinos, in common with all "subject peoples," were sincere in their desire for sovereignty. Nor did Lim accept the imperialist claim that the United States governed solely for the benefit of the Filipinos; it maintained possession "in order to have a commanding voice in the destinies of the Orient."[4]

Lim's criticism also highlights the perverse unwillingness of planners in Washington and Manila to subject the issue of Philippine defense to dispassionate and pragmatic discussion. Occasionally officers could take a large view and assert the unpleasant realities. In 1920 colonels Briant H. Wells and Stanley D. Embick argued the United States had no crucial economic or strategic interests west of Hawaii and, in opposing a WPD proposal to increase the Philippine garrison, Hugh A. Drum argued: "Unquestionably the Philippine Islands are the most vulnerable of American possessions overseas. They are, however, the least important."[5] But such forthrightness was unusual, and although Drum's memo was approved, the implications of his argument were never explored.

For the most part, as has been detailed, for the first decade after World War I the General Staff was content to repeat old arguments—Asian trade, containing Japan, moral duty—without questioning whether any of them were still valid. In particular, the unwavering belief that a Philippine naval base was essential both to protect U.S. Far Eastern interests and to allow the United States to fight a naval war with Japan continued to dominate military thinking. Over and over, officers in Manila and Washington would emphasize that only the possession of a base at Manila Bay would allow the U.S. fleet to launch an immediate offensive against Japan. In 1922, after much discussion, the Joint Board retained the prewar mission of the local army and navy forces: "to defend Manila and Manila Bay." Behind the declared mission lay other, hidden missions. Members of the JANPC argued that although Manila Bay would probably fall to Japan before the arrival of the fleet, "it is believed that the sacrifice of all our forces, both naval and military, would be justified by the damage done our enemy." Besides this spoiling role, a gallant defense would rally popular support: "An easily won success in effect would stimulate Japanese morale and depress the morale of our own people. A stout resistance by our own forces that would entail heavy Japanese losses in lives and ships would be a blow to Japanese morale and serve as an inspiration to Americans."[6] The mission to hold Manila and Manila Bay lasted until 1928, when the Local Joint Defense Planning Committee informed the War Department that the garrison was too weak to conduct offensive operations in Luzon and that the attempt to hold Manila would endanger the defense of Corregidor. The Joint Board finally restricted the army's mission to "hold the entrances to Manila Bay" with, as a secondary priority, "to hold the Manila Bay area as long as possible."[7]

The Philippine Department's defense plans of the 1920s sought to balance the nation's Orange plan with its own mission, and the reality of minimal resources. Washington's lack of tangible support taught department planners to be skeptical of promises of immediate relief. But even their realistic appraisal of a bleak future did not allow them to draw the logical conclusion— that the army's continued presence in the archipelago served little purpose. Instead, they continued to approach Philippine defense as a tactical problem. They tinkered and adjusted, analyzed and critiqued, but almost never questioned whether the Philippines should be defended at all, or to what purpose. The first postwar studies, written in 1920 and 1921, postulated Japan's landing 30,000 to 60,000 troops ten days after the war began. Corregidor's defenders would remain behind their guns to guard against a naval attack, but the mobile forces would "harass the enemy while actually landing, delay and impede his advance, and make opportune counteroffensives."[8] The 1923 study was similar: the mobile forces would conduct an "active defense by offensive and defensive operations," retiring to Corregidor and Bataan "only to save the bulk of the Mobile Forces from annihilation or capture," and then "defend to the last the islands at the entrance to Manila Bay."[9] The 1924 basic project discussed waging a "offensive-defensive" campaign in Central Luzon, urging its commanders to "move out and oppose the advance of a hostile force," but it also required that the mobile forces conserve themselves for a "final stand" at Bataan to protect the coast defenses.[10] Such conflicting goals may indicate that planners were determined either to give field commanders complete tactical freedom or to insure that whatever happened they could not be blamed.

In part the Philippine Department's plans reflected the U.S. Army's experience in World War I. Recognizing that the defense was tactically stronger but that the attacker maintained the initiative and higher morale, army officers sought to combine the two into vague "offensive-defensive" tactics. It also was an attempt to incorporate U.S. beach defense doctrine, based on William G. Haan's 1919 "Positive System of Coast Defense," which outlined a defense-in-depth of medium and light artillery, machine guns, and obstacles to channel the invaders into killing zones and mobile reserves to drive them back with counterattacks.[11] But, perhaps more than anything else, departmental plans represented a series of unsuccessful attempts to blend the Carabao Army's disparate elements into a coherent defensive scheme. As one department commander bluntly put it, "the Mission and the Force assigned to carry out the Mission are not harmonized."[12] It was "impracticable to make up any War Plan worthy of the name based on the present garrison and its organization. . . . The embarrassment that faces a Department commander in the Philippines now is that he is allowed more than enough men to garrison the fortified islands, but not enough to hold the back door to Manila Bay and to the fortified islands. What shall he do with the small residue of combat troops left over after providing a garrison for the fortified islands?"[13]

The Philippine defense projects of the early 1920s were never approved by the War Department. Instead, they circulated among the General Staff's various branches for comment. Before a consensus could be reached, a new project would arrive and the revision process began again. In 1925, WPD director Brigadier General LeRoy Eltinge concluded the undertaking was a waste of effort. The Philippine Department had produced several excellent studies, but because of the postwar army's weakness and the uncertainty over whether the islands would be retained, it was "hopeless" to think they would ever be implemented. Eltinge concluded that to all intents and purposes "there is no existing Project" and he "regard[ed] any expenditure of funds on or assignment of personnel to the Philippines as being in the nature of a sop to public sentiment made with the full knowledge that, from a military point of view, the funds and personnel are being sacrificed to political considerations."[14]

Perhaps because the War Department was unable to act, it devoted little attention to insuring that the projects submitted by the Philippine Department harmonized with national strategy. In fact, there were considerable differences between the two. Whereas the early 1920s the U.S. Army's Orange plans called for the defenders to hold Manila Bay for a relieving force, Philippine officers outlined a defense that incorporated most of Luzon. Whereas from 1923 on Washington anticipated extensive local recruitment, the department made no provision for Filipino participation beyond recruiting the Scouts to wartime strength.[15] Whereas the U.S. Army's 1923 Orange plan envisioned the rapid deployment of a 50,000-man Philippine relief force, the Philippine Department's 1924 basic project, citing the "growing sentiment in America that not only is the continuation of American sovereignty in the Philippines an economical burden, but is a growing menace to the peace of the nation and its military prestige," assumed instead:

> In the event of war, the people of the United States cannot be depended on for a determined effort to undertake a hazardous, early reinforcement expedition, involving serious national consequences in case of failure, for the relief of the forces on duty in the Philippines. For the same reasons, it is believed that a long costly struggle to retake the Islands in case of capture, will not receive the support of the American public. This puts the chief burden of the defense of the Islands square on the shoulders of the local military, naval and government authorities. Apparently they must plan to bear the brunt of the defense of the Islands until supremacy of the American navy is asserted in the Western Pacific and not build their defense structure on the hope of an early reinforcement from the United States.[16]

Such statements reveal that among the top planners in Manila the conviction had grown that Washington was unwilling or unable to assist them. They would have to fight alone against overwhelming odds, lacking even the certainty that their defeat would be avenged. Such a mordant view no doubt contributed to the willingness of some overseas planners to modify or ignore War Department directives, and to create their own defensive schemes independently of the Orange plans.

In July 1928, Major General William Lassiter arrived as commanding general of the Philippine Department with a specific mandate to revise its defense plans. In June the Joint Board had changed the garrison's assignment from defending Manila and Manila Bay to holding Manila Bay, and Lassiter was sent out to implement this new mission. As a former WPD director, Lassiter knew that owing to the general agreement that the Philippines was doomed, Washington had "permit[ted] the Philippine problem to drift . . . for many years past";[17] indeed, as he confessed, "heretofore I have always regarded this problem as a more or less hopeless one."[18] But, as with so many officers who served in the islands, Lassiter soon became convinced that his successors had simply approached the problem from the wrong perspective. With new insight and new weapons, the Philippines, or at least Manila Bay, might still be saved.

Lassiter's interest in a complete revision of the archipelago's defense prompted some officers to volunteer opinions that were so candid as to verge on insubordination. The irrepressible commander of the Philippine Division, Major General Johnson Hagood, confessed: "I have never seen anybody who believed in the present Orange Plan or would take responsibility for it, either in the Philippines or in Washington, the Philippine authorities always claiming that the essential defects were due to instructions from above and the Washington authorities claiming these defects were due to failure on the part of local commanders to take full advantage of the authority and responsibility conferred upon them." Should war ever come, he intended to "disregard the whole proposition" and immediately retreat to the fortresses in Manila Bay.[19] As had Morrison over a decade earlier, Hagood opposed any mobile defense in the Luzon countryside for both practical and humanitarian reasons. The defenders could accomplish only minimal delay at the cost of appalling destruction and suffering: "in the opinion of many, myself included, the American forces should not be permitted to engage in any such futile devastation of the country." Hagood was equally blunt about the possibility of support from the U.S. Navy, which he characterized as an "indeterminate factor. The size, composition and operations of the American naval forces in the Pacific upon the outbreak of war cannot be determined in advance, and any determinations, understandings or agreements entered into at this time with the naval authorities would have no binding effect upon those in authority at the time when the emergency arose."[20] In short, Hagood believed the Philippine garrison was on its own and no faith could be placed in either Washington or the navy; any current war plans based on joint-service cooperation or the immediate relief of the islands would be revoked by those called upon to execute them.

To Lassiter, Hagood's call to abandon everything except Manila Bay was both militarily and politically unsound. Such views accorded with the perception that closing the bay's entrance by fortifications and mines was, in common military parlance, the "key stone of the defense." But Luzon's new road system connected Manila to the coasts—and the invasion beaches—"thus giving Manila Bay a back entrance which must be considered in addition to the front entrance."[21] Moreover, World War I had shown that submarines, chemical agents, and airplanes negated much of the strength of coastal fortifications. Should Japan establish air superiority over Luzon, it could close Manila Bay without ever putting a soldier or gun along its shore. Lassiter believed a solution to the Philippine defense problem rested on two factors: adequate manpower and improved technology. Governor Wood's death, and his replacement by the tactful and popular Henry Stimson, had removed a major source of Filipino opposition to military participation, and Lassiter was convinced "that the Filipino would welcome the adoption of the Reserve System and my view is that we have everything to gain and nothing to lose by making the Filipinos feel that it is up to them to participate in the defense of their country."[22] As had earlier Philippine commanders, Lassiter pointed out the garrison was unbalanced, it had too few men to defend all of Manila Bay but too many to hole up in Corregidor. By integrating reservists with the Regulars in the Philippine Scouts, the defenders could field a 10,000-man force of highly mobile and well-armed infantry, which could throw back the attackers on the beaches. The ground power gained from this Filipino army would be complemented by a large force of submarines and aircraft. As Japan could not risk invading the Philippines until it had control of both air and sea, the prospect of a costly battle of attrition might deter it altogether, and if not, then the defending naval, air, and mobile forces would "meet the enemy where he is most vulnerable, namely, at sea and while landing on the beach."[23]

Lassiter's scheme aroused much interest in Washington, especially the reserve provisions. Chief of Staff Summerall accepted Lassiter's view that the responsibility for the archipelago's defense must rest with its population. He believed that the Organized Reserve system authorized by the 1920 Defense Act could be extended to the Philippines at minimal expense. But whereas Lassiter believed that units made up entirely of reservists would be unreliable and wanted to integrate reservists with the Regulars of the Philippine Division, Summerall suggested the army study the project, basing its estimate on raising a division a year. In ten years this incremental process would produce a 150,000-man force that might well repel any invasion of Luzon and could certainly protect Manila Bay—if it could be funded. Congress, which did not even provide minimal support for American reserves, was showing a growing inclination to sever all economic and financial ties with the Philippines. The chief of staff deplored this on both military and moral grounds: "Even should we abandon the Philippines, it would be obligatory upon us to leave them with an organized military for their own defense."[24]

Lassiter's successor, Douglas MacArthur, took command in October 1928, inheriting the broad outline of a defensive scheme based on air power, Filipino reserves, and beach defense. MacArthur's contribution lay in expanding his predecessor's concepts and setting them forth in the 1929 Philippine Department's Basic War Plan Orange. This plan was based on the premise that the defenders would be required to hold out unassisted for six months against a Japanese invasion force of between 40,000 and 80,000 men. The Japanese would probably attack coincident with a declaration of war, or immediately afterward, in December or January, when their own troops were fresh from their fall maneuvers and the Philippine forces were still recovering from the enforced idleness of the rainy season, and they would probably land at Lingayen Gulf. To meet this threat, "our only possible course is to strike the enemy with all available force where he is weakest, namely *at the beach*."[25] Perhaps following Summerall, MacArthur's "Main Plan" envisioned a ten-year program that by 1939 would produce a three-division army of 76,000. These forces—60,000 of whom would be Filipino reserves—would be deployed in three sector commands and charged with defending all of Luzon. Following the tactics outlined in Haan's "Positive System," MacArthur proposed a defense in depth. Submarines and an air group of one bombardment and three pursuit squadrons would attack the enemy at sea. As they approached the beaches, the enemy transports would be raked by the beach cordon troops of the Departmental Artillery and Machine Gun Brigade. With their transports damaged and their troops pinned down on the beaches and demoralized, the invaders would be smashed by the counterattacking mobile forces and driven into the sea.[26]

As a design to raise large numbers of Filipino forces, as a tactical scheme to fight a defense in depth, and as an integration of submarine, air, mobile, and fixed defenses, the 1929 Basic War Plan Orange was an ambitious effort. However, despite MacArthur's claim that the "contemplated plans were elastic and capable of application at any crisis," the "Main Plan" was in actuality a "project," a preliminary blueprint of the preparations necessary for a conflict in 1939, ten years hence; it was not a practical or realistic plan to defend the Philippines with their current resources. MacArthur's provisions for the immediate present—the "Auxiliary Plan"—postulated the same defense on the beaches, the same raising of three Filipino divisions, the same organizational structure, as did the Main Plan. It did call for slightly smaller numbers—only 23,600 Filipinos would be immediately recruited and 3,300 more would flock to the colors each month—but the only provision for mobilizing this manpower was to instruct the civil authorities to funnel recruits forward to Fort Stotsenburg. In short, the Auxiliary Plan assumed that the defenders could establish a recruitment system, train and arm thousands of new recruits, and transport and emplace dozens of field pieces and machine guns in the two weeks before the main Japanese invasion was expected to arrive. MacArthur had stood the entire process on its head; he had drawn up a plan of defense based on nonexistent troops, weapons, supplies, housing, and finances. For his scheme to work required not only a legal ruling that Filipino reserves were eligible for funding under the 1920 Defense Act, but that these reserves be funded at a time when Congress showed little inclination to allocate even enough money to keep the U.S. reserve system alive.[27] MacArthur's Basic War Plan Orange was a pipe dream, and the fact that it went unchallenged exemplifies the independent course pursued by overseas commanders and the absence of oversight by Washington.

The 1929 plan marks the culmination of a decade of debate over the defense of the Philippines. Frustrated by Washington's paralysis over earlier plans, officers weighed surrealistic expectations of fulfilling a clearly impossible mission—the prolonged defense of Manila and Manila Bay—while also coping with army-wide shortages, a reduction in the garrison to 4,000 Americans and 7,000 Scouts, the increasing obsolescence of the Manila Bay defenses, the new threats of chemical warfare and aviation, and the growing indications that the U.S. Army would sometime, perhaps quite soon, depart the Philippines forever. As Lassiter had acknowledged, the Carabao Army was too small to defend Luzon, yet too large to be entirely sheltered behind the Manila Bay fortifications. He also recognized that if the garrison was expected to hold out for several months, it was doubtful that Corregidor could withstand prolonged bombing. Lassiter thus had turned from the simple problem of defending Corregidor to the much greater one of protecting all of Luzon. His solution was to use aviation and submarines, and to double the available land forces by creating a Filipino reserve division. MacArthur took this basic scheme and raised it to grandiose heights—three infantry divisions, a special beach defense force, and an extensive reserve system. The prospect was intoxicating, for if his 1929 plan succeeded, the United States would avoid not only the humiliating defeat of its Philippine forces but also pressure for the immediate relief of the islands. Indeed, the Philippine forces might be able to deliver a costly and demoralizing defeat to the enemy within the first months of the war. But the very scope of the 1929 plan was its weakness: it relied on nonexistent funds and resources, and upon the dubious willingness of Filipino civil officials and citizens to identify with the United States, to serve, and if needs be die, in the army of a nation from which the majority wished to be independent.

In contrast to the army in the Philippines, which had never recovered its prewar strength, and whose ability to fulfill its mission was repeatedly questioned, there was consensus throughout the interwar era on the strategic importance of Hawaii and on the mission of its garrison. As one Army War College committee explained, the difference between the two possessions was clear: "our interests in the Philippines are merely that of a beneficent paternalism. Hawaii remains at the forefront of our defense of the Pacific Coast and is vital to us."[28] Similarly, the mission of the army—"to defend the Naval base at Pearl Harbor against: 1) Damage from naval or aerial bombardment or by enemy sympathizers 2) Attack by enemy expeditionary force or forces supported or unsupported by an enemy fleet or fleets"—remained virtually unchanged after 1919.[29]

The end of the world war did, however, prompt a reappraisal of the existing defenses. In 1919 Hawaii's first postwar defense board reported that new warship guns, aided by better fire control and aerial target direction, outranged Oahu's coastal artillery. The board found the land defenses equally weak; not only were there insufficient troops to prevent enemy landing parties from taking the harbor from the rear, but the roads necessary for troops to move overland and counterattack were "so inadequate that they may be considered practically non-existent." Finally, it drew attention to the War Department's slowness in supplying antiaircraft defenses: of the 110 three-inch guns promised for this purpose, only 15 obsolete models had arrived.[30]

Perhaps spurred by the board's pessimistic report, in November 1919 the War Plans Division directed Hawaiian Department commander Charles G. Morton to submit an "Oahu Defense Project" outlining the current status of his defenses. Morton responded with a request that the War Department first inform him what his mission was and what a defense project consisted of, the WPD having forgotten to do so. He was sent a copy of a the recently approved coast defense doctrine and instructions that Hawaii must be secured against attack by either Japan or an Anglo-Japanese alliance. In the event of an Orange war, the U.S. fleet would arrive in Hawaiian waters within a month, but if the nation faced an Anglo-Japanese coalition, the fleet would concentrate in the Atlantic and Oahu must hold out for 120 days. In either case, the fleet would be used for operations at sea and Morton could have only local naval forces for direct defense of Oahu.[31]

In response, Morton submitted a "Project for the Defense of Oahu" on 20 January 1920. Following the worst-case scenario, Haan's "Positive System of

Coast Defense," and his own understanding that a campaign on Oahu would resemble his recent experiences on the western front, Morton sought to structure a defense in depth to delay, halt, and then repulse an enemy attack. He proposed using the army's new sixteen-inch rifled cannons to deter capital ships from the harbors and the southern coast. This would force the enemy to disembark over the reefs on the north or east shores, where he would run a gauntlet of artillery and machine gun fire laid down by beach cordons. When he was most disorganized, the bulk of the mobile forces, traveling over a newly built road network, would launch a smashing counterattack and drive him into the sea. Morton therefore requested a full combat division of four infantry regiments and a field artillery brigade, a cavalry regiment to handle any internal threat, an increase in coast artillery, and a large road construction budget.[32]

The fate of the 1920 project is instructive, for it illustrates the stultifying micromanagement and lack of tangible support that Pacific defense projects encountered. Morton soon discovered that the Hawaiian district engineer had submitted his own estimates for fortifications, roads, and bridges, which drastically altered the general's defensive scheme. In Washington, the bureau chiefs criticized those parts which fell under their particular expertise. The chief of the Coast Artillery first recommended that twelve-inch mortars replace the Morton's proposed sixteen-inch batteries; then he decided that sixteen-inch guns were indeed suitable, but he wanted them placed at another location. The WPD's Lassiter noted a conflict with the 1916 Defense Act—the last major defense legislation that applied to Hawaii—and questioned whether implementing Morton's project not only threatened the allotted appropriations but, by canceling earlier plans to station a brigade at Shafter, left both Honolulu and Pearl open to attack by the "alien population."[33] Next came the news that Congress had cut the appropriation for defense roads from almost $600,000 to $70,000. This vitiated Morton's entire defensive scheme, for without roads he could not retain the bulk of his mobile forces at Schofield and then transport them to the beachhead for a counterattack. As a further complication, the War Department, caught up in the debate over manpower which finally culminated in the 1920 National Defense Act, demanded Morton revise the project but refused to inform him of the proposed size or composition of Oahu's peacetime garrison. Eventually, according to the project's historian, "General Morton quite properly put the buck up to them."[34] The mangled 1920 project was never adopted by the War Department, and it remained little more than a theoretical exercise, a symbol of the interference and absence of clear direction from Washington.

Morton's successor, Summerall, who commanded the department between 1921 and 1924, was reported to have taken as a slogan "they shall not land" and to have forbidden the use of the word "defense."[35] With Morton's work gathering dust in Washington, Summerall began drawing up the 1924 Project for the Defense of Oahu. This focused almost exclusively on repelling an attempt to seize the naval bases by invasion. It assumed the enemy (baldly identified as "Orange") must achieve tactical surprise and that the defenders would have no warning. The enemy must also secure control of the sea and air, and would thus either need to bring aircraft carriers or seize a neighboring island to establish airbases. Once this was done, Orange would begin a series of attacks to neutralize Pearl Harbor, with air raids on military facilities and utilities, and small landings at night to disrupt the defenders. The final invasion would be in an area where the enemy could rapidly expand the beachhead, almost certainly the North Shore.

Against this contingency, Summerall planned for a complete and integrated defense, incorporating aviation, coast artillery, and mobile forces. The air force was to prevent the establishment of an airdrome and "to find the enemy air force and destroy it and carry out destructive attacks against sea or ground organizations."[36] This would require 304 airplanes, including 152 pursuit planes and 80 bombers, and air bases on Oahu and the other islands. Summerall requested new guns for the coastal fortresses and $9 million for ordnance, roads, searchlights, and signal equipment. He outlined a scheme for using civilian labor during wartime to lay contact mines and barbed wire, construct field fortifications, expand airdromes, and otherwise prepare Oahu's physical defenses. Immediately upon mobilization, the garrison would be reinforced from the mainland to three divisions (72,000 men) and distributed into two sector commands—Schofield and Honolulu.

Summerall sought to mix flexibility with centralization, establishing a task-oriented command and control system. From his headquarters at Schofield, the departmental commander could oversee air attacks, antiaircraft defense, and coastal artillery, but each sector was assigned a "battle commander" who coordinated its artillery and could call for fire support, including the one-ton shells of the sixteen-inch coast defense cannon. Following Haan's precepts, Summerall's plan called for defense-in-depth: the attacker would face successive attacks from air, artillery, the beach cordons, and the sector reserve. If he did land and maintain his cohesion, he still faced the heavy guns of the coast artillery, clouds of mustard gas, counterattacking infantry and tanks, and then the final "deep zone defense of the area between Diamond Head and Pearl Harbor, including the naval reservation and Honolulu, which would be held to the last."[37] Like MacArthur's 1929 project, Summerall's 1924 project contained one major flaw—it was based on nonexistent manpower. The current

Orange plan did not provide for the large number of reinforcements Summerall needed, and his plan, although "correct in theory and principal . . . lacks the necessary battle power to carry out the mission should the enemy gain a foothold at one or more points on our coast, because it depends too strongly for its success on the man power to be procured locally."[38] Both MacArthur and Summerall thus produced innovative and detailed tactical schemes that could not be implemented with the resources available.

The bulwark of coast defense remained the heavy gun, which reached its apogee in the 1919-model sixteen-inch rifle—a 79-foot, 187-ton behemoth that could fire a 2,340 pound projectile 50,000 yards with devastating accuracy. Manila Bay's armament was frozen by the Washington Treaties, but between 1921 and 1924 two of these guns were installed at Fort Weaver across the Pearl Harbor channel from Fort Kamemeha. In the 1930s two more, slightly less powerful sixteen-inchers were placed at Fort Barrette in the highlands northwest of Pearl.[39] However, by the end of the decade one Hawaiian Department staff officer noted "there may be no effective fire from our fixed batteries against a landing. No one really knows what modern aerial or sea bombardment will be able to accomplish against fixed batteries protected by some [antiaircraft] guns."[40] He even wondered whether a combination of aerial attack, poison gas, improved warship gunnery, and sabotage might allow the Japanese to neutralize Oahu's fixed coast defense batteries and launch a direct sea attack on Honolulu Harbor—a possibility that had not been considered for twenty years.[41] In response to such concerns, Hawaii's coast defense commanders placed some of their fixed batteries on inactive status and transferred the gunners to mobile antiaircraft artillery, 155-millimeter cannon, and eight-inch railway guns, which could be deployed around Oahu. The threat of aerial attack contributed to the steady erosion of the traditional divisions between coast and field artillery and between harbor and beach defense, leading to more efficient and flexible artillery coverage on Oahu.[42]

But however strong the loyalty to old ways and old weapons, one revolutionary new method of carnage from World War I received prolonged attention. Poison gas appeared to provide an essential tool for beach defense, forcing the enemy to wade ashore in a deadly cloud, channeling him into killing zones, and denying him the protection of defiles and low ground. Philippine war plans, such as MacArthur's 1929 Orange plan, predicted: "Offensive operations using chemical agents will be carried on by the Air Corps, the Artillery, and the Chemical Troops."[43] Although the United States had formally declared it would not be the first to use lethal chemical agents, Philippine commanders were under the impression that "responsibility for the use of toxic gasses in the defense of the Philippines rests with the Department Commander, and decision will be made by the Department Commander as to its use when the emergency arises."[44] As was true in much of Philippine defense planning, reality intervened. Chemical agents and the equipment used to repel them broke down so rapidly in the archipelago's climate that by 1936 virtually none of the Carabao Army's gas masks, clothing, or chemicals were usable. Despite continual pleas, Washington steadfastly refused to ship sufficient chemical weapons to the Philippines.

Hawaiian officers also planned to use gas in massive quantities: the 1921 defense project called for 144 tons of chlorine, 80 tons of phosgene, 32 tons of chloropicrin, 16 tons of mustard gas, 2,500 toxic smoke candles, 1,750 mortar bombs filled with brombenzylcyanide, and an additional 14,000 chemical mortar bombs.[45] By the 1930s, Oahu housed "the largest known concentrated reserve of lethal gas in the world": 854 tons of chemical poisons, 88 chemical mortars, and 7,713 chemical shells.[46] In 1935 the army established a chemical filling plant in Oahu and by 1937 it was able to produce the 176 to 213 tons of mustard gas required by the defense project.[47] Behind the airplanes and big guns and beach defenses, chemical warfare loomed as the final resort for the Pacific's guardians.

The readiness to use chemical weapons is disturbing. In fairness, it must be remembered that many of these officers were veterans of World War I and had been exposed to the effects of chemical warfare. They recognized, on both a practical and an emotional level, the consequences of their position. Moreover, they were convinced that the Japanese would not hesitate to use toxic chemicals.[48] Tactically, their ideas had some merit in Hawaii. Massive quantities of chemical agents might have concealed the defenders' guns and field fortifications, blanketed inland waters and beaches, interfered with the attackers' fire support, denied the cover of depressions and valleys to the enemy, and allowed the defenders to concentrate their strength. It would have forced the invaders to come ashore in protective clothing and gas masks, greatly hampering their mobility and efficiency. The defenders too would have had to fight encumbered by masks and deluged by gas, but they were familiar with the terrain, their artillery and machine guns would already have been ranged and sighted, and they could fire blind with much more effective results. Whether justified on practical grounds, this ready acceptance of chemical warfare is chilling. The cost in civilian lives would have been appalling and the promiscuous dumping of chemical poisons on Oahu would have been an ecological disaster. The willingness of Pacific Army officers to destroy in order to save is a sobering reminder that within the hollow shell of the interwar army, there was a grim and ruthless determination.

Hawaii's defenses were tested in April 1925 by Joint Army and Navy Exercise

No. 3, which involved some 50,000 soldiers, sailors, and marines. After a great deal of aerial skirmishing between the defenders and the fleet, the exercise culminated in a successful landing on the North Shore, whereupon the umpires called it off and declared the invaders victorious. The exercises revealed much that was good and much that was bad about Oahu's defenses. Following the tactical scheme outlined in Summerall's 1924 project, the harbor defenders remained behind their guns; the mobile forces established a sector defense, placing beach cordons at possible landing places and retaining the bulk of their personnel at Schofield Barracks. The Coast Artillery at Pearl and Honolulu vindicated itself by driving off an attack by enemy battleships. For the mobile forces, the exercise was simply a repetition of their usual field exercises and they performed well.

The exercises also revealed deep divisions between the services. The commander of Hawaii's coast defenses was both amused and appalled at his naval opponents' inability to comprehend the power of heavy coastal guns. In one instance four battleships slowly steamed by, pretending to bombard the shoreline, oblivious to the presence of land batteries that would soon have reduced them to smoldering hulks.[49] Interservice rivalry was so rampant that the Air Service umpire declared "it was obvious . . . that the object of the Navy was to use this Exercise as an example of why coast protection should be turned over to the Navy and Naval Aviation."[50] In the joint area of air defense, communications between the Hawaiian Department and Pearl Harbor's 14th Naval District broke down completely. For some time Summerall and his naval counterpart had feuded over a number of issues; according to one observer they "could not cooperate in anything, not even calling on each other."[51] Summerall's successor had done nothing to overcome this estrangement. The refusal to cooperate doomed the defense: after the invading force landed airplanes and established a base on the island of Molokai, the army commander sought to launch a combined attack against them, but his naval counterpart refused, on the grounds that his airplanes were required to protect Pearl Harbor. The resulting delay proved fatal, as enemy air forces eliminated the defenders' air cover.[52]

In the next few years subsequent plans and projects sought to integrate the lessons of the Joint Exercise into Hawaiian defense. The basic outlines of Summerall's 1924 framework remained; later studies probed such issues as infantry tactics, naval support, clear delineation of beach cordons and sector defenses, appraisals of vulnerable beaches and their support, chemical warfare, and so on. The predictions of Japanese attack became both more detailed and more alarming, postulating the arrival of the enemy fleet and a devastating air attack concurrent with a declaration of war, followed by a naval bombardment, and then an invasion of 100,000 soldiers. Against such a threat, in 1929 the defenders could muster but 14,000 soldiers and eighteen airplanes.[53] The imbalance was excused, at least to Washington, by the shift in the 1928 Orange plan away from a direct rush to Manila Bay and to the immediate reinforcement of Panama and Hawaii. Unfortunately, neither in Hawaii nor Washington was the crucial issue of interservice cooperation addressed: each service continued to base much of its defense plans on the other's cooperation without insuring that its erstwhile allies intended to comply.

The Philippines maneuvers were characterized by less interservice rivalry, but revealed even more defensive problems. As Lassiter noted, the forces in the archipelago were unbalanced: there were too few mobile forces in the Philippine Division to stage a successful defense of Luzon and too many to take shelter in Corregidor. Major Raymond Lee outlined the disparity between its training and how it would actually fight: "For some time, both in map problems and maneuvers, the defensive force in the Philippines has been handled, in general, according to the ordinary methods of the typical division in open warfare, with the further assumption that it is backed up by a quickly mobilized civilian population, such as exists in the United States." But the Philippine Division was not really a division in either size or power, as one of its brigades was inactive and the other consisted of infantry, cavalry, and field artillery regiments understrength and given only the lightest equipment. Moreover, there was no reserve force or any provision for bringing the division up to war strength. Nevertheless, Lee noted, it was "annually maneuvered as a division and is placed in situations where the only result in a Japanese invasion would be its complete elimination from future participation."[54] One division commander, Johnson Hagood, disparagingly summarized the annual maneuvers: "We marched to the north, and went through the motions of preparing some kind of defense and upon receiving word that we were being attacked by superior forces, we fell back to Manila, destroying (in theory) the bridges as we went along."[55] In 1927, bored with constant defeat, he announced that the Japanese fleet had abandoned the invading army, then led a triumphal counteroffensive. Others, more solemn, failed to find much humor in the pervasive unreality.

Both in the Philippines and Hawaii commanders struggled with minuscule interwar budgets, depleted manpower, and inadequate matériel. The Philippine Division lacked trucks, communications equipment, chemical warfare supplies, and firepower—one of its two artillery battalions was equipped with the same light mountain guns and mules in use when Pershing last fought the Moros.[56] Firing practice in Hawaii was rare, both because of tourist complaints and of expense; each time the gunners at Fort Weaver fired one of their sixteen-inch cannon it cost $2,500, more than an $18-a-month buck private made in a decade. Fuel was so restricted that the only time the Hawaiian Division's tanks moved was during inspections, when they drove to and from their designated places in line.[57]

Lacking the means, and therefore perhaps the desire, for preparing for real war, the contingents of the Pacific Army came to devote much of their attention to spit-and-polish, immaculate appearance, and frequent parades and ceremonies. The Schofield reviews, with the Hawaiian Division marching past, tents meticulously lined up in neat rows, and equipment gleaming, were the delight of visitors. Only a few noticed that as late as 1931 nearly all its equipment was of World War I vintage. Conditions in the Philippines were even more extreme: one officer witnessed a soldier being carried upright by his battery mates so that he wouldn't wrinkle his trousers walking to mount guard. The 31st Infantry boasted it was "one of the best turned out regiments in the United States Army"[58] and "the cynosure of all eyes, of not only the officials of the Philippine government but those of all visiting foreign officials and of officers of the armies and navies from all over the world."[59] Such precision was, of course, the result of constant practice; in October 1922, for example, one of its companies spent 25 percent of its training time on close-order drill. Not surprisingly, in 1924 its commanding officer rated only 6 percent of his soldiers as proficient in general field training and an inspector reported, "in general much of the time allotted to training appears to be wasted. . . . Probably not more than 50% . . . is used in actual instruction and practice."[60]

The inspector's comment highlights the discrepancy between what the Pacific Army's combat troops were supposed to do and what they actually did. Fatigue work, a euphemism for menial labor, constituted an inordinate amount of a soldier's duties. In 1923, for example, the Hawaiian Division's infantry received no training at all because it had to unload, repack, and store 50,000 tons of War Reserve materials, most of which soon rotted away. One intensive survey of the training program in the 27th Infantry for January 1924 revealed that a quarter of its men were sick, in jail, or on detached duty; out of 154,700 man-hours allocated to the 27th for training that month, it lost 93,635 to fatigues, school, guard duty, post and regimental assignments, and special service.[61] In 1929 during one six-month period, 1,060 soldiers from Fort Kamehameha spent 629 man-days on roads and grounds, warehouse duties, and maintenance, and another 2,995 man-days on construction, dikes, railroads, fences. In 1931, an average of 15 percent of the troops in Schofield was detached for labor, school, or other duties.[62] The widespread use of soldiers as laborers did produce beautiful army posts and allowed modestly paid officers to enjoy a comfortable life-style, but it hardly conformed to Root's assertion that the purpose of an army was to prepare for war.

During the 1920s Pacific Army officers attempted to resolve the discrepancy between their ambitious missions and their limited means. The nation's postwar military retrenchment rendered both the Pineapple and Carabao armies hollow forces, unable to fulfill the tasks assigned them. To complicate the picture further, Washington required detailed plans and projects for the defense of the possessions, but overseas planners soon learned the War Department lacked either the desire or the ability to implement their proposals. The result was that Pacific defense planning was often based either on patently unrealistic premises—as evidenced by the studies submitted by Summerall and MacArthur—or became cynically fatalistic, as Hagood's comments attest. New tactics and technology offered some hope to rectify weaknesses and provide a distant chance against Japan's impressive army. Commanders who assimilated the lessons of the western front could use their mobile forces to turn the beaches into killing zones. They could envision well-trained beach cordons and massed counterattacks hurling back invaders. But again the gap between requirements and means arose. The garrisons in Hawaii and the Philippines lacked the manpower to execute the imaginative war plans its commanders devised for it. The end of the decade found the Pacific Army little improved and neither in Hawaii nor the Philippines could there be much optimism that the next decade would be any better.

CHAPTER 9

Army Aviation and Pacific Defense

To some officers, the Pacific Army's interwar problems had a simple solution that was relatively cheap and rendered beach cordons, coast artillery, field exercises, and most defense plans superfluous. Almost from its inception, the airplane represented both a new threat and a savior. As early as 1909, General William P. Duvall warned of the danger that aerial bombardment presented to Corregidor and requested antiaircraft guns, airplanes, and observation balloons to defend the fortress.[1] Recognizing the importance of aviation to coast defense, the General Staff accorded the overseas fortresses top priority, and in April 1915 assigned the army's first three aviation companies to Hawaii, the Philippines, and the Canal Zone.[2] In the Philippines, a seaplane base was established at Kindley Field on Corregidor with a few hydroplanes, often inoperative from crashes or lack of parts; other fields were designated at Stotsenburg (Clark Field) and Manila (Nichols Field). In Hawaii, a local board selected Ford Island (later named Luke Field) in the center of Pearl Harbor as the best location for assisting the coast defenses. On 13 March 1917 the 6th Aero Squadron arrived with two airplanes, one of which was soon destroyed. By this time, the crisis with Germany had all but shifted attention away from the Pacific. Secure from attack and lacking either military or pork-barrel benefits, the overseas departments were excluded by Congress from much of the wartime legislation establishing hangers, barracks, airfields, and fuel depots in the continental United States.[3]

In some respects, Pacific Army aviation never recovered from the neglect that occurred during the world war. In the Philippines, Corregidor's cramped and hilly terrain rendered the term "Kindley Field" a misnomer, as only seaplanes could take off from it, and then only during the six months when the monsoon was not blowing. Clark Field was primitive and unsafe and Nichols was even worse, each consisting of a sod runway and a few barracks. Cabcaben, on the Bataan Peninsula, was a superior site; there airplanes could assist in Manila Bay's defense while protected against land attack. But despite pressure from local commanders, the development of a main air base at Cabcaben remained in limbo. With funds for airfield construction virtually nonexistent after the Washington Treaties, airmen devoted much of their time to locating emergency landing fields and identifying possible air bases for future development.[4] In Hawaii, the situation was equally bad. Both the small subsidiary station for pursuit aircraft at Schofield's Wheeler Field and the main air base of Luke Field on Ford Island were inadequate. The latter soon became the object of a bitter interservice fight: although the island had been purchased by the army in 1917, the navy took advantage of wartime joint occupancy regulations to stake its own claim and then refused either to evacuate or to pay its share of the island's cost. Soon navy dirigible sheds, hangers, barracks, a fuel depot, and two separate airfields overcrowded the small island. To exacerbate matters further, in 1919 the army revised the original plans calling for one squadron of ten aircraft upward to three squadrons and twenty-four aircraft. As airplanes increased in size and power, Luke Field became increasingly unsatisfactory. It was so narrow that planes were in constant danger of collision, and the presence of ships and installations in the flight path prevented takeoff with live bombs. By 1924 both the army and navy conceded that Ford Island was hopelessly inadequate. Its only redeeming feature was that the services had each sunk $2 million in buildings and utilities; as there was no money for further construction, Luke had to suffice.[5]

Military aviation in the Pacific was further retarded by a colossal administrative blunder. Although the Joint Board did not determine the exact size and composition of the overseas departments until 1923, the JANPC, seeking to reduce the logistical demands of a Pacific war, seized on the idea of stockpiling vast War Reserves in the Pacific territories. The result of this was a massive dumping of surplus equipment: between 4 March 1919 and 31 March 1922, 250 DH-4 airplanes alone were shipped to Oahu. They arrived at army ports that were deluged with other War Reserve material. Most had been in storage—often badly packed—for as long as four years. Semisoaked in seawater, they then lay on the docks exposed to the elements until the understaffed Air Service personnel could repair and recrate the airframes, put the fragile wings up in dry storage, and drain and overhaul the engines. The effort required was enormous: in 1921, the air officer for the Philippine Department estimated it would take 800 man-hours to inspect and repair each of the 190 airplanes in the War Reserve. Since neither the manpower nor the time was available, the reserve materials remained in storage, where one officer estimated they deteriorated at the rate of $6,000 a month.[6] A similar situation existed in Hawaii until late 1924, when Joint Exercise No. 3 required that all the War Reserve airplanes be put into commission. The results were appalling. Warehouse after warehouse yielded rotten frames, warped propellers, broken wings, and frozen engines. Not one of the fifty-seven complete DH-4 airplanes that had been stored at Luke Field in 1918 was now salvageable—an estimated loss of $500,000. At the Wheeler Field warehouse, sixty-four DH-4s were unpacked; of these, fourteen were judged able to participate in the maneuvers. By 1926 Hawaii's air officer had concluded "there are no planes of any kind in the War Reserve."[7] If nothing else, this fiasco convinced the War Department that future stockpiling should consist only of materials that could be maintained within the existing facilities.

From quite early onward it appears to have been the air command's policy to keep new models within the continental United States and send only "proven" models overseas.[8] But given the limited budgets for aircraft development and a Congress whose policies almost destroyed the nation's aviation industry, by the time an airplane had proved itself on the mainland, it was usually obsolete and unfit for combat. Replacement aircraft arrived years after they had been promised—some without notice that they had been shipped—and missing essential pieces and spare parts. Kindley's prewar seaplanes, described in 1924 as "of little or no value from a tactical standpoint" were never replaced, and pilots at Clark Field used homemade bomb sights to drop coconuts.[9] During one drill in 1921 sixteen DH-4s were ordered readied for war: of these, four proved unable to taxi to the flying line; only half of the remainder had guns, and none had bomb racks.[10] That year the Philippine Department's air officer informed one board that in case of war the defenders could muster ten airplanes, but had the enemy "a single squadron of modern pursuit planes, the whole Air Force of the Philippines, would, of course, last only a few days."[11] In 1924 the 28th, the sole bomber squadron in the islands, had but thirteen DH-4 airplanes; in order to man them it had to borrow all the pilots from two other units. Twelve years later, the squadron had but six obsolete Keystone bombers, prompting the department commander to write "the effectiveness of our present air force is next to nothing."[12] Hunter Harris, who served with the 28th between 1937 and 1940, described the archipelago's air forces as "pitifully small," with "second-line aircraft" that were "one generation" behind those in the United States.[13]

In Hawaii the situation was almost as bad. Despite the Hawaiian Department Air Service's boast in 1925 that it could protect Oahu so that "the only ground troops necessary to defend Pearl Harbor would be those needed to handle the large alien population," in 1926 the 23rd Bombing Squadron reported it had only seven planes in commission and that many of these were unsafe because of a lack of spare parts; further, the 4th Observation Squadron had just six airplanes, all obsolete and hazardous DH-4s.[14] Five years later, the average number of operable aircraft in Oahu's combat squadrons was six airplanes, and some had only four.[15] When Hugh A. Drum took over the Hawaiian Department in March 1935 he discovered that of his command's 100 airplanes, 80 were over four years old, and 40 were over five years old. After a number of accidents, an Air Corps board grounded all Drum's observation and attack airplanes and reduced flying time for the obsolete pursuit and bomber airplanes so drastically that his pilots could barely qualify for flight pay. For much of 1936 the department had only 33 airplanes, half its authorized complement. Harold C. Davidson, who served in Hawaii in the late 1930s, recalled his squadron was equipped with bombers that were "absolutely useless for war,"[16] while pursuit pilot Bruce Holloway's squadron flew the P-26, "which was pretty, but it was essentially worthless." In 1939, Holloway's unit was reequipped with the P-36, which "was a little less worthless, but not much."[17] Not until the last-minute buildup in 1941 would Hawaii's pilots even begin to receive the most modern warplanes; but even then supply problems kept many of them grounded: on 6 December only 125 of the army's 234 airplanes on Oahu were operational.[18]

Nor were the problems limited to airplanes alone. Inadequate equipment contributed to a general lackadaisical attitude toward service. One Air Corps specialist, recently arrived from the United States, was appalled at the ignorance and laziness of the aircrews in the Philippines. Norris Harbold, the air officer at Nichols Field between 1937 and 1939, remembered that "the whole atmosphere of the place was directed towards just occupation but not [toward] any real preparations for combat."[19] Philippine airfields were little more than dirt and sod fields, totally unsuited for aircraft such as the B-17, or even some of the fighters, that were coming into production by the end of the decade.

Although most pilots believed that the best use of aviation was through the strategic bombing of enemy industry, the Air Service—renamed the Air Corps in 1926—embraced coast defense as a way to stake its claim for a separate air force with an independent mission. Nor surprisingly, this encroachment was looked on with some suspicion by the branch charged with protecting the coasts and there was more than a little resentment. The Philippine Department's air officer remarked in 1923 that despite the proven value of aerial spotting for long-range gunnery, the Coast Artillery was "still not sold" on the need for aviation and that "Air Service cooperation is usually tolerated rather than relied on."[20] The gunners' suspicions had some merit: throughout the 1920s aviators were unable to reconcile their weapon's potential with its performance. During 1923 and 1924 the chief of Coast Artillery and the chief of the Air Service sponsored a series of tests to determine the vulnerability of coast defenses to bombing and the range at which bombing was more effective than guns for defense against the enemy fleet. The Hawaiian tests demonstrated that even in peacetime the airplane was an erratic weapon: only one out of four one-ton bombs dropped at 15,000 feet on an undefended and almost stationary battleship hit their target.[21] Nevertheless, the Air Corps argued its superiority as a coast defense force and in 1931 an agreement between Chief of Staff MacArthur and Chief of Naval Operations Pratt gave the army first responsibility for this mission. Although the MacArthur-Pratt agreement did not survive the tenure of its authors, the Air Corps used their coast defense obligations to justify funding for a long-range heavy bomber.

Despite strong disagreements over the role and capabilities of aircraft, when charged with a specific task, ground and air officers cooperated most of the time. In 1924, for example, close communications were maintained between the Coast Artillery and the Air Service branches through joint classes and lectures; using aerial spotting, gunners reached new levels of accuracy.[22] Aviators also worked with the Coast Artillery's antiaircraft regiments, a duty that required that they fly a predetermined flight pattern towing a long target. Such training was dangerous; crashes were common and fatalities not unusual. During one exercise, when a young officer named Wood flew his airplane through a high tension line of 160,000 volts and miraculously survived, his superior dryly remarked that "Wood is a non-conductor of electricity."[23]

Long before Pearl Harbor, the threat of attack by enemy aircraft had found its way into all defense discussions, altering the debate and driving new problems to the fore. Less than two decades after Duvall's warning, observers concluded that the army must totally reevaluate its defense planning in the Philippines for, as Lieutenant Colonel Earl L. Canaday noted, "every plan of defense for the Philippine Islands is based on holding Corregidor. Corregidor cannot be held against an enemy who has control of the Air."[24] Colonel C. W. Exton of the Chemical Warfare Service agreed that "an enemy must be prevented from landing and establishing an air base within 100 miles of Corregidor, if that fortress is to be held under conditions of gas warfare."[25] Further, if Japanese warplanes controlled the air over Manila Bay, the defense of Corregidor would still not secure a safe anchorage for the relieving American fleet. For years the citadel of Corregidor had, in fortification parlance, been called the keep to Manila Bay, but with the airplane, as one officer explained, "now we have two keeps to Manila Bay—Corregidor and the air—and two keeps to Corregidor—Bataan and the air. If you have two keys to a house, the possession of only one doesn't give the owner any greater security."[26] In 1928, General Lassiter urged a complete overhaul of the archipelago's defense plans based largely on the danger of air attack: "The point then to be strongly stressed is that with modern developments in aviation, the center of gravity of our system of defense has shifted. An enemy can entirely disregard the fortified islands and still gain his essential purpose. *Whether our object is to keep a protected anchorage for our main fleet or merely to keep the flag flying on Corregidor, we must address ourselves to keeping an enemy from getting firmly established with a powerful air force in central Luzon.*"[27]

Similar concerns dominated defensive strategy in Hawaii. In 1920 the Joint Board recognized "[t]here are some places in the Hawaiian Islands from which an enemy might launch a surprise air attack upon Pearl Harbor."[28] Four years later, Major Arnold Krogstad warned of such an attack: "With oriental sacrificial fanaticism, enemy planes operating from points to the limit of their gas capacity could with only a few planes cut 2,400 miles from the range of our Navy by putting the oil base out of commission."[29] By 1931 Lassiter, now commanding the Hawaiian Department, concluded that "the most probable form of hostile attack on Oahu in the early stages of Pacific War would be a sea-air raid intended to destroy or damage naval installations here."[30]

In assessing the danger posed by enemy aviation, the threat of carrier attack was discounted until 1927, when Japan's first fleet carrier was completed. At first, and with some reason, army aviators argued that weight and size restrictions on carrier airplanes gave land-based aviation an insurmountable advantage: in 1931 one Air Corps' chief of training and operations declared that if only four of the defender's bombers reached their objective, they would destroy every one of Japan's carriers.[31] Those who actually had to prepare for a carrier attack were far less sanguine and after 1930 the destruction of enemy aircraft carriers became the first priority of Hawaii's air defense. Staff studies and actual maneuvers alike showed that unless forewarned, the defending air force would have no option but to suffer the first strike and hope the survivors could follow the attackers back to the carriers and destroy them. By 1934, both Hawaiian Department staff and students at the Air Corps Tactical School had deduced that Japanese carriers could concentrate 324 airplanes against Oahu's 123. Colonel Edward M. Markham's exhaustive survey of the Hawaiian Islands' defenses in 1937 reported that the military consensus was that war would "commence without a period of 'strained relations,' the initial attack taking the form of powerful, driving air raids against the installations and personnel of Pearl Harbor and our airdromes."[32] A year before the Japanese attack, department commander Charles D. Herron predicted that carriers would approach at night, launching their airplanes to strike the naval base at dawn, in an attempt to destroy the defenders' air forces. Against such an attack, neither antiaircraft weapons nor hastily scrambled pursuit planes would be sufficient; the defenders must establish an extensive long-range reconnaissance patrol and an efficient early-warning communications system. Chief of Staff George C. Marshall concurred and directed that Herron's postulates form the basis for Hawaii's air defenses. Unfortunately, the plans were still in their embryonic state in 1941.[33]

Hawaii's vulnerability to carrier raids had been graphically illustrated in 1932, when, during Grand Joint Exercise No. 4, the invading side's two aircraft carriers delivered a strong attack at dawn on Sunday, 7 February. The aggressors were credited with destroying several defending airplanes on the ground and with seizing temporary control of the air over Oahu. The similarities to Japan's later attack have led some authors to castigate the army leadership or even to suggest that the Japanese copied the American carrier tactics.[34] But to contemporary officers, the lessons of the maneuvers, so clear in hindsight, were obscured by a multiplicity of other factors. The 1932 exercises had been designed primarily to test Oahu's defenses against invasion, U.S. Navy fleet tactics, and the amphibious warfare doctrine of the Marine Corps. They were based on the scenario that Oahu had been conquered by the enemy (Black) and the United States (Blue) must recapture it; this provided a rationale for Oahu's defenders to test their tactical plans and also allowed the U.S. Navy and Marines to practice attacking a defended island. The umpires, surprised by the aerial attack of 7 February, failed to understand its implications for a number of reasons, perhaps the greatest of which was that the carrier attack was not delivered against the naval base at Pearl Harbor, but, as the reports make clear, "on enemy aviation and its bases."[35] The U.S. Navy's carrier airplanes did achieve a successful surprise attack on Luke Field, located on Ford Island and so geographically within Pearl Harbor, but they did not attack the Pearl Harbor naval base itself. Indeed, to have done so would have been strategic imbecility, since Blue had to capture these facilities intact, whereas they were of little use to the Black defenders.

A second factor that may have lulled observers is that the strike was far from decisive: perhaps anticipating such an attack, the Black commander, Briant H. Wells, had dispersed and camouflaged his airplanes, and the attackers were credited with the destruction of only fifteen of them. Moreover, the events immediately following the carrier attack demonstrated the high cost of such operations. Both Blue carriers were attacked by a Hawaii-based submarine shortly after launching their surprise attack. Later, Wells's airplanes located and bombed them; they were judged to have suffered heavy damage. Indeed,

Oahu's army aviators claimed they had sunk both carriers, one of them twice. As a result, army and navy umpires overlooked the enormous implications of the successful strike and, by an understandable but fatal irony, concluded: "It is doubtful if air attacks can be launched against Oahu in the face of strong defensive aviation without subjecting the attacking carriers to the danger of material damage and consequent great losses to the attacking air force."[36]

Other maneuvers provided similarly ambivalent lessons, demonstrating that the defenses were indeed vulnerable to carrier raids, but displaying even more clearly—for all too receptive eyes—the cost to the aggressor. In cases where the defense was clearly porous—as in a 1932 departmental exercise when six navy airplanes raided Pearl Harbor without challenge from the defenders—the lessons were less than clear. In this particular instance, the Air Corps blamed the navy for the failure of its offshore patrols and its poor communications: although a U.S. Navy patrol plane had picked up the enemy flight, it took almost twenty minutes to decode the alarm and pass it on to the waiting pursuit squadrons.[37] In other exercises, which demonstrated that, unless they received early warning, pursuit plans and antiaircraft artillery would have difficulty protecting Pearl Harbor, the solution appeared simple, but impracticable. Thus one department commander reported of the 1934 exercises: "our best defense against hostile air attack on Oahu is believed to be bombing attacks on carriers, before hostile planes are launched or afterward, or both. Based on the soundness of this premise the system of offshore intelligence must guarantee the discovery of the carrier from 100 to 300 miles at sea."[38] As noted earlier, the weaknesses of air and artillery defense against a surprise attack, and the desperate need for long-range reconnaissance, were reported again in 1940 by General Herron. But correcting the deficiencies revealed in the maneuvers would have imposed high costs: altering aircraft production schedules, dispersing the continental strategic bomber force, delaying the reequipment of mainland pursuit squadrons, and forcing a showdown with the navy over responsibility for offshore reconnaissance. Moreover, the joint maneuvers and tactical exercises appeared to demonstrate that Oahu's air defenses were a formidable deterrent. In a joint exercise in 1936 Oahu's air force located the approaching warships within three hours and, according to the army, destroyed all three of the aircraft carriers. After a similar exercise a year later, Drum concluded that "numerous instances emphasized the difficulties and serious weaknesses of carrier based aviation in so far as massed attack against land defenses is concerned."[39]

Perhaps the greatest defect in Hawaii's air defenses, displayed during the maneuvers but never adequately addressed, was the protracted inability of Hawaii's army and navy commands to develop joint defense policies. Much of the problem originated in the bitter interwar feud between the navy and the Air Corps over coastal defense, a conflict that made army officers, and Air Corps officers in particular, perceive any encroachment on their prerogatives as part of the navy's persistent campaign to take over coast defense aviation. Efforts to mediate were unsuccessful and both services interpreted joint agreements as they wished. Technically, joint relations were governed by the principle of "paramount interest," whereby the navy controlled Hawaii's air when the fleet was at Pearl and the army controlled it when the defense of Oahu was at issue. In reality, both army and navy commanders consistently cited their own service missions as precluding cooperation, but complained when the other service did likewise. This contributed not only to interservice sniping, but to a disastrous complacency that the other service was responsible for filling gaps in the defenses. Army planners in Washington accepted their naval colleagues' repeated assurances that the presence of the battle fleet would be sufficient to guard Oahu; they do not appear to have considered the possibility that the fleet itself might need to be protected. Thus, for example, in 1935 one of the reasons the WPD rejected General Drum's efforts to build up Oahu's air defenses was that "if the Fleet is strategically present and free to act . . . [a] serious attack is scarcely to be anticipated and could be readily met."[40]

The Hawaiian Department's tactical plans, and even the joint defense plans drawn up in the mid-1930s, retained many of these areas of overlapping responsibility, but never delineated overall command. Local officers received little guidance from Washington: efforts to solve one problem sometimes frustrated compromise in another, as when the Joint Board rejected a proposal for the Pearl Harbor command to mount twenty-four surplus antiaircraft guns because the defense of naval bases was entirely an army responsibility. Even more confusing was the formula developed in the Joint Board's 1935 "Joint Action of the Army and Navy." This assigned to the army the protection of permanent naval bases and "direct defense of the coast," but recognized the navy's paramount interest in defeating enemy forces approaching the coast, a jurisdiction that passed to the army only when it became apparent that the enemy intended to attack a shore objective. In operations within a designated Defensive Coastal Area, such as Hawaii, the paramount interest rested with the army except when the presumed objective was shipping, in which case it was a navy responsibility. Moreover, when the fleet "is strategically present and free to act, paramount interest at sea rests with the Navy" but "when enemy forces approach close enough to threaten or launch a direct attack against our territory, and the Fleet . . . is not strategically present, or is not free to act," then paramount interest shifted to the army, and the navy's task was that of support. The army interpreted the 1935 agreement to mean that anything that involved "over-the-horizon operations by surface, sub-surface, and air craft, information of hostile forces approaching from overseas" was the responsibility of the navy.[41] Clearly the formula was a prescription for disaster: in December 1941 the fleet was in port and the enemy threat was at sea, the navy had the mission of long-range reconnaissance, but it was the army that was charged with defending the naval base and Oahu's air space. As one department commander openly admitted, during wartime army and navy cooperation depended more on the personalities of the officers than on any doctrine. Unfortunately, as the Pearl Harbor inquiries would reveal, in 1941 Oahu's army and navy commanders enjoyed cordial social relations but had not coordinated air defense.[42]

Exacerbating this interservice rivalry were disagreements between the Hawaiian Department and the 14th Naval District, which administered the Pearl Harbor base. Efforts to work out compromises followed the pattern set in 1926, when an extended discussion over a variety of joint air defense issues ended in a complete deadlock. The army demanded the navy be responsible for long-range reconnaissance at sea, while at the same time maintaining that its own bombers could do the job better. The navy wanted army aviators restricted to supporting the land defenses. The ongoing battle over ownership of Luke Field poisoned relations: the navy complained that army aircraft ignored safety precautions and the army complained of constant petty harassment, such as the navy's occasional refusal to ferry army personnel to Ford Island.[43] Even more infuriating to the army was the navy's persistent effort to block the acquisition of property next to Pearl Harbor for what would eventually become Hickam Air Field on the grounds that the navy might someday require this area itself. Feelings ran high, for both services perceived the conflict in almost apocalyptic terms. To Lieutenant Robert J. Brown, "Any move to turn over Ford's Island to the Navy Air Service involved our entire policy of coastal defense and will be the entering wedge of the Navy to eventually control the entire U.S. Air Force. This lays the foundation for a militaristic oligarchy controlling the sea and air power contrary to all principles of American government."[44] Brown's paranoia was misplaced, but the navy's position in Hawaii—that the army provide air defense for Pearl but under no circumstances inconvenience naval activities or take over the overwater reconnaissance patrols—was unreasonable, impractical, and ultimately disastrous.

Interservice rivalry frustrated joint action and contributed to an atmosphere of mutual suspicion. In 1935, when the navy stationed several long-range patrol planes at Pearl, Drum accused it of trying to form an Advanced Striking Force, which would not only preempt the strategic bombing mission assigned to the General Headquarters (GHQ) Air Force of the U.S. Army Air Corps, but the air defense of Oahu. He wrote MacArthur, "We are indeed facing a serious problem with the Navy's determination to secure air supremacy in these islands. We must block them by all means."[45] As would become tragically clear in 1941, the two services never resolved the crucial issue of who was responsible for long-range overwater reconnaissance. Drum's solution, which illustrates the willingness of local commanders to use national issues for their own gain, was to have GHQ Air Force station its bombers in Hawaii and for the army to assume the navy's overwater patrolling duties. When the Joint Board rejected this, Drum's chief of staff portrayed it as a disastrous defeat: the refusal to authorize long-range air patrols "really admits that the Army has nothing to do but hold the islands for seventy days until the Navy arrives and they will then handle the situation. . . . we are permitting the Navy to do a mission which is the Army's in peace and war. . . . As I read between the lines I see a steady infiltration of Navy control, which if we do not combat it, will result in due time in the navy writing the defense plans for the Hawaiian Islands."[46]

It is clear, then, that contrary to prevalent opinion, the army did anticipate an aircraft carrier attack on Hawaii and frequently rehearsed its defense. The problem was not, as critics have charged, that ground-bound generals dismissed both aviation and the aircraft carrier. Nor was the problem that short-sighted and narrow-minded officers refused to recognize the implications of such incidents as the 1932 carrier raid on Oahu. Rather the opposite is true. The army took the threat of a Japanese air attack so seriously it devoted a great deal of attention to planning and testing Oahu's air defenses. The trouble was that the results of these tests, which would appear so obvious after 7 December 1941, were equivocal and ambiguous to those called upon to interpret them at the time. Further complicating an accurate assessment was interservice rivalry, which led army and navy officers to view Hawaiian air defense as a valuable prize in a continuous turf war. The navy's successful carrier raid in the 1932 exercise was downplayed by army umpires, just as the army's successful strikes on the carriers were ignored by naval officers. In 1934 and 1935, joint exercises that might have tested Hawaii's air defenses were twice frustrated by the navy's refusal to allow the defender's air force any mission but antisubmarine warfare and providing an escort when the fleet entered Pearl Harbor.[47] Similarly, the chief of staff of the Hawaiian Air Force later claimed that in 1940 and 1941 he repeatedly tried to involve the navy in planning for joint air defense but was told the fleet could secure the base by itself.[48] The disaster at Pearl Harbor was due less to the military's lack of foresight and imagination than to its persistent failure to put aside differences and cooperate for the common defense.

At the same time it emerged as the dominant threat to the overseas territories, aviation also beckoned as their potential savior. As early as 1920, one Hawaiian Department air officer predicted that "the defense of the Hawaiian Islands will be primarily from the air and will be based on the bombing and destruction of [the] enemy fleet and transports before a landing on Oahu can be effected."[49] In 1921 Major General Mason Patrick, chief of the Air Service, urged that the Philippines be provided with a force of 237 airplanes, a number he believed sufficient to defend Manila Bay, prevent amphibious landings, strike at the enemy fleet, and even bomb Formosa, thereby causing Japan to seek an armistice. Major John P. Smith argued that the Philippines could serve for "a raid on Japan's wooden cities by aeroplanes"—an idea that would be revived in 1940.[50] According to one officer, the 1923 Chesapeake Bay experiments, in which airplanes sank captured warships, "indicate[d] clearly the effectiveness of aerial attack against vessels, and the lessons learned as a result of such experiments definitely establish[ed] the fact that one of the most efficient auxiliary means to be emphasized in the defense of the Insular Possessions and the Panama Canal from sea attack is the use of bombs dropped from aircraft."[51] With the combination of enthusiasm and impracticality that typified prewar military aviators, the 1924 plan for the Philippines' lone fighter squadron, the 3rd Pursuit, called for the "destruction of all resources of a hostile nation within striking distance of the Philippine Islands, and the defense of our own resources from hostile aggression."[52]

One of the most visionary spokesmen for the airplane's potential, both as threat and protector, was Brigadier General William Mitchell, who in late 1923 set out for a tour of the Pacific's air defenses. The ensuing report has become legendary, in part because of its prediction of a Japanese air attack on Pearl Harbor. As with many of Mitchell's predictions, his Pearl Harbor attack was a curious mixture of the prescient and the preposterous. For example, although he was correct in the relatively minor prediction of a dawn attack, he was completely wrong in anticipating that the Japanese navy would remain in home waters and that there was "nothing whatever to fear from so-called naval airplane carriers, because not only can they not operate efficiently on the high seas but, even if they could, they cannot place sufficient aircraft in the air at one time to insure a concerted operation."[53] In Mitchell's scenario the Japanese loaded ten submarines with six pursuit planes each and ferried them across the Pacific to the isolated Hawaiian island of Niihau. After a secret air base was built, the pursuit airplanes would be joined by 100 bombers flying in from Midway. This combined air fleet would then deliver a series of devastating attacks with gas and explosives on the Ford Island airdrome, Pearl Harbor fuel tanks, Schofield Barracks, and Honolulu Harbor.[54] There was only one way to avert this danger. The army must station some 650 airplanes on Hawaii, build airfields on outlying islands, and take over all patrolling duties within a 200-mile radius of the Islands.[55]

Mitchell might have secured a more favorable reception for his views had he not peppered his report on Hawaii with such comments as "in proportion to the strength and ability of the United States, the organization, command, training, and supply of the air forces in Hawaii were by far the poorest that I inspected in any country."[56] Department commander Summerall fired back a seven-page response to Chief of Air Service Patrick denouncing Mitchell's "superficial impressions and academic discussions" and termed his report "unwarranted," "misleading," "not thoroughly informed," and "in error."[57] In a slyly vindictive anecdote, Summerall recounted that Mitchell had announced he would fly from Oahu to Kauai and back along the very route he later assured readers that hundreds of Japanese aviators could fly without loss. When high winds prevented this flight, Mitchell decided to take a boat over to Kauai and then fly back, but, having arrived in Kauai, complete with airplane, Mitchell had again found the weather too dangerous and returned by ship. Patrick, perhaps aware that Summerall was a leading candidate for chief of staff, soothed him by describing Mitchell's piece as a "theoretical treatise" useful perhaps a decade hence when airplane development was further advanced.[58]

A decade after Mitchell's report, Hawaiian Department commander Drum presented a radical new scheme for defending Hawaii by air. Like his friend MacArthur, Drum had little regard for the decisions of his Washington superiors and insisted that "no matter how the Joint Board writes its conception of the mission of these islands in national defense, the Pearl Harbor naval base is not the sole or only objective of the defense."[59] He proposed that the garrison's mission be shifted from protecting Pearl Harbor to serving as the center of an "active barrier" linking Alaska, Panama, and the West Coast in a "defensive sea area" patrolled and defended by the army's new long-range bombers.[60] Hawaii's air forces should be increased by additional observation and pursuit squadrons and by strengthening its bomber force from 18 to 117—all of them the most modern airplanes available—as well as by building airfields on the outlying islands. Finally, in accord with the MacArthur-Pratt agreement, the army must be given control of all air reconnaissance in the Hawaiian theater, a 300-mile radius from the islands, and naval aviation be strictly confined to fleet activities.[61]

Although parts of Drum's study appealed to Washington strategists, the proposal was rejected. The WPD's director, Stanley D. Embick, approved Drum's advocacy of a Alaska-Hawaii-Panama defensive perimeter but was unwilling to entrust Pacific defense to a weapon as unproven as the airplane. Nor did he believe that Hawaii's primary strategic role was to be the center of a 3,000-mile patrol area: the mission of Hawaii's air force was the "direct defense of Hawaiian Islands."[62] Embick's conclusions were supported by a WPD study that concluded—with remarkably poor foresight—that Oahu's "security is assured so long as our Fleet is strategically present and free to act." The WPD was unconvinced by Drum's insistence that Hawaii could be held by a reinforced military garrison. Rather it believed that without naval relief "Oahu could probably not maintain itself indefinitely against determined attacks, especially since it could be cut off from the mainland and effectively isolated." Noting that the recent agreement on "Joint Action of the Army and Navy" gave the navy responsibility for "over-the-horizon operations" and for "information of hostile forces approaching from overseas," the WPD argued "the Army can not and should not shoulder the Navy's part of the burden."[63]

Drum encountered equal resistance from the one group that, on the face of it, should have upheld him. Although the Air Corps shared his conviction that the airplane was the ultimate coast defense weapon, and that more airplanes were needed, it balked at subordinating bombers to local defense. Major General Frank M. Andrews, head of the nation's strategic bombing reserve—GHQ Air Force—had earlier enlisted Drum's support to withdraw bombers from tactical commands and concentrate them for Pacific defense. But Andrews wanted this bomber force stationed in the continental United States, free to deploy against any foe, while Drum insisted it be stationed in Hawaii. Moreover, Drum challenged the contention advanced by the Air Corps that it could reinforce Hawaii by air and complained that "the overseas garrisons are being sacrificed to build up the GHQ Air Force, located in the mainland." Such would be strategic folly: "no possible emergency in Europe or any other part of the world can spring up demanding such immediate action by the GHQ Air Force in the mainland as may be required by the air forces in these islands."[64] The Air Corps hearkened back to Mahan: like the battle fleet, its bombers must be concentrated for a knockout blow and should never be committed to positional defense.

With the outbreak of war in Europe there was a rapid, and unsuccessful attempt to revive the Pacific air forces. In part this was a result of the huge growth in the Air Corps after 1939, but much of it was due to a new confidence that air power was finally able to live up to the promise of defending the overseas outposts. The Pacific forces now had first call on airplanes, including the precious B-17 heavy bombers.[65] The most dramatic effort was in the Philippines. In 1940 the War Department shifted from its long-standing policy of ignoring the archipelago to investigating the possibility of stationing an enormous force of 441 airplanes on Luzon, including a squadron of B-17s.[66] According to Secretary of War Henry L. Stimson, in July and August 1941 the Japanese movement on French Indochina prompted a crisis in Japanese-American relations that coincided with a new optimism that the Philippines might serve as a base for air attacks on Japan. Chief of Staff Marshall, who had earlier written off the islands, now concluded they were of "great strategic importance, as they constitute both a Naval and Air Base upon the immediate flank of the Japanese southern movement."[67] Citing the "contagious optimism of General Douglas MacArthur" and the "sudden and startling success" of the B-17 in England, military officials convinced Stimson that the Philippines "could become a self-sustaining fortress capable of blockading the China Sea by air power."[68] In November, Marshall told correspondent Robert Sherrod that the Americans were pouring aircraft into the Philippines and trying to inform Japan's civilian leaders of the danger posed by bombing raids on Japanese cities. Sherrod was impressed with Marshall's briefing and confided to his editor that should war occur, the United States "will fight mercilessly. Flying fortresses will be dispatched immediately to set the paper cities of Japan on fire. There wont [sic] be any hesitation about bombing civilians—it will be all-out."[69]

As 7 December demonstrated, the results of this frenzied effort to put the nation's Pacific defenses in order fell short of expectations. The influx of men and equipment and the release of millions of dollars could not overcome decades of neglect. Samuel E. Anderson remembered that the buildup of Hawaii's air defenses began in 1939, but when he left two years later the system was still in its infancy, with an untried combat control center, officers on the mainland for training, and the first radar barely installed. The Philippines air defense system was almost nonexistent; indeed, in 1940 WPD planners estimated it would cost $23 million to build airfields able to handle the P-40s and B-17s necessary for the archipelago's protection.[70] It was all but impossible for the Hawaiian and Philippine departments to organize the newly arrived pursuit and bombardment squadrons into a coherent air defense. Many of their pilots had just earned their wings and required hours of training in formation flying, tactics, and gunnery. The dozens of airplanes that arrived on the docks of Manila and Honolulu did not translate into immediate combat strength: they had to be uncrated, assembled, and tested, a process that often took months and was hampered by a dearth of spare parts and ammunition. In Hawaii only six of the twelve B-17s were in commission on 7 December. When the experienced pilots of 35th Pursuit Group arrived in the Philippines barely three weeks before the Japanese attack, they discovered that the only aircraft available were obsolete and badly worn P-35s, an airplane none of them had ever flown. Despite MacArthur's enthusiastic pronouncements, Colonel Harold H. George proved accurate when he told his fighter pilots on 6 December 1941, "You are not necessarily a suicide squadron, but you are Goddamn near it!"[71]

CHAPTER 10

The Last Years of the Pacific Army

As noted earlier, except for the different ethnic composition of the troops, an observer in 1930 would have been hard pressed to tell the Hawaiian and Philippine forces apart. But by 1940 the situation had changed dramatically. During the 1930s, Hawaii was finally recognized as the center of America's Pacific defenses, the outlying bastion of a perimeter than ran from Alaska to Panama. In contrast, the Philippines lay in strategic limbo, the subject of a bitter clash between those who wanted to withdraw as soon as decently possible and those who favored increasing the nation's military commitment. In Hawaii, the decade witnessed a slow but steadily growing influx of men and matériel and public works projects that directly benefited the health and combat ability of the garrison. By the end of the decade, it was generally agreed that the Hawaiian garrison was ready for any challenge. The Philippines remained in flux, with the islands' defense policy changing virtually with each new commander. Cautious realists, convinced the garrison was doomed, recommended that the Carabao Army immediately take up defensive positions on the Bataan Peninsula to defend Manila Bay. Enthusiastic optimists, convinced that aviation and Filipino manpower had finally reversed the archipelago's decades-long military inferiority to Japan, urged that the defenders meet the enemy on the beaches. The result was constant shifts in defense plans and an inordinate amount of confusion over what exactly the Philippine forces were supposed to do. More dangerously, there was a growing trend toward independence, even insubordination, as Philippine commanders went their own way and Washington failed to curb them.

As the lyrics of "Manila's Own" 31st Infantry Regiment's march proclaimed,

American soldiers were "a Yankee clan in a foreign land," a land only slightly less alien to these khaki-clad "sundowners" than it had been to the soldiers who arrived in 1898.[1] At the beginning of the 1930s, support for maintaining ground forces in the islands was weakened by the army's financial woes during the Depression, the Democrats' 1932 landslide, increased Japanese military power, and the growing movement for Philippine independence. However, until 1935, the last year of MacArthur's term as chief of staff, the War Department and the Joint Board continued to argue for the islands' retention, to insist they could be defended, and to plan for their immediate relief in wartime.[2] But such arguments were no longer either popular or justifiable. With the Tydings-McDuffie Act of 1934, Congress mandated the creation of an independent Philippine republic in 1946, and in 1935 the caretaker Commonwealth government was sworn in. Its first action was to pass a defense bill organizing its own army. Soon the Carabao Army began to break up, as Filipino soldiers transferred to Commonwealth service. By 1940, the American forces were in the process of shifting from guardians of empire to military advisors, striving to create native armed forces that could assume the burden of protecting the archipelago when the last U.S. Army transport sailed away.

Throughout the 1930s, the military threat to the Philippine Islands remained the same: a Japanese invasion of overwhelming strength, perhaps initiated by a surprise attack on the Manila Bay defenses, that would occur either prior to or simultaneous with a declaration of war. Planners envisioned an invasion force of at least four divisions (80,000 troops) landing either at Bataan, Lingayen Gulf, or one of the bays in Southern Luzon, with concomitant feints at other locations. Once ashore, the enemy would swiftly build an air base and launch an offensive to capture the Manila Bay defenses as rapidly as possible.[3] If anything had changed since the 1920s, it was that Japanese military prowess had increased. Having rejected the Washington Treaties, Japan had undertaken a rapid naval and military buildup. By the mid-1930s, Philippine Department war plans rated "the strength and efficiency of the Orange Army . . . greater than at any time in recent years": Japan's troops were veterans of years of warfare in China, its high command experienced, its transport and logistics excellent, and its morale and training the equal of American Regulars and better than the Scouts.[4]

Despite Japan's growing strength, the garrison's fundamental purpose—to hold Manila Bay as a base for the U.S. fleet and relieving expeditionary force—remained overambitious. In 1936 the Joint Board changed this to "delay the enemy at Subic Bay and elsewhere as may be practicable without jeopardizing the timely withdrawal of mobile ground forces to the Bataan Peninsula; and to defend the entrance to Manila Bay."[5] This shift acknowledged earlier estimates of the navy's ability to relieve the garrison within forty-five days as unrealistic; the Manila Bay defenses must hold out for at least six months. In Washington, army and navy planners recognized it might actually take between two and three years for the American fleet to reach the islands. Thus, as throughout its existence, the Philippine garrison's appointed task bore little relation to its capabilities.[6]

Unlike the Philippines, Hawaii's strategic importance was never questioned. Indeed, in some ways, it became even more vital in the 1930s as the United States began to withdraw from the Philippines. Officers accepted Lieutenant Colonel Samuel T. Mackall's argument that holding Hawaii conveyed two vital advantages. Offensively, it was the "first step in an advance to the western Pacific." Defensively, it was an "outpost to our line of resistance in the Pacific coast, and no hostile force could invade the coast without first securing possession of the islands. No hostile force based on the island in the Pacific more distant from our coast than is Hawaii could operate against the coast with much prospect of success."[7] A 1935 WPD study agreed that the islands were "our most westerly possession capable of a prolonged defense" and of "great strategic value primarily from a naval point of view, since it facilitates our control of the Eastern North Pacific, as well as offensive operations to the westward."[8] This emphasis on Hawaii's double mission was no coincidence: regardless of whether they favored a strong military presence in the Philippines and a war plan based on an immediate offensive into the western Pacific or a Alaska-Hawaii-Panama defensive perimeter and a war plan based on continental defense, officers recognized that Hawaii was essential.

At the beginning of the 1930s, the Hawaiian Department still retained the mission assigned by the Joint Board in 1919: "protect the naval base at Pearl Harbor against naval or aerial bombardment, against enemy sympathizers, and against hostile expeditionary forces, supported or unsupported by a hostile fleet."[9] This mission—drawn up when the garrison numbered but 4,700 officers and men and when the U.S. fleet was divided between two oceans, the Philippines still very much an American possession, and the Anglo-Japanese alliance still in force—called for the garrison to maintain an independent defense for four months. By 1940, conditions had greatly changed: over 25,000 troops guarded Oahu, the battle fleet was in the Pacific, the newly formed strategic air reserve offered the hope that Hawaii might be protected and reinforced by air, the Orange plans called for the immediate reinforcement of Hawaii, and Japan had become the sole threat. In 1934 the Joint Board expanded the Pineapple Army's task to "defend Pearl Harbor Naval base against a) damage from naval and aerial bombardment or by enemy sympathizers. b) attack by an enemy expeditionary force or forces supported or unsupported by enemy fleet or fleets."[10] This accorded with the board's view that the peril of invasion was far less serious than the danger of a surprise attack by naval gunfire, air raid, blocking operations, or sabotage. In 1936, it assigned the joint army-navy mission "to hold Oahu as a main outlying naval base," with the army's task "to hold Oahu against attacks by sea, land, and air forces and against hostile sympathizers."[11] At the same time, the growing power of the U.S. Navy led the board to reduce the number of days that Oahu's defenders need plan for a self-sustained defense from 120 to 70. With the decision to station the Pacific Fleet at Pearl, the mission was changed in February 1941 to include protection of the fleet while it was in port.[12]

Hawaii's commanders developed a fairly realistic approach to the threat. As the 1933 joint army-navy local defense plan acknowledged, the strategic importance of the Hawaiian Islands, and especially Pearl Harbor, in a Pacific war make it obvious that Japan would "possibly prior to a declaration of war and almost surely early in the war, endeavor to cripple the naval facilities in these Islands in order to delay, if not to prevent, the operation of our fleet to the westward."[13] In contrast to the extensive debate that raged in the Philippines between citadel and beach defense, throughout the 1930s the basic tactical framework for land defense established by Summerall in 1924—sector defense, beach cordons, supporting firepower, and mobile reinforcements—remained largely unchallenged. Reflecting the dictates of Washington and their own appreciation of the worst case scenario, successive Hawaiian Department commanders devoted the bulk of their attention to defending against invasion, naval bombardment, and internal uprising. As is too often overlooked, probably not until 1941 was the Imperial Japanese Navy's aerial arm capable of the shattering stroke it delivered on 7 December: it did not have enough aircraft carriers, it had no carrier tactical organization, its airplanes lacked sufficient range, and it did not have suitable bombs and torpedoes. Throughout the 1930s, however, if it had been able to overcome the considerable logistical problems, the Japanese navy did have the ability both to bombard Pearl Harbor from the sea and to deliver an amphibious attack on Oahu. Based on the information available to them, therefore, Hawaii's defenders were justified in continuing their efforts to protect the coasts from such threats. Although in retrospect their emphasis was mistaken, the fault was not military incompetence, laziness, or an arrogant dismissal of Japanese capabilities. Rather it represented a plausible and reasoned response to the military situation at the time.

The Hawaiian Department in the 1930s was fortunate to be commanded by many of the army's leading intellects—Fox Conner (1928–30), William Lassiter (1930–31), Briant H. Wells (1931–34), Hugh A. Drum (1935–37), and

Charles D. Herron (1940–41)—and they fostered the practice, at least in their staffs, of intensive and critical examination. Experimentation was constant, so that succeeding commanders built upon their forerunners' efforts. The concurrent improvement of Oahu's road system and the arrival of motorized field artillery, trucks, and tanks allowed commanders to increase the firepower of the beach cordons and to withdraw to create a larger and more mobile reserve.[14] Conner's 1930 Primary Tactical Plan abandoned efforts to guard every beach in favor of building up firepower on the most vulnerable landing points. By 1928 each mile of defended waterfront was assigned twenty machine guns, sited to begin firing at 1,800 yards, so that "the shallow waters and beaches are literally flailed with fire."[15] The beach defenses were further strengthened with dozens of 75-millimeter guns, able to hit waterborne targets at 4,000 feet, shift positions rapidly, and then fire again. Lassiter refined air-ground and infantry-artillery coordination. Wells improved marksmanship and conducted a series of tests that demonstrated the strength of Oahu's defenses.[16] Drum further increased the defenders' firepower and restructured the sector commands. Herron made an extensive study of both the existing and past tactical plans and, having concluded that the general concepts for land defense were sound, focused on gunnery, rapid deployment of the reserve, and physical training.[17]

The land defenses of Oahu were tested repeatedly in field problems, tactical exercises, and departmental and joint maneuvers. These revealed that the tactical plan was sound, but the mobile forces were too few to execute it. In Grand Joint Exercise No. 4 in 1932, the defenders' lack of manpower forced them to uncover the west coast, allowing a constructive force of two divisions, in reality fewer than 1,300 soldiers and marines, to make an unopposed landing. Despite having been surprised, within twelve hours the defenders had committed an infantry brigade to a counterattack and were firing on the beachhead with six batteries of 75-millimeter guns, five batteries of 155-millimeter howitzers, two batteries of 155-millimeter cannon, and two twelve-inch mortars. A prominent Marine expert on amphibious assault who witnessed the maneuvers concluded a real attack would have been repulsed with horrible casualties. Nevertheless, the Hawaiian Department's commander concluded that Oahu must be reinforced, particularly by infantry. The department maneuvers a year later repeated this lesson. The attackers brushed away the weak defensive cordon, which could not delay them sufficiently for artillery to be called in.[18] Although the garrison was increased to 18,500 in 1936, the lack of infantry continued to plague commanders until 1940, when the nation's rearmament allowed the War Department to send thousands of troops to the islands. By the time of the Japanese attack the garrison of Oahu stood at some 43,000 soldiers, many of them recent draftees or local recruits. With sufficient troops manning hundreds of machine guns, field artillery pieces, chemical warfare weapons, and beach defenses, the mobile forces of the Hawaiian Division, now broken into the 24th and 25th Divisions, were a formidable deterrent to invasion.

Hawaii's coast defenses remained relatively unchanged during the 1930s, in part because they were believed to be more than adequate to repel any attack on the two crucial harbors. Nevertheless, as tensions with Japan increased through the decade, local officers devoted much attention to maximizing their firepower and effectiveness. Some, following the Coast Artillery's traditional emphasis, believed the primary danger lay in battleship bombardment and favored placing more sixteen-inch guns near Pearl Harbor. Others feared invasion from the north and west coasts and urged the deployment of large numbers of eight-inch railroad artillery and 155-millimeter guns throughout the island. Ultimately, the army compromised: in 1934 twelve eight-inch railroad guns arrived, and Fort Barrette, a single battery fort mounting two sixteen-inch guns, was established near Makakilo Gulch, overlooking the west lochs of Pearl Harbor.[19] That same year the Hawaii Separate Coast Artillery Brigade completed a network of fire-control stations, allowing observers to call down heavy artillery on any beach in the island. Although they were never tested, there is no reason to doubt contemporary analysis that "an enemy fleet or convoy could come within range of the southern defenses only at great hazard to capital ships and transports" and that the Oahu's other coasts could be covered with "considerable fire."[20]

Less faith could be placed in Oahu's ground-based antiaircraft defenses, which tactical exercises had repeatedly demonstrated were inadequate. Successive department commanders warned the War Department that without effective long-range reconnaissance or pursuit airplanes, Oahu's protection from air attack fell to machine guns and three-inch cannon, and there were far too few of these to do the job. Hawaiian commanders begged for antiaircraft guns to cover Oahu: typical was Drum's 1935 insistence that the department's three-inch guns and fifty-caliber machine guns be increased from 24 each to 536 and 132 respectively.[21] Despite repeated demands, until the 1940 buildup, Oahu's antiaircraft capability resided largely in the 64th Coast Artillery Regiment, whose primary task was to protect Pearl Harbor, and in the World War I–vintage machine guns and light artillery pieces emplaced next to the fortifications. As the pilots who towed the long target sleeves during firing practice continually emphasized, Oahu's antiaircraft defenses were entirely inadequate; even under ideal conditions, it was a rare gunner who could hit an aerial target.[22]

In Hawaii, the 1930s witnessed a profound change in the Pineapple Army. Money, previously so tight, began to pour in the last half of the decade; by 1938 one officer estimated the War Department had spent over $160 million on Hawaii's defenses and was spending a further $18 million a year. A series of public works projects finally built modern barracks for the long-suffering soldiers at Schofield and, more important, constructed Hickam Air Field and a road system capable of carrying the Hawaiian Division to any threatened beach. Training time increased, new weapons and equipment arrived, and there was a consensus "that beyond a doubt, an emergency would find all members of combat units of this command so trained they could efficiently perform any combat duty which they could reasonably be expected to undertake."[23]

In contrast to the relatively steady, if selective, improvement in the Hawaiian garrison, Philippine defense remained uncertain and variable. During MacArthur's tenure as chief of staff, the army's Pacific strategy centered on an aggressive offensive against Japan based, in part, on the immediate reinforcement of the Philippines. This shift occurred despite the opposition of the Philippine commanders themselves, who not only warned that the local defenses were unable to hold out even for the limited time envisioned by Washington, but questioned whether it was strategically sound to defend the islands at all. As had occurred in 1929 with MacArthur's Philippine defense plan, those charged with defending the archipelago made military plans that were radically different from the Orange plans being developed in Washington. Even more dangerous, War Department officers recognized this dichotomy but refused to force compliance on their overseas subordinates: a WPD director blandly wrote the chief of staff during a controversy with the Philippines command that the "preparation of *plans* is a responsibility of the Department Commander and the War Department has never amended the local commander's plan."[24]

In his first year as chief of staff, MacArthur made some effort to push his Philippine Department 1929 Basic War Plan, informing the secretary of war of the need to raise 45,000 local troops and expostulating that "the Philippines can be successfully defended by the employment of native manpower against any probable attack."[25] But at the same time, he directed the WPD to undertake a study of U.S. policy in the Philippines based, in part, on the assumption that it was "not practicable to build up a local defense for the Philippines that would be strong enough to hold out against a determined attack for an indefinite period without relief from the United States."[26] Whatever his real sentiments, MacArthur soon found he could barely wheedle sufficient funds to maintain the Regular Army; obtaining appropriations for raising his proposed three Filipino reserve divisions was manifestly impossible. MacArthur then turned his attention to inserting a two-division relief force for the Philippines via Suez and securing Chief of Naval Operations Pratt's agreement that upon the outbreak of war there would be a "quick movement of the U.S. Fleet to the Philippine area."[27]

In the Philippines, MacArthur's 1929 plan had barely survived his departure. The 1931 Philippine defense project noted that the "War Department approve[d] in principle" the 1929 plan, but that there was no money to implement it.[28] In 1932 Philippine Department commander Major General Ewing E. Booth, declared the 1929 plan not only based on nonexistent manpower, but fundamentally flawed. The underlying tactical principles were those of Haan's decade-old "Positive System of Coast Defense" and they followed its organization of defense in depth by sector, beach defense cordons, and supporting forces. Haan had estimated it required 8,088 combatant troops to defend a twenty-mile beach front, and then only with support by motorized transport, copious amounts of field artillery and machine guns, excellent communications with the rear, aviation, railroad guns, naval support, and all the other matériel of modern warfare. But the U.S. forces in the Philippines had virtually none of these. To guard roughly 100 miles of accessible beaches there were some 6,500 mobile forces, who lacked heavy artillery, tanks, chemical warfare equipment, and reserves. Nor did Booth approve of the 1929 plan's proposal to use the Carabao Army's scarce manpower as cadres for new Filipino divisions. Rejecting its call for a full mobilization of local manpower, he determined that "initial operations must be conducted mainly with existing units. Fighting strength must be conserved."[29] Therefore the Philippine Department's 1932 Orange plan relegated mobilization of a Filipino division from the "First Phase"—the initial three weeks of war—to the second phase of operations, including the caveat that this would occur only "if time and a reserve of trained man-power permits."[30] Since local planners concluded that Manila itself would fall before the First Phase was over, postponing the mobilization of Filipino manpower in effect made much of the 1929 plan irrelevant.

Booth's reservations are symptomatic of the strong revisionist sentiment of the time. In April 1933, Stanley D. Embick, the commanding general of the Harbor Defenses of Manila and Subic Bays, said that an extensive study of the nation's Pacific policies since 1907 convinced him that "the Philippine Islands have become a military liability of a constantly increasing gravity." In what must have been a painful admission for a coast artilleryman intimately involved with both their planning and construction, he declared that the strategic importance of the Manila Bay fortifications was "relatively negligible." He concluded that "to carry out the present Orange Plan—with its provisions for the early dispatch of our fleet to Philippine waters—would literally be an act of madness."[31]

In a covering letter, Booth concurred with Embick: "there appears to be no tactical or strategical reason for [Corregidor's] defense. The sole purpose . . . is to keep the American Flag flying in Manila Bay." He believed that the nation's "unsound military policy" was due to a variety of factors: "diplomatic considerations" dictated the defense of Manila Bay; "political conditions" required a colonial garrison; and "economic conditions" mandated that the cost of this military presence be reduced.[32] But Booth cautioned that subordinating sensible strategy to nonmilitary considerations entailed substantial risks: an Asian nation attacking the archipelago would force the United States into a unwanted, costly, and distant war to defend an insignificant possession. More seriously, he feared an aroused American population would ignore military realities and demand the immediate dispatch of a relief expedition, with disastrous military consequences.

Like Embick, Booth favored an independent and neutral Philippines, the withdrawal of all American military forces, and the creation of a Alaska-Hawaii-Panama defensive perimeter. He interpreted the garrison's mission to defend Manila Bay in very restrictive terms; the Philippine Department's plans should focus only on protecting the fortifications with as little expenditure of men and money as possible. His 1933 Orange Plan reduced the 1929 proposal to create three Filipino divisions down to a modest increase of 1,717 recruits to bring the harbor defenses up to wartime strength. It rejected sector and beach defense: at the first sign of Japanese attack, soldiers would set to work transferring supplies, equipment, and men to Bataan and Corregidor. Mobile operations would be strictly limited: the 31st Infantry would immediately deploy to Corregidor as a beach defense force, while the Philippine Division concentrated near Stotsenburg and delayed the enemy, insuring that its own route to Bataan was never severed. When driven back, it would take up prepared positions along the Mariveles peaks, sufficiently deep to prevent the enemy from shelling Corregidor, and hold out as long as possible.

In many respects, the 1933 plan was a reversion to the Corregidor-first strategy adopted prior to World War I. Its reliance on citadel defense was due not only to Embick's assurance that the fortress could withstand a year-long siege, but also to the strategic legacy of J. Franklin Bell. Booth had served with Bell in two tours in the islands; he probably did not need the reminder of another disciple, Johnson Hagood, that "the fundamental principle upon which Bell operated was that the defense of the Philippine Islands, in the last analysis, consisted of the defense of Corregidor Island."[33] But there was more than pipe dreams and nostalgia in the 1933 plan. In 1932, 1934, and 1935 it was tested in the departmental maneuvers; according to Booth's successor, these "conclusively proved it is possible to hold the defensive position selected and from that position as a base to oppose a hostile advance from the north by successive delaying actions."[34] Of equal importance, the 1933 plan fulfilled Booth's goal of reconciling the nation's political, economic and diplomatic goals with its minimal military resources in the Philippines.

Washington's reaction to Booth's revision of the 1929 plan is interesting. Booth wrote a personal letter to WPD director Charles E. Kilbourne denying he had "scrapped" MacArthur's 1929 plan. Rather, he had focused on the areas that the 1929 plan had glossed over—in particular the First Phase of the "Auxiliary Plan" which concerned the Philippine Department's reaction to immediate Japanese attack. Kilbourne was not fooled. In a letter to MacArthur, he drew attention to the fact that Booth's letter came at a time when the army and navy were discussing MacArthur's proposal to reinforce the Philippine garrison with two divisions sent through the Suez Canal: a plan that both Booth and Embick considered "almost suicidal."[35] He noted the differences between the two plans. Whereas MacArthur's 1929 plan was predicated on a Filipino army that existed only on paper, Booth's scheme made use only of existing forces. Whereas the 1929 plan called for throwing the invaders back on the beaches, Booth argued that the best the garrison could do was hold a 20,000-foot perimeter at the tip of the Bataan Peninsula. More significantly, Embick and Booth maintained the defense of the Philippines was a strategic mistake and that best policy was to withdraw to a Alaska-Hawaii-Panama perimeter. Kilbourne believed Booth had submitted Embick's views, and his own supporting letter, to force Washington both to reconsider the plans for reinforcement and to acknowledge the wide gulf between the garrison's mission and its capabilities.

In response to the Booth-Embick proposition, Kilbourne wrote a long and closely reasoned memorandum to MacArthur. He noted that Japan had materially increased its military and naval strength since the 1928 war plan and "undoubtedly could overcome such resistance as could be made by our present mobile forces in the Philippines[,] successfully land on Luzon, and invest the Manila Bay from the landward side. Then, by utilizing her chain of islands she could rapidly establish, in the Manila Bay area[,] an air force of sufficient strength to make extremely hazardous any attempt to occupy Manila Bay by our naval forces and any attempt to [relieve] Luzon with reinforcements." However, Japan might not choose to risk the losses to its warships and aircraft that an attack on Manila Bay might entail until the U.S. battle fleet was destroyed. Should Orange delay major operations on Luzon long enough for the relief expedition to arrive, there was a "reasonable chance" that the United

States could repel the invasion, with benefits that would be incalculable: "Manila Bay, in spite of the lack of naval repair facilities, has exceptional value in the furtherance of the ultimate plan. Not only the resources of Luzon would be available to the fleet, but protected by the fortifications and a strong land-based air force, Manila Bay could be developed into a satisfactory fleet base which would be a long step toward a prompt and favorable decision in the war."[36] In any case, Kilbourne argued, the discussion was somewhat academic. Even under the most optimistic timetable, the Philippines would not become independent until 1946 and until then the United States was responsible for the islands' defense.

The positions outlined in the Embick-Booth and Kilbourne papers reveal in microcosm the persistent debate over the Philippines in the last decade before the war. To Embick and Booth, the weakening of the U.S. position in the Far East, the unsuitability and exposed position of Manila Bay as a base, and the growth of Japanese power made the defense of the Manila Bay strategically suspect, and the dispatch of the U.S. fleet to its relief "an act of madness." Believing the Philippines were indefensible and the nation's Far Eastern interests negligible, they wanted to withdraw to an easily defensible and strategically vital Alaska-Hawaii-Panama line. Kilbourne believed the United States still had vital interests in the Far East and that the Philippines were so valuable as a base that great risks were justified. Moreover, it was the army's task to fulfill the policies of its political masters; since the U.S. government's policy was to defend the Philippines until independence, the army's duty was to carry this out. It does not appear to have occurred to Kilbourne that the nation's political leaders might well wish to revise a policy if they were told that those charged with executing it were convinced their task was hopeless.

Booth's successor, Major General Frank Parker, was a staunch imperialist who believed that the nation should retain the Philippines to insure stability in Asia, to protect Far Eastern markets, and to continue the moral tutelage of the Filipinos. But whatever his emotional commitment to the retention of the islands, Parker was both professional enough, and realist enough, to accept that the best that could happen was for the garrison to sell itself as dearly as possible. New developments in military technology, the decision to grant independence to the Philippines, and the change in the Asian balance of power had "nullified" the value of Corregidor and made its defense "futile."[37] A visit to Japan impressed him with that country's military power, and he concurred with his intelligence officer's assessment that the Japanese armed forces were aggressive, well trained, and superbly led.[38] In coordinating the revision of the department's Orange plan in 1934 and 1935, Parker followed Booth's basic operational design. This acceptance was bolstered by his own staff's assessment that whatever the immediate tactical benefits of striking the enemy as he landed, beach defense was precluded by the primary mission "to hold the entrances to Manila Bay" and the necessity of assuring both that supplies be sufficient and that soldiers never be committed "at such a distance that any force might cut off our retirement to Bataan."[39] If the United States was unwilling to commit enough men and military resources to defend its vital interests in the islands, it should withdraw immediately and not expose itself to the danger of humiliating defeat. Like Booth, Parker sought to force Washington to make the basic decision as to whether the Philippines should be defended. In March 1934 he and the commander of the Asiatic Fleet, Admiral F. B. Upham, penned a joint declaration stating that, with the existing forces, the garrison's mission under the Orange plan was "impossible of accomplishment."[40]

Washington's response to the Parker-Upham letter was much the same as its response to the Embick-Booth warning. Kilbourne acknowledged the decline in America's position in Asia and the present Philippine garrison's inability to hold Manila Bay. But if the defenders could be reinforced by two divisions, there was "reasonable assurance that Manila Bay can be held." Were this done, Manila Bay would serve as a base and the U.S. fleet could "undertake immediate operations in the western Pacific."[41] The JANPC contributed a fourteen-page memo that reaffirmed that the strategic concepts behind the Orange plan itself were good, but failed to address the Parker-Upham caveat that the existing forces were unable to execute those concepts.[42] The Joint Board followed the JANPC in drawing a sharp distinction between the mission of the Philippine garrison, which it declared "sound," and its inability to accomplish it. The board's solution was to transfer the 15th Infantry from China to Manila, rebuild the harbor defenses, increase the air force from some 30 to 155 airplanes, and construct air bases throughout the islands.[43] In retrospect, it is difficult not to conclude that the board was writing for the record, advocating policies that had little chance of approval. For over a decade Republican administrations, though firmly committed to retention, had done nothing to halt the slow decline in the Philippines' defenses. Yet the board professed to believe that a Democratic Congress and president, grappling with the Depression, committed to Philippine independence, and determined to avoid provoking Japan, would shoulder a much heavier military commitment in the Far East.

When Malin Craig replaced MacArthur as chief of staff in 1935, the pendulum abruptly swung the other way. Craig's director of the War Plans Division was Embick, whose opposition to Philippine defense and whose commitment to a Alaska-Hawaii-Panama defense line were already well known. As noted earlier, one of Embick's first actions on taking charge of the WPD was to table MacArthur's plan for the reinforcement of the Philippines. He then supported Krueger's prolonged battle with the navy members of the JANPC to prevent an immediate offensive into the western Pacific, eventually threatening to reveal this plan to Congress. He was insistent that the "maintenance in the Philippine Islands of military forces adequate to defend a base is wholly impracticable. To create a base that is inadequately defended is to assume a military liability of incalculable magnitude. Such a base would not facilitate our operations in a war conducted by us alone against Japan. It would be lost immediately after the opening of hostilities."[44] To Embick, the solution was to hold the garrison at the minimum level necessary for appearances until independence, and then withdraw as fast as possible.

Ironically, at the very time Washington was adopting the defensive policies urged by its former Philippine commanders, a new commander in the archipelago was moving in the opposite direction. Major General Lucius R. Holbrook became commanding general of the Philippine Department late in 1935, a tour that, portentously, coincided with the arrival of MacArthur as military advisor to the Philippine Commonwealth. Holbrook and MacArthur clashed over equipment and personnel, but they shared an unswerving belief in their ability to defend the archipelago. Holbrook soon came to the conviction that "the most delicate international military situation that confronts the United States Government today is found *right here* and that the most hazardous period for us is *right now*." He wrote his superiors letters that combined threat with enticement: "Should we be defeated by a foreign power, the American people would never forgive the War Department for not having adopted timely and adequate measures for successful defense of the Manila Bay Areas in so far as this is readily within its power. . . . I believe that victory is within our grasp—if timely and adequate preparation is made, and this is an insignificant cost as compared with defeat."[45]

MacArthur's position as military advisor to a Filipino government preparing for total independence in 1945 did not change his conviction that the United States must maintain its military presence in the Philippines. He had no patience with those who advocated withdrawal to the Alaska-Hawaii-Panama defense perimeter, dismissing it as "the big defeatist line."[46] Writing to Hawaiian commander Hugh A. Drum in 1936, he declared that America's "real line of defense" was a Philippines-Alaska perimeter, with Hawaii serving as a "supporting base" for both. This would allow the U.S. Navy to maneuver, freely control the "major strategic lines of communication in the Pacific Ocean," nullify Japan's possession of the Mandated Islands, and place America in "a position of such mastery in the Pacific as to give pause to any forces of aggression." By unstinting assistance to the Commonwealth's Philippine Army and by building and maintaining air and naval bases in Alaska and the Philippines, "the United States can look with perfect serenity upon the developments in the Pacific situation in the decades to come."[47]

The two generals also shared a conviction that the provisions of the Tydings-McDuffie Act, which allowed the president of the United States to call into service all Commonwealth armed forces, made them, in Holbrook's words, "an ever increasing potential Reserve for the American forces in the Philippines." In his efforts to "help develop MacArthur's Army as a reserve force for myself," Holbrook instituted a double assignment system so that each recruit was attached to both a Commonwealth Army and a U.S. Army Organized Reserve unit.[48] He had already announced he was completely revising the Philippine Department's defense projects and plans to conform to "the role the [Commonwealth's] Philippine Army will play in the defense of the Philippines from now on."[49] MacArthur agreed: "The Commonwealth Army, as the reserve element of the American forces during the next ten years, builds up and secures the left flank of our Pacific position which has heretofore been so weak as to create a definite defeatist conception, and even attitude, on our part."[50]

Given their shared conviction that the Philippines should be the primary focus of U.S. Pacific defense and that the Philippine Army could provide the necessary manpower, it is not surprising that the two generals also shared a common disdain for the retreat-to-Bataan tactics of the 1933 Orange plan. MacArthur had already demonstrated his belief that the existing war plans could be freely dispensed with, and he continued to go his independent way. Writing to Captain Bonner Fellers in 1939, he confessed his unfamiliarity with the nation's current Orange plan but assumed it was "the same old plan that was antiquated even before my own tenure as Chief of Staff. Fortunately, the man who is in command at the time will be the man who will determine the main features of campaign. If he is a big man he will pay no more attention to the stereotyped plans that may be filed in the dusty pigeon holes of the War Department than their merit warrants."[51]

Holbrook also had little patience with plans to confine operations to the defense of Manila Bay. Complaining that "my entire staff had become absolutely imbued with the idea of a hopeless defense, visualizing nothing of the future," he set to work "inculcating as fast as possible the idea of an active offensive with no idea of retreat but with a view to whipping the enemy at the beach and employing our best troops for that purpose."[52] The general proposed a new strategy—which he first modestly termed the "Holbrook plan"— formalized in 1936 as the Philippine Department's First Phase Plan Orange.

Luzon was divided into three sectors: the North Sector would cover an attack from Lingayen Gulf, the South Sector an attack between Batangas and Tayabas, and the West Sector an attack on Bataan and the harbor defenses. A motorized reserve would reinforce the threatened sector. Since the department's mobile forces were clearly inadequate to throw back an estimated invasion force of 125,000 Japanese—the South Sector's entire combat contingent was scarcely 1,000 men—the 1936 plan required that "full use will be made of all personnel of the Philippine Army when made available under the provisions of the Tydings-McDuffie Act."[53] To assist this, the G-1 (Personnel) Annex of the plan included a copy of an executive order to be signed by the Philippine president placing the Commonwealth army under the commanding general of the Philippine Department and ordering the recruits to go to mobilization centers where they would be inducted into the U.S. Army with the ranks and grades previously assigned them.

The 1936 plan marked a return to the 1929 plan and a major, and perhaps irrevocable step toward the Philippines-wide defense attempted by MacArthur in December 1941. The rationale for this more inclusive mission as outlined in the department's G-3 (Operations and Plans) Annex would be accepted virtually unchanged by later planners. According to this analysis, the immediate transfer of all troops to the Bataan–Manila Bay area conferred only two advantages: complying with the assigned mission and placing the mobile troops in their final position in good physical condition. The numerous disadvantages included failing to fulfill other subsidiary missions that might be contemplated; abandoning airfields and supplies, with the consequent curtailment of aerial support; yielding Luzon and Manila unchallenged; allowing Japan access to the shoreline of Manila Bay, whence it could shell Forts Frank and Drum; demoralizing the Filipino population; bringing the United States into worldwide contempt; and making no use of the Commonwealth's armed forces. Against this dismal picture, the G-3 offered a second scenario: meeting the Japanese at the shore with beach cordons and using the bulk of the Philippine Division for counterattack; only if the enemy advanced from its beachhead would the mobile forces withdraw to Bataan. Such a plan offered the advantages of permitting the air force more time for operations, it confronted the enemy on the beach where he was most vulnerable, and it delayed the enemy and thus allowed more time to mobilize and employ the Philippine Army. Against these numerous advantages was offset the temporary splitting of the Philippine Department's limited Regular component into sector and training commands.[54]

Like MacArthur's 1929 effort, Holbrook's 1936 plan was in actuality a project, based not on current realities—the dominant factor in Booth's 1933 plan—

but rather on the future, when MacArthur's efforts had produced tens of thousands of well-trained, well-equipped, and highly motivated Filipino soldiers. As in 1929, the 1936 plan evaded the question of what would happen should war come before such Filipino reserves were ready. Like the 1929 plan, it ignored the paucity of equipment, supplies, and weapons to outfit these hypothetical native armies. In reality, there were only sufficient supplies in 1936 to support a total of 30,000 soldiers, and then only if they remained close to the supply depots of Manila Bay. Moreover, despite Holbrook's complaint that "considering the limited quantity of obsolete or obsolescent equipment available, the effectiveness of our present air force is next to nothing," and despite Washington's clear declaration that the Philippines could expect little more in the future, the 1936 plan called for an aggressive air campaign against enemy transports and warships.[55] Finally, like the 1929 plan, it was breathtakingly optimistic, envisioning little friction either in mobilizing and deploying thousands of reservists or in defending the beaches against an opponent with a crushing superiority in manpower, airpower, and firepower. Its conceptual basis was little more than the impractical enthusiasm expressed in Holbrook's declaration: "We should no longer plan a losing fight, but forget the slogan 'When do we retreat?' We must meet the enemy at the beach and whip him there. We must be there first."[56]

By the time Holbrook submitted his plan, it had slowly dawned on some General Staff officers that their Philippine commanders were going their own way. In July 1936, Lieutenant Colonel J. H. Cunningham of WPD wrote a memo to Krueger pointing out, with massive understatement, that the defense situation in the Philippines was "somewhat confused." The War Department's long-standing policy was to maintain the combat strength and mission of the archipelago's garrison at status quo and to retain all combat forces under the direct authority of the commanding general of the Philippine Department. But the War Department had also granted wide powers to MacArthur and informed the department commander that one of his primary tasks was to support the military advisor. To complicate the situation further, in a series of "obviously inspired articles" MacArthur claimed his plans to create a Filipino army had the full support of the department commander and the General Staff. The latter, at least, was manifestly untrue, for the General Staff had never approved the Philippine Defense Act. Cunningham confessed he was unable to determine MacArthur's motives for spreading such reports, "unless it is an attempt to tie in the United States permanently with responsibility for Philippine defense. If this is the case, it seems to me that General MacArthur's future intentions are a matter of concern to the War Department."[57]

Shortly after Cunningham warned of MacArthur's independent course, Chief of Staff Craig discovered the same trend in the "Holbrook Plan." Craig was no stranger to the problems of Philippine defense, having served with the Philippine Division under Hagood and commanded the harbor defenses of Manila and Subic Bays in 1922, where his fixed-defenses expert had been Embick. Faced with the approaching global war, Craig was determined to place the nation's army in a position of immediate readiness and had little enthusiasm for expending precious men, equipment, or supplies in a peripheral region of dubious strategic value. He was unimpressed by the barrage of repetitive letters from MacArthur and Holbrook, by their complaints of Washington's lethargy, their incessant demands for more resources, or by their remonstrances that dire consequences were inevitable should their requirements not be met immediately. Although Craig agreed with Holbrook "in principle" that until the Philippines received full independence in 1946, U.S. military strength should not be diminished, he warned that "the practical difficulties of translating this view into reality are considerable," especially since the War Department "had to integrate remedial measures with even more pressing shortages in other quarters."[58]

Craig objected especially to Holbrook's scheme to revise defense planning and projects so as to integrate fully the Philippine Army. Although he expressed himself gratified with that organization's progress, he cautioned that "sober reflection appears to indicate that it would be hazardous for us to place too much reliance, at least for the present, upon that army in carrying our defense mission in the Islands" since change in the Commonwealth government "might well make such reliance illusory." Moreover, he stressed that Holbrook's plans were in conflict with national goals: "preparations for using the Philippine Army as part of our own defense forces could scarcely be kept secret" and would hamper State Department efforts to secure the neutralization of the Philippines.[59] Above all, he recognized that Holbrook's wish to incorporate the Philippine Army into defense planning was in direct conflict with the Joint Board's 19 May 1936 decision to restrict the army's mission to such delaying action as was possible without in any way threatening the retreat to Bataan. On two occasions he remonstrated with Holbrook that Philippine defense planning must be based on this revised mission and must not be subordinated to creating a role for the Commonwealth forces.[60]

Craig's attempt to shift Philippine defense planning back to the more modest objectives envisioned by the Joint Board and the 1933 plan was of limited success. Craig could, and did, continue to abide by the War Department's policy of keeping Philippine units at current strength and maintaining the harbor defenses, but making no increases in men or matériel. He monitored and approved the nation's strategic policy, outlined by Embick and Walter Krueger of the War Plans Division, of withdrawing from the Philippines to a Alaska-Hawaii-Panama line. He supported Embick in his battles with the navy over the retention of Philippine bases and helped persuade Roosevelt to reject this option. He endorsed the 1938 Joint Army and Navy Basic War Plan Orange, which further limited the mission of the Philippine garrison to delaying the enemy at Subic and to defending the entrance to Manila Bay, and declared that the Philippine Department would fight "augmented only by such personnel and facilities as are available locally."[61] The chief of staff was well aware that adherence to this plan virtually guaranteed the fall of the Philippines, for, as Krueger informed him, "the idea of a definite period of self-sustained defense is no longer a part of our present concept of the defense of the Philippines in an Orange war, nor is it authorized under any approved Joint Board Action now in force. Whatever form the new Joint Army and Navy Basic War Plan Orange may take, it is highly improbable, as matters now stand, that expeditionary forces will be sent to the Philippines in the early stages of an Orange war. Even if the dispatch of such forces were contemplated, it would be impossible to predict, with any degree of accuracy, when they would arrive."[62]

From the available documentation, it is clear that neither Craig nor the General Staff encouraged Holbrook and MacArthur in their revision of the Philippine defense plans. Indeed, Craig sent clear messages, at least to Holbrook, emphatically disapproving of them. How then did the Holbrook-MacArthur scheme for defending the archipelago—a scheme so counter to the army's wishes, the Orange plans, and the nation's foreign policy—slip past Washington's supervision? Unfortunately, the evidence does not provide a clear answer. A charitable explanation is that the Herculean task of rectifying the nation's appalling neglect of its defenses precluded the War Department from more than cursory attention to areas of such limited strategic value as the Philippines. Given the War Department's long history of refusing to interfere in local defense plans, even when they were clearly contradictory to the national war plans, it would have been unusual for Craig to demand his Philippine subordinates follow his lead. A more cynical interpretation is that Philippine vulnerability and the approaching independence of the islands engendered a belief that since all defense plans were futile, local commanders should be left alone. But until conclusive evidence emerges to settle these conjectures, the provisional judgment must be that Craig erred in not forcing a showdown with Holbrook and MacArthur. He allowed the discussion over the "Holbrook plan" to be kept informal—the generals addressed each other as "My dear"—and did not request the General Staff to comment on what were clearly substantial revisions in the Philippine plans. Having been alerted that his subordinates were charting their own course, Craig failed to insist that they comply with his directives. He did not assert his prerogatives, or even his duty, as chief of staff and demand obedience; instead he let the issue drift. By his timidity, Craig allowed Holbrook to discard the Booth-Parker defense plan that conformed both to the Philippine garrison's military capabilities and to the nation's strategic policy and to substitute for it a poorly conceived and overoptimistic plan based on a scenario that might be created a decade hence. Craig also set an unfortunate precedent in the War Department's dealing with MacArthur, who quickly learned that, although his military superiors might deny him equipment and personnel, they would neither enforce compliance nor attempt supervision. Indeed, because of Craig's unwillingness to demand obedience, MacArthur would later, with some justice, complain that he had attempted to implement an approved defense plan with inadequate means.

Craig's lack of direction allowed Philippine commanders to continue to pursue their own vision. In 1938 the Army and Navy Joint Defense Plan for the Philippine Islands Coastal Frontier and the Philippine Defense Project expanded the basic premises of Holbrook's 1936 Orange plan. Both called for the Philippine Division, designated the Initial Protective Force, to be divided into three sector commands—North, South, and West—and deployed to protect the "vital areas of Central Luzon," or Lingayen Gulf, Batangas and Tayabas Bay, and the Bataan coastline. Should the Protective Force fail to hold the beaches, it would fight a series of delaying actions, buying time for the Commonwealth forces to be mobilized and sworn into U.S. service. These newly federalized recruits would then be assigned to new Philippine Scout organizations, eventually comprising a small corps of two divisions. The 1938 Philippine scenarios were thus based on the full and free utilization of the Philippine Army and were completely at variance with Craig's instructions to Holbrook.[63]

The Philippine Department's 1940 Orange plan marks a final step away from the Corregidor-first strategy. Based on a scenario in which the first elements of a Japanese expedition would begin landing on Luzon's beaches and striking for Manila no more than forty-eight hours after a declaration of war, it proposed three alternatives. The first two of these were identical to the options listed in the 1936 Orange plan: to retreat immediately to Bataan or to meet the invaders at the beach with small-sector commands and then fight delaying actions until forced into the zone defenses at Bataan. The third option was to employ the major portion of the mobile forces for beach defense and seek "to eject the enemy, or, failing to do this, to limit his beachhead operations energetically until forced to withdraw." In the meantime, the Philippine Army would be mobilized and used "to the fullest extent possible," eventually replacing the initial defenders, who would then be held in reserve. This would permit time for air operations, for gathering supplies, for the organization of Bataan's defense, and for the full use of the Commonwealth forces. It would also improve morale, cultivate an offensive spirit, and "bind the Filipino people more closely to our cause." Against this was the sole disadvantage that the mobile forces would initially be dispersed. The Philippine Department's planners, concluding that any defense plan must meet the enemy on the beaches and allow for the mobilization of the Philippine Army, advocated the third option. They reconciled this aggressive defense with their assigned mission—to "delay the enemy at Subic Bay and elsewhere as may be practicable without jeopardizing the timely withdrawal of mobile ground forces to the Bataan Peninsula; and to defend the entrance to Manila Bay"— by reasoning that "the assigned War Department mission can best be accomplished by administering a crushing defeat to Orange at the beaches, thus obviating the necessity for delaying actions, withdrawals and a final occupation of Bataan. Such a defeat is possible and practicable under this plan."[64]

In view of the controversy that later arose over MacArthur's last-minute alteration of the 1940 Orange plan for one that emphasized the defense of the entire archipelago, with extensive use of airpower and the Philippine Army, it is important to remember that by 1940, and perhaps as early as 1936, the Philippine high command had rejected a strategy of immediate retreat to Bataan and instead had committed itself to an aggressive, mobile defense intended to hold the enemy on the beaches and to make full use of Filipino forces. Scholars who have focused only on the differences between the 1940 plan and MacArthur's 1941 plan have failed to notice that MacArthur's decision was less a sharp break than a further, and perhaps logical, extrapolation of Holbrook's 1936 plan. In retrospect, the surprising thing is not that the War Department countenanced MacArthur's 1941 revisions, but that it allowed its Philippine commanders to develop war plans that were clearly at variance with the nation's Orange plans and with its own desire to rid itself of the burden of Philippine defense.[65]

That Philippine Department officers chose to base so much of their defense plans on the Commonwealth army is puzzling, given their ambivalence about Filipino troops. Ever since the passage of the Jones Act, army officers had been forced to consider the eventual creation of a Filipino army. Pershing's 1922 instructions to the Philippine Department commander had given official sanction to the creation of such an army while at the same time emphasizing the desirability of Filipino reserves for the garrison's current needs. MacArthur's 1929 Philippine Department Basic War Plan had acknowledged that, because "upon the loyalty and response of the Filipino people depends the success of our mission, it is of primary importance that every effort be made in times of peace to insure their loyalty and to inculcate in them the basic understanding that the defense of their country rests upon them."[66] But throughout the 1920s the lack of finances and the questionable applicability of the 1920 Defense Act to the islands had frustrated the creation of a reserve force. Even when the reserve organization was eventually declared legal, there was insufficient money for anything but a few college ROTC programs and a reserve roster of retired Scouts and resident Americans. In the words of Major James H. Tierney, "no insular force can be created after war has been declared that can have any influence in the defense of the Islands. Not only will it lack officers, arms and equipment, but it will lack time to organize and be trained." Recognizing this, the realists who drew up the 1933 Orange plan had proposed to augment the existing forces with fewer than 2,000 recruits.[67]

When strong congressional sentiment for Philippine independence intensified in the 1930s, the subject of the islands' future armed forces became of great interest in the Philippines and United States. Despite the War Department's order that "no action will be taken which could affect, in any way, the initiative of the Filipinos in determining the character of the defensive forces to be developed," there was extensive discussion in Manila.[68] Veterans of the anti-American resistance, National Guardsmen, and Scout officers such as Vicente Lim outlined a variety of proposals. Several high-ranking authorities, including Parker, Embick, Craig, and Philippine Commissioner Frank Murphy believed the Philippines should trust to an international neutrality agreement and maintain only a small paramilitary constabulary. Some wanted a very limited military mobilization that would supply sufficient recruits to bring the Philippine Division and harbor defenses up to their full war strength of 30,000, a figure that also considered the limited equipment and supplies in the department.[69]

In early 1934 Chief of Staff MacArthur and the soon-to-be president of the Commonwealth, Manuel Quezon worked out an agreement whereby MacArthur would become military advisor of the new government. MacArthur assured Quezon that with 10 million pesos he could build a Philippine defense force strong enough to deter any invader. The following year, MacArthur assigned Dwight Eisenhower, James B. Ord, and a special War College committee to draw up a plan for the Commonwealth armed forces. Although there was extensive and informed discussion of the proper military organization for the Commonwealth in the Philippines, the Americans did not seek Filipino input. Their plan, after much cutting to keep it within the new government's limited budget, was presented by MacArthur in 1936 as the

"Report on National Defense in the Philippines" and accepted by President Quezon and the Commonwealth legislature. Under its provisions, the Philippine Army would consist of a small regular contingent of 11,000, whose primary purpose was to train reserves and provide technical expertise, and a reserve component of 400,000 trained male citizens between twenty-one and fifty, who would be organized into tactical units divided among ten military districts. The Philippines would also have an air force of fast bombers and fighters and a navy of torpedo boats to harass enemy expeditions and inflict disproportionate losses on his warships. Possibly with an eye to placating Filipino and Japanese officials, MacArthur argued his "plan completely negates any possibility of employing the Army in aggressive action and makes no attempt to maintain a more militaristic objective than the development of each island in the Archipelago as a citadel of defensive strength."[70]

Accordingly, after 1935 there were two military organizations in the Philippines, the U.S. Army's Philippine Department and the emerging Commonwealth or Philippine Army. Both reported to the War Department and both clamored for supplies, men, and equipment; both viewed themselves as the archipelago's primary military institution, and each considered the other as a provider of necessary goods and services. The Philippine Department's commander was in an impossible position, for in October 1935 when MacArthur left Washington he carried with him orders that emphasized the creation of the Philippine Army as one of the U.S. government's top priorities. But by 1936 U.S. support for the Philippine military had greatly diminished; the arms and equipment that MacArthur believed he had been promised never arrived.[71] Perhaps as a result of this setback, MacArthur and his staff placed more demands on the Carabao Army. The Philippine Department lost equipment and facilities to the new army, and training and preparedness suffered. Regulars objected that solid and combat-ready units were being sacrificed to create a mass militia of dubious value. Echoing the struggle of the earlier years between civil and military authorities, commanders complained they were being plundered of essential personnel as training cadres for the Commonwealth forces. MacArthur and his staff had close friends among the department staff, and one biographer has described relations between the two offices as "sensitive but reasonably harmonious during the period 1938–40."[72] But privately, according to Eisenhower, most American officers professed to find the whole idea of a Filipino army "somewhat ridiculous."[73]

In addition to uneven relations with the Philippine Department, the Military Mission was hampered by both internal and external problems. MacArthur left Eisenhower and Ord to administer the creation of the Philippine Army, he rarely worked in his office, and, save for occasional visits to camps and reviews; he spent most of his time with his new family. This often led to considerable stress between the sanguine MacArthur and his more practical and increasingly disillusioned staff. Eisenhower wrote that once when he and Ord protested MacArthur's decision to call up 200,000 recruits because there were no facilities to handle them, the general had subjected them to "one of his regular shouting tirades."[74] Nor could MacArthur control Quezon, who proved as mercurial in supporting the army as in his other political positions. Eisenhower acidly commented that the Philippine Army's difficulties were "mainly occasioned by the almost total lack of administrative ability in the higher officials of the government and the army. From the President down each official seems to act individually and on the spur of the moment without respect to any detail in which he is interested, and without regard for possible effects upon other activities or upon the army as a whole."[75]

Despite general enthusiasm for an army of their own, Filipinos voiced legitimate and accurate criticisms of the form it was taking. MacArthur shunned virtually all input and his social and professional contacts were limited to a small coterie of political and business leaders. He had little interaction with the Filipinos who officered and manned the Commonwealth forces and in whom he expressed such confidence. Notwithstanding his incessant flow of optimistic pronouncements, informed Filipinos suspected his plans were "based largely on probabilities and not on possibilities, on what he expected would happen rather than what could happen."[76] Vicente Lim, a West Pointer, War College graduate, and future general in the Philippine Army, was convinced MacArthur was fixated on the numbers of recruits in training camps and failing to ascertain whether they were actually being trained. Like many Filipinos, he believed MacArthur had permitted Quezon free rein to pick the Philippine Army's commanders, with the result that the upper ranks were dominated by political loyalists of limited ability. And, like many Scout officers, Lim thought the Commonwealth must first create a solid cadre of trained soldiers and an educated officer corps before it could hope to instruct and command thousands of peasant conscripts. MacArthur's aloofness, his blatantly unrealistic press releases, his controversial policies, his extravagant salary, and his isolation from his troops gained him little internal support within the Philippine Army; ultimately his authority was completely dependent on Quezon. By 1939 this prop was crumbling. Quezon became disillusioned and sought to appease Japan: he slashed military funding, cut the number of reservists, and demanded that the United States remain responsible for Philippine defense. Convinced his military advisor had deceived him, the Commonwealth president limited his meetings with MacArthur and privately ridiculed his plans.[77]

The dissension in Manila was mirrored in relations with Washington. MacArthur and the supporters of the Philippine Army were, and subsequently remained, bitter in their denunciations of Washington's failure to offer "meaningful assistance" in the form of weapons, supplies, and expertise.[78] From Washington's perspective, the tail was wagging the dog. Instead of taking the burden of defense off the United States, the Commonwealth Army made incessant demands for more equipment and money. Particularly galling was the knowledge that MacArthur, as a recent chief of staff, knew perfectly well that his requests could be met only at great cost and by jeopardizing the United States's own rearmament. As the voluminous correspondence on the subject of supplying the Philippine Army makes clear, the issue was not nearly as simple as sending obsolete and unneeded equipment to the archipelago. Much of the matériel in question was essential to the Regular Army's expansion from 139,000 in 1935 to 258,000 in 1940, or equally necessary for the National Guard and Organized Reserves. To the Roosevelt administration, still in the throes of the Depression, and to a Congress that had supported Philippine independence for budgetary reasons, the Commonwealth's efforts to bill the United States not only for equipping its army, but for shipping and transport as well, were insupportable.[79]

Moreover, there were some in Washington who protested that the Commonwealth's military buildup jeopardized its neutrality and threatened the Far Eastern balance of power.[80] Craig doubted that the Philippine Army actually represented the solution to the archipelago's defense, and he was markedly unenthusiastic about the Holbrook-MacArthur proposal to use it in the event of war. His skepticism was shared in the War Department: even MacArthur's close friend, Brigadier Charles Burnett, told the War College in 1939 that the Philippine Army "would form no formidable obstacle" to an invasion and believed its main value was to assist the "social development" of the Filipino peasant.[81] Save for the ever sanguine MacArthur, this disparaging view of the Philippine Army was shared by most of the officers who worked with it. Eisenhower and others admired the enthusiasm and morale of the recruits, but recognized the enormous obstacles they faced—corruption, favoritism, unqualified officers and noncoms, inadequate equipment, no natural defenses, inconsistent financial and political support—and that these would take years to overcome. At the beginning of 1940, the Commonwealth forces numbered 109,000, few with more than minimal training, equipped with castoff rifles and artillery, and with insufficient ammunition, transport, or supplies.[82]

As the Philippine Army suffered through its birthing pains, the Carabao Army remained pathetically weak: in 1934 there were 611 officers and 10,543 enlisted men, of whom nearly all the officers and 4,086 of the enlisted men were Americans.[83] The Philippines were accorded a low priority in supplies, and the equipment that did exist was often inappropriate: poking around Pettit Barracks in Zamboanga, one officer found boxes containing everything from cavalry harness to sleigh bells.[84] Except for the 31st Infantry, all combat commands were at 30 to 50 percent of their wartime strength. One inspector reported of Stotsenburg's garrison in 1933 that it had "neither the armament, the equipment, nor the strength to accomplish combat missions that would normally be expected of its organization as designated on paper."[85] His comment could just as easily have been applied to virtually any unit in the department during the decade.

Whereas Hawaiian defense steadily improved, the center of Philippine defense for most of the 1930s remained the Manila Bay fortifications. The Washington Treaties restricted the army from doing more than preserving the existing defenses—a task that cost $2.6 million a year. Financial stringency was the order of the day, at one point reducing garrison officers to collecting bottles and scrap in order to purchase barbed wire. The tactical exercises that might have tested air and gas defense were never held: the War Department refused to grant the necessary funding. In an effort to save money and manpower, Fort Wint in Subic Bay and several smaller batteries in the Manila Bay defenses were left to caretaking detachments. But successive harbor defense commanders managed to circumvent both the treaties and budgetary restrictions and succeeded in digging the huge Malinta Tunnel, which provided essential shelter against air attack. Surveys throughout the decade concluded that the $58 million fortifications, despite their deteriorating condition and their obsolete armament, were more than sufficient to deter any attack by the enemy battle fleet. There was far more debate over Manila Bay's vulnerability to aerial bombardment, chemical warfare, and shore-based artillery. Some commanders, such as Frank Parker, believed these new dangers rendered Corregidor indefensible, but others, such as coast artillerymen Hagood and Embick, claimed it might hold out for a year.[86]

Discussion of the tactical strength of the Manila Bay harbor defenses was not nearly as acerbic as the debate over their strategic importance. From the beginning, they had been something of an anomaly: fortifications designed to defend a nonexistent naval base at a location the navy itself opposed. They had been assumed to be essential, not only to protect the harbor that the fleet would need after it fought its way across the Pacific, but to safeguard U.S. interests in Asia. But with the Philippines headed toward independence and with clear threats to national security emerging in Japan and Germany, the United States needed to decide which of its overseas interests were worth fighting for. Ironically, some of those who most strongly defended the fortifications' tactical value denigrated their strategic importance. While serving as Corregidor's commander, Embick argued that enemy aircraft and heavy artillery would prevent an American fleet from sheltering in the bay. All the fortifications could do was "serve only the minor, and relatively negligible, end of denying to the naval vessels of an enemy the free use of Manila Bay."[87]

Officers encountered a similarly bleak situation when they viewed the mobile forces of the Philippines. Realistic training was curtailed by lack of money and men. Edward Almond, who commanded a battalion of the 45th Regiment in 1933, complained that most of his time was taken up in administrative chores: only in the brief dry season could he "actually train the battalion in things that I had been practicing in theory and had practiced in the war that ended in 1918."[88] For much of the 1930s, the bulk of the Philippine Division's firepower was still mule-carried pack howitzers, and during the 1934 maneuvers the 24th Field Artillery's field transportation consisted of two trucks and a Ford car. The 1936 maneuvers, designed to test both the new motorized transport and the Holbrook plan, required the division to take up beach defense positions at Lingayen and Subic Bays, before retreating through the Bataan Peninsula. Although demonstrating its new mobility, the maneuvers also showed its pathetic combat strength—the 23rd Brigade, the division's only active combat unit, fielded but 619 infantry and 75 artillerymen. The following year the War Department would not even grant the department $5,000 for extra gas and oil for maneuvers.[89] Ultimately, there were just too few soldiers, too little equipment, too great an area to protect, and too little support, for the mobile forces to fulfill their mission.

The rapid escalation of Japanese-American tensions in 1940 abruptly ended the slow decline of the archipelago's defenses and led to an abrupt volte-face in the army's, and the nation's, two-decade withdrawal from its Philippine commitment. Washington, desperate to shore up its Pacific defenses, reversed its policy of neglect and poured money, matériel, and manpower overseas. Secretary of War Stimson urged that all possible efforts be taken to improve the Philippine defenses. Chief of Staff George C. Marshall wrote on 16 July 1941: "At the present time, with Japan's known preparations to move South, the Philippines become of great strategic importance, as they constitute both a Naval and Air Base upon the immediate flank of the Japanese southern movement."[90] Marshall, Stimson, and others hoped that the long-range B-17 bomber would not only close the sea-lanes to invaders, but could threaten Japanese cities. Recalled to active service in July 1941 as commander of the U.S. Army Forces in the Far East, MacArthur immediately set to work implementing his oft-expressed conviction that he could save the Philippines. He revived Lassiter's ambitious plan to use air power for defense and to threaten Japanese sea communications: by December 1941 he had received 35 B-17s (three times as many as Hawaii) and 159 modern pursuit airplanes. Pacific transports shuttled in thousands of reinforcements, so that when the Japanese attacked, his American contingent had increased to almost 19,000 with another 19,000 en route. These forces were augmented by the newly mobilized Philippine Army. Ever optimistic, MacArthur demanded enormous quantities of supplies, weapons, equipment, transportation, and ammunition. He modified the existing defense plan to include all the islands, established regional tactical commands, and pressed for defense of the beaches.

MacArthur failed to inspire his subordinates with similar confidence. Brigadier General Bradford Chynoweth, who arrived in Manila in November 1941 and had an audience with him, was appalled at the incompetence he found: "In retrospect, I can see that General MacArthur was in complete fog about his Army and his subordinates. Yet because of his colossal *magnetism*, I left that encounter feeling *inspired!*"[91] But when Chynoweth turned to his duties, he found an air of almost surrealistic lassitude pervaded the army. There were only the most rudimentary efforts to put Manila Bay's defenses in order, to store food, or to establish defensive positions. The Commonwealth armed forces, amalgamated into U.S. Army Forces in the Far East, underwent a chaotic mobilization that resembled more the gathering of an armed horde than the preparation of a modern army. Officers and their soldiers often spoke different languages, and many could not even understand the Regulars assigned to advise them. There were few weapons, fewer firing ranges, and even less ammunition. Nor were the Regulars doing much more: soldiers continued the relaxed schedule of colonial soldiering, drilling in the morning and devoting the afternoons to fatigue duty and athletics. In May 1941, the commander of the Philippine Division, Brigadier General Jonathan M. Wainwright, reported that his typical workday consisted of an hour's horseback ride in the morning, followed by breakfast, observing the troops, a visit to his office, luncheon at one, and afternoons devoted to golf or, occasionally, office work.[92]

For four decades, the Filipinos and Americans in the Carabao Army had provided an adequate colonial garrison. Meticulously drilled, dressed in their tailored uniforms, and filled with long-service soldiers, they were the most impressive symbols of American overlordship. The military parades and athletic contests, the imposing fortifications in Manila Bay, and the snap and precision of its soldiers, drew the admiration of foreign and domestic observers. But the Carabao Army was never more than a hollow deterrent to the primary danger that it confronted, a Japanese invasion. At best capable of a stubborn defense around Manila Bay's fortifications, it was manifestly inadequate for the ambitious task envisioned by Holbrook and MacArthur. Moreover, the fortifications themselves, although tactically impressive, were strategically insignificant. By the mid-1930s neither army nor navy planners advocated the direct thrust to Manila that alone would have justified the prolonged defense of Corregidor. Indeed, there was a consensus that the United States should withdraw from the Philippines and retrench to a Alaska-Hawaii-Panama perimeter. For a variety of reasons, this rational strategy was not implemented. Instead, Washington allowed its Philippine commanders to develop an ambitious and implausible plan of defense based on an untried army and nonexistent weaponry. That the battle for Luzon would end in defeat was, as the realistic former department commander Ewing E. Booth noted in 1942, "no surprise to those who knew the conditions in the Philippines."[93] Tragically, the failure of individual commanders, Washington's vacillation, and Japanese brutality would mean that this defeat was accompanied by an unnecessary amount of privation, suffering, and death.

Hawaii, on the other hand, had long been viewed as the bastion of American defense in the Pacific. By the end of the decade, the Pineapple Army had made great strides toward fulfilling its mission of protecting the naval base at Pearl and the Island of Oahu from attack. The emplacement of new coastal guns, the increase in mobile forces, the deployment of new weapons, and the constant training and exercises had all but removed the possibility of a successful invasion and led credence to the boast of Chief of Staff Marshall and Secretary of War Stimson that Oahu was the best-defended fortress in the world. Indeed, the fantasies of novelists aside, it is most likely that had the Japanese invaded Oahu—and even had their aviation been able to secure command of the sky—they would have been slaughtered on the beaches in truly catastrophic numbers. Nor, as has been discussed earlier, did ground-bound army planners willfully ignore the danger posed by carrier aviation. The Pineapple Army's ultimate failure lay not in willful stupidity or military conservatism, but in a variety of other factors. Interservice and intraservice disagreements, lack of suitable aircraft, and, most important, the apparent lesson of field exercises that Oahu's garrison would inflict severe damage on the attacker all contributed to the army's inability to appreciate the seriousness of the danger or the weakness of its defenses. When these long-standing problems were coupled with the individual mistakes, poor communications, and bad fortune that plagued the Hawaiian forces on 7 December 1941, the result was a shocking, unexpected, and humiliating defeat.

CONCLUSION

On 7 December 1941, at a little before 8 A.M., Japanese aircraft attacked the recently arrived U.S. Pacific Fleet at Pearl Harbor and Oahu's military and naval facilities. In two waves, coming in from the north—some even tracing the long-anticipated invasion route down the Leilehua Plain—they proceeded to strafe, bomb, and torpedo the fleet, the naval base, and the airfields. In two hours, they destroyed or damaged 188 of Oahu's 394 aircraft, sank or crippled eighteen warships, and killed 2,403 American servicemen. The defenders fought with great personal courage but the resistance was fragmented and disorganized. Most of the Army Air Corps's 221 fighters and bombers were caught on the ground and destroyed, only 30 pursuit planes took to the air to fight. Of Oahu's twenty-seven antiaircraft batteries, only four were fired during the attack. A few hours after their comrades had attacked Pearl Harbor, Japanese pilots struck at the American forces in the Philippines, and once again achieved both surprise and devastating success. On 10 December the first Japanese invaders landed on Luzon's beaches and by Christmas the American and Filipino forces were in full retreat. On 9 April 1942 the starving remnants on Bataan surrendered; a month later the Corregidor garrison capitulated and by 9 June all organized army resistance in the Philippines had ceased. Although they held out far longer than expected, and by their heroism and sacrifice rallied and inspired their countrymen, the defenders paid a terrible cost. Battle, disease, starvation, and the brutality of their captors all but annihilated the Philippine Army.

The drama of these early battles and the bitter controversies over responsibility for the American debacle has captured the historical imagination for half a century. In contravention of Napoleon's axiom, these are defeats that have spawned a thousand fathers. But in seeking answers to the debacles of 1941, historians have rarely pushed their investigations back beyond 1940. Indeed, beyond a few crumbling ruins of coast defenses and colorful and often apocryphal soldiers' tales of jungle patrols, tropical locales, and exotic maidens, the Pacific Army has all but disappeared from our memory.

The acquisition of Hawaii and the Philippines in 1898 was a major turning point for the U.S. Army. For over a century the Regular Army had served as a small coast defense force and frontier constabulary, charged with a mission to defend the continental United States against internal and external threats and serving as the core of the much larger citizen-soldier armies raised in wartime. Prior to the war with Spain, the army had no plans for overseas expansion or any imperialist dreams. With the Pacific empire came new responsibilities and commitments, calling forth not only a major reorganization, but the creation of a distinct colonial army. The postconquest army found itself in a unique and difficult situation, required to defend two overseas bases against an empire with superior military and naval power in the western Pacific. For almost forty years, officers in Washington, Manila, and Honolulu sought to overcome the tactical and strategic problems posed by the Japanese threat. Their difficulties were exacerbated by shifting politics, the uncertain status of the Philippines, minuscule budgets, public and political indifference, and inadequate manpower. The army also had to deal with internal problems— service competition, administrative reform, technological change—as well as a world war, and the persistent debate over the importance of the Pacific territories to the nation's interests.

In Hawaii, the U.S. Army faced what initially seemed a relatively simple and familiar engineering problem: the fortification of two harbors. Only after the 1907 Japanese-American War Scare did the defense of Oahu take on the further dimension of protection against landing parties, invasion, and rebellion. Unlike the Philippines, there was never any debate over Hawaii's necessity to national security; its value was apparent to all. But, as in the Philippines, there was strong disagreement over whether to adopt a position defense to protect Pearl and Honolulu harbors or attempt to repel the enemy on the beaches. Unlike Luzon, on Oahu, the options eventually blended. The island's geography allowed the defenders to concentrate on only the most vulnerable beaches, and military technology, in the form of the heavy siege artillery piece, pushed defense lines back further and further until they incorporated these very coasts. Building the fortifications at Pearl and Honolulu fixed the army's coast defense tactics, and land tactics were essentially set by 1924. Ironically, the airplane, and especially the carrier-borne airplane, reopened the whole problem. Aviation promised to extend Hawaii's defensive perimeter hundreds of miles out to sea, but enemy carriers presented a potential threat that was still unresolved when the Japanese struck.

In the Philippines, the U.S. Army was placed in a far more difficult position. First, the army had to overcome Filipino conventional forces, regional guerrilla resistance, brigandage, tribal violence, and religious uprisings; in the process it developed effective small-war tactics and took the first steps in recruiting what eventually became a sizable native contingent. Second, it had to hold the archipelago against Japan. Successive administrations, particularly those of the 1920s, demanded an American presence in the Far East and the retention of the Philippines. They gambled, successfully, that the Carabao Army, starved of the necessary manpower and matériel, would not be called upon to back up the nation's commitments with force. And while the War Department established the basic framework of defense against seaborne raids— coastal fortifications and mobile garrisons—it proved unable to obtain the steady stream of men, matériel, and new technology necessary to meet the rapidly evolving threats from land and air.

The army did little to ease the predicament in which it had been placed by its civilian superiors. Indeed, if anything it contributed to the illusion that the Philippines could and should be defended. As early as 1907 it was clear that Japan could launch an invasion with sufficient forces to overwhelm the defenders and conquer most, if not all, of Luzon. The Americans had three options: to acknowledge the colony's vulnerability and station only a small colonial force to preserve internal order and repel a raid; to abandon everything but Manila Bay; or to defend Manila Bay and other strategic objectives— initially Manila and later all of Luzon. For most of the American occupation, the military debate essentially revolved around the last two options. Those who favored the second alternative claimed that the defense of the islands ultimately rested on the U.S. Navy's ability to control the surrounding waters. If Corregidor and its outworks could hold out until relieved, the defenders would have accomplished their mission: to provide the safe haven that the battle fleet required to go immediately on the offensive in the western Pacific. Those who pressed for defending Manila or all of Luzon argued that even if the army held Corregidor, Japanese artillery (and later aircraft) could deny Manila Bay to the American fleet. All of Luzon must be defended, and this, in turn, required a mass Filipino army. Only rarely would a dissident voice the first option, that the islands were of insignificant military and economic value and the army's limited resources badly needed elsewhere. Although this last view gained currency among a number of key planners during the mid-1930s, these realists were unable to impose their views on either the army or local commanders.

The danger from outside was exacerbated by the danger from within. From its beginnings, the Pacific Army shouldered a dual mission: both to protect the native populations and to guard against insurrection. First during the conquest of the Philippines and later in the long pacification campaigns, the army served as the ultimate sanction of the insular government. Although its coercive role ended with the pacification of the Moros, it remained a constant and formidable presence. Army posts were located both to deter the invasion and to keep the population under control. Army intelligence agencies investigated suspected subversives, in the process adding to the military's hyperawareness of subversion, and departmental staffs drew up extensive plans to deal with rebellion. Behind the Pacific Army's snappy appearance and drill there was a clear reminder to civilians that this was a force to be respected.

Some historians have criticized the army for focusing so intensely on the dangers posed by the local population. But even allowing for the army's strong ethnocentric bias, its intelligence services discovered ample evidence for the presumption that the Filipinos, like the Japanese Americans, might assist the invaders in the event of an attack. In view of the size of this threat, army plans to counter uprisings and sabotage after World War I were rather modest and restrained. One need only look at the conduct of Japanese or French colonial forces toward actual or potential rebels to appreciate just how humane the Americans were. Moreover, to focus exclusively on instances of army prejudice is to overlook the generally harmonious relations between soldiers and civilians. Much of this good feeling was due to the army's early commitment to social reform. One may criticize officers for their casual dismissal of native rights and dignity, but one can only applaud their willingness to suffer disease, financial hardship, and professional setbacks in order to help the nation's colonial wards. The army built roads, dams, wells, schools, and marketplaces. In dozens of very practical ways, the army improved the lives of Filipinos and Hawaiians: it established health clinics and trade fairs, treated the sick, taught children and adults to read and write, improved agricultural production through planting new crops, quarantines, and crop dusting, and, in the Philippines, stamped out brigandage and sect violence. Army athletics and parades were tremendously popular among the local populations; newspapers reported game scores and thousands of spectators flocked to boxing matches and track meets. For many Hawaiians and Filipinos, the army was a proud symbol of their connection with United States.

In practical terms, the Pacific Army's sensitivity to internal threats had a far more baneful effect than "dehumanizing" the local populations: it vitiated its efforts to prepare for the external danger. Given the navy's refusal to commit its battle fleet and the army's inability to station sufficient forces overseas, the obvious solution to the defense problem was to incorporate the territories' populations into the armed forces. But with the singular exception of the

Philippine Scouts, the United States did not follow the example of Great Britain and France and raise a distinct colonial army composed of native troops. Nor did it create a reserve force that could bolster the Regulars in time of war. Fear of treason and army ethnocentrism, as well as lack of funding and political support, hampered all efforts to enlist the local populations. When local officers such as MacArthur, Wells, and Herron did urge that more trust be placed in the indigenous populations, they were frustrated by Washington. By the time the approaching independence of the Philippines and the growing danger of Japan finally made the creation of a Filipino army imperative, it was too late. Instead of providing a large and well-trained reserve, the Philippine Army proved poorly armed, inadequately trained, and, from the highest levels on down, erratically commanded. One can speculate on what might have been had the manpower provisions of MacArthur's Orange plan been adopted in 1929 or debate the merits and demerits of his decision to defend Luzon on the beaches, but such what-ifs obscure the far greater issue of the army's failure to prepare the local populations for their own defense.

It is the contention of this book that contrary to the popular view, the U.S. Army recognized the danger posed by Japan very early, and in policy studies, military exercises, and war games, officers foresaw the events of 1941 with sometimes uncanny accuracy. But a variety of factors—inadequate manpower and resources, changes in weaponry and tactics, low budgets, public and political indifference, intraservice and interservice dissension between local commanders and Washington—all hindered the development of adequate defenses for the Pacific territories. Critics might ascribe the army's inability to come up with a cogent solution to the "military mind"—conservative, impervious to new ideas, and unable to deal with conflicting data. But simple explanations are unsatisfactory. Certainly there were a number of questionable decisions and several outright blunders. But there was never a dearth of thought or competence; if anything the reverse was true. The voluminous records on planning offer impressive testimony to the intelligence, innovation, and critical spirit of army officers. Summerall developed a tactical system that stood for almost two decades. Hugh A. Drum was even more radical than many airmen in proposing that Oahu be defended by air. Hawaiian Department commanders Wells and Herron were far in advance of their mainland colleagues in advocating the recruitment of nisei soldiers. Similarly, in the Philippines, if charismatic officers such as Wood and MacArthur, or strategists such as Bell and Lassiter, or brilliant coast defense specialists such as Embick and Hagood had not been so energetic, so competent, so capable of overcoming the almost impossible barriers they faced, the army might have abandoned the struggle. But over and over, faced with specific problems—enemy battleships, siege artillery, infantry, airplanes—officers worked out solutions that appeared both plausible and practical. Indeed, their successful focus on an endless series of immediate and tangible problems encouraged them to believe that with more men, new technology, or new tactics they might ultimately find the solutions to other, much greater dilemmas.

U.S. Army Manpower, 1902–1941

Year	Army Total	Philippines Total	Philippincs: U.S. Troops	Philippines: Scouts	Ilawaii: U.S. Troops
1902	75,028	29,238	24,238	5,000	c. 210
1903	70,552	21,217	16,346	4,871	c. 210
1904	69,817	17,810	12,723	5,087	229
1905	66,956	18,375	13,194	5,181	c. 210
1906	68,372	19,574	14,415	5,159	c. 234
1907	63,624	16,613	11,508	5,105	c. 234
1908	76,428	17,835	12,441	5,394	c. 234
1909	85,263	19,439	13,693	5,746	c. 600
1910	80,678	17,834	12,282	5,552	1,371
1911	83,315	17,455	11,875	5,580	2,229
1912	91,461	19,010	13,007	5,995	4,039
1913	93,301	16,659	11,097	5,562	7,111
1914	97,760	14,778	9,500	5,278	8,195
1915	105,993	18,521	12,909	5,612	9,521
1916	105,107	17,669	11,813	5,788	8,491
1917	250,357	19,979	13,795	5,702	12,463
1918	2,379,579	16,137	9,399	6,738	10,306
1919	846,498	14,200	5,255	8,159	6,694
1920	201,918	20,282	13,173	7,109	4,798
1921	228,650	13,251	5,524	7,112	15,638
1922	146,507	13,869	6,939	6,930	10,369

Year	Army Total	Philippines Total	Philippines: U.S. Troops	Philippines: Scouts	Hawaii: U.S. Troops
1923	131,254	11,527	4,415	7,112	14,513
1924	140,943	11,808	4,575	7,233	13,096
1925	135,254	11,285	4,601	6,684	14,717
1926	133,443	12,189	5,019	7,170	14,433
1927	133,268	11,388	4,430	6,958	13,774
1928	134,505	10,943	4,457	6,486	14,083
1929	137,529	11,337	4,770	6,567	14,228
1930	137,645	11,232	4,690	6,542	15,155
1931	138,817	11,152	4,660	6,492	14,843
1932	132,399	11,744	5,207	6,537	14,223
1933	135,015	11,140	4,982	6,458	14,728
1934	136,975	11,130	4,762	6,368	14,294
1935	137,966	11,615	5,187	6,428	14,821
1936	166,121	11,323	4,893	6,430	18,702
1937	178,108	10,932	4,520	6,412	18,516
1938	183,455	11,083	4,690	6,393	21,777
1939	187,893	10,920	4,514	6,406	21,475
1940	267,767	c. 11,000	c. 4,500	c. 6,500	c. 25,000
1941	1,461,000	22,532	10,569	11,963	42,857

Sources: *Annual Report of the War Department*, 1902–1941; Hawaiian and Philippine Department annual reports, RG 407; Mark S. Watson, *Chief of Staff: Prewar Plans and Preparations* (Washington, D.C.: Historical Division, Department of the Army, 1950), pp. 16, 474. Due to different accounting practices, there are discrepancies in manpower figures between these sources.

NOTES

Abbreviations

AAC—Army Air Corps
AAF—Army Air Force
AC/S—Assistant Chief of Staff
ACTS—Air Corps Tactical School
Adj.—Adjutant
AFHRA—U.S. Air Force Historical Research Agency
AG—Adjutant General
AGO—Adjutant General's Office Document Number
ANJ—Army and Navy Journal
AS—Air Service
ASPO—Army Strategical Plan Orange
AWC—Army War College
AWCCA—Army War College Curriculum Archives, Military History Institute
AWCCLC—Army War College, Curriculum Locator Cards, Military History Institute
AWCIR—Army War College Instructional Records, RG 165
BDP—Basic Defense Plan
BF—Bulky File
BWPO—Basic War Plan Orange
CA—Coast Artillery
CAC—Coast Artillery Corps
CARL—Combined Arms Research Library
CAWC—Course at Army War College
CCDF—Classified Central Decimal Files
CDF—Central Decimal Files
CDMSB—Coast Defenses of Manila and Subic Bays
CG—Commanding General
CO—Commanding Officer
C/S—Chief of Staff
CWS—Chemical Warfare Service
DL—Department of Luzon
DM—Department of Mindanao
DP—Division of the Philippines
DV—Department of the Visayas
E—National Archives Record Group Inventory Entry Number
F—File Number
FY—Fiscal Year
GB—General Board

GCM—General Court Martial
GO—General Order
GS—General Staff
HD—Hawaiian Department
HDMSB—Harbor Defenses of Manila and Subic Bays
HDN—Hawaiian Division
HDR—Hawaiian Department Records, RG 338
HNG—Hawaii National Guard
HQ—Headquarters
HSA—Hawaii State Archives, Honolulu.
IG—Inspector General
JANPC—Joint Army and Navy Planning Committee
JB—Joint Board
MID—Military Intelligence Division
M/S—Military Secretary
MS—Manuscript
OCS—Office of the Chief of Staff
PC—Philippine Constabulary
PD—Philippine Department
PDN—Philippine Division
PDP—Philipine Defense Project
PF—Project Files
PSD—Philippines Division
R—Microfilm Roll
RG—Record Group
RWD—*Annual Report of the War Department*
SCF—Security Classified Files
SN—Secretary of Navy
SPN—*Strategical Planning in the Navy*
SPWPC—Special Projects, War Plans—Color, 1920–48, RG 407
SW—Secretary of War
T.H.—Territory of Hawaii
WCD—War College Division
WPD—War Plans Division
WPO—War Plan Orange

Chapter One

1. Van Deusen, "Which Are More Needed," p. 990. Wagner, "Military Necessities of the United States," pp. 238–42; Cooke, "Our Army and Navy," pp. 426–30; Gibbon, "The Danger to Our Country," pp. 16–28; Abrahamson, *America Arms for a New Century*, pp. 29–40; Cosmas, *An Army for Empire*, pp. 35–41; Weigley, *Towards an American Army*, pp. 145–47.

2. William T. Sherman to Emory Upton, 12 July 1875, quoted in Upton, *Armies of Asia and Europe*, p. v.

3. Quoted in Petillo, *Douglas MacArthur*, p. 45.

4. Theodore Roosevelt to Francis V. Greene, 27 Sept. 1897, Greene Papers; Upton, *Armies of Asia and Europe*, pp. 1–12; Sanger, "Artillery in the East," pp. 231–32; Abbot, "Recent Japanese Manoevers," pp. 748–50; Stephan, *Hawaii under the Rising Sun*, pp. 55–56.

5. John M. Schofield to My Dear General [William T. Sherman], 15 Feb. 1873, Box 78, Schofield Papers. Tate, *Hawaii: Reciprocity or Annexation*, pp. 114–15.

6. Burton S. Alexander to A. A. Humphreys, 11 Mar. 1872, Box 78, Schofield Papers.

7. Military Information Division, *Hawaiian Islands*, pp. 9–10. The Military Information Division was retitled the Intelligence Office, Philippine Department, and in 1922 designated the Military Intelligence Division. Throughout this period officers referred to the intelligence office as MID.

8. "Hawaiian Islands," pp. 215–16. J.C.B., "Hawaiian Islands," pp. 682–83. An examination of official correspondence in the Records of the U.S. Army Adjutant General's Office (RG 94) reveals virtually no discussion of the Hawaiian Islands prior to the dispatch of troops in 1898.

9. John M. Schofield, "The Hawaiian Islands," [1898?], Box 93, Schofield Papers. G. L. Gillespie to Senior Officer, JB, 5 Dec. 1904, JB 304, Series 23, R 5, M 1421.

10. Slocum, "Annexation of Hawaii," p. 209.

11. Reeves, "Hawaiian Islands," pp. 171–208.

12. Cosmas, *An Army for Empire*, pp. 119–21, 199–200; Trask, *War with Spain*, pp. 383–86. Totals for expeditionary manpower from Entry 194, RG 94. The official designations for the U.S. Army forces in the Philippines are somewhat confusing. Very simply, the first troops to arrive in the islands were part of the Department of the Pacific and the 8th Army Corps. This cumbersome title was simplified on 29 March 1900 to the Division of the Philippines and on 22 December 1903 to the Philippines Division. On 9 October 1913, the U.S. Army garrison in the islands was renamed the Philippine Department. In 1921 the mobile forces were designated the Philippine Division. Throughout this period army officers continued to use earlier designations or even make up their own.

13. ANJ 36 (24 Sept. 1898). "In the Hands of Americans," *Pacific Commercial Advertiser* (2 June 1898); "Manila Brigade No. 2 Calls Here," *Pacific Commercial Advertiser* (24 June 1898); Acting SW to John S. Sherman, 24 Sept. 1898, AGO 128821, RG 94; J. Johnson Ray to SW, 29 Sept. 1898, AGO 147328, RG 94; William C. Addleman, "History of the United States Army in Hawaii, 1840 to 1939" [1940], E 6048, RG 395; Trask, *War with Spain*, pp. 388–89; Bailey, "United States and Hawaii," pp. 553–56; Osborne, *Empire Can Wait*.

14. Wang Wei Pin to E. A. Mott-Smith, 27 Oct. 1898; William Ennis to AG, Department of California, 28 Apr. 1900; H. M. Brown to Samuel M. Mills, 10 Jan. 1900, all filed in AGO 296674, RG 94.

15. Sanford B. Dole to Samuel M. Mills, 20 Jan. 1900; William M. Sternberg, 13 Feb. 1900, endorsement on Samuel M. Mills to AG, 19 Jan. 1900, Order No. 13, 20 Jan. 1900, all filed in AGO 309569, RG 94; Frederic V. Abbott to John R. Slattery, 3 Jan. 1906, U.S. Departments—War Department File, Governors' Correspondence—C. R. Carter, HSA.

16. Trask, *War with Spain*, pp. 391–422; Gates, *Schoolbooks and Krags*, pp. 3–42, 54–70.

17. Lyman W. V. Kennon to Henry C. Corbin, 26 Oct. 1899, Box 1A, Corbin Papers.

18. James Parker, "Some Random Notes," p. 340.

19. For histories of the Philippine War, see Gates, *Schoolbooks and Krags*; Linn, *U.S. Army and Counterinsurgency*; Sexton, *Soldiers in the Sun*; Taylor, "History of the Philippine Insurrection."

20. Memoranda: Showing Provinces, Districts, and Islands in the Philippine Archipelago, in which there has been no conditions requiring military interference . . . from reports of the Military Governor, 24 May 1902, F 4865-6, RG 350. On the southwestern Luzon and Samar campaigns, see Gates, *Schoolbooks and Krags*, pp. 248–65; May, *Battle for Batangas*; Linn, *U.S. Army and Counterinsurgency*, pp. 118–61; Linn, "Struggle for Samar."

21. Wooster, *Military and U.S. Indian Policy*, pp. 204–6.

22. Sexton, *Soldiers in the Sun*, pp. 105–6. Bacon, "Is Our Army Degenerate?"; James Parker, *Old Army*, pp. 105–6. An essential reference is Coffman, *The Old Army*.

23. Henry T. Allen to John A. Johnston, 21 Jan. 1902, Box 7, Allen Papers. Taylor, "History

of the Philippine Insurrection," p. 30HS, M 719; Linn, *U.S. Army and Counterinsurgency*, p. 22.

24. John H. Parker to Theodore Roosevelt, 18 Nov. 1900, Series 1, R 7, Roosevelt Papers.

25. Barr Questionnaire.

26. Bullard, "Citizen Soldier," pp. 153–67.

27. Church, "Increasing Desertions," p. 855.

28. "Insular Notes," p. 448.

29. Ganoe, *History of the United States Army*, p. 406.

30. Principal Wars and Other Belligerent Incidents, Philippine Insurrection File, No. 2159, Legislative and Policy Precedent Files, 1943–75, RG 407.

31. Chynoweth, *Bellamy Park*, pp. 25–26.

32. Samuel S. Sumner to AG, Department of Southern Luzon, 28 Sept. 1901, E 2349, RG 395.

33. Wagner, *Service of Security and Information*, p. 100; Bordwell, *Law of War between Belligerents*, pp. 155, 229–33.

34. Clifton Diary, 24 Jan. 1902, Clifton Papers.

35. "General Bell Defends the Army," *ANJ* 44 (23 Mar. 1907).

36. Root, *Military and Colonial Policy*, pp. 92–93; Jessup, *Elihu Root*, pp. 337–43; Joseph Stockton to George V. H. Moseley, 19 Aug. 1902, Scrapbook, Box 9, Moseley Papers; Samuel B. M. Young, "Our Soldiers in the Philippines," 13 Nov. 1902, Box B, Young Papers; Howard, "Is Cruelty Inseparable from War."

37. Edwin F. Glenn to Matthew F. Steele, 10 Feb. 1903, Box 17, Steele Papers.

38. "Insular Notes," p. 448.

39. Proceedings of a Board of Officers to Inquire into Allegations made by Maj. Cornelius Gardener, 13th U.S. Infantry in His Report of Dec. 16, 1901, AGO 421607, RG 94; Nelson A. Miles to SW, 19 Feb. 1903, AGO 389439, RG 94; Fairfull, "General Nelson Miles"; Wooster, *Nelson A. Miles*, p. 245.

40. Arthur Murray to Henry T. Allen, 12 May 1902, Box 7, Allen Papers.

41. Luke Wright to William H. Taft, 19 Apr. 1902, Box 164, Root Papers. Welch, "American Atrocities."

42. William H. Taft to Elihu Root, 18 Aug. 1900, Series 21, Taft Papers.

43. Petillo, *Douglas MacArthur*, pp. 52–63. Both protagonists have their champions, see Young, *General's General*, pp. 257–90; Minger, *William Howard Taft*, pp. 42–50.

44. John R. White, *Bullets and Bolos*, p. 51.

45. "American Army," pp. 643–45. Seaman, "U.S. Army Ration," p. 375.

46. Reichmann, "In Pace Para Bellum," pp. 6–7.

47. U.S. Congress, Senate, *Affairs in the Philippine Islands*, p. 867.

48. Glenn, "Some Things Our Infantry Requires," p. 130.

49. John H. Parker, "What Shall We Do," pp. 662–70.

Chapter Two

1. *Manila Times* (23 July 1902). Luke E. Wright to Elihu Root, 20 July 1902, Box 2, Edwards Papers.

2. William E. W. McKinley to John F. Guilfoyle, 27 Aug. 1903, F 4865-16, RG 350.

3. *Manila Times* (25 July 1906).

4. William H. Taft to Clarence R. Edwards, 16 Apr. 1903, Box 2, Edwards Papers.

5. Coolidge, *U.S. As a World Power*, p. 155.

6. Woodruff, "Normal Malay."

7. Leonard Wood to Theodore Roosevelt, 26 July 1906, Box 37, Wood Papers.

8. J. M. Sheriden, Conditions As to Peace and Order, Dec., 1906, F 2490-48, RG 350.

9. Brands, *Bound to Empire*, pp. 60–79; Karnow, *In Our Image*, pp. 196–211; Grunder and Livezey, *Philippines and the United States*, pp. 78–145. An excellent source for U.S. efforts is Glenn A. May, *Social Engineering*.

10. *RWD* 1903, 1:33.

11. *RWD* 1904, 1:264–74; *RWD* 1905, 1:423–37; Woolard, "Philippine Scouts," pp. 88–110, 121–43.

12. Henry T. Allen to W. Cameron Forbes, Supplemental Report, 1 July to 20 Sept. 1904, 22 Sept. 1904, Box 8, Allen Papers. Luke E. Wright to Elihu Root, 20 July 1902, Box 2, Edwards Papers; William H. Taft to Elihu Root, 14 Apr. 1903, F 4865-15, RG 350; Luke E. Wright to William H. Taft, 27 Apr. 1904, Box 3, Edwards Papers; *RWD* 1903, 1:32–33.

13. Thomas A. Hendrick to Theodore Roosevelt, 30 Sept. 1904, Box 4, Edwards Papers.

14. *ANJ* 43 (23 Sept. 1905); Cornelius D. E. Willcox to C/S, PSD, 24 Feb. 1910, AGO 1645979, RG 94; Luke E. Wright to William H. Taft, 2 Jan. 1905, Box 5, Edwards Papers; Smythe, *Guerrilla Warrior*, pp. 79–80.

15. DP, GO 152, 7 July 1902, E 2070, RG 395. Grunder and Livezey, *Philippines and the United States*, pp. 78–79.

16. Tasker H. Bliss, Memorandum: Rearrangement of Scout Stations in the Department of Luzon, making the companies available for service in Negros and Leyte, 17 Nov. 1905, No. 263160, E 2670, RG 395.

17. *RWD* 1904, 3:235. Daniel J. Moynihan to AG, DV, 17 Feb. 1904, No. 893-B, E 2498, RG 395; William H. Carter to AG, PSD, 27 Feb. 1904, No. 893-C, E 2498, RG 395; L. R. Wilfrey to Secretary of Commerce and Police, 18 Dec. 1905, E 3002, RG 395.

18. "Major Carrington's Fate," *Manila Times* (23 Feb. 1905); "Justice for the Army," *ANJ* 42 (25 Feb. 1905).

19. "Lessons of the Grafton Case," *ANJ* 44 (18 June 1907). "Soldiers' Rights in the Philippines," *ANJ* 42 (4 Feb. 1905); Sigerfoos, "Are Members."

20. William H. Taft to SW, 30 Nov. 1903, F 4865-20, RG 350.

21. *RWD* 1904, 3:206. Charles E. Magoon to SW, Report on the Use of the Philippine Scouts in Securing the Execution of the Civil Laws in Force in the Philippine Islands, 29 Nov. 1902, F 1877, RG 350; George V. H. Moseley, Memorandum, 1903, Box 38, Moseley Papers; Twichell, *Allen*, pp. 129–32; Woolard, "Philippine Scouts," pp. 93–100.

22. Annual Report for the Year Ending 30 June 1905 by Brigadier General Henry T. Allen, Chief, Philippine Constabulary, 1905, Box 32, Allen Papers. Henry T. Allen to Anon., 1904, Box 8, Allen Papers; Bliss, Memorandum: Rearrangement of Scout Stations.

23. John S. Guilfoyle to Robert W. Mearns, 29 Mar. 1905, Box 1, Mearns Papers.

24. Leonard Wood to Henry C. Corbin, 23 Feb. 1905, Box 36, Wood Papers. Anon. [Robert W. Mearns] to M/S, PSN, 31 May and 4 July 1905, Box 1, Mearns Papers; William H. Johnston, "First Battalion Philippine Scouts," pp. 28–39; Woolard, "Philippine Scouts," pp. 125–37.

25. Woolard, "Philippine Scouts," pp. 109–10.

26. William H. Taft to Henry T. Allen, 4 Sept. 1905, Box 1, Mearns Papers.

27. Bliss Diary, 1905, pp. 40–41, Bliss Papers.

28. Frederick W. Sibley to AG, DL, 27 Jan. 1905, No. 19438-gg, E 2670, RG 395. Coats, "Philippine Constabulary," pp. 139–67.

29. Frederick W. Sibley to AG, DL, 24 Feb. 1905, No. 19438-2, E 2670, RG 395.

30. Wallace C. Taylor to AG, PC, Report of Third District, Philippine Constabulary, 19 July 1905, Box 32, Allen Papers. Contemporaries used a variety of spellings—Pulahanes, Pulahans, Pulajans, Pulajanes; I have chosen one of the most common. For background on Samar, see Cruikshank, *Samar: 1768–1898*.

31. Statement of Pantaleon Hobayen, 18 Jan. 1905, No. 3412-CN, E 2498, RG 395; *ANJ* 42 (4 Mar. 1905); Arens, "Early Pulahan Movement," pp. 57–109; McCoy, "Baylan."

32. Hugh D. Wise to M/S, DV, 2 June 1906, E 2074, RG 395. John A. Paegelow to Adj., San Julian, 25 June 1906, No. 6100-N, E 2498, RG 395; Statement of Fruto Minsan—Pulajan, 1904 Diary, Box 1, Allen Papers; Statements of Captured Pulahanes, E 2698, RG 395; "The Situation in Samar," *ANJ* 43 (21 July 1906).

33. Franklin S. Hutton to M/S, DV, 3 Dec. 1906, Box 1, E 2712, RG 395. For descriptions of Pulahan tactics, see Norman E. Cook to M/S, 6 Feb. 1905, No. 3412-DH, E 2498, RG 395; Hamilton, "Jungle Tactics," pp. 25–27; Wise, "Notes on Field Service," p. 14; Coats, "Philippine Constabulary," pp. 315–19.

34. Norman E. Cook to Henry T. Allen, 12 Jan. 1905, No. 3412-AV, E 2498, RG 395; Stanley P. Hyatt, "Fair and Frank Criticism," *Manila Times* (16 Mar. 1905); *RWD* 1905, 3:285–86; Forbes Journal, 10 Aug. 1904, 1:37, Forbes Papers; Woolard, "Philippine Scouts," pp. 137–39; Coats, "Philippine Constabulary," pp. 310–51.

35. Henry T. Allen to W. Cameron Forbes, 18 Dec. 1904, Box 1, Allen Papers. Henry T. Allen, Proclamation, 20 Feb. 1905, E 2929, RG 395; M/S to CO, Camp Connell, 3 Jan. 1905, No. 2, E 5452, RG 395; Henry T. Allen to W. Cameron Forbes, 14 Mar. 1905, Box 8, Allen Papers; Henry T. Allen to CO, Lloriente, 5 Apr. 1905, No. 3412-DJ, E 2498, RG 395.

36. Allen Diary, 7, 9, 16–18, 21 Mar. 1905, Box 1, Allen Papers.

37. Henry C. Ide to Leonard Wood, 2 June 1905, No. 6100-6, E 2498, RG 395. Luke E. Wright to William H. Taft, 2 Jan. 1905, Box 5, Edwards Papers; W. Cameron Forbes to Leonard Wood, 10 Feb. 1905, Box 36, Wood Papers; *Manila Times* (4 Feb. 1905); Twichell, *Allen*, p. 134. Lieutenant Albert W. Foreman's reports are filed in No. 3412, E 2498, RG 395.

38. *RWD* 1905, 3:264; *ANJ* 42 (29 July 1905).

39. *RWD* 1905, 3:257–60; George Curry to CO, Tarangnan, 31 July 1905, No. 84, E 5452, RG 395; Emil Speth to M/S, DV, 31 Aug. 1906, No. 52, E 5397, RG 395; Norman E. Cook to E. E. Fuller, 21 Oct. 1905, No. 6, E 2708, RG 395; Cornelius Gardener to CO, Hinalasan, 15 June 1905, E 2928, RG 395; Charles R. Howland to J. T. Ware, 20 Nov. 1905, No. 113, E 3855, RG 395; Franklin S. Hutton to M/S, 29 May 1906, No. 6100-4, E 2398, RG 395.

40. Norman E. Cook to CO, Taft, Sub: Instructions of Governor Curry, 12 Apr. 1906, No. 149, E 3855, RG 395. William H. Johnston to M/S, 8 Apr. 1906, Box 38, Wood Papers; "Black Treachery of the Samar Pulajanes," *Manila Times* (26 Mar. 1906); Sturtevant, *Popular Uprisings*, p. 130; Coats, "Philippine Constabulary," pp. 344–45.

41. Samuel V. Ham to M/S, 14 Dec. 1906, No. 9000-4-AU, E 2498, RG 395; Jesse M. Lee, Personal Memorandum, 21 Mar. 1907, AGO 1250150, RG 94; *Manila Times* (21 June and 1 Aug. 1906); Arens, "Early Pulahan Movement," pp. 74–78.

42. Frederick A. Smith to Leonard Wood, 20 Dec. 1906, Box 38, Wood Papers; Proceedings of a Board of Officers . . . Borongan, Samar, 1 Dec. 1906, No. 6100-6, E 2498, RG 395. The chief in question, Otoy, was finally killed in 1911.

43. Memo: Principal engagements, with dates and number of casualties, WCD 9136-2, E 296, RG 165.

44. On parallels between the West and Moroland; see George M. Barbour to Leonard Wood, 27 Nov. 1903, Box 33, Wood Papers; Frank McCoy to John P. Taylor, 25 Sept. 1903, Box 10, McCoy Papers; George W. Davis, Notes on the Government of the Country Inhabited by Non-Christians in Mindanao and the Neighboring Islands, 25 Aug. 1902, F 132, E 300, RG 165; "Dato of the Malanos," Drum Papers; Tan, "Sulu under the Eagle's Shadow," pp. 56–57; Mastura, "American Presence in Mindanao," pp. 31–32. For some of the romantic works on the Moros, see Dobbs, *Kris and Krag*; Victor Hurley, *Swish of the Kris*; Cloman, *Myself and a Few Moros*; Russel, "Tales of a Tawi Tawi Garrison," pp. 210–17; Hogan, "Sultan of Sulu," pp. 636–41. For treatments of the U.S. Army and the Moros, see Gowing, "Mandate in Moroland"; Jornacion, "Time of Eagles"; Thompson, "Governors of the Moro Province." For an example of how the Moro conflicts became a staple of veterans' stories, see Jones, *From Here to Eternity*, p. 14.

45. Hugh L. Scott to Leonard Wood, 9 Mar. 1905, Box 36, Wood Papers.

46. Benjamin Foulois to Dear Mother, 7 Feb. 1905, Box 4, Foulois Papers.

47. Bullard, "Road Building," p. 819.

48. Pershing Diary, 4 Dec. 1911, Box 1, Pershing Papers.

49. *RWD* 1902, 1, pt. 9:495.

50. Benjamin Foulois to Dear Mother, 7 Feb. 1905, Box 4, Foulois Papers. Hugh L. Scott to Leonard Wood, 9 Mar. 1905, Box 36, Wood Papers; Bateman, "Military Taming of the Moro," pp. 259–66.

51. Smythe, *Guerrilla Warrior*, p. 104.

52. Gowing, "Mandate in Moroland," pp. 318–23.

53. Leonard Wood to Theodore Roosevelt, 20 Sept. 1903, Box 32, Wood Papers; Leonard Wood to Luke E. Wright, 12 July 1904, Box 34, Wood Papers; Gowing, "Mandate in Moroland," pp. 385–94; Lane, *Armed Progressive*, pp. 123–30.

54. "From Reveille to Retreat: An Autobiography," p. 141, Helmick Papers.

55. Adna R. Chaffee to Samuel S. Sumner, 5 Sept. 1902, Box 1, Corbin Papers.

56. John J. Pershing to George W. Davis, 1902, Notebook, Box 1, Pershing Papers.

57. John J. Pershing to Samuel S. Sumner, 7 and 9 Apr. 1903, Notebook 1903, Box 1, Pershing Papers. Smythe, *Guerrilla Warrior*, pp. 66–110; Vandiver, *Black Jack*, 1:303–18; Gowing, "Mandate in Moroland," pp. 352–59.

58. Bullard Diary, 8 Oct. 1904, Bullard Papers.

59. Lane, *Armed Progressive*, pp. 124–25; Millett, *The General*, pp. 175–77.

60. Leonard Wood to Theodore Roosevelt, 3 Aug. 1903, Box 32, Wood Papers.

61. Leonard Wood to Horace Fletcher, 26 Dec. 1903, Box 32, Wood Papers. Bacevich, "Disagreeable Work," pp. 49–61. The number of Moro casualites in the 1903 Jolo expedition is unclear. Wood stated 500, but in his diary he estimated as many as 1,200; see Thompson, "Governors of the Moro Province," p. 57.

62. Leonard Wood to Theodore Roosevelt, 7 Dec. 1903 and 5 Jan. 1904, Box 33, Wood Papers. Luke E. Wright to William H. Taft, 27 Apr. 1904, Box 3, Edwards Papers; Forbes Journal, 23 Oct. 1904, 1:88, Forbes Papers; *RWD* 1906, 3:280.

63. Harold P. Howard to Adj., 20 Jan. 1905, F 6, Box 1, Howard Papers. Hugh L. Scott to Leonard Wood, 17 Apr. 1905, Box 36, Wood Papers. Much of the correspondence on Bud Dajo is filed with AGO 1143147, RG 94.

64. Sanford, "Battle of Bud Dajo," p. 12. Bacevich, *Diplomat in Khaki*, pp. 36–38; Lane, *Armed Progressive*, pp. 127–30; John R. White, *Bullets and Bolos*, pp. 299–313; Gowing, "Mandate in Moroland," pp. 482–90.

65. Horace Fletcher to Tasker H. Bliss, 24 July 1906, Scrapbook, Bliss Papers. The number of Moro casualties at Bud Dajo was never ascertained, but estimates vary from 600 to as many as 1,800; see Sanford, "Battle of Bud Dajo," pp. 12, 17. The army had fifteen soldiers killed and fifty-two wounded at Bud Dajo.

66. "The Moro Battle," *The Independent* 60 (15 Mar. 1906), pp. 637; "The Battle in Jolo," *Outlook* 82 (17 Mar. 1906), pp. 582–83; Gowing, "Mandate in Moroland," pp. 486–89.

67. Edgar Z. Steever to Tasker H. Bliss, 23 Aug. 1906, Scrapbook, Bliss Papers. *ANJ* 46 (23 Jan. 1909); Gowing, "Mandate in Moroland," pp. 495–577.

68. *RWD* 1907, 3:290.

69. John N. Merrill to Dear Mama, 19 Oct. 1907, Merrill Family Papers.

70. Pershing Diary, 14 Dec. 1911, Box 1, Pershing Papers.

71. Smythe, *Guerrilla Warrior*, pp. 169–73.

72. Gowing, "Mandate in Moroland," pp. 635–38.

73. Return of Casualties in Jolo Field Force in Action at Bud Bagsak and Sahipi's Cotta on June 11 to 15, 1913, E 2076, RG 395; Smythe, *Guerrilla Warrior*, pp. 186–204; Vandiver, *Black Jack*, 1:559–67.

74. J. Franklin Bell, Report on Military Situation, Moro Province and Division of the Philippines, 9 Nov. and 15 Dec. 1913, AWC 8116-2, E 296, RG 165.

75. Hamilton, "Jungle Tactics," p. 23. Crane, "Our New Infantry Drill Regulations," p. 241; *RWD* 1906, 3:209.

76. Bradley G. Ruttencutter to Adj., 4th District, 20 Jan. 1907, E 3004, RG 395.

77. Franklin S. Hutton to M/S, DV, 3 Dec. 1906, E 2712, RG 395; Israel R. Costello to Adj., 5th District, 22 Jan. 1907, E 5220, RG 395; Harry E. Knight to M/S, DV, 25 Jan. 1907, E 5220, RG 395; Hamilton, "Jungle Tactics," pp. 27–28; *RWD* 1905, 3:288; Interview, pp. 14–15, McLaughlin Papers.

78. Report of Colonel D. J. Baker Jr., Assistant Chief Commanding Provisional District, Philippines Constabulary, on Work Done in That District since its Organization up to July 31, 1905, F 1184-60, RG 350.

79. Summary of Expeditions and Results. Samar, P.I., June 13th to Dec. 15th 1906, No. 100, E 3861, RG 395. Frederick A. Smith to M/S, DV, 26 July 1906, No. 6100-4, E 2498, RG 395; Hugh D. Wise to Frederick A. Smith, Journal of Events, 19 Dec. 1906, E 2074, RG 395; *RWD* 1906, 3:273.

80. Bibliographical File: Philippines.

81. W. P. Baker to Chief, P.C., 6 Aug. 1905, No. 19438-4, E 2670, RG 395.

82. HQ, DV, GO 28, 27 June 1906, E 2505, RG 395. Bradley G. Ruttencutter to Adj., 4th District, 20 Jan. 1907, E 3004, RG 395; Bullard, "Road Building"; Bateman, "Military Road Making."

83. Augustus H. Bishop to Adj., 11 June 1907, No. 118, E 5212, RG 395.

84. George Bell to Adj., Field Forces, Leyte, 16 June 1906, Box 37, Wood Papers. *RWD* 1907, 3:217–19.

85. DV, Field Orders No. 3, 28 Mar. 1903, Box 38, Moseley Papers.

86. George T. Langhorne to Leonard Wood, 23 Aug. 1905, Box 36, Wood Papers.

87. Edgar Z. Steever to Tasker H. Bliss, 23 Aug. 1906, Scrapbook, Bliss Papers. Gowing, "Mandate in Moroland," pp. 360–61.

88. Leonard Wood to Tasker H. Bliss, 17 July 1906, Scrapbook, Bliss Papers.

89. Circular No. 1, HQ, Troops in the Field, Island of Leyte, 13 Aug. 1906, E 3236, RG 395.

90. Israel R. Costello to Adj., 5th District, 22 Jan. 1907, E 5220, RG 395; Ralph Van Deman, Sub: Translation, June 1902, F 223, M 1023; Bradley G. Ruttencutter to Adj., 4th District, 20 Jan. 1907, E 3004, RG 395; Franklin S. Hutton to M/S, DV, 3 Dec. 1906, E 2712, RG 395; Harry E. Knight to M/S, 25 Jan. 1907, E 5220, RG 395.

91. Taylor, "History of the Philippine Insurrection"; Farrell, "An Abandoned Approach"; Gates, "Official Historian."

92. Charles G. Morton, "Organization, Use and Equipment of Machine Guns," Apr. 1905, AWC Special Study No. 1, Serial No. 12, E 299, RG 165.

93. Bullard, "Army in Cuba," p. 157.

94. Leonard Wood to AG, 1 July 1907, Box 40, Wood Papers.

95. Jesse M. Cullison, Handling Troops in the Tropics, in Francis W. Mansfield to AG, 7 Apr. 1909, AGO 1512366, RG 94.

96. William H. Johnston, "First Battalion," p. 38.

97. Daniel H. Brush to AG, PSD, 2 Apr. 1911, AGO 1748020, RG 94; Vandiver, *Black Jack*, 1:560.

Chapter Three

1. "Monkeys Have No Tails," Vol. 1, p. 2, Ivins Papers.

2. *RWD* 1917, 1:129.

3. Root, *Military and Colonial Policy*, pp. 351–52.

4. On the Root reforms, see Abrahamson, *America Arms*; Weigley, *History of the U.S. Army*, pp. 313–34; Jessup, *Elihu Root*, pp. 220–40; Lane, *Armed Progressive*, pp. 148–55; Karsten, "Armed Progressives," pp. 197–232; Roberts, "Reform and Revitalization," pp. 197–203; Zais, "Struggle for a Twentieth Century Army."

5. Carter, "Elihu Root," p. 117.

6. GO 107, 17 July 1903, E 284, RG 165. Tasker H. Bliss to Chief, 2nd Division, 20 Apr. 1904, No. 157, E 291, RG 165.

7. Testimony of William H. Taft, U.S. Congress, Senate, *Hearings . . . 1906–7*, p. 39.

8. *RWD* 1911, 1:15.

9. James Parker, *Old Army*, pp. 371–72. Wooster, *Nelson A. Miles*, pp. 242–44; Ransom, "Nelson A. Miles," pp. 173–83.

10. "Right Oblique" to Editor, *ANJ* 44 (2 Mar. 1907). Charles W. Larned to Editor, *ANJ* 43 (10 Feb. 1906); "What Is the Matter with Our Army," *ANJ* 45 (28 Dec. 1907).

11. *RWD* 1905, 1:397–98. Kerrick, "Our Military Resources," pp. 293–316; Glassford, "Preparation for Defense," pp. 68–81.

12. *RWD* 1911, 1:152.

13. Malone, "Capture of New York," p. 933. For similar sentiments, see Hugh Johnson, "Lamb Rampant"; Pettit, "How Far Does Democracy."

14. James J. Thomsen to Marvin C. Hepler, 17 Jan. 1904, Hepler Papers. "The Regeneration of the Army," *ANJ* 43 (27 Jan. 1906); *RWD* 1904, 1:255–56; Rhodes, "Experiences of Our Army," pp. 217–18.

15. *RWD* 1904, 1:226.

16. Hagood, *Circular*, p. 14. As with most U.S. Army statistics, there are discrepancies; see *RWD* 1905, 1:451–52; *RWD* 1914, 1:276.

17. *RWD* 1907, 1:18. For information on enlisted life, see Hagood, *Circular*; J. Franklin Bell, "The Army As a Life Occupation for Enlisted Men," *Report of the Secretary of War, 1907*, pp. 62–109; Jesse M. Lee, Personal Memorandum Submitted to the Honorable, the Secretary of War, 21 Mar. 1907, AGO 1250150, RG 94.

18. Millard, "Shame of Our Army," p. 420. "Army Training and Desertion," *ANJ* 44 (2 Mar. 1907); Hagood, *Circular*, pp. 14–15; *RWD* 1907, 1:230; *RWD* 1908, 1:294–95; Raines, "Major General J. Franklin Bell," pp. 485–91.

19. Stratemeyer, *Under MacArthur in Luzon*. King, "American Soldier," pp. 1401–8; Saltzman, "How May Public Opinion."

20. Adams, "Education of Trooper Brown," p. 11.

21. Millard, "Shame of Our Army," p. 419.

22. "What's the Matter with the Army," *ANJ* 44 (16 Feb. 1907).

23. Stephen C. Mills to Clark E. Carr, 9 Mar. 1909, Mills Papers. Hagood, *Circular*, p. 26. For Roosevelt's interference, see Raines, "Major General J. Franklin Bell," pp. 1–5, 118; "The President's Warning," *ANJ* 42 (15 July 1905); James Parker, *Old Army*, pp. 386–87. On complaints of favoritism, see Arthur L. Wagner to Henry T. Allen, 18 Jan. 1905, Box 8, Allen Papers; Carter, "General Staff," p. 564; "What Is the Matter with Our Army," *ANJ* 45 (28 Dec. 1907).

24. Rhodes, "Experiences of Our Army," p. 218. Root, *Military and Colonial Policy*, p. 394.

25. *RWD* 1903, 1:140. *RWD* 1906, 3:212.

26. *RWD* 1909, 1:295. Figures from *RWD* 1905, 1:361–62; *RWD* 1909, 1:13.

27. "An Army without Officers," *ANJ* 45 (13 Feb. 1909). *RWD* 1909, 1:211–12.

28. Seaman, "Native Troops," p. 860. For contemporary views on native forces, see Swift, "Peon or Soldier"; Rhodes, "Utilization of Native Troops"; Ward, "Utilization of Native Troops"; Moseley, "A Colonial Army"; Munro, "Philippine Native Scouts"; William H. Johnston, "Philippine Infantry."

29. William H. Johnston, "First Battalion," p. 34; Henry T. Allen to Clarence Edwards, 31 Jan. 1903, Box 8, Allen Papers; James C. Rhea to Adj., 30 Oct. 1913, AGO 2105160, RG 94.

30. "The Territory of Hawaii," *ANJ* 42 (2 Aug. 1905); J. W. Jones to Adj., HNG, 3 Dec. 1903, F Arthur MacArthur—M37CB, 1866, R 277, M 1064.

31. Charles D. Rhodes to Johnson Hagood, 5 Oct. 1907, in Hagood, *Circular*, p. 99. Meixsel, "U.S. Army Policy," pp. 9–13.

32. *ANJ* 44 (29 Dec. 1906). George W. Davis to Adna R. Chaffee, 17 Apr. 1902, Box 1, Corbin Papers. For a favorable evaluation of black soldiers in the Philippines, see "Record of the 24th Infantry," *Manila Times* (29 June 1902).

33. "Dato of the Malanos," Drum Papers. J. Franklin Bell to Leonard Wood, 15 May 1906, Box 36, Wood Papers; David P. Barrows to Chairman of Philippine Civil Service Board, 12 Jan. 1905, Box 5, Edwards Papers; Meixsel, "U.S. Army Policy," pp. 13–15.

34. Joseph Tucker to Editor, *Manila Times* (24 June 1902). *Manila Times* (15 July 1902); Coolidge, *United States As a World Power*, pp. 73–74.

35. Recommendation for Cavalry and Infantry regiments to replace regiments to be relieved during 1907 in the Philippines, 26 Nov. 1907, OCS 19, E 5, RG 165.

36. Henry L. Stimson to Sidney Ballou, 16 Dec. 1912, OCS 9678, E 5, RG 165. On the excellent performance of black troops, see George Williams, Memorandum Report of Observations in Leyte, [1906], Box 38, Wood Papers.

37. Bliss Diary, 1905, Bliss Papers.

38. *RWD* 1908, 3:233.

39. Campbell B. Hodges to Mother, 11 Feb. and 2 May 1904, Hodges Papers.

40. Testimony of William H. Carter, in U.S. Congress, Senate, *Hearings . . . on Bill 8129*, p. 11.

41. Palmer, *America in Arms*, p. 139.

42. John M. Palmer, Report on a Scheme for a Well Balanced Army (Supplemental Study), 31 Oct. 1911, AWC 6368-41, E 296, RG 165. Holley, *General John M. Palmer*, pp. 205–11. For a detailed study of the origins of the Colonial Army, see Meixsel, "U.S. Army Policy," pp. 46–57.

43. *RWD* 1912, 1:16–17.

44. "Report of the Land Forces of the United States," 1912, F 25532, RG 350.

45. Leonard Wood to SW, Sub: Reorganization of the Philippines garrison, 7 Feb. 1912; Leonard Wood to Asst. AG, 20 Feb. 1912; War Department, GO 8, 30 Mar. 1912; all in OCS 8397, E 5, RG 165. Hawaii's Colonial Army garrison in 1913 comprised the following regiments: 1st Infantry; 2nd Infantry (2 battalions); 20th Infantry (1 battalion); 25th Infantry; 4th Cavalry; and 1st Field Artillery (2 batteries).

46. R. H. R. Loughborough to CG, PD, Sub: Annual Report, District of Luzon, 30 June 1913, AWC 3676, RG 165.

47. F. C. Marshall to CO, 15th Cavalry, Sub: Review of Regimental Training and Recommendation of Future Training, 25 Jan. 1917, AWC 8438-16, RG 165. Notes by General Wotherspoon, 1913, AWC 7881-4, RG 165; J. E. McMahon to C/S, Sub: Status of Non-commissioned Officers in Foreign Service, 29 July 1913, OCS 7881-1, E 296, RG 165; Hugh L. Scott to SW, 13 May 1915, AGO 2290794, RG 94; War Department, GO 36, 9 June 1915, AWC 9047-4, RG 165; Meixsel, "U.S. Army Policy," pp. 73–86.

48. V. M. Elmore to CO, HD, Sub: Annual Report, 1 July 1922, R 120, HDR; Jarvis J. Bain to AC/S, WPD, Sub: Inspection of the Hawaiian Department Made by Maj. Jarvis J. Bain, General Staff, Feb. 17–28, 1924, AGO 333.1 (HD), E 37, RG 407.

49. Major General Commanding to AG, Sub: Annual Report, FY 1921, 30 July 1921, AGO 319.2, E 37, RG 407.

50. Edward M. Lewis to AG, Sub: Annual Report, HD, FY 1926, 30 June 1926, AGO 319.12 HD (6-30-26), RG 407.

51. George L. Febiger to CG, HDN, Sub: Annual Inspection of Schofield Barracks, FY 1931, 24 June 1931, AGO 333.1, E 11, RG 159. Fox Conner to AG, Annual Report, FY 1930, 28 July 1930, AGO 319.12 (7-28-30) HD, RG 407; William Lassiter to AG, Annual Report, FY 1931, 22 Aug. 1931, AGO 319.12 (8-22-31) HD, RG 407.

52. J. L. Parkinson to CG, PD, Sub: Inspection of Post of Manila, 13 June 1931, AGO 333.1, Box 133, RG 159.

53. William H. Raymond, Study of Cost of U.S. Army in Insular Possessions, 1912–1913, [1914?], AWC 7330, RG 165; Montgomery M. Macomb to C/S, Sub: Policy to Be Followed in Returning Troops from Foreign Service, 12 Apr. 1915, AWC 9047-1, RG 165; Meixsel, "U.S. Army Policy," p. 67.

54. Douglas MacArthur to Fanniebelle Stuart, 17 Apr. 1908, F 5, Box 1, RG 10, MacArthur Papers.

55. Willeford, *Something about a Soldier*, p. 61.

56. Hugh Straughn, History of the Intelligence Office, PD, 1919, MID 10560-152-187, RG 165. Prior to 1920, Hawaii was a two-year tour.

57. Oral History, p. 14, Larsen Papers.

58. Russell A. Eberhardt to Brian M. Linn, Jan. 7, 1993, in author's possession.

59. *RWD* 1916, 1:198. Weckerling, "Natives of Northern Luzon," pp. 141–44; Blumenson, *Patton Papers*, pp. 214–16, 291–92; "Military Marriages," pp. 811–12; "The Marriage Question in the Army," *ANJ* 42 (18 Feb. 1905).

60. "Information on Philippine Service," pp. 429–30.

61. Maus, *Army Officer on Leave*, p. 35.

62. Shunk, *Army Woman*, pp. 7–8.

63. White Diary, June 1927, White Papers.

64. "An Army Wife" to Editor, *ANJ* 53 (21 Oct. 1905).

65. White Diary, 15 June 1927, White Papers. "Some Brutal Suggestions," *ANJ* 45 (12 Oct. 1907); Nazarro Oral History, p. 21.

66. Deichelmann Oral History, pp. 30–31.

67. *Manila Times* (14 Jan. 1903); "Justice for the Enlisted Man," *ANJ* 44 (19 Jan. 1907); "Still Another Army Wife" to Editor, *ANJ* 53 (25 Nov. 1905); Willeford, *Something about a Soldier*, pp. 23–28, 153–62.

68. Nazarro Oral History, pp. 21–22; Deichelmann Oral History, pp. 30–31; *ANJ* 43 (17 July 1906); "Iwilei Wrecked by Colored Troops," *Pacific Coast Advertiser* (14 Jan. 1916).

69. Russell A. Eberhardt to Brian M. Linn, 7 Jan. 1993; Robert W. Keeney to Brian M. Linn, 4 Feb. 1994, both in author's possession.

70. "Story about a Soldier," p. 123, Koch Papers.

71. "Monkeys Have No Tails," Vol. 4, pp. 33–37.

72. "The Territory of Hawaii," *ANJ* 42 (2 Aug. 1905); Arthur MacArthur to AG, 2 Feb. 1904, AGO 453450, RG 94.

73. "The 21st at Camp Connell," *ANJ* 42 (24 Jun. 1905). "A Tour of the Visayas," *ANJ* 42 (28 Jan. 1905); *ANJ* 43 (16 Sept. 1905).

74. *ANJ* 44 (20 July 1907).

75. Throughout its existence Stotsenburg was referred to as both "Camp Stotsenburg" and "Fort Stotsenburg." For consistency, the more common term of Fort Stotsenburg will be used.

76. Proceedings of a Board of Officers convened at Camp McKinley, Hawaiian Territory, 18 Dec. 1902, AGO 257654, RG 94; Proceedings of a Board of Officers . . . , 26 Nov. 1903, AGO 453450, RG 94; William C. Addleman, "History of the United States Army in Hawaii, 1840 to 1939" [1940], E 6048, RG 395, pp. 3, 9.

77. George A. Nugent to IG, Sub: Inspection of Harbor Defenses of Pearl Harbor, 20 May 1927, AGO 333.1 (HD), Box 143, RG 159. W. P. Kendall to Surgeon General, Sub:

Annual Report, 1919, 21 Jan. 1920, AGO 319.12, RG 112; G. R. Allen to CG, HD, Sub: Annual Inspection, Harbor Defenses of Pearl Harbor, T.H., FY 1935, 10 May 1936, AGO 333.1, Box 143, RG 159.

78. Howard C. Fields to Brian M. Linn, 4 Mar. 1994, in author's possession.

79. Dana T. Merrill, Survey and Inspection of Harbor Defenses of Honolulu, T.H., FY 1934, 21 May 1934, AGO 333.1, Box 142, RG 159; Christian, "Harbor Defenses of Honolulu," pp. 483–84.

80. Conner, *What Father Forbad*, pp. 158–59.

81. Shea, *Army Wife*, pp. 254–55.

82. Addleman, "History," p. 13. "The Fifth Cavalry in Hawaii," ANJ 46 (27 Feb. 1909); Nedbalek, *Wahiawa*, pp. 39–41.

83. Hawaiian Defense Project, Basic Document, 1928, E 6061, Box 2, RG 395. J. B. McDonald to CG, HD, Sub: Annual garrison inspection of Schofield Barracks, T.H., 7 Apr. 1915, Box 275, E 11, RG 159; William Lassiter to C/S, Sub: Project for the Defense of Oahu, 26 Feb. 1920, AGO 660.2, CCDF, RG 407; Joseph P. Aleshire to CG, HD, Sub: Economic Survey, Schofield Barracks, T.H., 10 Aug. 1928, AGO 333.1, E 11, RG 159; "$11 Million for Army Building Here Is Sought," *Honolulu Advertiser* (2 Dec. 1924); Nedbalek, *Wahiawa*, pp. 59–60.

84. Statement by Major General H. A. Drum, Commanding General Hawaiian Department, to House Military Appropriations Committee, n.d., F HD, Box 21, Drum Papers. Briant H. Wells to AG, Sub: Annual Report, FY 1932, 16 July 1932, AGO 319.12 (7-16-32), RG 407; W. A. Pickering to CG, HD, Sub: Annual Inspection, Schofield Barracks, T.H., 30 June 1933 and 30 June 1935, AGO 333.1, Box 276, E 11, RG 159.

85. Robert W. Keeney to Brian M. Linn, 16 Feb. 1994; Alfred N. Poirier to Brian M. Linn, 7 Apr. 1994, both in author's possession.

86. "Story about a Soldier," p. 78. Memoirs, p. 10, Scott Papers; RWD 1906, 3:209; Fred Ainsworth to CG, PD, 16 Sept. 1910, AWC 6270, RG 165; ANJ 42 (3 Sept. 1904); Meixsel, "U.S. Army Policy," pp. 24–28.

87. Green, "Coast Artillery Life"; Gleeck, *Manila Americans*, p. 248.

88. Shunk, *Army Woman*, pp. 32–41.

89. Inspection of Fort Stotsenburg, P.I., including Clark Field, 31 Oct. 1935, AGO 333.1, Box 134, RG 159; Tuttle, "Camp Stotsenburg."

90. Michael J. Campbell MS, pp. 68–69, Olson Papers; J. L. Parkinson to CG, PD, Sub: Inspection of Post of Manila, 13 June 1931, AGO 333.1, Box 13, RG 159; "Conditions in the Philippines."

91. Hawaiian Department, *Digest of Information*.

92. "Monkeys Have No Tails," Vol. 2, p. 49.

93. C. H. Conrad to CG, PD, Sub: Annual Inspection of Post of Manila, 19 May 1924, AGO 333.1, Box 133, RG 159.

94. Office of Quartermaser General to AG, 28 Jan. 1925, AGO 319.12 HD, E 37, RG 407.

95. George L. Febiger to CG, HD, Sub: Annual Inspection, Schofield Barracks, T.H., FY 1931, 24 June 1931, AGO 333.1, E 11, RG 159; Jay L. Benedict to CG, HD, Sub: Annual Report, FY 1932, 8 July 1932, R 121, HDR; and Russell A. Eberhardt to Brian M. Linn, Jan. 7, 1993; Carmine Del Giudice to Brian M. Linn, 14 Nov. 1992, both in author's possession.

96. Woodruff, *Effects of Tropical Light*.

97. ANJ 43 (9 June 1906).

98. "Infantry Veteran" to Editor, ANJ 44 (27 July 1907).

99. Jesse M. Cullison, Handling Troops in the Tropics, in Francis W. Mansfield to AG, 7 Apr. 1909, AGO 1512366, RG 94. George D. Freeman to Officer in Charge of Laboratory, Medical Museum, 26 Sept. 1905, E 5450, RG 395; Alexander Brodie to COs, 20 Oct. 1906, E 2712, RG 395; *RWD* 1912, 3:87–89.

100. *ANJ* 46 (27 Feb. 1909).

101. Charles L. Williams to Father, 11 Feb. 1916, Williams Family Papers.

102. Edward Bowser to Mother, 8 Sept. 1941. Edward Bowser to Mother, 17 Sept. 1941, Bowser Papers.

103. Alfred Smith to M/S, 16 Aug. 1905, No. 98, E 2926, RG 395. Noah Overly to Frederick A. Smith, 12 Sept. 1906, No. 125, E 2699, RG 395; Oliver P. Robinson to M/S, 24 June 1905, E 2928, RG 395; Glenn, "Some Things," pp. 127–28; Seaman, "Native Troops," pp. 847–60.

104. *RWD* 1914 1:381; R. G. Ebert to Surgeon General, Sub: Annual Report, 1917, 19 Jan. 1918, AGO 319.1-2, RG 112; Edward M. Lewis to AG, Sub: Annual Report, HD, FY 1926, 30 June 1926, AGO 319. 12 (6-30-26) HD, RG 407; Hawaiian Department, *Digest of Information*.

105. *ANJ* 46 (12 Dec. 1908). Breeden, "Army and Public Health," p. 91.

106. Memoir, pp. 58–59, Reeder Papers.

107. Howard C. Fields to Brian M. Linn, 4 Mar. 1994. John N. Merrill to Dear Maude, 8 Nov. 1903, Merrill Family Papers; Campbell B. Hodges to Mother, 11 Feb. 1904, Hodges Papers; 1905 Diary, Bliss Papers; Charles L. Williams to Dear Father and Mother, 15 July 1917, Williams Family Papers; "The American Soldier in the Orient," *ANJ* 42 (17 July 1905); Munson, "Ideal Ration," pp. 309–46.

108. George V. H. Moseley to Walter C. Short, 19 Nov. 1926, Box 5, Moseley Papers. "Monkeys Have No Tails," Vol. 5, pp. 52–53.

109. Bayley, "Life at Hickam, 1940." For enlisted men's views on the poor quality of food, see GCM of Samuel Rosinoff, Dan B. Hogan, Joseph Silva, Michael A. Zilemper, Peter J. Eustace, and Edward Peno, GCM 105462, RG 153; GCM of Robert W. Driscoll, John F. Nolan, John Blyn, and William D. O'Brien, GCM 190320, RG 153.

110. Eli A. Helmick to Charles S. Farnsworth, 22 Mar. 1923, F HD, E 11, RG 159.

111. Robert W. Keeney to Brian M. Linn, 4 Feb. 1994. HQ, Inspector General, HD to Inspector General, Sub: Annual Report, 31 June 1930, R 121, HDR; Walter N. Poirier to Brian M. Linn, 7 Apr. 1994; Thomas J. Wells to Brian M. Linn, 25 Jan. 1994.

112. George L. Febiger to CG, HD, Sub: Annual Inspection, Schofield Barracks, T.H., FY 1931, 24 June 1931, AGO 333 1, Box 1, E 11, RG 159; Inspection of Major Arthur A. Lane, 1925, WPD 2027-11, RG 165; Sub: Annual Report, HD, FY 1924, 14 Nov. 1924, AGO 319.12 HD, E 37, RG 407; HD, Estimate of the Situation, Joint Defense Plan—Hawaiian Theater, 1935, Box 10, E 6051, RG 395.

113. "Story of a Soldier," pp. 74–76.

114. Hugh A. Drum to AG, Sub: Secret Defense Considerations, 25 May 1937, Box 21, F HD, Drum Papers; William M. Cruikshank, WPD to C/S, Sub: Letter from Alfred Carter, Parker Ranch, 28 Sept. 1920, OCS 623, E 8, RG 165. For extensive comments on the problems of supplying Hawaii and growing local foodstuffs, see the correspondence in AGO 403 (3-7-36) HD, RG 407.

Chapter Four

1. On U.S. military thought, see Weigley, *Towards an American Army*; Millis, *American Military Thought*, pp. 127–36, 196–206. On U.S. coast defenses, see Browning, *Two If by Sea*; Clary, *Fortress America*; Lewis, *Seacoast Fortifications*; Hamburger, "Technology, Doctrine and Politics."

2. William C. Langfitt to SW, 13 Feb. 1899, AGO 188909, RG 94.

3. Report of a Board Convened in 1901 to Report on the Defenses of Pearl Harbor and Honolulu Harbor, 13 Nov. 1901, AWC Serial No. 126, E 299, RG 165. G. L. Gillespie to Senior Officer, JB, 5 Dec. 1904, JB 304, Series 23, R 5, M 1421; J. G. Breckinridge to AG, 17

July 1901, AGO 401283, RG 94; Arthur S. Conklin, "Historical Sketch of the Defense of Oahu by the United States. From the Annexation of the Hawaiian Islands, July 1898, to July, 1912," 1913, copy in Military History Institute Library.

4. *RWD* 1905, 1:27. Braisted, *U.S. Navy in the Pacific, 1897–1907*, pp. 115–36. The army would later discover that Kolekole Pass provided access from the Waianae Coast to the Leilehua Plateau.

5. G. L. Gillespie to Senior Officer, JB, 5 Dec. 1904, JB 304, Series 23, R 5; 2 Dec. 1904 Minutes, JB Copy Book, R 21, both in M 1421. The Taft Board recommended four twelve-inch cannons at the entrance of Pearl Harbor, two fourteen-inch cannons at Honolulu Harbor, eight twelve-inch mortars at Diamond Head, eight twelve-inch mortars at Queen Emma's Beach, two three-inch cannons to cover the minefields at Pearl Harbor, and two three-inch cannons to cover the minefields at Honolulu; see National Defense Board, Committee Number One, 29 Jan. 1907, GB 403, F 1904–1905, RG 80.

6. Enoch H. Crowder, Memorandum Report, 7 June 1903, AGO 257564, RG 94. The Mackenzie Board's findings are in Proceedings of a Board of Officers . . . , 26 Nov. 1903, AGO 453450, RG 94.

7. J. W. Jones to Adj., HNG, 3 Dec. 1903, F Arthur MacArthur, M37CB, 1866, R 277, M 1064.

8. Arthur MacArthur to AG, 2 Feb. 1904, AGO 453450, RG 94.

9. Leonard Wood later misquoted Crowder's 7 June 1903 memorandum as emphasizing the threat posed by "alien inhabitants," but this phrase does not appear in the original; see Leonard Wood to SW, Sub: Policy of General Staff, U.S. Army, Regarding Strength of Garrison, Island of Oahu, Hawaiian Islands, 13 Feb. 1913, OCS 8628, E 5, RG 165.

10. Report of the Proper Military Policy of the United States, *RWD* 1916, 1:217.

11. Quoted in SW to SN, 27 Mar. 1911, AGO 2152083, RG 94.

12. Tasker H. Bliss to Secretary, JB, 10 June 1904, JB 325, R 9, M 1421.

13. Munroe McFarlane, Analysis and Discussion, Map Problem No. 30, Part 3—Problems and Exercises, Vol. 55, CAWC 1914–15, Box 5, AWCIR.

14. C. H. Mason, "Our Military Needs," 1 May 1912, AWC 7280-25, RG 165.

15. Testimony of General Leonard Wood, U.S. Congress. House. *Hearings to Increase the Efficiency of the Military Establishment*, 2:742.

16. SW to SN, 27 Mar. 1911, AGO 2152083, RG 94. Braisted, *U.S. Navy in the Pacific, 1897–1909*, pp. 115–36.

17. GB 405, 15 June 1903, Vol. 2, RG 80. *RWD* 1906, 3:245. For material detailing the discussion of the location of the naval bases, see GB 404-1, F 1900–1904, RG 80.

18. George Dewey to SN, 19 Dec. 1903, JB Copy Book, R 21, M 1421. For the Taft Board report, see National Defense Board, Committee Number One, 29 Jan. 1907, GB 403, F 1904–1905, RG 80. On Pacific fortifications, see Braisted, *U.S. Navy in Pacific, 1897–1909*, pp. 175–79; Dorrance, *Fort Kamehameha*, pp. 8–12; Lewis, *Seacoast Fortifications*, pp. 89–100; Hamburger, "Technology, Doctrine, and Politics," pp. 136–41. On navy plans to defend Subic, see Dion Williams, "Defense of Our New Naval Stations"; Chief Intelligence Officer, Office of Naval Intelligence to William D. Beach, 7 Dec. 1904, Vol. 32, E 69, RG 38; Spector, *Admiral of the New Empire*, p. 165.

19. Leonard Wood to William M. Folger, 29 June 1904, Box 34, Wood Papers; "Is Subig Bay a Mistake?" *ANJ* 42 (10 Sept. 1904); J. Franklin Bell to SW, 21 Dec. 1907, F 6073, AWC 310B, Thomas Files, RG 165; Johnson Hagood, Memorandum, 10 Jun. 1913, F 4, Box 186, Hagood Papers.

20. William M. Folger to SN, 1 June 1904, Box 34, Wood Papers. Tasker H. Bliss to Leonard Wood, 14 Mar. 1905, Box 36, Wood Papers; GB No. 404, 14 Aug. 1904, Vol. 3, RG 80.

21. Johnson Hagood to General Townsley, Sub: Coast Defenses of Manila and Subig

Bays, June 1917, F 4, Box 186, Hagood Papers. Harry W. Hawthorne, "The Transportation and Mounting of Heavy Guns . . . ," 1906, AWC Study No. 29, Serial 91, E 299, RG 165; Spector, *Admiral of the New Empire*, pp. 168–69; Hamburger, "Technology, Doctrine, and Politics," p. 173.

22. ANJ 42 (17 June 1905). William A. Folger to Leonard Wood, 3 June 1904, Box 34, Wood Papers; Frederick Funston to M/S, 9 June 1905; John McClellan to M/S, 7 July 1905, both filed in AGO 1028799, RG 94.

23. Leonard Wood to SW, Sub: Policy of General Staff . . . Hawaiian Islands.

24. "Navy" to Editor, ANJ 44 (13 July 1907).

25. Leonard Wood to Hugh L. Scott, 3 Apr. 1907, Box 57, Scott Papers. Leonard Wood to SW, 13 Apr. 1907, Box 39, Wood Papers.

26. William Loeb to J. Franklin Bell, 3 Mar. 1907, MID 1766-17, RG 165; T. W. Jones, "A Report Compiled from Reports and Other Data Showing the Activities of Japanese and Japanese Officials in Relation to the United States and Her Possessions," 6 Nov. 1907, AWC 1766-30, RG 165; "Japan and the United States," ANJ 44 (4 May 1907). On the War Scare, see Braisted, *U.S. Navy in the Pacific, 1897–1909*, pp. 191–215; Clinard, *Japan's Influence*, pp. 54–56; Iriye, *Pacific Estrangement*, pp. 146–48; Neu, *An Uncertain Friendship*, pp. 83–149; Stephan, *Hawaii under the Rising Sun*, pp. 55–68; Weigley, *Towards an American Army*, pp. 155–56.

27. AWC Problem No. 12: Measures to be taken to meet a sudden attack by Japan under existing conditions, 12 June 1907, Orange and Blue Problem, CAWC 1906–7, AWCCA. J. Franklin Bell to George A. Converse, 9 Jan. 1907, AWC, Miscellaneous Correspondence, Reports, Etc., in Regard to the Relative Advantages of Subig Bay and Manila Bay as a Naval Base in the Philippines, [1909?], Serial 43, E 299, RG 165 [hereafter cited as Subic Bay File].

28. SN to SW, 4 Mar. 1907, Subic Bay File.

29. AG to CG, PD, 6 July 1907, AGO 1260092. 6 June 1907 Minutes, JB Copy Book, R 21, M 1421; War between United States and Japan, steps to be taken, 18 June 1907, JB 325, R 1, M 1421.

30. William W. Wotherspoon to My dear Mills [Stephen C. Mills], 29 Oct. 1907, Subic Bay File.

31. J. Franklin Bell to SW, 5 Sept. 1907, Subic Bay File.

32. GB 405, 3 Oct. 1907, Vol. 5, RG 80.

33. Leonard Wood to AG, 23 Dec. 1907, AGO 1260092, RG 94. Stephen C. Mills to William W. Wotherspoon, 5 Oct. 1907, Mills Papers; 29 Jan. 1908 Minutes, JB Copy Book, R 21, M 1421; E. T. Wilson, Memorandum on the Subject of the Land Defense of Subig Bay, Nov. 1907, Subic Bay File; William W. Wotherspoon, Memorandum on the Naval Base in the Philippine Islands and Its Protection from Capture or Destruction by the Army, 21 Nov. 1907, Subic Bay File; Louis Morton, "Military and Naval Preparation," pp. 99–104.

34. Theodore Roosevelt to SW, 11 Feb. 1908, R 6, M 1421. 29 and 31 Jan. 1908 Minutes, JB Copy Book, R 21, M 1421.

35. Wotherspoon, Memorandum on the Naval Base. Braisted, *U.S. Navy in the Pacific, 1897–1909*, pp. 221–23.

36. W. L. Rodgers, H. D. Todd, and S. A. Cheyney, "The Value of the Hawaiian Islands As a Military Base and Its Adaption and Equipment for This Purpose, with Remarks on Other Secondary Bases in the Pacific," 4 Mar. 1908, AWC Serial 126, E 299, RG 165. Braisted, *U.S. Navy in Pacific, 1897–1909*, p. 222.

37. J. P. Story, introduction to Lea, *Valor of Ignorance*, p. xlviii. Fitzpatrick, *Coming Conflict of Nations*; Thomas Millard, *America and the Far Eastern Question*. For a discussion of war literature, see Iriye, *Pacific Estrangement*, pp. 146–48; Stephan, *Hawaii under the Rising Sun*, pp. 55–68; Weigley, *Towards an American Army*, pp. 155–56.

38. Diary and Comments, Problem Involving War between Orange and Blue, Orange and Blue Problem, CAWC 1906–7 and 1907–8, AWCCA.

39. Military Monograph on Japan, 1910, Orange and Blue Problem, Part 1, CAWC 1909–10, AWCCA. For War College views on a Japanese-American war, see Diary and Comments; Waldo E. Ayer, Defense of Hawaii and Panama, and Withdrawal from Alaska, 19 July 1909; Beaumont B. Buck, Defense of Philippine Islands, 21 July 1909; C. St. John Chubb and H. C. Hodges, Orange General Plan for Operations in the Philippines and Guam, 21 July 1909; P. Clayton, Plan for the Landing and Occupation of the Island of Oahu by a Mixed Brigade of the Orange Army, 4 Aug. 1909; Map Maneuvers in Philippine Islands, 19 Oct. 1909, all in Orange and Blue Problem, Course in Military Art, CAWC 1908–9, AWCCA; Lyman W. V. Kennon, Strategical Plans for the Defense of the Hawaiian Islands; Charles M. O'Conner, The Military Geography of the Island of Oahu, T.H., Orange and Blue Problem, both in CAWC 1909–10, AWCCA; War Plan: Plan in Case of War in the Pacific before the Panama Canal Is Completed, 19 May 1913, AWC 7820, RG 165; C. Crawford to General Staff Officer, 10 Apr. 1915, AWC 4853-51, RG 165; Part 3: Problems and Exercises, no volume no., CAWC 1913–14, AWCIR; Part 5: Lectures, Vol. 66, CAWC 1916–1917, AWCIR.

40. Benjamin A. Poore, Orange vs. Blue Session, Part 5—Lectures, Vol. 57, CAWC 1914–15, AWCIR.

41. Ibid.

42. Mahan, *Influence of Seapower*, p. 72. On Mahan, see Crowl, "Alfred Thayer Mahan"; Weigley, *American Way of War*, pp. 174–91.

43. Report of the Joint Board in the Matter of the Establishment of a Naval Station in the Philippine Islands, 8 Nov. 1909, R 21, M 1421. Emphasis in original.

44. Edward S. Miller, *War Plan Orange*, pp. 68–76; Braisted, *U.S. Navy in the Pacific, 1909–1922*, pp. 72–76, 246–62.

45. Frederick Funston to AG, 28 Apr. 1913, AWC 6266-24, RG 165. Arthur Murray to C/S, 2 Oct. 1909, OCS 4458, E 5, RG 165; Mason, "Our Military Needs"; Dan C. Kingman, Memorandum on Report on the Defenses of the Philippine Islands, 20 Dec. 1915, AWC 4853-54, RG 165; "Notes on the Philippines," 1915, Box 20, Steele Papers.

46. William H. Carter to AG, 21 May 1915, AWC 6266-82, RG 165. History of the Hawaiian Department Primary Tactical Plan, 1940, Box 2, HDR; Newton D. Baker to SN, Sub: Naval Members of Oahu Defense Board, 16 Mar. 1917, AWC 6266-87, RG 165; Braisted, *U.S. Navy in Pacific, 1909–22*, p. 224.

47. CG, PD to AG, 19 May 1913, AGO 2040609, RG 94. T. E. Merrill to Secretary, Sub: Conference, Naval War College, 1910, 27 Nov. 1910, AWC 16295-1, RG 165.

48. Leonard Wood to Johnson Hagood, 8 Oct. 1914, File 5, Entry 176, Hagood Papers.

49. Discussion by Major DeRosey C. Cabell, Map Problem No. 42, Vol. 3, CAWC 1913–1914, Box 3, AWCIR.

50. National Coast Defense Board, Committee No. 1, 29 Jan. 1907, General Board 403, Box 11, RG 80. Report of Committee No. 1, National Coast Defense Board, 6 Feb. 1907, Subic Bay File; Leonard Wood to AG, 23 Dec. 1907, AGO 1260092, RG 94; William W. Wotherspoon to J. Franklin Bell, 28 Oct. 1907, Subic Bay File. The National Coast Defense Board recommended at Lasisi Point, two twelve-inch cannons and three three-inch cannons; at Corregidor, four twelve-inch mortars and three three-inch cannons; at Caballo, four fourteen-inch cannons; at El Fraile, two fourteen-inch cannons; at Carabao, two fourteen-inch cannons and eight twelve-inch mortars, in addition to permanent minefields.

51. J. Franklin Bell to Erasmus R. Weaver, 23 Sept. 1913, Copy, F 2, Box 176, Hagood Papers; Johnson Hagood to E. E. Booth, 23 Jan. 1932, F 5, Box 186, Hagood Papers. For Duvall's views, see William P. Duvall to AG, 13 Sept. 1910, E 25, AGO 1602803, RG 94; C. H. McKinstry to CG, PSD, 5 Dec. 1910, AGO 1682853, E 25, RG 94; Report of the

Fortification Board on the Revision of the Project for the Land Defenses of Manila, 9 Dec. 1910, AGO 1750126, RG 94; Braisted, *U.S. Navy in the Pacific, 1909–1922*, pp. 65–66.

52. AG to CG, PSD, 26 Dec. 1911, AGO 1861622, E 25, RG 94. Report of the Fortification Board on the Permanent Defense of Corregidor, Caballo, El Fraile and Carabao Islands against Landing Parties, 6 Sept. 1910, AGO 1602803, E 25, RG 94. Leonard Wood, Memorandum for General Wotherspoon, Sub: Policy Relative to the Defense of the Philippine Islands, 16 June 1911, OCS 6991, E 5, RG 165; Leonard Wood to AG, 18 Dec. 1911, AGO 1861622, E 25, RG 94; Johnson Hagood to CG, PD, Sub: Coast Defense Maneuvers, 29 May 1914, AWC 4853-60, RG 165.

53. Charles L. Williams to Father, 24 Jan. 1916, Williams Family Papers. Proceedings of the Defense Board, 19 Nov. 1911, AGO 1602803, RG 94; Johnson Hagood, Memorandum, 10 June 1913, F 4, Box 186, Hagood Papers; Johnson Hagood, "Down the Big Road," pp. 165–66, Hagood Family Papers. The reports and proceedings of the Manila Bay defense board are located in AGO 1416707, RG 94. In 1916 the Harbor Defenses of Manila listed as complete or nearly complete the following ordnance: Fort Mills on Corregidor had six twelve-inch rifles, two ten-inch rifles, twelve twelve-inch mortars, five six-inch guns, and six three-inch guns; Fort Hughes on Caballo Island had two fourteen-inch guns and eight twelve-inch mortars; Fort Frank on Carabao Island had two fourteen-inch guns, two six-inch rifles, two three-inch guns, and four twelve-inch mortars; see State of Defense Project for the Philippines, 10 Oct. 1916, AWC 8921-15, RG 165.

54. Honolulu was protected by Fort Ruger on Diamond Head (twelve twelve-inch mortars, two five-inch guns, four four-point-seven-inch guns); Fort DeRussy at Waikiki (two fourteen-inch guns, two six-inch guns) and Fort Armstrong at Honolulu Harbor (two three-inch guns). Pearl Harbor's main defense was Fort Kamehameha (two twelve-inch guns, eight twelve-inch mortars, four six-inch guns, four three-inch guns); see State of Defense Project for Oahu on Oct. 10, 1916, AWC 8921-15, RG 165; *RWD* 1905 1:27; J. Franklin Bell to Acting SW, Sub: Preliminary Report on Project for Land Defense of Fortifications and Naval Station, Island of Oahu, 13 Aug. 1908, AGO 1383705, E 25, RG 94; Dorrance, *Fort Kamehameha*, pp. 7–13.

55. John W. Ruckman, The Philippine Islands, 1914, AWC 8438-27, RG 165.

56. Cited in Conklin, "Historical Sketch," p. 19.

57. William W. Wotherspoon to C/S, 15 July 1914, Sub: Land Defense of the Bataan Peninsula, 15 July 1914, OCS 11330, E 5, RG 165. Johnson Hagood to CG, PD, Sub: Coast Defense Maneuvers, 1914, 29 May 1914, AWC 4853-60, RG 165; Harrison Hall to CO, CDMSB, 17 Mar. 1914, AGO 2171793, RG 94.

58. C. J. Bailey to AG, Sub: Defense of Corregidor against Guns on Mariveles, 11 Nov. 1916, AWC 4853-76, RG 165.

59. Hugh L. Scott to AG, Sub: Corregidor Garrison, 24 Feb. 1915, AGO 2212633, E 25, RG 94. The War Department exacerbated these problems by dumping obsolete material overseas. In one incident, the War Department arbitrarily exchanged Corregidor's allotment of twenty-six three-inch guns for forty three-point-two-inch guns. Not only were the latter obsolete, but they could not fit into the emplacements; further, they required much larger gun crews. Perhaps most important, they could not be fired accurately over water, and thus could not fulfill their assigned task of deterring enemy landing parties; see J. Franklin Bell to AG, 16 June 1911, AGO 1810553, E 25, RG 94.

60. Rodgers, Todd, and Cheyney, "Value of the Hawaiian Islands."

61. Report on the Defensive Plans of the Island of Oahu, T.H., 1910, AWC 6266-1, RG 165; Reports by Committees of Officers, 1910–11, AWC 6266-10, RG 165.

62. Arthur Murray to AG, 11 Apr. 1910, AGO 1642686, E 25, RG 94. George D. Moore, William H. Chapman, Charles W. Exton, and Austin M. Pardee, Land Defense of Oahu, 15 Mar. 1910, AGO 1642682, RG 94; Conklin, "Historical Sketch," pp. 13–16.

63. Arthur Murray to AG, 18 Dec. 1911, AWC 6266-11, RG 165. Conklin, "Historical Sketch," pp. 21–22.

64. The Defense of Oahu: Report of a Board of Officers Convened at Honolulu, Territory of Hawaii, July 31, 1912, 6 Sept. 1912, AWC 6266-13, RG 165 [First Macomb Board]. Hunter Liggett to C/S, Sub: Additional Mortar Batteries and Other Fixed Defenses on the Island of Oahu, 31 Jan. 1912, AWC 6266-11, RG 165; James J. Dowling to Sidney M. Ballou, 18 Feb. 1909; Guy Rothwell to Sidney M. Ballou, 19 Feb. 1909; Sidney M. Ballou to Walter L. Finley, 10 Mar. 1909, all in AGO 114231, RG 94; Conklin, "Historical Sketch," pp. 24–25, 28–30.

65. Stephen Foote, Omar Bundy, and William D. Connor to C/S, Sub: Armament for fixed defenses of Oahu, 4 Nov. 1913, AWC 2966, RG 165.

66. Erasmus M. Weaver to C/S, Sub: Coast defenses of Hawaii, 14 Feb. 1913, AWC 6266-14, RG 165; John Biddle to C/S, Sub: Defenses of Oahu, 5 Nov. 1913, AWC 6266-20, RG 165; John M. Palmer to C/S, Sub: Report of a Board of Officers on the Land Defenses of Pearl Harbor, 1 Dec. 1912, AWC 6266-14, RG 165; William Crozier to C/S, Sub: Report of Board of Officers on the Defense of Oahu, 18 Jan. 1913, AWC 6266-15, RG 165; "Down the Big Road," p. 337.

67. Frederick Funston to AG, 2 July 1913, AWC 6266-20, RG 165. The Defense of Oahu. Report of a Board of Officers Convened at Honolulu, T.H., Apr. 21, 1913, AWC 6266-38, RG 165 [Second Macomb Board].

68. Warren T. Hannum, The Defense of Oahu, 4 Dec. 1914, AWC 6266-42, RG 165.

69. William H. Carter to AG, 21 May 1915, AWC 6266-82, RG 165.

70. Report of the Oahu Defense Board . . . to Meet a Modern Naval Attack, 2 June 1916, AWC 6266-82, RG 165.

71. R. R. Raymond to Chief of Engineers, 19 Sept. 1916, AWC 6266-84, RG 165.

72. Extract from the Report of the Joint Conference on the Defense of Oahu, Apr. 1916, AWC 6266-72, RG 165. Committee on Mainland Defense to Defense Board, Sub: Plans for Defensive Lines on Mariveles, 8 Sept. 1914, AGO 2304019, RG 94.

73. Montgomery M. Macomb to C/S, Sub: Defense against Hostile Landings, 24 May 1916, AWC 6266-71, RG 165.

74. Report of the Fortification Board of the Defense of the Philippine Islands, 28 Mar. 1911, AGO 1750126, E 25, RG 94.

75. John M. Palmer to C/S Sub: A Scheme for a Well Balanced Army, 31 Oct. 1911, OCS 8244, E 5, RG 165.

76. AG to CG, PD, 26 Dec. 1911, AGO 1861622, E 25, RG 94.

77. Proceedings of a Board of Officers . . . in the Philippine Islands, 9 May 1915, AWC 4853-54, RG 165. Braisted, U.S. Navy and the Pacific, 1909–1922, pp. 250–51.

78. Report on the Defenses of the Philippine Islands, [1915–16], AWC 4853-54, RG 165.

79. E. S. Kellog, Some Truths about Corregidor, 30 June 1915, GB 403-1915, Box 12, RG 80. Emphasis in original.

80. John F. Morrison to CG, PD, Sub: The Military Situation in the Philippines, 1916, AWC 8438-16, RG 165.

81. Montgomery M. Macomb, Memorandum on the Defenses of the Philippines, 12 Oct. 1916, AWC 4853-64, RG 165. For other comments on the Liggett Board, see Stanley D. Embick, Memorandum for the Board of Review, 15 Nov. 1915; Dan C. Kingman, Memorandum on Report on the Defenses of the Philippine Islands, 20 Dec. 1915; William Crozier, Memorandum for the Board of Review, 4 Jan. 1916, all filed in AWC 4853-64, RG 165.

82. Statement of a Proper Military Policy for the United States, 11 Sept. 1915, AWC 9053-90, RG 165.

83. Report of a Joint Board of Co-operation of the Army and Navy in the Philippines, 10

Nov. 1917, Series 49, JB 303, F-49, E 284, RG 165. Hunter Liggett to AG, Sub: Defense of the Philippine Islands against Attack by a First-Class Power, Based in the Orient, 29 Sept. 1916, AGO 2494259, E 25, RG 94; Paul Foley, Report of the Staff Ride of the United States Army through Central Luzon Valley, Jan. 1916, GB 403 Jan.–June 1916, Box 12, RG 80.

84. Montgomery M. Macomb to C/S, Sub: Joint Mission of Military and Naval forces in the Philippines after Declaration of War, 5 Oct. 1916, AWC 4853-67, RG 165.

85. Joint Mission of Military and Naval forces in the Philippines: Dissent of Colonel W. H. Johnston, 18 Sept. 1916, AWC 4853-67, RG 165.

86. P. D. Lochridge, Memo, 16 Sept. 1916, AWC 4583-67, RG 165.

87. Montgomery M. Macomb, Comments on War College Division Memo, Sub: Joint Mission of Military and Naval Forces in the Philippines, 11 Oct. 1916, AWC 4583-67, RG 165. Emphasis in original.

88. Montgomery M. Macomb to C/S, Sub: Joint Mission of Military and Naval Forces in the Philippines after the Declaration of War, 15 Oct. 1916, AWC 4853-67, RG 165. Emphasis in original.

89. Leonard Wood to Theodore Roosevelt, 26 June 1906, Box 37, Wood Papers. HQ, PSD, GO 19, 24 Mar. 1906, Box 57, Scott Papers; Field Problem: Camp Stotsenburg, July 1905, Box 38, Moseley Papers; J. Franklin Bell, Report on Military Situation, Moro Province and Division of the Philippines, 9 Nov. and 15 Dec. 1913, AWC 8116-2, E 296, RG 165.

90. Leonard Wood to SW, 16 Nov. 1907, Box 39, Wood Papers; RWD 1908 1:203–5; C. W. Kennedy to C/S, Sub: Status of Officers, Philippine Scouts, 28 Nov. 1916, AWC 9136-10, E 296, RG 165; Woolard, "Philippine Scouts," pp. 139–54.

91. Fort William McKinley, GO 36, 15 June 1907, Box 371, Pershing Papers. [John J. Pershing] to AG, 9 Oct. 1907, Box 279, Pershing Papers; Military Posts in the Philippines— Fort Wm. McKinley, [1907?], Box 371, Pershing Papers; RWD 1906, 3:215; RWD 1907, 3:235. For complaints about maneuvers in the continental United States, see "Joint Maneuvers in Virginia," ANJ 42 (10 Sept. 1904); "Echoes of the Maneuvers," ANJ 42 (24 Sept. 1904); James Parker, Old Army, p. 384.

92. RWD 1907, 3:328. Request that attendance at military meets in the Philippines Division be held duty same as rifle competitions, 8 Feb. 1907, OCS 187, E 5, RG 165; Philippines Free Press (17 and 24 Feb. 1907); John J. Pershing to AG, 1 Oct. 1907, Box 278, Pershing Papers.

93. Harrison Hall to CO, Coast Defenses of Manila Bay, 17 Mar. 1914, AGO 2171793, E 25, RG 94; Johnson Hagood to CG, PD, Sub: Coast Defense Maneuvers, 1914, 29 May 1914, AWC 4853-60, RG 165; Chief Umpire's Report, Exercise No. 2, Philippine Maneuver Campaign, Jan. 22 to Feb. 5, 1914, AWC 8438-5, RG 165. On maneuvers, see [John J. Pershing] to Chief Umpire of Maneuvers, 13 Mar. and 12 Oct. 1910, Box 279, Pershing Papers; William P. Duvall, Confidential Report: Maneuvers, Philippines Division, 1910, AGO 1710830, RG 94; Sharpe, "Campaign at Dinaluphin," pp. 13–24; Frederick Funston to AG, PSD, June 1912, E 2680, RG 395.

94. Chief Umpire's Report, Exercise No. 2, Philippine Maneuver Campaign, Jan. 22 to Feb. 5, 1914, AWC 8438-5, RG 165. William H. Carter to AG, Sub: Co-operation of Navy in Problem of Defense of Oahu, 15 Sept. 1914, AGO 2215141, RG 94; William H. Carter to AG, Sub: Report of Annual Tactical Inspection, 11 Dec. 1914, AGO 2241606, RG 94.

95. "Down the Big Road," p. 167. Johnson Hagood to CG, PD, Sub: Coast Defense Maneuvers, 1914, 29 May 1914, AWC 4853-60; "Memories of the Service," p. 128, John H. Parker Papers.

96. Mason, "Our Military Needs." Report of the Fortification Board of the Defense of the Philippine Islands, 28 Mar. 1911, AGO 1750126, E 25, RG 94; Cornelius D. Willcox to C/S, PSD, 24 Feb. 1910, AGO 1645979, RG 94; Hugh Straughn, History of the Intelligence Office, Philippine Department, 1919, MID 10560-152-187, RG 165.

97. Report of Committee No. 1, National Coast Defense Board, 6 Feb. 1907, Subic Bay File.

98. Consuelo A. Seone to AG, 9 June 1909, AWC 5379-6, RG 165. Nicholas W. Campanole, Report of Confidential Mission in the Hawaiian Islands, Feb. 18–May 18, 1912. With Reference to the Japanese Situation by 1st Lieut. N. W. Campanole, 1st U.S. Infty., AWC 7501-1, RG 165.

99. Walter S. Schuyler to Henry T. Allen, 8 Sept. 1911, AGO 1856409, RG 94.

100. Moore, Chapman, Exton, and Pardee, Land Defense of Oahu; Willard A. Holbrook to Francis J. Koestner, Reports of Committees of Officers, 1910–11, AWC 6266-10, RG 165. On Army War Collge views, see Lyman W. V. Kennon, Strategical Plan for the Defense of the Hawaiian Islands, Orange and Blue Problem, Part 4, Vol. 12, CAWC 1909–10, AWCCA; Waldo E. Ayer, Defense of Hawaii and Panama, and withdrawal from Alaska, 19 July 1909, Orange and Blue Problem, Parts 1 and 2, Course in Military Art, CAWC 1908–9, AWCCA.

101. The Defense of Oahu. Report of a Board of Officers Convened at Honolulu, Territory of Hawaii, July 31, 1912, 6 Sept. 1912, AWC 6266-13W, RG 165. Hannum, The Defense of Oahu.

102. Schofield, "Notes on 'The Legitimate in War,'" p. 2. Gates, Schoolbooks and Krags, pp. 83–84.

103. Chester, "Musings of a Superannuated Soldier," pp. 391–92.

104. William P. Duvall to AG, 3 Jan. 1910, AGO 1562452, RG 94; William P. Duvall to AG, 10 Feb. 1910, AGO 1618517, E 25, RG 94.

105. 'S' to My Dear General, 9 Feb. 1911, AWC 5288-14, RG 165.

106. HQ, PSD, Secret Service File, 1909, AWC 6595, E 296, RG 165; Philippine Constabulary, For the perusal of the Secretary of War only, [Nov.–Dec.] 1909, AGO 1562452, RG 94.

107. James G. Harbord to Clarence R. Edwards, 23 May 1910, Vol. 3, Harbord Papers. James G. Harbord to Leonard Wood, 16 Apr. 1910, Vol. 3, Harbord Papers; Kawada and Suganami, Japanese Spies, 1910, AWC 6595-15, RG 165; Philippines Free Press (2 Apr. 1910).

108. Forbes Journal, 18 June 1913, Vol. 5, pp. 261–62, Forbes Papers. Frederick Funston to AG, Sub: Plans of Defense for Hawaiian Islands, 28 Apr. 1913, AWC 6266-24, RG 165; "Down the Big Road," p. 162; "Story about Soldier," pp. 78–79, Koch Papers; Clinard, Japan's Influence, pp. 105–6, 112–13.

109. Bell, Report on Military Situation.

110. A. L. Mills to SW, Sub: Recommendations with Regard to Boards Organized for Conducting General Defense and Coast Defense, 9 Jan. 1915, AGO 2267902, RG 94.

111. Montgomery M. Macomb to C/S, Sub: Strength of the Defenses at the Entrance to Manila Bay, 12 Oct. 1915, AWC 4853-56, RG 165.

112. J. Franklin Bell to AG, 16 June 1911, AGO 1810553, E 25, RG 94.

113. Leonard Wood to AG, 23 Dec. 1907, AGO 1260092, RG 94; Wotherspoon, Memorandum on the naval base. For instructions on local defense plans, see Montgomery M. Macomb to C/S, Sub: Plans for the Defense of the Philippine Islands, Oahu and Panama Canal, 8 Feb. 1915, AWC 8921-2, RG 165.

114. Hagood, "Down the Big Road," p. 164. Johnson Hagood to CG, PD, Sub: Coast Defense Maneuvers, 29 May 1914, AWC 4853-60, RG 165. For plans to put mobile forces on Corregidor, see J. Franklin Bell to AG, 29 Apr. 1911, AGO 1750126, E 25, RG 94; Proceedings of the Defense Board, 27 Nov. 1912, AGO 1602803, RG 94; J. Franklin Bell to Erasmus R. Weaver, 23 Sept. 1913, Copy, F 2, Box 176, Hagood Papers; R. R. Day to CG, PD, Sub: Annual Garrison Inspection of the Coast Defenses of Manila Bay, 27 Nov. 1914, AGO 333.1, Box 143, E 11, RG 159.

115. Thomas H. Barry to AG, Sub: General Officer for Command of the Coast Defenses

of Manila Bay, 2 July 1914, AGO 2179759, E 25, RG 94. Hagood, "Down the Big Road," p. 169. There was also strong criticism of the "Corregidor first" strategy at the Army War College, where the majority of students favored meeting the enemy on the beaches; see Munroe McFarlane, Analysis and Discussion: Map Problem No. 30, Part 3—Problems and Exercises, pp. 123–40, Vol. 55, CAWC 1914–15, Box 5, AWCIR.

116. Ernest Hinds to CG, PD, 23 Aug. 1916, AWC 4853-69, RG 165.

117. Frank McIntyre to C/S, Sub: Return of Troops from the Philippine Islands, 27 Aug. 1917, AWC 8438-19, RG 165. Robert K. Evans to AG, Sub: Annual Report for the Fiscal Year Ending June 30, 1918, 25 July 1918, AGO 319.12 PD, E 37, RG 407; Meixsel, "U.S. Army Policy," pp. 94–95.

118. OCS to AG, Sub: Discharge of Major General A. P. Blocksom, 16 Apr. 1918, AGO 322.08 HD, E 37, RG 407.

119. Charles L. Williams to Father and Mother, 13 Feb. 1918, Williams Family Papers; CO, 1st Infantry to CG, HD, Sub: Report of Disposition of Troops, 9 Feb. 1917, R 229, HDR.

120. Joseph E. Kuhn to C/S, Sub: Reserves in Philippine Department, 8 Feb. 1917, AWC 8438-16, RG 165; Reserves for the Philippine Department, 9 Feb. 1917, OCS 13058, E 8, RG 165; Lytle Brown to AG, Sub: Concerning Status of Philippine Scout Officers Who May Be Appointed to the Regular Army, 24 July 1918, OCS 1133, E 8, RG 165; WPD to C/S, Sub: Reduction in Strength of Philippine Scouts, Feb. 1920, OCS 1133, E 8, RG 165.

121. Campanole, Report of Confidential Mission; Governor of Hawaii to SW, 16 Jan. 1909, War Department File, Governors' Correspondence—Walter F. Frear, HSA.

122. Lucius E. Pinkham to Franklin K. Lane, 15 Nov. 1915, AGO 2340215, RG 94. Governor of Hawaii to SW, 7 Aug. 1916, Army 1916–17 File, U.S. Departments, Governors' Correspondence—Lucius E. Pinkham, HSA; Inspector General, Hawaii National Guard to Chief, Division of Militia Affairs, Sub: Organized Militia—Hawaii, 6 May 1915, AWC 9126, E 296, RG 165; Wakefield, "History of the Hawaii National Guard," pp. 108–20.

123. Robert K. Evans to AG, Sub: Hawaiian and Filipino Enlisted Personnel, 17 Oct. 1916, AGO 322.04, E 6035, RG 395; A Bill Authorizing the President to Commission the Commanding General and the Adjutant General of the Hawaiian Militia, 12 Jan. 1916, OCS 12294, E 5, RG 165.

124. Robert C. Richardson, Filipino Manpower in the Time of War, 31 July 1923, F 273A-2, AWCCA. Fourth Philippine Legislature, Special Session 1917, Senate No. 119, 7 Mar. 1917, OCS 1183, E 8, RG 165; Lytle Brown to C/S, Sub: Philippine National Guard, 22 June 1918, OCS 1133, E 8, RG 165; Francis J. Kernan to C/S, Sub: Confidential Report on Relations of Military to Civil Authorities during the First Half of Aug. 1920, 17 Aug. 1920, AGO 319.1 PD, E 37, RG 407; Military Memoirs, pp. 122–25, Kernan Papers; Gleeck, *Manila Americans*, p. 117; Harrison, *Corner-Stone of Philippine Independence*, pp. 161–68; Jose, "Philippine National Guard"; Quezon, *Good Fight*, pp. 133–35; Meixsel, "Army for Independence," pp. 11–17; Woolard, "Philippine Scouts," pp. 169–84.

125. Newton D. Baker to Lucius E. Pinkham, 3 Apr. 1917 and Newton D. Baker to Chairman, Committee on Military Affairs, House of Representatives, 17 Apr. 1917, OCS 12350, E 5, RG 165; President, 27 May 1918, OCS 623, E 8, RG 165; Eligibility of Filipinos and Japanese for Membership in the Militia of Hawaii, 29 Apr. 1916, OCS 12530, E 5, RG 165; Wakefield, "History of the Hawaii National Guard," pp. 122–28.

126. John A. Baird, History of the Activities of the Intelligence Office, Hawaiian Department, 31 Jan. 1919, MID 10560-152-194, RG 165. Wakukawa, *A History of the Japanese*, pp. 203–4.

127. Education (Illiteracy in the Army), AGO 350.5, Box 4, E 6035, RG 395; Schedule for Machine Gun Company, 2nd Hawaiian Infantry, 1918; HQ, 2nd Hawaiian Infantry, Drill Schedule for Month of Oct. 1918, both in R 205, HDR.

Chapter Five

1. Pritchett, "Army Canteen," p. 678.
2. Thomas H. Barry, Recommendations for Cavalry and Infantry Regiments to Replace Regiments to Be Relieved during 1907 in the Philippines, 26 Nov. 1906, OCS 19, E 5, RG 165. On military social history, see Coffman, *Old Army*; Noble, *Eagle and the Dragon*; Rickey, *Forty Miles a Day*.
3. "The Tragedy in Jolo," *ANJ* 43 (17 Mar. 1906).
4. E. A. Mott-Smith to SW, 23 Dec. 1907, U.S. Departments—War Department File, Governors' Correspondence—Walter F. Frear, HSA; William H. Carter to C/S, Sub: Annual report of Commanding General, District of Hawaii, 3 Nov. 1911, OCS 7910, E 5, RG 165.
5. Hunt, *History of the Twenty-Seventh Infantry*. N. M. Green to Frank McCoy, 25 Mar. 1906, Mar.–Apr. 1906 File, Box 11, McCoy Papers; Sothern, "Athletics in the Philippines," p. 387; Thorne Strayer to CG, PD, Sub: Annual Inspection of the Post of Manila, 1934, AGO 333.1, Box 133, RG 159. On U.S. Army athletics, see Pope, "An Army of Athletes."
6. Joseph F. Janda to Post Commanders, Sub: Sportsmanship in the Army, 21 Mar. 1921, R 104, HDR; HQ, Schofield Barracks, Athletic Memorandum No. 11, 28 Feb. 1938, E 6075, RG 395; HQ, Schofield Barracks, Bulletin No. 1: Sportsmanship, 2 Jan. 1934, E 6058, RG 395; Russell A. Eberhardt to Brian M. Linn, 7 Jan. 1993; Robert W. Keeney to Brian M. Linn, 4 Feb. 1994, both in author's possession.
7. Report of Lt. Col. R. L. Landers, AC/S, G-1, for Welfare, 21 July 1922, R 120, HDR.
8. Edward M. Lewis to AG, Sub: Annual Report, HD, FY 1926, 30 June 1926, AGO 319.12 HD (6-30-26), RG 407. Astin, "Soldiering in the Hawaiian Islands," p. 452.
9. Robert K. Tompkins to Brian M. Linn, 11 Mar. 1994, in author's possession.
10. Oral History, pp. 13–14, 18–19, Larsen Papers.
11. Robert W. Keeney to Brian M. Linn, 16 Feb. 1994, in author's possession.
12. Walter Maciejowski to Brian M. Linn, 6 Jan. 1993, in author's possession.
13. HQ, HD, Training Memo No. 3, 22 Sept. 1936, Box 23, E 6049, RG 395.
14. J. M. Kimborough to Inspector General, Sub: Annual Inspection and Survey, 4 Sept. 1928, AGO 333.1, Box 133, RG 159. Edward M. Almond, Annual Report of the President, Fort McKinley Dramatic Club, 1 Dec. 1931, Edward M. Almond Papers.
15. Dana T. Merrill to CG, HD, Sub: Survey and Inspection of Harbor Defenses of Pearl Harbor for FY 1929, 12 Mar. 1929, AGO 333.1 (Pearl Harbor), Box 143, RG 159; O. L. Stephens, Sub: The Luke Field Post Exchange, 1924, AGO 331.3, PF-HD, RG 18; Department Morale Office to Chief, Morale Branch, Sub: Monthly Morale Report, July 1921, 20 Aug. 1921, AGO 322.06 HD, E 37, RG 407.
16. Edward M. Lewis to AG, Sub: Annual Report, HD, FY 1926, 30 June 1926, AGO 319.12 HD (6-30-26), RG 407. Department Morale Office to Chief, Morale Branch, Sub: Monthly Morale Report, Dec. 1920, 28 Jan. 1920, AGO 322.06 HD, E 37, RG 407; Report of Lt. Col. R. L. Landers, AC/S, G-1, for Welfare, 21 July 1922, R 120, HDR.
17. R. W. Thacker to Camp General, Sub: Morale Report for Feb. 1920, 1 Mar. 1920, R 103, HDR.
18. W. A. Pickering to CG, HD, Sub: Annual Inspection, Schofield Barracks, T.H., FY 1933, 30 June 1933, AGO 333.1, Box 276, E 11, RG 159. Dana T. Merrill to CG, HD, Sub: Survey of Hawaiian Division and Post of Schofield Barracks, FY 1929, 26 Dec. 1929, AGO 333.1, E 11, RG 159; Astin, "Soldiering in the Hawaiian Islands," pp. 452–53; Robert W. Keeney to Brian M. Linn, 4 Feb. 1994.
19. Meixsel, "U.S. Army Policy," pp. 20–37; Luke E. Wright to William H. Taft, 27 Apr. 1904, Box 3, Edwards Papers; Weckerling, "Our Own Simla." For one soldier's adventures on leave at Fort John Hay, see Willeford, *Something about a Soldier*, pp. 108–31.

20. Horan, "A Week at Kilauea"; Astin, "Soldiering in the Hawaiian Islands," pp. 454–55.

21. "Manila Notes," *ANJ* 44 (3 Aug. 1907).

22. Forbes Journal, 17 Nov. 1909, 6 and 13 Feb., 1910, Vol. 3, pp. 345, 409, 416, Forbes Papers; *Philippines Free Press* (13 Feb. 1909); CG, HD, Sub: Annual Report, HD, FY 1922, 8 Aug. 1922, AGO 319.12 HD, E 37, RG 407.

23. Diary of Floyd L. Parks, 1926, Box 1, Parks Papers.

24. Pearce, "Coast Artillery in the Philippines"; Green, "Coast Artillery Life," p. 447.

25. "Sojourn in Zamboanga," Darnell Papers.

26. Maus, *Army Officer*, p. 4.

27. Gleeck, "American Club Life," pp. 26–39; Gleeck Jr., *Manila Americans*, pp. 63–65; Harrison, *Corner-Stone*, p. 149.

28. CO, Luke Field to Ira A. Rader, 29 Aug. 1924, AGO 331.3, PF-HD, RG 18. Personal Memoirs, Yeo Papers; H. O. Williams to CG, HD, Sub: Annual Garrison Inspection of Schofield Barracks, 27 June 1916, E 11, RG 159; CO, Schofield Barracks to CG, HD, Sub: Irregularities and Deficiencies, Annual Garrison Inspection, 13 July 1916, E 11, RG 159; Fenn, "Polo for Infantry," pp. 149–50.

29. Paine, "Polo in the Philippines," pp. 417–18. 14th Cavalry Polo Association Tournament, 24 Oct. 1910, Scrapbook, Bell Papers; Matthew F. Steele to My precious girls, 15 Feb. 1910, Box 9, Steele Papers; Memoir, pp. 53–54, Reeder Papers; "A Brief Narrative of the Life of Guy V. Henry, Jr.," p. 52, Henry Papers.

30. J. M. Kimbrough to CG, PD, 2 Nov. 1928, AGO 333.1, Box 133, RG 159. W. R. Riley to CO, Post of Manila, Sub: Irregularities and Deficiencies, 11 Oct. 1928, AGO 333.1, Box 133, RG 159. *ANJ* 44 (20 July 1907). Conner, *What Father Forbad*, pp. 160–61.

31. Conner, *What Father Forbad*, p. 180. "The Ladies' Reading Club of Schofield Barracks," Pamphlet, Personal Correspondence, 1918–58, Leland S. Hobbs Papers; "The 21st at Camp Connell," *ANJ* 42 (24 June 1905); "Notes on Parang," *ANJ* 45 (23 Nov. 1907); "With the 'Four Hundred' of Manila," *ANJ* 42 (29 Oct. 1904). The *Army and Navy Journal* between 1902 and 1941 is an excellent source of material on army society, particularly in the columns on "Hawaii" and "Manila Notes."

32. Conner, *What Father Forbad*, p. 173. Barcus Oral History, pp. 43–44.

33. Thomas F. Millard, *America and the Far Eastern Question*, p. 405.

34. Daws, *Shoal of Time*, p. 317.

35. Slackman, *Target: Pearl Harbor*, pp. 34–44, 281.

36. Report of Lt. Col. R. L. Landers, AC/S, G-1, for Welfare, 21 July 1922, R 120, HDR.

37. Oral History, pp. 13, 18–19, Larsen Papers. Ira C. Eaker Interview, 1972, Eaker Papers; Cron Diary, 8 Sept. 1931, Cron Papers; Walter F. Dillingham to Dear George [Patton], 10 June 1926, Box 26, Patton Papers.

38. Annual Report of the Hawaiian Division, FY 1922, 8 Aug. 1922, AGO 319.12 HD, E 37, RG 407; B. E. Wullie to C/S, Sub: Lending Cement, Honolulu, T.H., 10 Dec. 1919, AWC 8915-17, RG 165; E. C. Worthington to CG, HD, 21 Jan. 1920, R 103, HDR; Edward M. Lewis to AG, Sub: Annual Report, HD, FY 1926, 30 June 1926, AGO 319.12 HD (6-30-26), RG 407; *Paradise of the Pacific* 49 (Mar. 1937), pp. 21–22, 31–32; 18th Composite Wing, Annual Report, 1932, AGO 319.1, PF-HD, RG 18.

39. "Hawaii's Soldier-Citizens an Integrated Part of Community," *Honolulu Advertiser* (17 July 1924); CG, HD, Sub: Annual Report, HD, FY 1922, 8 Aug. 1922, AGO 319.12 HD, E 37, RG 407.

40. "Good News," *Honolulu Advertiser* (1 May 1934). "Maj. Gen. Briant H. Wells, Citizen of Hawaii," *Honolulu Advertiser* (30 Sept. 1934).

41. Lawrence M. Judd to Ray Lyman Wilder, 17 May 1932, Miscellaneous Files—Ala Moana Case, Governors' Papers—L. M. Judd, HSA. Thomas J. Wells to Brian M. Linn, 25 Jan. 1994, in author's possession. Most treatments of the Massie Case fail to distinguish

between the army and the navy; see Daws, *Shoal of Time*, pp. 319–27; Slackman, *Target: Pearl Harbor*, p. 37.

42. "Good News," *Honolulu Advertiser* (11 July 1933). AG Memo, 5 Nov. 1932, R 256, HDR; HQ, Schofield Barracks, Bulletin No. 3, 28 Mar. 1930, E 6058, RG 395; Hunter, "Murder, Rape, and Carpetbaggers."

43. Charles G. Morton to All officers on duty at Headquarters, Hawaiian Department, or in command of stations on Oahu, Sub: Policy of the Department Commander on the Subjects Specified, 21 July 1919, AG 319, Box 2, E 6051, RG 365.

44. Shea, *Army Wife*, pp. 257–58.

45. W. A. Pickering to CG, HD, Sub: Annual Inspection, Schofield Barracks, T.H., FY 1935, 30 June 1935, AGO 333.1., E 11, RG159. Christian, "Harbor Defenses of Honolulu," pp. 483–84.

46. S. A. Wood, "Racial Problem in Hawaii," p. 434.

47. "Down the Big Road," pp. 270–72, Hagood Family Papers.

48. John R. White, *Bullets and Bolos*, p. 233. For other criticisms of women in the colonies, see Crow, *America and the Philippines*, pp. 231–34; Gleeck Jr., *Manila Americans*, pp. 6–11; Brownell, "Impressions of Manila," p. 53. For a penetrating study of colonial male stereotypes of women, see Callaway, *Gender, Culture and Empire*.

49. John C. H. Lee, A Policy for the Philippines, 1 Sept. 1921, MID 6530-138, RG 165; C. H. Conrad to C/S, 24 June 1924, AGO 333.1, Box 153, RG 159.

50. Vicente Lim, "The Philippine Islands: A Military Asset," 29 Apr. 1929, F 357-54, AWCCA.

51. The Political Situation in the Philippines, HD, Brown Plan, 1924, Box 1, E 6051, RG 395.

52. Briant H. Wells to AG, Sub: Report on Matters Pertaining to the Defense of Oahu, 22 Sept. 1922, AGO 320 HD (1-9-23), E 37, RG 407.

53. CG, HD to AG, Sub: Annual Report, FY 1920, 23 July 1920, AGO 319.12 HD, E 37, RG 407.

54. HQ, HD, GO 38, 19 Aug. 1913, E 3061, RG 395.

55. HQ, HD, Circular No. 45, 7 July 1921, R 205, HDR.

56. Memoirs, pp. 69–75, Campbell Papers.

57. C. B. Hazeltine to C/S, HD, 7 Sept. 1922, R 104, HDR.

58. R. B. Ellis to AC/S, HD, Sub: Annual Report, 1925, 21 July 1925, R 121, HDR.

59. Adj. to CO, Fort Shafter, 1st endorsement on G. M. Halloran to CO, Fort Shafter, Sub: Report of Riot on Night of Dec. 25, 1916, 27 Dec. 1916, R 103, HDR; C. B. Hazeltine to C/S, HD, 7 Sept. 1922, R 104, HDR; Office Memo No. 2, 29 Dec. 1919, R 103, HDR; "Seemed Like Bowery in Old Days," *Honolulu Advertiser* (6 Sept. 1922).

60. Russell A. Eberhardt to Brian M. Linn, 7 Jan. 1993.

61. Edward M. Lewis to AG, Sub: Annual Report, Hawaiian Division, FY 1926, 30 June 1926, AGO 319.12 HD (6-30-26), RG 407.

62. Howard C. Fields to Brian M. Linn, 4 Mar. 1994.

63. Joseph Y. K. Akaina Interview, *Waikiki, 1900–1985*, 1:11. Walter Maciejowski to Brian M. Linn, 6 Jan. 1993.

64. R. E. Fraile to CG, HCAD, Sub: A Near Riot of Soldiers and Civilians in Waikiki, 17 Jan. 1925; A. R. Taylor to CO, Hawaiian Depot Area, 24 Jan. 1925; Statement of Frank Henderson, 14 Jan. 1925; Statement of Robert Kennard, 15 Jan. 1925; all in R 106, HDR; Wallace Amioka Interview, *Remembering Kakaako*, p. 50.

65. "A Friend of the Army Girl," ANJ 42 (28 Feb. 1905). Johnson Hagood, "What about the Philippines," (1938), F 19, Box 11, Hagood Papers; Coolidge, *United States as a World Power*, p. 161.

66. Basic Plan (Brown) for Military Activities in the Event of a Native Uprising in the Philippine Islands, 1923, F 321, Box 88, AG SPWPC, E 365, RG 407.

67. Hugh A. Drum, Speech at Meeting of the Chaplain's Association, 1935, Vol. 7, Box 33, Drum Papers.

68. W. D. Ketcham to Secretary, GS, Sub: The Use of Native Military Forces in the Philippine Islands, 26 Mar. 1918, OCS 1183, RG 165.

69. PDN, Standing Orders No. 600-750, Personnel: Recruiting for the Regular Army, 19 Oct. 1925, 300.4, PF-PD, RG 18. For a fictional account of Manila's army community and the issue of intermarriage, see Putnam, *Daniel Everton*.

70. Willard A. Holbrook to Charles J. Crane, 14 Aug. 1901, E 2483, RG 395.

71. *ANJ* 44 (1 Sept. 1906).

72. Gleeck Jr., *Manila Americans*, p. 56.

73. Charles G. Treat to James G. Harbord, Sub: Changes in Personnel and Animals in the Garrison of the Philippine Islands, 21 Oct. 1921, AGO 320.2, E 37, RG 407.

74. Inspection of the Post of Manila, 1924–25, AGO 333.1, Box 133, RG 159.

75. Russell A. Eberhardt to Brian M. Linn, 16 Feb. 1993, in author's possession. "Some Phases of the Querida Question," *Manila Times* (6 Aug. 1902); Willeford, *Something about a Soldier*, pp. 62–63. For references to "shack jobs" in Hawaii, see E. W. Morton to CG, Honolulu, 30 Sept. 1919, R 103, HDR; John A. Board to C/S, 11 July 1919, R 103, HDR; Howard C. Fields to Brian M. Linn, 1 Feb. 1994, in author's possession.

76. Edward Bowser to Dear Mother, Oct. 1941, Bowser Papers.

77. J. L. Parkinson to CG, PDN, Sub: Inspection of Post of Manila, 13 June 1931, AGO 333.1, RG 159. Terami-Wada, "Kerayuki-san of Manila," pp. 299–312.

78. "I Hired Out to Fight," Montgomery Papers. Willeford, *Something about a Soldier*, pp. 83–85.

79. Honolulu Social Survey, *Report . . . on the Social Evil*, p. 11. Greer, "Collarbone and the Social Evil," pp. 3–17; Hori, "Japanese Prostitution in Hawaii," pp. 113–24.

80. "Visit to the Red Light District" [n.d.], Waldron Papers.

81. R. B. Ellis to AC/S, HD, Sub: Annual Report 1925, 21 July 1925, R 121, HDR. H. C. Gibner to CG, Schofield Barracks, Sub: Investigation of Unnatural Sexual Practices, 16 Nov. 1933, R 106, HDR; Eugene Kennedy Interview, *Waikiki, 1900–85*, 4:1249–50; Willeford, *Something about a Soldier*, pp. 164–67.

82. R. H. R. Loughborough to CG, PD, Sub: Annual Report, District of Luzon, 30 June 1913, E 3676, RG 395.

83. Asst. AG, Circular 10, 18 Mar. 1902, *ANJ* 39 (29 Mar. 1902). *RWD* 1908, 2:119; *RWD* 1914, 1:381; Leonard Wood to Tasker H. Bliss, 26 June 1906, Scrapbook, Bliss Papers.

84. "Manila's Greatest Need," *ANJ* 42 (12 Aug. 1905).

85. W. P. Kendall to CG, HD, Sub: Annual Report, 14 July 1916, R 120, HDR; Gleeck Jr., *Manila Americans*, p. 6.

86. *RWD* 1911, 3:224.

87. *RWD* 1910, 1:392.

88. Honolulu Social Survey, *Report . . . on the Social Evil*, p. 10.

89. HD, GO 26, 26 Aug. 1914, E 2061, RG 395; HQ, HD, GO 38, 19 Aug. 1913, E 3061, RG 395; C. Willcox to Surgeon General, Sub: Annual Report, 1922, 12 Jan. 1921, 319.1-2, HD AA, Box 4, RG 112. The prophylactic treatment is described in Willeford, *Something about a Soldier*, p. 83.

90. Russell A. Eberhardt to Brian M. Linn, 5 Mar. 1993, in author's possession.

91. Charles R. Darnell to Surgeon General, Sub: Annual Report, 1923, HD, 31 Feb. 1923, 319.12, Box 4, RG 112. Department Surgeon to CO, Honolulu District, Sub: Annual Report, 30 June 1922, R 120, HDR; T. S. Bratton to Surgeon General, Sub: Annual Report, 31 Jan. 1927, AGO 319.12, Box 4, RG 112.

92. C. H. Conrad to CG, PD, Sub: Annual Inspection of Post of Manila, 19 May 1924 and 23 Jan. 1926; H. C. Merriam to CG, PD, Sub: Inspection of Post of Manila, 18 Aug. 1934, all in AGO 333.1, Box 133, RG 159.

93. Statistics Covering Arrests by the Hawaiian Military Police, FY 1925, R 121, HDR. Statistics were compiled by totaling the yearly number of general courts-martial for the entire U.S. Army and for the Hawaiian and Philippine departments in the General Court Martial Ledger Sheets, RG 153. Some soldiers were charged for multiple offenses and others had their conviction overturned by higher authorities. It is likely that many soldiers suspected of homosexuality received administrative discharges, but it is impossible to locate statistical documentation.

94. Assistant to Judge Advocate, Review of Record of Trial, 5 Feb. 1918, GCM of Ellis Wakeland, GCM 109223, RG 153.

95. GCM of Jack Milliken, GCM 208976, p. 30. For other examples of social sanctions, see E. J. Walsh, Review of Record of Trial by Division Judge Advocate, 31 Oct. 1936, GCM of Charles Grey, CGM 205553; GCM of Clay C. Whittle, GCM 149153, pp. 32–37, 51; Testimony of Albert Kellenbenz, GCM of Albert Kellenbenz, GCM 195908, pp. 24–25; Testimony of Thad Johnson, GCM of Frank K. Cuff, GCM 152802, p. 60; all in RG 153.

96. Testimony of Lynwood H. Reynolds, GCM of Edwin F. Meckes, Buford H. Hall, and Leslie E. Aspinall, GCM 188724, p. 18. Testimony of George Farnsworth, GCM of Bert J. Hardy, Chetwyn Grant, Leon du Mell, and Curtis G. Cottle, GCM 177311, p. 11, all in RG 153.

97. Statement of Pfc. Andrew Suda, Battery G, 64th CA, 21 Oct. 1933, R 106, HDR. Jones, *From Here to Eternity*, pp. 6, 134–37, 336–61.

98. W. P. Connally, Review of an Investigation of the Undersigned in Cases Involving Sodomy in Which Several Soldiers Have Been the Victims of Perverts of the Lowest Order in Honolulu in Recent Months, 25 Oct. 1933, R 106, HDR. E. J. Walsh, Review of Staff Judge Advocate of Trial by Court Martial, GCM of Rupert W. Barnett, GCM 209932; GCM of Earl C. Pugh, GCM 148131, both in RG 153.

99. Testimony of Neal Van Overen, Wakeland GCM, pp. 10–12. For other cases of soldiers' being ostracized or denounced, see Whittle GCM; GCM of Charles W. Brown, GCM 209102; E. J. Walsh, Review of Staff Judge Advocate on Record of Trial by Court Martial: U.S. vs. Elmer T. Neathery, 8 Mar. 1939, GCM of Elmer T. Neathery, CGM 209393, all in RG 153.

100. Testimony of Levy Johnson, Cuff GCM, p. 67. Testimony of Floyd W. Hunter, Whittle GCM, pp. 38–43.

101. Cited in E. J. Walsh, Review of Staff Judge Advocate on Record of Trial by Court Martial, 12 Nov. 1938, GCM of James W. Sullivan, GCM 210854, RG 153.

102. Testimony of Pvt. Frederick C. Zorn, Kellenbenz GCM, p. 20.

103. For examples of convictions that appear based largely on entrapment or on prejudiced testimony, see GCM of Welsey M. Bird, GCM 153065; GCM of William C. Chandler, GCM 150884; GCM of Eston Moore, GCM 150626; GCM of Martin P. Murphy, GCM 209167; GCM of Reuben C. Wilhoit, GCM 210087; GCM of Eugene Quintal and Englebert Unterburger, GCM 202663; GCM of Edward S. Lobel, GCM 209101; GCM of Raymond Soderquist and Laudislaus Wojciekowski, GCM 188432; Whittle GCM, all in RG 153.

104. Review by Assistant Staff Judge Advocate, 24 Nov. 1931, GCM of Francis Clinton Cabree, CGM 197708, RG 153.

105. In 1922 the army made attempted sodomy—a euphemism for attempted male rape— a separate offense. Between July 1922 and June 1941, there were 140 courts-martial for this offense in the U.S. Army (20 acquittals), 34 in Hawaii (4 acquittals) and 6 in the Philippines (1 acquittal). The data for heterosexual rape are fragmentary and there are no statistics in

the courts-martial ledger sheets for many of the years between 1918 and 1941. The data that are available indicate the Hawaiian Department had 4 general courts-martial for rape (2 acquittals) and the Philippine Department had 7 (5 acquittals). These figures are from General Court Martial Ledger Sheets, RG 153.

106. Testimony of Patrick McHenry, GCM of Kenneth W. Hickman, GCM 145153. Sworn Testimony of Witnesses Taken at the Investigation of Charges against: Private Harley J. Stewart, GCM of Harley J. Stewart, GCM 197279; GCM of Leonard R. Roberts, GCM 164359; GCM of Frank J. Papatone, GCM 164360; Leslie R. Spalding, et al., GCM 177310; Hardy, Grant, du Mell, and Cottle GCM; Meckes, Hall, and Aspinall, GCM; GCM of Charles R. Stewart and Clyde Martin, GCM 191247, all in RG 153.

107. GCM of John M. Mason and Shird M. Millsaps, GCM 196578.

108. Testimony of Capt. John G. Cook, GCM of Ivory Oakes, GCM 170861, pp. 101–3.

109. Oakes GCM, p. 280.

110. Connally, Review of an Investigation.

111. J. L. Parkinson to CG, PDN, Sub: Inspection of Post of Manila, 13 June 1931, ACO 333.1, RG 159.

112. Michael J. Campbell Memoirs, pp. 70–71, Olsen Papers. GCM of Ellsworth Shaw, GCM 162137, RG 153; Willeford, *Something about a Soldier*, pp. 99–100.

113. Connally, Review of an Investigation. E. W. Timberlake to CO, 64th CA, 10 Nov. 1933, R 106, HDR; Testimony of Chester M. Rooney, Kellenbenz GCM, p. 17. A fictional account of one such investigation appears in Jones, *From Here to Eternity*, pp. 472–77.

114. Joseph H. Davis to SW, 30 Jan. 1914, AGO 2123803, RG 94.

115. HQ, HD, Memorandum No. 10, 14 Sept. 1917, E 3061, RG 395.

116. General Courts Martial Ledger Sheets, RG 153. In contrast, between 1920 and 1925 a total of 95 soldiers were court-martialed for using narcotics in the Canal Zone command.

117. A. B. Eckerdt to Wallace Ryder Farrington, 28 Feb. 1925, Anti-Narcotic Conference, Governors' Correspondence—Wallace R. Farrington, HSA.

118. R. B. Ellis to AC/S, G-1, HD, Sub: Annual Report, FY 1925, 21 July 1925, R 121, HDR.

119. John N. Merrill to Dear Papa, 20 Nov. 1903, Riggs Family Papers.

120. U.S. Congress, Senate, *Sales of Intoxicating Liquors*, pp. 7–10, 20–22, 25–26; Cruz, *America's Colonial Desk*, p. 478.

121. RWD 1914, 1.226. RWD 1908, 2:119; RWD 1909, 1:306–8; RWD 1912, 3:87–89; RWD 1914, 1:320.

122. U.S. Congress, House, *Sale of Beer and Light Wines*, pp. 19–20.

123. Edward Davis to AG, Department of California, 16 July 1902, AGO 361008, RG 94. William B. Pistole to Judge Advocate, Sub: Annual Report, 1 July 1922, R 120, HDR; "Notes on Okolehao," 1922, Box 4, Summerall Papers.

124. C. Willcox to Surgeon General, Sub: Annual Report, 1921, 12 Jan. 1922, AGO 319.1-2, RG 112.

125. S. C. Huber to Charles C. Morton, 7 Oct. 1921, R 103, HDR. E. C. Williams to AC/S, Sub: Report of Military Police Operations, 30 June 1924, R 121, HDR.

126. Charles G. Morton to Governor of Hawaii, 7 July 1921, R 104, HDR. Department Engineer to CG, HD, 10 July 1922, R 103, HDR; Department Morale Office to Chief, Morale Branch, Sub: Monthly Morale Report, July 1921, 20 Aug. 1921, AGO 322.06 HD, E 37, RG 407.

127. Russell A. Eberhardt to Brian M. Linn, 7 Jan. 1993; Howard C. Fields to Brian M. Linn, 3 Mar. 1994, in author's possession.

128. "Okolehao Blamed for Soldier and Civilian Brawls," *Pacific Commercial Advertiser* (28 Dec. 1919). "Iwilei Wrecked by Colored Troops," *Pacific Commercial Advertiser* (14 Jan. 1916); "Xmas Celebration Ends in Calaboose," *Pacific Commercial Advertiser* (27 Dec. 1916).

129. A. J. Pederson to CG, HD, 8 Mar. 1921, R 104, HDR.

130. Edward M. Lewis to AG, Sub: Annual Report, HD, FY 1926, 30 June 1926, AGO 319.12 HD (6-30-26), RG 407.

131. E. C. Williams to AC/S, G-1, Sub: Report of Military Police Operations, 30 June 1924, R 121, HDR.

132. D. L. Howell to CG, HD, Sub: Fight between Soldiers and Police, Monday night, Dec. 25th, 1916, 27 Dec. 1916, R 103, HDR.

133. Frederick S. Strong to Chairman, Police Commission, 15 Apr. 1917, R 103, HDR. Statement of Sgt. Joseph H. Huf, included in L. M. Brett to CG, HD, Sub: Mistreatment of Enlisted Men by Honolulu Police, 1 Apr. 1917, R 103; Crosby Elliott to C/S, 7 Nov. 1921, R 104; G. M. Halloran to CO, Fort Shafter, Sub: Report of Riot on Night of Dec. 25, 1916, 27 Dec. 1916, R 103, all in HDR.

134. C. B. Hazeltine to C/S, HDN, 7 Sept. 1922, R 104, HDR.

135. E. C. Williams to AC/S, HDN, Sub: Annual Report 1925, 21 July 1925, R 121, HDR. Edward M. Lewis to AG, Sub: Annual Report, HDN, FY 1926, 30 June 1926, 319.12 HD (6-30-26), RG 407. The army also negotiated an agreement with the City and County of Honolulu allowing the military jurisdiction in all cases except traffic offenses, R. B. Ellis to AC/S, Hawaiian Division, Sub: Annual Report 1925, 21 July 1925, R 121, HDR.

136. Walter Maciejowski to Brian M. Linn, 6 Jan. 1993.

137. Howard C. Fields to Brian M. Linn, 3 Mar. 1994.

138. Fox Conner to AG, Sub: Annual Report, FY 1929, 30 June 1929, AGO 319.12 (6-30-29) HD, RG 407.

Chapter Six

1. Lytle Brown to C/S, Sub: Ultimate Philippine Garrison, 2 June 1919, AWC 8438-26, RG 165; Peyton C. March to AG, Sub: Ultimate Philippine Department Garrison, 24 June 1919, OCS 1133, E 8, RG 165; AG to CG, PD, Sub: Philippine Garrison, 11 Oct. 1920, AGO 330.2 PD, RG 407; J. R. Lindsey to C/S, Sub: Annual Report, FY 1924, 28 Nov. 1924, AGO 319.12 (9-3-24), RG 407; Briant H. Wells to C/S, Sub: Peace and War Garrisons and War Reserve Supplies, PD, 1921, AGO 320.2 PD (10-1-20), E 37, RG 407. On the 1920 Defense Act, see Millett and Maslowski, *For the Common Defense*, pp. 365–67; Weigley, *History of the U.S. Army*, pp. 396–403; Holley, *General John M. Palmer*, pp. 464–97, 509–18. Until 1938 the Philippine Department also shared responsibility for two battalions of the 15th Infantry in China—about 950 officers and men.

2. John L. DeWitt to C/S, Sub: Report of the Operations and Training Division, General Staff, 17 Dec. 1923, WPD 1549, RG 165; John L. DeWitt to C/S, Sub: Annual Report of the Operations and Training Division (G-3) for FY, 1923, 29 Jan. 1924, WPD 1549, RG 165; AG to CG, PD, Sub: Reorganization of Philippine Garrison, 17 July 1922, AGO 320.2, E 37, RG 407.

3. Hugh A. Drum to C/S, Sub: Missions of the Regular Army, 15 Feb. 1924, WPD 1549, RG 165.

4. Weigley, *History of the U.S. Army*, pp. 406–9, 415–19; Watson, *War Department: Chief of Staff*, pp. 23–31.

5. "Monkeys Have No Tails," Vol. 5, p. 46, Ivins Papers. "Sojourn in Zamboanga," pp. 43–47, Darnell Papers.

6. C/S, PD to AC/S, WPD, Sub: Current Estimate of the Strategic Situation in the Philippine Islands, 1 Oct. 1924, WPD 1031-9, RG 165. Campbell King to C/S, Sub: Philippine Scout Enlisted Personnel, 26 Oct. 1928, AGO 660.2 PS (10-11-28), RG 407; Eli A. Helmick to AC/S, G-2, Sub: Comments Affecting G-2 in the Philippines and China, 18 Dec. 1925, MID 2055-34, RG 165; D. Clayton James, *Years of MacArthur*, pp. 302–3.

7. "The Mutiny of the Philippine Scouts in 1924—Personal Statement," 1 Nov. 1969, Carraway Papers; AC/S: Copy of Memo, WPD, 19 Mar. 1925, Carraway Papers.

8. J. H. McRae to AG, Sub: Annual Report of the CG, PD, 30 July 1925, AGO 319.12, E 37, RG 407. Memoirs, Alvarado Papers.

9. G-3 Estimate of the Situation, PD, First Phase Plan Orange, 1934, F 171, SPWPC, E 365, RG 407. Clarence Dougherty to Hugh A. Drum, 7 Dec. 1937, Box 9, Drum Papers; Interview with Edward M. Almond, p. 40, Almond Papers; Memoirs, Yeo Papers.

10. Robert C. Richardson, Filipino Manpower in Time of War, 31 July 1923, CAWC 1922–23, AWCIR, RG 165.

11. Edward M. Lewis to AG, Sub: Report on Joint Army and Navy Exercise No. 3, 21 July 1925, WPD 1678-57, RG 165. In 1927, for example, the Hawaii National Guard's 1,727 members included 498 Hawaiians, 206 Japanese, 184 Filipinos, 167 Portuguese, 152 Chinese, 139 Puerto Ricans, and 129 Caucasians. The 1923 decision by the Territorial Attorney General that foreign-born Filipinos were ineligible for the Guard led to over 500 being discharged; see Reports of the Adjutant General of Hawaii, July 1, 1917 to June 30, 1935, E 6050, RG 395; Wakefield, "Hawaii National Guard," pp. 145–46.

12. Geoffrey P. Baldwin, The Defense of Hawaii, 28 Mar. 1928, AWC Class 1927–28, F 349-54, AWCCA. Eli A. Helmick to John L. Hines, 28 Mar. 1923, Box 275, HD, E 11, RG 159; G-3 Appendix, Basic Defense Plan, Oahu, 1924, Box 1, E 6051, RG 395; A. W. Bradbury to AC/S, G-3, Sub: What is the Efficiency of the National Guard? 20 May 1925, R 228, HDR.

13. AG to Judge Advocate General, Sub: Legal Aspect of the Development of Native Forces in the Philippines, 16 Oct. 1928; E. A. Kreger to CG, PD, Sub: Applicability of Section 55, National Defense Act, to the Philippines; both in AGO 660.2 PD (8-21-28), RG 407; Meixsel, "An Army for Independence," pp. 97–98.

14. George W. Read to AG, Sub: Annual Report, CG, PD, FY 1924, 30 July 1924, AGO 319.12, E 37, RG 407. William Lassiter to Deputy C/S, Sub: Annual Report, PD, 1922, 24 Mar. 1923, AGO 319.12, E 37, RG 407; Hugh A. Drum to AC/S, WPD, Sub: Study on the Extension to the Philippine Islands of the Provisions of the National Defense Act Relating to the Reserves, 30 Dec. 1935, AGO 660.2 PDP, RG 407.

15. Carpenter, "Toward the Development," pp. 24–26; John P. Smith, Statistical Data on the Philippine Islands . . . from the Military Point of View, 1921, F Philippines Wood-Forbes, Box 82, McCoy Papers; Memoirs, pp. 121–49, Kernan Papers.

16. Exhibit E to Report of Major Jarvis J. Bain on Inspection trip to Philippine Islands, 30 Apr. 1924, AGO 333 9 PD (8-25-24), CDF, RG 407.

17. Robert C. Richardson, Sub: The Creation of a Federal Reserve of Natives in the Philippine Islands, 25 Nov. 1921, AGO 320.2 (11-25-21), E 37, RG 407.

18. G-1 Appendix, Basic Project for the Defense of the Philippine Islands, 1924, AGO 660.2 (2-27-22), E 37, RG 407.

19. G-2 Annex, Basic Project for the Defense of the Philippine Islands, 1924, AGO 660.2 (2-27-22), E 37, RG 407.

20. George W. Read to AG, Sub: Annual Report, CG, PD, FY 1924, 30 July 1924, AGO 319.

21. William Lassiter to Charles P. Summerall, 6 July 1928, AGO 660.2 PD (12-2-27), RG 407. Meixsel, "An Army for Independence," pp. 103–6.

22. PD, BWPO, 1929, F 206X, SPWPC, E 365, RG 407. MacArthur to AG, 15 Oct. 1928, telegram, AGO 660.2 PD (8-21-28), RG 407; George S. Simonds to C/S, Sub: Defense Plans for the Philippine Islands, 6 Nov. 1928, AGO 660.2 PD (8-21-28), RG 407.

23. G-3 Appendix, PD, 1929, F 209X; Artillery and Machine Gun Beach Defense Annex, PD, BWPO, 1929, F 222X; Chemical Warfare Annex, PD, BWPO, 1929, 213X, all in SPWPC, E 365, RG 407; Meixsel, "An Army for Independence," pp. 110–11.

24. AG to MacArthur, 29 Dec. 1928, AGO 660.2 PD (8-21-28), RG 407.

25. Charles P. Summerall to AG, 20 May 1924, E 6051, RG 395. Briant H. Wells to C/S, Sub: Personnel of Reserve Corps for Garrison of Oahu, 24 Mar. 1922, AGO 381 (11-4-21), CDF 1917–25, AGO 407; HD, Annual Report, FY 1926, 30 June 1926, AGO 319.12 HD (6-30-26), RG 407. Summerall's sentiments found their way into succeeding assessments, sometimes verbatim; see HD, Estimate of the Situation, Army Operating Defense Plan—Hawaiian Theater, 1936, F 107, SPWPC, E 365, RG 407; Estimate of the Political and Economic Situation—Hawaiian Theater, Joint Defense Plan, 1933, Box 4, E 6051, RG 395; HD, Estimate of the Situation, Army Operating Defense Plan—Hawaiian Theater, 1939, F 132, SPWPC, E 365, RG 407.

26. Charles P. Summerall to AG, 20 May 1924, E 6051, RG 395.

27. Basic Project for the Defense of Oahu, 1924, E 6051, RG 395.

28. Estimate of the Situation, HD, BDP, Red-Orange Situation, 1924, E 6051, RG 395. Emphasis in original.

29. Charles P. Summerall to AG, 20 May 1924, E 6051, RG 395. Emphasis in original.

30. Edward M. Lewis to C/S, Sub: Report on Subjects from the Viewpoint of Operations . . . , 19 May 1925, WPD 2027, RG 165.

31. Charles E. Kilbourne to C/S, Sub: Promotion of Reserve Corps Officers in Hawaiian Department, 15 Sept. 1934; Hugh A. Drum to AC/S, WPD, Sub: Infantry Reserve in Hawaii, 13 Dec. 1934, both in AGO 320 HD (4-23-31), RG 407.

32. E. S. Hartshorn to C/S, Sub: Hawaiian Service Command, 30 Apr. 1937, No. 19803-6, E 12, RG 165; Mobilization Plan, Honolulu District—Hawaiian Service Command, 1937, E 6053, RG 395; Hugh A. Drum to AG, Sub: Defense Considerations, HD, 25 May 1937, Box 21, Drum Papers; Robert L. Eichelberger to AG, Sub: Hawaiian Service Command—Reserve, 5 Aug. 1937, No. 19803-5, E 12, RG 165; Walter Krueger to C/S, Sub: Defensive Considerations, HD, 16 Oct. 1937, WPD 3878-3, RG 165.

33. Memo: G-1/7082, 22 Oct. 1924, AGO 325 HD, E 37, RG 407.

34. Charles G. Morton to AG, Hawaii 28 Oct. 1920; Charles G. Morton to AG, Sub: Japanese Reserve Corps Officers, 10 Sept. 1920; Dennis E. Nolan to Director, Operations Division, Sub: Japanese Reserve Officers, 8 Oct. 1920; Joseph L. Collins to Director, Operations Division, Sub: Japanese Reserve Corps Officers, 23 Nov. 1920, all in MID 1766-S-83, RG 165.

35. LeRoy Eltinge to C/S, Sub: Enlistment in the National Guard of Hawaii of American Citizens of Japanese Descent, 3 Feb. 1925, AGO 323.5, E 37, RG 407; HD Intelligence Summary, Officers Reserve Corps, HD, 15 Dec. 1934, WPD 3615, RG 165; Reports of the Adjutant General of Hawaii, July 1, 1917 to June 30, 1935, E 6050, RG 395.

36. Charles P. Summerall to AG, Sub: National Guard in Hawaii, 30 Oct. 1924, AGO 323.5, E 37, RG 407.

37. H. L. Landers, Report of Officer in Charge, R.O.T.C. Affairs, FY 1924, 30 June 1924, R 121, HDR; Charles T. Menoher to AG, Sub: National Guard of Hawaii, 21 Nov. 1924, AGO 323.5, E 37, RG 407; Fox Conner to AG, Sub: R.O.T.C. Inspection, 17 June 1928, AGO 333.9 HD (6-17-28), RG 407.

38. Proceedings of a Board of Officers Appointed to Make a Survey of the Developments of the National Guard and Other Civilian Components of the Army in the Hawaiian Department, 23 May 1931, AGO 320 HD (4-23-31), RG 407; Charles E. Kilbourne to C/S, Sub: Promotion of Reserve Corps Officers in Hawaiian Department, 15 Sept. 1934, AGO 320 HD (4-23-31), RG 407.

39. Briant H. Wells to Douglas MacArthur, 23 July 1934, WPD 3768, RG 165.

40. Reports of the Adjutant General of Hawaii, July 1, 1917 to June 30, 1935, E 6050, RG 395. Stanley D. Embick to C/S, Sub: Promotion of Reserve Corps Officers in Hawaiian Department, 17 Aug. 1935, WPD 3768, RG 165; G-1 Appendix, Joint Defense Plan—Hawaiian Theater, Basic Document, 1933, E 6051, RG 395; Charles E. Kilbourne, WPD to C/S,

Sub: Infantry Reserves, HD, 9 Nov. 1934, WPD 3615-2, RG 165; Intelligence Summary, Officers Reserve Corps, Hawaiian Department, 15 Dec. 1934, WPD 3615, RG 165.

41. Charles D. Herron to AG, Sub: Hawaiian Department Reserve Officers of Japanese Extraction, 23 Dec. 1938, AGO 320 HD (4-23-31), RG 407. Herron's observations on the divisions within Hawaii's Japanese community were quite astute; see Stephan, *Hawaii under the Rising Sun*, pp. 32–54.

42. Enclosures in L. D. Gasser to C/S, Sub: Hawaiian Department Reserve Officers of Japanese Extraction, 7 Feb. 1939, AGO 380 HD (4-23-31), RG 407. Charles Burnett to AC/S, G-1, Sub: Letter of CG, HD, dated Dec. 23, 1938, with reference to Hawaiian Reserve Officers of Japanese Extraction, 28 Jan. 1939, AGO 320 HD (4-23-31), RG 407.

43. AG to All Corps Areas and Department Commanders, 1 Aug. 1940, WPD 3768-3, RG 165.

44. "Gen. Short Says No Racial Lines in Reserve Call," *Honolulu Star Bulletin* (20 Feb. 1941).

45. [W. Cameron Forbes] to SW, 12 Nov. 1921, MID 2657 Z 2, RG 165; AG to CG, PD, 27 July 1922, AGO 660.2 PD 2/22, RG 407; Dissent of Major John J. Kingman, JANPC to JB, Sub: The Defense of the Philippine Islands, 13 Apr. 1922, F179, E 258, RG 165; Stanley C. Vestal, "The Use in Battle of Allies, Auxiliaries, Colored Troops, and Troops Raised in the Insular Possessions," Lecture 30 Apr. 1924, Command Course, CAWC 1923–24, F 270-46, AWCCA; James H. Tierney, The Defense of the Philippine Islands, 1 Apr. 1928, F 349-33, AWCCA.

46. Leonard Wood to Wallace R. Farrington, 13 Sept. 1926; Report by Lieutenant Colonel R. A. Duckworth-Ford to his Excellency, the Governor General of the Philippine Islands, 4 Nov. 1926, both in Philippine Islands File, U.S. Departments, Governors' Correspondence—Wallace R. Farrington, HSA; J. W. McRae to AG, Sub: Annual Report of the Commanding General, Philippine Department, 30 July 1925, AGO 319.12, E 37, RG 407; Francis H. French to AG, Sub: Annual Report, FY ending 30 June 1919, 26 July 1919, AGO 319.12, E 37, RG 407; MID, PD, Philippine Islands, Estimate of the Psychologic [*sic*] Situation, 30 Mar. 1921, F 3020, Box 1842, E 77, RG 165. A large collection of internal security reports can be found in MID, Regional File, 1922–44, Philippine Islands, Boxes 1838 to 1842, E 77, RG 165.

47. Basic Plan (Brown) for Military Activities in the Event of a Native Uprising in the Philippine Islands, 1923, F 321, SPWPC, E 365, RG 407. This plan was originally titled "Basic Plan (White)" and retitled, either in Manila or Washington.

48. Ibid.

49. Army Strategical Plan—Brown, 1931, War Plan—Brown, F 318, SPWPC, E 365, RG 407; Defense Commanders Plan of the Manila Defenses, War Plan—Brown, 1932, F 313, SPWPC, E 365, RG 407; Plan of 31st U.S. Infantry in case of local disturbances directed against Malacanan, War Plan—Brown, 1933, F 313, SPWPC, E 365, RG 407; Walter Krueger to CG, PD, 23 June 1937, F 4548-2, War Plan Brown, WPD, RG 165.

50. Confidential Note, Exhibit B, J. W. Heard to President, Board of Officers, 8 Feb. 1919, AGO 660.12 HD, E 37, RG 407. Proceedings of a Board of Officers which met at Honolulu, T.H., pursuant to the following order: Special Orders No. 5, HQ, HD, 4 Mar. 1919, AGO 660.12 HD, E 37, RG 407. In 1919 Washington specified the Hawaiian Department's postwar mission was the defense of Pearl Harbor against both external threat and "enemy sympathizers"; see William G. Haan to AG, Sub: Revision of Defense Projects and Plans, Hawaiian Department, 31 Dec. 1919, AGO 600.2, CGDF 1919–39, Box 1, RG 407.

51. E. D. Anderson to C/S 13 Mar. 1920, OCS 623, E 8, RG 165. Daws, *Shoal of Time*, pp. 305–6.

52. A. A. Hopkins, Confidential Survey, Territory of Hawaii: Japanese Activities, 31 Jan. 1921, MID 1766-S-97, RG 165.

53. George M. Brooke to Director, Military Intelligence, 7 Apr. 1920, MID 1766-S-72, RG 165. G-2, HD [George M. Brooke], The Economic Situation in Hawaii as Relating to Japanese Activity, 10 Feb. 1921, MID 1766-S-95/1, RG 165; HQ, HD, G-2, Digest of Facts and Statements Collected in the Office of the Assistant Chief of Staff for Military Intelligence, Hawaiian Department, with Reference to the Japanese Situation, [1921?], MID 1766-S-95/3, RG 165. The song that troubled Brooke—"Momotaro"—is still taught to Hawaii's schoolchildren.

54. Address by Major General C. P. Summerall to the Makiki Church, 12 Nov. 1922, Box 27, Summerall Papers. Charles P. Summerall to AG, 20 May 1924, E 6051, RG 395.

55. S. A. Wood, The Japanese Situation in Hawaii, 27 July 1921, MID 1766-S-111/3, RG 165. A somewhat more moderate version of this report appears in S. A. Wood, "Racial Problem."

56. Estimate of the Political and Economic Situation, Hawaiian Islands, Joint Defense Plan, 1933, F 116, SPWPC, E 365, RG 407; Kuykendall and Day, Hawaii: A History, p. 244.

57. Charles G. Morton, "The Defense of Hawaii," 17 Oct. 1921, Lecture, F 215-42, AWCCA. On the ambivalent loyalties of Hawaii's Japanese, see Stephan, Hawaii under the Rising Sun, pp. 14–15, 23–40. For a strongly antimilitary view of the Japanese labor movement, see Okihiro, Cane Fires.

58. Report: Filipino Secret Societies, 9 Jan. 1924; Stephen O. Fuqua to AC/S, G-2, Sub: Filipino fraternal organizations, 10 Nov. 1924, both in MID 10582-85-7, RG 165; L. M. Judd to Fox Conner, 27 Mar. 1930, Japanese Propaganda File, U.S. Departments, Governors' Correspondence—L. M. Judd, HSA. Army fears of radical contamination may have peaked in 1925 when two soldiers, members of the Hawaiian Communist League, were jailed for organizing an American Union of Soldiers, Sailors, and Marines; see Young Worker (30 May 1925 and 6 June 1925), MID 10110-PP-74, RG 165; A. G. Lott to C/S, Sub: Points of Special Interest in the Hawaiian Department, Deemed of Sufficient Importance for the Present Attention of the Chief of Staff, 2 Apr. 1925, Box 39, Hines Papers.

59. HD, Basic Plan White, 1924, E 6051, RG 395.

60. HD, Annex No. 3, Military Intelligence, White Plan: Military Aid to Civil Authorities during Domestic Disturbances in Hawaiian Islands, 1928, E 6051, RG 395.

61. White Plan: Military Aid to Civil Authorities during Domestic Disturbances in Hawaiian Islands, 1928, E 6051, RG 395.

62. HD, White Plan, 1932, E 6051, RG 395.

63. H. Gooding Field, Report on Internment and Segregation of Japanese Residents on Island of Oahu (City and County of Honolulu) and in City of Honolulu Respectively in Event of Emergency, 22 Nov. 1920, E 6051, RG 395.

64. Morton, "Defense of Hawaii."

65. HD, Estimate of the Situation, BDP, Red-Orange Situation, 1924, E 6051, RG 395. WPD Annex, Basic Project for the Defense of Oahu, 1924, E 6051, RG 395.

66. G-2 Appendix, Joint Defense Plan—Hawaiian Theater, 1933, F 118, SPWPC, E 365, RG 407. Appendix 2: Intelligence, HD, White Plan, 1932, Box 7, E 6051, RG 395; Provost Marshal's Operations Annex, Joint Defense Plan—Hawaiian Theater, 1933, F 126, Box 55, RG 407.

67. Halstead Dorey to WPD, 30 Jan. 1935, WPD 3675-1, RG 165. Hugh A. Drum to AG, Sub: Defense Considerations, HD, 25 May 1937, Box 21, Drum Papers; Sherman Miles to AC/S, WPD, Sub: Control of the Japanese in Hawaii as Provided for in the Present Joint Defense Plan, Hawaiian Theatre, 22 Oct. 1934, WPD 3675, RG 165. One author asserted that U.S. Army officers wanted to intern Hawaii's Japanese but businessmen opposed this; however, there is no evidence to support his claim. See Barber, Hawaii: Restless Rampart, pp. 245–46.

68. Annex No. 6: Provost Marshal, Operations Orders, Joint Defense Plan—Hawaiian

Theater, 1936, F 110, SPWPC, E 365, RG 407. For internal security plans: E-Plan—Employment of Troops to Control Enemy Sympathizers in the Hawaiian Islands, 1929, Box 4, E 6051, RG 395; G-1 Appendix, HD, Joint Defense Plan—Hawaiian Theater, 1933, F 117, SPWPC, E 365, RG 407; Provost Marshal Operations Annex, HD, Joint Defense Plan—Hawaiian Theater, 1933, F 126, SPWPC, E 365, RG 407; Annex No. 8: Search of Alien Communities, HD, Operations Orders, Joint Defense Plan—Hawaiian Theater, 1937, F 105, SPWPC, E 365, RG 407; Army Operating Defense Plans, Hawaiian Coastal Frontier, Operations Orders, 1938, Box 14, E 6051, RG 395.

69. [George S. Patton], Plan for Initial Seizure of Orange Nationals, [1935], Box 3, HDR. James G. Ord to Charles E. Kilbourne, n.d., Sub: Provost Marshal's Operations Annex, Joint Defense Plan—Hawaiian Theater, 1933, F 126, SPWPC, E 365, RG 407; Charles E. Kilbourne to James G. Ord, n.d., Sub: Provost Marshal's Operations Annex, Joint Defense Plan—Hawaiian Theater, 1933, F 126, SPWPC, E 365, RG 407.

70. Blumenson, *Patton*, p. 136.

71. Slackman, *Target: Pearl Harbor*, p. 38.

72. HD, Annex No. 1—Military Intelligence, WPO, 1927, E 6051, RG 395.

73. Samuel T. Mackall, The Defense of Hawaii, 14 Mar. 1929, F 357-56, AWCCA. Emphasis in original. HD, Estimate of the Situation: Japanese Population of Hawaii, 1933, MID 242-12-133, RG 165; Casey Hayes, Strategic Estimate of the Situation—Hawaiian Islands, 1930, E 6051, Box 5, RG 395.

74. Halstead Dorey to WPD, 30 Jan. 1935, WPD 3675-1, RG 165.

75. HQ, HD, Training Memo No. 3, 22 Sept. 1936, E 6044, Box 23, RG 395. Annex No. 6—Provost Marshal, HD, Operations Orders, Joint Defense Plan—Hawaiian Theater, 1937, F 105, SPWPC, E 365, RG 407; Scenario of the Problem, Report of Department Maneuvers, Apr.–May 1940, Box 2, HDR.

Chapter Seven

1. Braisted, *U.S. Navy in the Pacific, 1909–1922*, pp. 289–490; Edward S. Miller, *War Plan Orange*, 108–14.

2. WPD was created in Feb. 1918 as the primary planning agency for the General Staff. In 1921 it was made the fifth section of the General Staff and given the additional task of overseeing and coordinating the needs of the overseas garrisons. For most of the interwar period, WPD had a staff of about a dozen officers; see Walter Krueger, "The Detailed Working of the War Plans Division, Its Tasks and Their Methods of Execution," 18 Oct. 1924, Lecture, WPD Course, Vol. 8, Part 1, AWC 1924-25, AWCIR; Cline, *War Department: Washington Command Post*, pp. 8–39.

3. "Notes on the Philippines," Steele Papers.

4. Charles D. Rhodes, "The Problem of the Pacific," 1921. Francis J. Kernan, "Political and Military Relations of the Philippine Islands to the United States," 27 Apr. 1921, both in Philippines Wood-Forbes 1921, Box 82, McCoy Papers.

5. William G. Haan to AG, Sub: Revision of Defense Projects and Plans, Hawaiian Department, 31 Dec. 1919, AGO 600.2, CCDF, RG 407; E. R. Stone to AG, Sub: Plans and Projects, 18 June 1925, WPD 2024, RG 165; Brief History of the Hawaiian Defense Project, [1936], Box 10, E 6051, RG 395.

6. Jarvis J. Bain, Inspection of the Philippine Department made by Major J. J. Bain, G.S., 25 Aug. 1924, AGO 333.9 (PD), E 37, RG 407.

7. Haan to AG, Sub: Revision of Defense Projects.

8. Minutes: Conference, Jan. 13, 1925, Room 259, State, War and Navy Building, WPD 2011-1, RG 165; Walter Krueger to AC/S, Sub: Agenda for Conference re—Project for the Installation of Four 16″ guns at Schofield Barracks for the Defense of Oahu, 12 Jan. 1925,

WPD 2011, RG 165; Charles E. Kilbourne to C/S, Sub: First Phase Plan—Orange, PD, 1933, 25 Oct. 1933, WPD 3251-14, RG 165; Meixsel, "An Army for Independence," pp. 88–89.

9. W. F. Clark to C/S, Sub: Projects and Plans for National Defense and Their Development, 2 May 1919, AWC 8921-18, RG 165; Weigley, *American Way of War*, p. 245; Edward S. Miller, *War Plan Orange*, pp. 83–84. For most of the interwar period, the Joint Board's permanent members were the army chief of staff, deputy chief of staff, and assistant chief of staff of the War Plans Division and the navy's chief of naval operations, assistant chief of naval operations, and the director of the Plans Division. The Joint Army and Navy Planning Committee consisted of three or more members each of the army's War Plans Division and the navy's Plans Division.

10. Harry E. Yarnell to John M. Palmer, 25 Apr. 1919, F 28, Box 2, E 284, RG 165. JANPC to JB, Sub: National Policy and War Plans, 28 Oct. 1919, Box 1, E 284, RG 165; Braisted, *U.S. Navy in Pacific, 1909–1922*, p. 470.

11. JANPC to JB, Oct. 1919, Sub: Strategy of the Pacific, F 28, Box 2, E 284, RG 165; Harry E. Yarnell to Army Members, JANPC, Sub: Joint Army and Navy Doctrine for Defense of the Seacoast against Landing Attacks, 9 Feb. 1920, F 4, E 284, RG 165; Braisted, *U.S. Navy in the Pacific, 1909–1922*, p. 474; Edward S. Miller, *War Plan Orange*, p. 84.

12. Peyton C. March to SW and SN, Sub: 'Strategy of the Pacific' and Policy in Connection Therewith, 18 Dec. 1919, AGO 381 (12-18-19), RG 407.

13. JANPC to JB, Sub: National Policy and War Plans, 28 Oct. 1919, Box 1, E 284, RG 165; John J. Kingman to Chief, G-3 Section, Sub: An Outline of the Development to Date of War Plan Orange, 15 Nov. 1922, F 368, WPO, WPD, RG 165.

14. Dingman, *Power in the Pacific*; Ellis, *Republican Foreign Policy*, pp. 79–136; Braisted, "Washington Conference"; Powers, "U.S. Army and the Washington Conference."

15. JANPC to JB, Sub: The Defense of the Philippine Islands, 13 Apr. 1922, JB 303, F 179, Box 5, E 258, RG 165. JB, Sub: Policy re Defense of Philippines. Effect of new Treaties, 17 May 1922, JB 303, Series 179, F 179, Box 6, E 258, RG 165.

16. Gole, "War Planning," p. 219.

17. JB, Sub: Defense of the Philippines, 7 July 1923, JB 305, Series 208, F 208, Box 7, E 284, RG 165.

18. JB, Sub: Retention of Military and Naval Bases in the Philippines, 15 Apr. 1924, JB 305, Series 229, F 229, Box 8, E 284, RG 165.

19. JANPC to JB, Sub: Relations with the Philippine Islands, and Military and Naval Bases in Case Independence Is Granted, 12 Mar. 1924, JB 305, Series 227, F 227, Box 8, E 284, RG 165.

20. Cited in James H. Tierney, Defense of the Philippine Islands, 1 Apr. 1928, F 349-33, AWCCA. Briant H. Wells to C/S, Sub: A Pacific Policy for the United States, 31 Oct. 1921, AGO 381 (11-2-21), CDF 1917–25, SCF, Box 50, RG 407.

21. Hugh A. Drum to C/S, Sub: Missions of the Regular Army, 15 Feb. 1924, WPD 1549, RG 165.

22. John W. Gulick to AC/S, Sub: Reorganization and Redistribution of the Regular Army at Its Present Strength, 11 June 1924, WPD 1549-2, RG 165. Kernan, "Political and Military Relations."

23. Robert Henderson, "Strategical Survey of the Western Atlantic, the Pacific and the Caribbean including Our Outlying Possessions," 14 Sept. 1925, Lecture, WPD Course, Vol. 10, CAWC 1925–26, AWCIR. Contemporary AWC war games reflect Henderson's views: see Report of Committee 19, Summary of the Estimate on the Orange Situation, 3 Nov. 1922, Course No. 29, G-2 Documents, CAWC 1922–23; Report of Sub-Committee No. 22, Disposition of an Expeditionary Corps, 25 Mar. 1926, Command Course, No. 30 and 31, Vol. 6, CAWC 1925–26, both in AWCIR.

24. John J. Pershing to C/S, Sub: Synopsis of Joint Army and Navy Estimates of the

Orange Situation, 7 July 1923, JB 325, Series 207, F 207, Box 7, E 258, RG 165; Joint Army and Navy Basic WPO, 1924, F 228, Box 8, E 284, RG 165; Walter Krueger, Draft of Joint Army and Navy Basic Plan Orange, 7 Nov. 1923, F 368, WPO, WPD, RG 165; Army Section to Navy Section, JANPC, Sub: War Plan Orange, 19 Mar. 1923, JB 325, Series 207, F 207, Box 7, E 258, RG 165. On U.S. Navy planning, see Edward S. Miller, *War Plan Orange*, pp. 122–31.

25. Joint Army and Navy BWPO, Aug. 1924, F 228, Box 8, E 284, RG 165.

26. Navy Draft: Joint Army and Navy BWPO, Jan. 1924, F 368, WPO, WPD, RG 165; Walter Krueger, Draft: Joint Army and Navy BWPO, 28 Feb. 1924, F 368, WPO, WPD, RG 165; Strategical Plan, Army WPO, 1925, F 230, Box 69, SPWPC, E 365, RG 407; JANPC to JB, Sub: Relations with the Philippine Islands.

27. JANPC Draft, Joint Army and Navy BWPO, 23 Nov. 1926, F 368, WPO, WPD, RG 165.

28. J. D. Reardan to Stanley D. Embick, 29 Apr. 1927; F. A. Ruggles to Chief, AS, Sub: Air Effort in the Orange and Red War Plans, July 1927; both in Development of Joint Estimate of the Situation—Orange (1927), F 232, SPWPC, E 365, RG 407.

29. ASPO, 1928, F 141, SPWPC, E 365, RG 407. Draft: Joint Army and Navy BWPO, 17 Apr. 1928, F 368, WPO, WPD, RG 165.

30. George S. Simonds to Frank A. Schofield, 10 Feb. 1928, F 2720-7, WPO, WPD, RG 165. Memo: Points Brought up for Discussion at the Joint Board Meeting, 9 Feb. 1928, F 280, Box 10, E 284, RG 165.

31. ASPO [WPD WPO 2], 1928, F 141, SPWPC, E 365, RG 407. Draft, Joint Army and Navy BWPO, 17 Apr. 1928, F 368, WPO, WPD, RG 165; Clement H. Wright, Memo: Organization of the Army Contingent, Initial Expeditionary Force (Orange), 8 Sept. 1928, Development of ASPO, 1928, F 237, SPWPC, E 365, RG 407; Stanley H. Ford to AC/S, WPD, Sub: Information assisting in the Development of the Orange Plan, 26 Feb. 1928, F 2720-8, WPO, WPD, RG 165.

32. ASPO [WPD WPO 2], 1928.

33. Section 1, Joint Army and Navy BWPO, Chapter 1, The General Scheme of the Navy Basic Plan Orange, Mar. 1929, Navy BWPO, R 2, *SPN*. Estimate of the Situation, Joint Army and Navy BWPO, 1929, F 226, SPWPC, E 365, RG 407; Forces for the Principal Theater of Operations; Concept of the War, Both in Navy BWPO, Mar. 1929, R 2, *SPN*.

34. Blue-Orange Joint Estimate of the Situation, Joint Army and Navy BWPO, 1929, F 226, SPWPC, E 365, RG 407.

35. Douglas MacArthur to SW, Sub: Military Value of the Philippine Islands to the United States, Oct. 1931, AGO 093.5 PI (10-2-31), RG 407. Friend, *Between Two Empires*, pp. 77–79.

36. JANPC to JB, Sub: Independence of the Philippine Islands; Effect of Withdrawal of Military Forces, 28 Feb. 1934, F 525, Box 16, E 284, RG 165.

37. Douglas MacArthur to Bonner Fellers, 1 June 1939, F 10, Box 2, RG 1, MacArthur Papers. On one occasion, Hoover told MacArthur that the United States "had a definite moral responsibility in regard to the Philippine people but at the same time they were a great liability"; see Moseley, "One Soldier's Journey," Vol. 2, p. 153, Moseley Papers.

38. Charles E. Kilbourne to Army Members, JANPC, Sub: Military Policy in the Philippine Islands, 1 May 1934, WPD 3251-18, RG 165.

39. George S. Simonds to AC/S, G-4, Sub: Possible Reduction in the Philippine Garrison, 16 July 1930, WPD 3251-7, RG 165.

40. Charles E. Kilbourne to C/S, Sub: Revision of ASPO, 14 Nov. 1933, Development File, ASPO, 1935 and 1936 Revision, F 238, SPWPC, E 365, RG 407. Memo: Orange, 13 June 1933, Development File, ASPO, 1935 and 1936 Revision, F 238, SPWPC, E 365, RG 407.

41. Marginalia on memo: Orange Plan with Relation to Four Army Plan, 18 Nov. 1932, WPO 2730-49, WPD, RG 165. Memo: Orange, 13 June 1933, Development File, ASPO, 1935 and 1936 Revision, F 238, SPWPC, E 365, RG 407; D. Clayton James, *Years of MacArthur*, pp. 367–68.

42. George S. Simonds to AC/S, G-4, Sub: Policy for the Philippine Department, 20 Jan. 1930, WPD 2316-11, RG 165.

43. Charles E. Kilbourne to G. V. H. Moseley, Sub: Extracts from a G-2 Estimate of Possible Orange Air Operations in the Philippine Islands, 12 Oct. 1932, encl. in Estimate of Situation, Joint Army and Navy, BWPO, 1929, F 226, SPWPC, E 365, RG 407.

44. Committee No. 6, Estimate of the Situation-Orange, G-2 Course, Vol. 2, CAWC 1930–31. H. H. Slaughter, "Japan," 8 Jan. 1937, Lecture, G-2 Course, Vol. 7, CAWC 1936–37; W. W. Crane, "The Japanese Empire," 10 Dec. 1931, Lecture, G-2 Course, Vol. 2, CAWC 1931–32; Charles Burnett, "The Japanese Empire in 1932," 5 Dec. 1932, Lecture, G-2 Course, Vol. 2, CAWC 1932–33, all in AWCIR. The argument that racism led prewar officers to denigrate Japan appears in Dower, *War without Mercy*; Kahn, "U.S. Views Germany and Japan," and May, "Conclusions," in Ernest R. May, *Knowing One's Enemies*, pp. 476–77, 497, 537; Slackman, *Target: Pearl Harbor*, pp. 34–44, 281.

45. Philippine Map Problem and Map Maneuver General Solution: Orange and Orange Command Group Assignments, Conduct of War Class, Vol. 6, CAWC 1930–31; Special Instructions for Map Study No. 3 (Orange), Conduct of War Course, Vol. 6, CAWC 1932–33; Theater Study No. 5, Western Pacific Area: Situations and Requirements, 15–21 Mar. 1934, WPD Course, Vol. 7, CAWC 1933–34; Situation and Requirements, Theater Study No. 2: Western Pacific, 5–18 Mar. 1936, WPD Course, Vol. 6, CAWC 1935–36; Map Problem No. 2: First Situation and Requirement, 25 May to 9 June 1937, Conduct of War, Vol. 5, CAWC 1936–37; Excerpts from Student WPO, Conduct of War, Vol. 5, CAWC 1936–37; all in AWCIR.

46. Gole, "War Planning," pp. xii–xiv, 30, 33–35.

47. Weigley, *History of the U.S. Army*, pp. 415–21; Edward S. Miller, *War Plan Orange*, pp. 182–83, 213–28.

48. Stanley D. Embick to CG, PD, Sub: Military Policy of U.S. in Philippine Islands, 19 Apr. 1933, AGO 093.5 PD (10-2031), CF, RG 407. Schaffer, "General Stanley D. Embick."

49. JANPC to Joint Board, Sub: Revision of Joint Army and Navy BWPO, 23 Apr. 1935, JB 325, Series 546, F 546, E 283, RG 165.

50. Douglas MacArthur to SW, Sub: Revision of Joint Army and Navy BWPO, 8 May 1935, JB 325, Series 546, E 285, RG 165. Edward S. Miller, *War Plan Orange*, p. 183.

51. Stanley D. Embick, Military Aspects of the Situation That Would Result from the Retention by the United States of a Military (Including Naval) Commitment in the Philippine Islands. Appendix A: Defense of the Philippine Islands by the United States, 2 Dec. 1935, F Philippine Islands Secret, Box 3, E 207, RG 107.

52. Sherman Miles, Memo: U.S. Military Position in the Far East, 1935, F 573, Box 17, E 284, RG 165.

53. W.K. [Walter Krueger], Memo: Our Policy in the Philippines, 28 Oct. 1935, F-573, Box 17, Entry 284, RG 165. Krueger made similar arguments before the JANPC; see Walter Krueger to C/S, Sub: Joint Board Case "Our Military and Naval Position in the Far East," 14 Feb. 1936, and JANPC, Development File, Sub: Our Military (including Naval) Position in the Far East, 17 Mar. 1936, F 573, Box 17, E 284, RG 165; Greene, "Military View," pp. 370–71.

54. A. S. Carpender, Memo for discussion in Joint Planning Committee, 17 Dec. 1935, F 573, Box 17, Entry 284, RG 165.

55. Navy Members, Joint Planning Committee to Joint Board, 6 Feb. 1936, Enclosure B

in Joint Planning Committee to Joint Board, Sub: Re-Examination of Our Military (Including Naval) Position in the Far East, JB 305, Series 573, Box 17, RG 165.

56. Army Section of the Joint Planning Committee to Joint Board, 5 Mar. 1936, Enclosure A, Joint Planning Committee to Joint Board, Sub: Re-Examination of Our Military (Including Naval) Position in the Far East, JB 305, Series 573, Box 17, RG 165.

57. Walter Krueger and A. S. Carpender. Joint Planning Committee to Joint Board, Sub: Re-Examination of Our Military (Including Naval) Position in the Far East, [Mar.?] 1936; Memorandum for Joint Planning Committee-Army, Sub: Re-Examination of Our Military (Including Naval) Position in the Far East, 19 May 1936, both in JB 305, Series 573, Box 17, RG 165.

58. Current Estimate of the Situation, ASPO, 1936, F 235, SPWPC, E 365, RG 407.

59. Stanley D. Embick to AC/S, WPD, Sub: Draft of directive to Planning Committee re New Orange Plan, 5 Nov. 1937, Development file for WPO (1938), F 225, SPWPC, E 365, RG 407. Edward S. Miller, *War Plan Orange*, pp. 223–25.

60. [Stanley D. Embick] C/S to Asst. SW, Sub: Military Priority Policy to Guide Industrial Planning, 25 Oct. 1937, Development File for WPO (1938), F 225, SPWPC, E 365, RG 407.

61. C/S to CNO, 3 Nov. 1937, Development File for WPO (1938), F 225, SPWPC, E 365, RG 407.

62. Walter Krueger to C/S, Sub: Some Thoughts on the Joint Basic War Plan Orange, 22 Nov. 1937, WPO 2720-103, WPD, RG 165.

63. C/S to ASW, Sub: Military Priority Policy.

64. Joint Army and Navy BWPO, 1938, F 223, SPWPC, E 365, RG 407. Emphasis omitted. For the debate over the 1938 plan, see Edward S. Miller, *War Plan Orange*, pp. 223–27; Matloff and Snell, *Strategic Planning*, pp. 2–3.

65. G-2 Course, Vol. 1, CAWC 1939–40, AWCIR. On the "Rainbow" plans, see Matloff and Snell, *Strategic Planning*, pp. 4–48; Gole, "War Planning"; Dwan, "Franklin D. Roosevelt," pp. 55–71.

66. War Department Concentration Plan Orange, 1940 (WPD WDCP-0-40), F 227, SPWPC, E 365, RG 407.

67. D. Clayton James, *Years of MacArthur*, pp. 588–92.

Chapter Eight

1. The primary units of the Hawaiian Division were the 21st Brigade (19th and 21st Infantry Regiments); 22nd Brigade (27th and 35th Infantry Regiments); 11th Field Artillery Brigade (8th, 11th, and 13th Field Artillery Regiments); and the 11th Tank Company. Hawaii's Coast Artillery went through a bewildering number of organizational adjustments, but in 1923 it consisted of the Hawaiian Coast Artillery District, which was subdivided into the Coast Defenses of Honolulu and Coast Defenses of Pearl Harbor, manned by seven companies each (in 1924 organized as the 15th and 16th Coast Artillery Regiments), as well as the 55th (motorized 155-millimeter guns) and 64th (antiaircraft) Coast Artillery Regiments and the 41st (8-inch railway guns) Coast Artillery Battalion. Hawaii's aviation organization, almost as unstable as that of the Coast Artillery, had in 1923 the 5th Composite Group (6th Pursuit and 23rd and 72nd Bombardment squadrons) at Luke Field and the 17th Composite Group (19th Pursuit and 4th Observation squadrons) at Wheeler Field, part of the Schofield garrison. The main forces in the Philippine Department were Harbor Defenses of Manila and Subic Bays (the American 59th and 60th and the Filipino 91st and 92nd Coast Artillery Regiments); the all-Filipino Philippine Division (45th and 57th Infantry, the 26th Cavalry, the 24th Field Artillery, the 14th Engineer, and the 12th

Medical Regiments); and the unattached American components, consisting of the 31st Infantry Regiment, a battalion of the 15th Infantry Regiment (two battalions were stationed in China), and the 2nd Observation, 3rd Pursuit, and 28th Bombardment squadrons. The composition of the Philippine Division shifted several times, with the 26th Cavalry often detached. In keeping with mainland practice during the interwar years, the Pacific Army's tables of organization seldom reflected the actual condition of units. Many organizations were kept at reduced strength, and others were either partially or completely "inactive" and consisted of little more than a few officers or noncommissioned officers. To confuse the issue further, the Scout battalions stationed at Zamboanga and Baguio were occasionally referred to as the 43rd Infantry Regiment.

2. JB 305, Series 208, Sub: Defense of the Philippines, 7 July 1923, F 208, Box 7, E 284, RG 165. Wheeler, "Republican Philippine Policy," pp. 377–90; Trani and Wilson, *Presidency of Warren G. Harding*, pp. 158–59.

3. Francis J. Kernan, "Political and Military Relations of the Philippine Islands to the United States," 27 Apr. 1921, Wood-Forbes 1921 File, Box 82, McCoy Papers. For the Wood-Forbes Mission and army responses, see Wood-Forbes 1921 File, Box 82, McCoy Papers; Bacevich, *Diplomat in Khaki*, pp. 93–99. For sample U.S. Army views on independence, see Eli A. Helmick to SW, 11 Dec. 1925, MID 2055-264, RG 165; Charles G. Treat to James G. Harbord, 12 Oct. 1921, AGO 320.2, E 37, RG 407; Report of Committee No. 5, The Region of the Pacific and the Region of the Caribbean, 1 Mar. 1923, F 254-5, AWCCA.

4. Vicente Lim, The Philippine Islands: A Military Asset, 29 Apr. 1929, F 357-54, AWCCA. On the Wood-Quezon controversy, see Bacevich, *Diplomat in Khaki*, pp. 100–13; Brands, *Bound to Empire*, pp. 125–37; Onorato, *Leonard Wood*.

5. Hugh A. Drum to C/S, Sub: Missions of the Regular Army, 15 Feb. 1924, WPD 1549, RG 165. The Embick-Wells report is cited in James H. Tierney, Defense of the Philippine Islands, 1 Apr. 1928, F 349-33, AWCCA.

6. JANPC to JB, Sub: Defense of the Philippine Islands, 13 Apr. 1922, F 179, Box 6, E 258, RG 165. AG to CG, PD, 27 July 1922, AGO 660.2 PD, RG 407; Leonard Wood to SW, 5 Feb. 1923, AGO 660.2 PD (2-5-23), RG 407.

7. George S. Simonds to C/S, Sub: Mission of the Armed Forces in the Philippine Islands, 25 June 1928, AGO 660.2 PD (12-2-27), RG 407. "Down the Big Road," p. 350, Hagood Family Papers; Johnson Hagood to William Lassiter, 20 May 1928, F 5, Box 186, Hagood Papers; Local Joint Defense Planning Committee to AG, Sub: Study of the Joint Mission of the Military and Naval Forces in the Philippines, 17 Mar. 1928, F 298, Box 11, E 284, RG 165; JANPC to JB, Sub: Revision of Joint Mission of Military and Naval Forces in the Philippine Islands, 5 June 1928, F 298, Box 11, E 284, RG 165; JB, Sub: Revision of Joint Mission of Military and Naval Forces in the Philippine Islands, 14 June 1928, JB 303, Series 298, F 298, Box 11, E 284, RG 165; PD, WPO, First Phase, 1934, F 198X, Box 11, SPWPC, E 365, RG 407.

8. Francis J. Kernan to AG, Sub: Confidential Report and Map of Lingayen Gulf, 7 June 1921, AGO 381 (6-7-21), RG 407. Proceedings of a Joint Army and Navy Board, PD, Oct. 1920, AGO 381 (11-29-20), SCF CDF 1917–25, RG 407; G-2 Estimate of the Situation for War Plan Orange, Dec. 1921, MID 242-12-15, RG 165.

9. George W. Read to AG, Sub: Air Base—Cabcaben, 19 June 1923, AGO 660.2, PDP 1923, RG 407; H. G. Bishop to AG, Sub: Project for the Defense of the Philippine Islands, 23 June 1923, AGO 660.2, PDP 1922, RG 407; George W. Read to AG, Sub: Defense Project, Philippine Islands, 27 Dec. 1923, AGO 660.2, PDP 1922, RG 407.

10. Air Service Annex, Basic Project for the Defense of the Philippine Islands, 1924, AGO 660.2 PD (2-27-22), E 37, RG 407.

11. William G. Haan, A Positive System of Coast Defense, 1919, AGO 660.2 (11-22-19), RG 407.

12. William Lassiter to George S. Simonds, 31 Aug. 1928, WPD 3251, RG 165.

13. Report on the Defense of the Philippine Islands by Major General Wm. Lassiter, 21 Aug. 1928, AGO 660.2 PD (8-21-28), RG 407.

14. LeRoy Eltinge to AG, Sub: Defense Project, Philippine Islands, 21 Aug. 1924, AGO 660.2, PDP 1922, RG 407. Francis J. Kernan to AG, Sub: Defects and Deficiencies in the Coast Defense District of Manila and Subic Bays, 7 June 1921, AGO 381, E 37, RG 407; Major Army Project—Philippine Project, 29 May 1925, MID 242-57, RG 165; LeRoy Eltinge to C/S, Sub: Annual Report, 31 Mar. 1925, AGO 310.12 (3-31-25), RG 407. Correspondence on the Philippine Defense Project is filed in AGO 660.2, PDP, Box 8, RG 407.

15. John J. Pershing to William M. Wright, 23 May 1923, AGO 320.2 PD (5-19-22), E 37, RG 407.

16. G-2 Appendix, Basic Project for the Defense of the Philippine Islands, 1924, AGO 660.2 (2-27-22), E 37, RG 407. The Basic Project was not technically an Orange plan, but it contains a detailed explanation of the Philippine Department's plans against Japanese invasion, as well as against internal rebellion (War Plan Brown); see Basic Project for the Defense of the Philippine Islands (1924), Part 1: Brief Estimate of the Situation, War Plan Brown, F 310, Box 87, SPWPC, E 365, RG 407.

17. William Lassiter to Charles P. Summerall, 30 Aug. 1928, AGO 660.2 PD (8-21-28), RG 407.

18. William Lassiter to Charles P. Summerall, 27 Sept. 1928, WPD 3251-1, RG 165.

19. Johnson Hagood to C/S, PD, Sub: Orange Plan, 13 July 1928, F 5, Box 186, Hagood Papers.

20. Johnson Hagood to William Lassiter, 20 May 1928, F 5, Box 186, Hagood Papers.

21. William Lassiter, Report of the Defense of the Philippine Islands, 21 Aug. 1928, WPD 3251, RG 165.

22. William Lassiter to Charles P. Summerall, 30 Aug. 1928, AGO 660.2 PD (8-21-28), RG 407. William Lassiter to Charles P. Summerall, 6 July 1928, AGO 660.2 PD (12-2-27), RG 407.

23. Lassiter, Report on the Defense.

24. Charles P. Summerall to AC/S, WPD, Sub: Defense of the Philippines, 1 Oct. 1928, WPD 3251, RG 165.

25. PD, BWPO, 1929, F 206X, Box 14, SPWPC, E 365, RG 407. Emphasis in original. According to Hagood, MacArthur was very hostile to Lassiter's plan and said he was doing all he could to change it; see "Down the Big Road," pp. 457–58. But WPD's director wrote that, "In brief General MacArthur agrees with the grand lines of General Lassiter's plans except that he considers mobile forces of one division inadequate"; see George S. Simonds to C/S, Sub: Defense Plans for the Philippine Islands, 6 Nov. 1928, WPD 3251, RG 165.

26. PD, BWPO, 1929, F 206X, Box 14; Artillery and Machine Gun Beach Defense Annex, PD, BWPO, 1929, F 222X, Box 14; Chemical Warfare Annex, PD, BWPO, 1929, F 213X, Box 13, all in SPWPC, E 365, RG 407.

27. [Douglas] MacArthur to AG, 21 Jan. 1929, AGO 660.2 PD (8-21-28), RG 407.

28. Report of Committee No. 5, The Region of the Pacific and the Region of the Caribbean, 1 Mar. 1923, F 254-5, AWCCA. R. E. Coontz to SW, Sub: Extent and Development of Pacific Bases Required for a Campaign in the Pacific, 15 July 1920, AGO 660.2 (7-15-20), RG 407; Survey of the Vital Strategic Areas of the United States and Its Overseas Possessions, WPD Course, Part 2: Committee Reports, Vol. 5, CAWC 1921–22, Box 16, AWCIR, RG 165; John L. Hines and Robert E. Coontz, Report of the Chief Umpires, Joint Army and Navy Exercises, Apr. 1925, Joint Problem No. 3, 13 May 1925, WPD 1678-57, RG 165.

29. William G. Haan to AG, Sub: Revision of Defense Projects and Plans, Hawaiian Department, 31 Dec. 1919, AGO 600.2, CCDF, RG 407. JB to SW, 19 May 1936, Sub: Mission, United States Forces, Hawaiian Islands, MID 242-12-155, RG 165.

30. Proceedings of a Board of Officers . . . Special Orders No. 5, HQ, HD, 4 Mar. 1919, AGO 660.12 HD, E 37, RG 407.

31. Haan to AG, Sub: Revision of Defense Projects and Plans.

32. Charles G. Morton to AG, Sub: Project for Defense of Oahu, 1 Jan. and 25 May 1920, AGO 660.2 HD, CCDF, RG 407; Brief History of the Hawaiian Defense Project, [1934], Box 10, E 6051, RG 395.

33. William Lassiter to C/S, Sub: Building Program, HD, 30 Mar. 1920, OCS 623, E 8, RG 165. William G. Haan to C/S, Sub: District Engineer, HD, 17 July 1920, OCS 623, E 8, RG 165; William J. Snow to Director, WPD, Sub: Project for the Defense of Oahu, 20 Feb. 1920, AGO 660.2 HD, CCDF, RG 407.

34. Brief History of the Hawaiian Defense Project, p. 2. Newton D. Baker to Chairman, Committee on Appropriations, 28 Apr. 1920, OCS 623, E 8, RG 165; H. O. Williams to CG, HD, Sub: Project for Defense of Oahu, 3 Mar. 1920, AGO 660.2 HD, CCDF, RG 407.

35. Eli A. Helmick to Frank W. Coe, 26 Mar. 1923, Box 275, E 11, RG 159. Frank W. Coe, Memo: Oahu, 6 Nov. 1919, OCS 623, E 8, RG 165; William Lassiter to C/S, Sub: Building Program, Hawaiian Department, 17 Mar. 1920, OCS 623, E 8, RG 165; Charles G. Morton, "The Defense of Hawaii," 17 Oct. 1921, Lecture, F 215-42, AWCCA.

36. Basic Project for the Defense of Oahu, 1924, E 6051, RG 395. Briant H. Wells to AG, Sub: Report on Matters Pertaining to the Defense of Oahu, 22 Sept. 1922, AGO 320 HD (1-9-23), E 37, RG 407; Briant H. Wells to C/S, Sub: Army Mission in Project for the Defense of Oahu, 29 Sept. 1923, WPD 1400, RG 165.

37. WPD Annex, Basic Project for the Defense of Oahu, 1924, E 6051, RG 395.

38. Charles P. Summerall to AG, 20 May 1924, E 6051, RG 395.

39. William Lassiter to C/S, Sub: Project for the Defense of Oahu, 26 Feb. 1920, AGO 660.2, CCDF, RG 407; LeRoy Eltinge to Charles P. Summerall, 9 Jan. 1925, WPD 2011, RG 165; Lewis, *Seacoast Fortifications*, p. 113; Howard C. Fields to Brian M. Linn, 1 Feb. 1994, in author's possession.

40. Sherman Miles to C/S, HD, Sub: Continuation of Study on Revision of Primary Tactical Plan, 18 Nov. 1929, HD, Primary Tactical Plan, 1930, Box 4, E 6051, RG 395.

41. Sherman Miles to C/S, HD, 14 Aug. 1929, F 462, Box 13, E 284, RG 165.

42. War Plans Course No. 7, Theatre Study No. 2, Hawaiian Islands, CAWC 1933–34, F 405 A-7, AWCCA; William J. Snow to Director, WPD, Sub: Project for the Defense of Oahu, 20 Feb. 1920, AGO 660.2, CCDF, RG 407; R. T. Ward to Chief, CAC, 18 Nov. 1926, A52-87, Box 5, RG 77; William M. Cruikshank to AG, Sub: Project for 36 155mm GPF Guns at Oahu, T.H., 20 Sept. 1920, AGO 660.2, CCDF, RG 407; Belote, "Rock in the 'Tween War Years," pp. 26–27.

43. BWPO, 1929: Chemical War Service Annex, F 206X, Box 14, SPWPC, E 365, RG 407. As chief of staff, MacArthur cited the needs of the Pacific garrisons in opposing restrictions on chemical warfare; see Douglas MacArthur to Secretary of State, 16 Feb. 1933, Limitation of Armaments File, Box 110, E 207, RG 107.

44. Lucius R. Holbrook to Malin Craig, 6 July 1936, AGO CF 660.2 PD (7-16-36), E 37, RG 407. CG, PD to AG, 3 Apr. 1926, AGO 381, SCF, AAF General File 1918–35, E 167, RG 18; Douglas B. Netherwood, Report on Airdrome Defense against Attack by Chemical Agents, 24 Mar. 1934, 145.93-149, AFHRA.

45. Memo: Chemical Warfare Annex to the Project for the Defenses of Oahu, 14 Oct. 1921, 1925, AGO 381 (10-15-21), Box 50, CDF 1917–25, RG 407. "A Study of the Use of Chemicals in the Defense of Oahu," 1933, Box 16, E 3061, RG 395; Charles P. Summerall to AG, Sub: Project for the Defense of Oahu: CWS Annex, 22 Dec. 1922, WPD 986-2, RG 165.

46. Walter Krueger to AC/S, WPD, Sub: Use of Chemical Agents in the Joint Army and Navy War Plan Orange, 15 Aug. 1934, F 542, Box 16, E 284, RG 165.

47. Charles E. Kilbourne to C/S, Sub: Use of Chemicals in the Defense of the Hawaiian Islands, 19 Oct. 1934, WPD 3490-1, RG 165; Map Problem No. 13, Chemical Warfare School, Edgewood Arsenal, JB, Sub: Use of Chemical Agents, 7 Nov. 1934, JB 325, Series 542, F 542, Box 16, E 284, RG 165; Walter Krueger to C/S, Sub: Defense Reserve of Mustard Gas for Hawaiian Department, 16 Mar. 1938, WPD 3490-18, RG 165.

48. Benjamin N. Booth, "The Defense of the Hawaiian Islands," 1 Apr. 1928, Lecture, F 349-6, AWCCA; Walter Krueger to AC/S, WPD, Sub: Use of Chemical Agents in the Joint Army and Navy War Plan Orange, 15 Aug. 1934, F 542, Box 16, E 284, RG 165.

49. "One Soldier's Journey," Vol. 2, p. 98, Moseley Papers.

50. C. J. Brant to Chief, AS, Sub: Report of Air Service Participation in Joint Army and Navy Exercise No. 3, 16 Jun. 1925, AGO 353, PF HD, RG 18.

51. Edward J. Foy, Joint Army and Navy Training, 2 Oct. 1939, G-3 Course, No. 14, AWCCA. T-Plan (Tactical), HD, BDP, Red-Orange Situation, 1924, E 6051, RG 395.

52. Charles M. Milliken, "The Communications and Intelligence Lessons of the Joint Army and Navy Maneuvers in Hawaii," 1931, Individual Research Paper No. 64, CARL; Edward R. Stone to C/S, Sub: Proposed Air Attack on Naval Blue Air Base at Molokai during Grand Joint Army and Navy Exercise No. 3, 3 Oct. 1925, WPD 1678-57, RG 165.

53. Primary Tactical Plan, Defense of Hawaiian Islands, 1926; HD, WPO, 1927; Primary Tactical Plan, Defense of Hawaiian Islands, 1928; Hawaiian Defense Project, Basic Document, 1928; all in E 6051, RG 395; Estimate of Situation, Joint Army and Navy BWPO, 1929, F 226, SPWPC, E 365, RG 407.

54. Raymond E. Lee, The Philippine Defense Problem, 1 Mar. 1927, F 235-82, AWCCA. "Down the Big Road," p. 360.

55. "Down the Big Road," p. 281. Philippine Division Diaries, 1923 and 1927, Box 430; 15th Infantry Regiment, 1st Battalion, Diary, 1927, Box 392; both in AWC 310, RG 165.

56. George W. Read to AG, Sub: Motorization of Field Artillery, 28 Dec. 1923 and 27 Jan. 1924; Sub: Rearming of One Battalion, 24th F.A.; William L. Snow to AG, 21 Feb. 1924, all in 1922 File, AGO 660.2 PDP, RG 407.

57. CG to AG, Sub: Annual Report 1920, 23 July 1920, AGO 319.12 HD, E 37, RG 407; Eli A. Helmick to Charles S. Farnsworth, 22 Mar. 1923, HD, E 11, RG 159; HQ, 27th Infantry, Training Circular 8, Sub: Brigade Inspection, 11 Jan. 1924, R 205, HDR; H. R. Perry to CG, HDN, Sub: Training Tests, 10 Mar. 1924, R 205, HDR; Fox Conner to AG, Sub: Annual Report, 1930, 28 July 1930, AGO 319.12 HD (7-28-30), RG 407; Diaries of Hawaiian Department and Coast Defenses, Boxes 390–91, AWC 310, RG 165.

58. Herbert E. Smith, "Soldier in the Philippines," p. 378. W. A. Pickering to CG, HD, Sub: Annual Inspection, Schofield Barracks, T.H., FY 1933, 30 June 1933, AGO 333.1, Box 276, E 11, RG 159; Memoirs, Yeo Papers.

59. Sothern, "Athletics in the Philippines," p. 393.

60. C. H. Conrad to CG, PD, Sub: Annual Inspection of Post of Manila, 19 May 1924, AGO 333.1, Box 133, RG 159.

61. H. L. Laubach to CG, Schofield Barracks, Sub: Report on Man Hours for Jan. 1924, 2 Feb. 1924, R 205, HDR. John T. Toffey to CG, 22nd Inf. Brigade, Sub: Results of Training . . . 35th Infantry, 10 Mar. 1924, R 205, HDR; E. M. Lewis to AG, Sub: Organization of the Hawaiian Garrison, 27 Mar. 1926, AGO 319.12 HD, E 37, RG 407; HQ, PD to AG, 3 Apr. 1926, AGO 381, SCF, E 167, RG 18.

62. Dana T. Merrill to CG, HD, Sub: Survey and Inspection of Harbor Defenses of Pearl Harbor for FY 1929, 12 Mar. 1929, AGO 333.1, Box 143, E 11, RG 159; G. L. Febiger to CG, HD, Sub: Annual Inspection, Schofield Barracks, T.H., FY 1931, 24 June 1931; Joseph P. Aleshire to CG, HD, Sub: Economic Survey, Schofield Barracks, T.H., 10 Aug. 1928; W. A. Pickering to CG, HD, Sub: Annual Inspection, Schofield Barracks, T.H., FY 1933, 30 June 1933, all in AGO 333.1, Box 276, E 11, RG 159.

Chapter Nine

1. William P. Duvall to AG, Sub: Defense of Manila and Manila Bay, 19 Oct. 1909; John T. Thompson to AG, 9 Dec. 1909, both filed in AGO 1592073, Box 1, E 25, RG 94. Some authors credit U.S. Navy officer Bradley Fiske's 1911 article as the first to discuss using aviation to defend the Pacific territories; see Sherry, *Rise of American Air Power*, p. 11.

2. Memo: Aviation organization for Overseas Possessions, 7 Apr. 1915, OCS 11782, E 5, RG 165. Leonard Wood to Quartermaster, Sub: Establishment of an Aviation Station in the Hawaiian Islands, 15 Oct. 1913, OCS 10657, E 5, RG 165. Until 1940, the Philippine Department's combat aviation consisted of the 3rd Pursuit and 28th Bombardment squadrons. Hawaii's combat aviation consisted of two pursuit squadrons (6th and 19th), two bombardment squadrons (23rd and 72nd), and, after 1930, one attack squadron (26th).

3. John B. Brooks to AG, Sub: 6th Aero Squadron, Signal Corps, 23 Aug. 1917, Early Aviation in Hawaii Folder, 15th Air Base Wing History Office, Hi.; AG to CG, HD, Sub: Construction of Barracks and Quarters in the Island of Oahu, 11 Nov. 1915, AGO 1383705, RG 94.

4. B. Q. Jones to CG, PD, Sub: Detachment of 2nd Observation Squadron at Paranaque Beach, 29 Aug. 1921, AGO 373, PF PD, RG 18; V. L. Burge to William Mitchell, Sub: Conditions at Kindley Field, 15 Jan. 1924, Box 42, Mitchell Papers; Harris Oral History, p. 58; LeRoy Eltinge to C/S, Sub: Cabcaben Air Base, P.I., Oct. 1924, 167.6-35, AFHRA; A. I. Eagle to Chief, AS, Sub: Exploration of the Center of the Island of Mindoro, 20 May 1926, AGO 373, PF PD, RG 18.

5. Report of Local Joint Planning Committee on Aerial Defense of the Hawaiian Islands, 18 Feb. 1924, F 245, Box 9, E 284, RG 165; Charles G. Morton to Commandant, U.S. Naval Station, Sub: Naval Flying Field, 8 Aug. 1919, R 255, HDR.

6. B. Q. Jones to Francis J. Kernan, Sub: Re-adjustment of Air Service Activities, 19 Aug. 1921, AGO 373, PF PD, RG 18; JANPC to JB, Sub: Army and Navy Aviation Programs, 27 Aug. 1923, JB 349, Series 206, F 206, E 257, RG 165; B. Q. Jones to Chief, AS, Sub: Activities Report, PD, 16 Oct. 1921, AGO 300, PF PD, RG 18; Stuart Heintzelman to C/S, Sub: Construction for Airplane Storage, Hawaiian Air Depot, 20 Apr. 1923, WPD 759-5, RG 165; Harry A. Smith to C/S, Sub: Storage of DH-4 Airplanes in Hawaii, 6 Oct. 1925, WPD 759-10, RG 165; J. P. Wade to AG, Sub: Air Service Activities Report, 10 Aug. 1925, AGO 319.1, PF PD, RG 18.

7. John H. Howard to Mason Patrick, 15 Nov. 1926, AGO 319.2, PF HD, RG 18. Fox Conner to AC/S, WPD, Sub: Air Service War Reserves, Hawaii, 18 Dec. 1924, AGO 381.4 (6-7-24), CDF 1917–25, RG 407; George E. Lovell to Arthur Lane, Sub: Report of War Reserves, AS, 1925, WPD 2027-11, RG 165.

8. O. Westover to ACS, WPD, 28 Mar. 1935; R. M. Jones to AG, 25 Feb. 1936, both filed in 145.93-149, AFHRA. Major, *Prize Possession*, p. 281. On interwar Congressional aviation policy; see Vander Meulen, *Politics of Aircraft*.

9. V. L. Burge to William Mitchell, Sub: Conditions at Kindley Field, 15 Jan. 1924, Box 42, Mitchell Papers. Interview, pp. 22–23, Eaker Papers; Jarvis J. Bain to AC/S, WPD, Sub: Inspection of PD, 25 Mar. 1927, WPD 1573-9, RG 165.

10. B. Q. Jones to Chief, AS, Activities Report, Aug. 16–21, 1 Sept. 1921, AGO 373, PF PD, RG 18.

11. Ira C. Eaker to Chief, AS, 27 May 1921, AGO 381, E 177, RG 18.

12. Lucius R. Holbrook to Malin Craig, 16 July 1936, AGO 660.2 PD (7-16-36), RG 407. Henry W. Harms to Chief, AC, Sub: Activities Report, 8 Mar. 1930, AGO 319.1, PF-PD, RG 18; Frank Parker to AG, 13 Nov. 1934, 145.93-159, AFHRA; Benjamin D. Foulois to AG, 13 Oct. 1934, 145.93-159, AFHRA; Map Study No. 3: Philippine Department. Situation and

Requirements, 13–21 Feb. 1936, WPD Course, Vol. 6, CAWC 1935–36, AWCIR, RG 165; JANPC, Sub: Study on the Range, Radius, and Carrying Capacity of Bombardment and Reconnaissance Planes Required by the Army Air Corps, 15 June 1938, F 628, E 284, RG 165.

13. Harris Oral History, pp. 54–55, 58. Combs Oral History, p. 41; Harbold Oral History, p. 22.

14. C. J. Brant to Chief, AS, Sub: Report of Air Service Participation in Joint Army and Navy Exercise No. 3, 16 June 1925, AGO 353, PF HD, RG 18. John H. Howard to Mason Patrick, 15 Nov. 1926, AGO 319.2, PF HD, RG 18.

15. Vincent B. Dixon to CO, 18th Composite Wing, 10 Dec. 1932, AGO 319.1, PF HD, RG 18.

16. Davidson Oral History, p. 428. Hugh A. Drum to Malin Craig, 4 Mar. 1936, Box 9, Drum Papers; Hugh A. Drum to AG, 19 Feb. 1936, 145.93-149, AFHRA.

17. Holloway Oral History, p. 39.

18. Fred L. Martin to Henry H. Arnold, 17 Dec. 1940; Henry H. Arnold to Fred L. Martin, 29 Jan. 1941, both in 145.93-150, AFHRA; Watson, *Chief of Staff*, p. 474.

19. Harbold Oral History, pp. 23–24. "I Hired Out to Fight," pp. 29–31, Montgomery Papers. On the drudgery of aircrews' service overseas, see Willeford, *Something about a Soldier*, pp. 28–132; Jones, *From Here To Eternity*, pp. 406–13.

20. B. G. Weir to CG, PD, 21 June 1923, AGO 353, PF PD, RG 18. B. Q. Jones to CG, PD, Sub: Inspection of Air Service at Paranaque Beach, 11 Jan. 1922, AGO 319.1, PF PD, RG 18. Ira C. Eaker Interview, pp. 20–22. For a similar comment from Hawaiian aviators; see H. J. Knerr to Director, Military Aeronautics, Sub: Coast Defense Target Practice, 29 Nov. 1919, AGO 353.17, PF HD, RG 18.

21. Albert Hegenberger to Walter H. Frank, 3 Mar. 1924, McNair Board and Auxiliary Reports, Part 5, 248.82-70, AFHRA. HD, Comparative Test Coast Artillery–Air Service, 1923–24, Box 2, E 6051, RG 395; AG to CG, HD, Sub: Report Required from CG, Hawaiian and Panama Canal Departments on Powers and Limitations of Coast Artillery and Air Service, 21 Apr. 1923, R 205, HDR; Hegenberger Oral History, pp. 19–20; Shiner, "Air Corps, the Navy, and Coast Defense."

22. V. L. Burge to William Mitchell, Sub: Conditions at Kindley Field, 5 Jan. 1924, Box 42, Mitchell Papers. Charles P. Summerall to Mason M. Patrick, 7 Apr. 1924, 1 AGO 319.2; Stanley D. Embick to CG, CDMSB, Sub: Cooperation of Air Service in Recent Artillery Firings, 12 Apr. 1924, AGO 353; J. S. Gullett, Report of Air Service Activities, 7 Apr. 1924, AGO 353; J. T. Conrad to AG, Sub: Air Service Activities Report, 10 Sept. 1925, AGO 319.1, all filed in PF PD, RG 18; Extract from a report of Lt. Col. A. L. Fuller on Aerial Position Finding, n.d. [1923], Box 2, E 6051, RG 395.

23. Earl H. Gorman to Chief, AS, Sub: Weekly News Items, 26 May 1922, E 6067, RG 395. John F. Curry to CG, HD, Sub: Summary of Air Service Activities, July 1, 1921 to July 1, 1922, 30 June 1922, R 120, HDR.

24. Earl L. Canady to William Mitchell, 13 July 1926, AGO 319.1, PF PD, RG 18.

25. C. W. Exton to Chief, CWS, 5 June 1926, AGO 381, SCF 1918–35, E 167, RG 18.

26. Critique, Joint Army-Navy War Game, 20 Mar. 1926, Command Course, Part 3, Vol. 6, CAWC 1925–26, AWCCA.

27. William Lassiter, Report of the Defense of the Philippine Islands, 21 Aug. 1928, WPD 3251, RG 165. Emphasis in original.

28. Joint Army and Navy Doctrine for the Protection of Seaports against the Attacks of Naval Vessels, 1 Jan. 1920, Joint Army . . . Naval Vessels Folder, Box 3, E 284, RG 165. Study of the Defense of Oahu, made pursuant to letter of instructions from Headquarters, Hawaiian Department, dated Mar. 7, 1916, AWC 6266-79, RG 165; Charles G. Morton to AG,

Sub: Project for Defense of Oahu, 1 Jan. 1920, AGO 660.2 HD, CCDF, RG 407; JB, Sub: Aerial Defense of the Hawaiian Islands, 12 Oct. 1922, JB 303, Series 125, F 185, Box 6, E 258, RG 165.

29. Arnold M. Krogstad to Chief, AS, Sub: Training for Year 1924, 14 Nov. 1924, AGO 353.9, PF HD, RG 18. Minutes, Conference, Jan. 13, 1925, Room 259, State, War and Navy Building, WPD 2011-1, RG 165. For the danger posed by carrier attacks, see Richmond K. Turner, "Naval Aviation," 6 Mar. 1930, Lecture, ACTS, 248.2011D-4, AFHRA; Annex No. 2: Air Corps Operations, HD, Primary Tactical Plan, 1930, E 6051, RG 395; Coast Defense, ACTS Course 1930–31, 248.2012A-6, AFHRA; Report of a Board of Officers, Apr. 1931, 145.93-149, AFHRA; Illustrative Problem: Defense against Carrier Attack, Course: Air Force, ACTS 1933–34, 248.2015A-9, AFHRA; Illustrative Problem No. 6: Air Defense of Hawaii, Air Force Course, ACTS, 1933–34, 248.602-25, AFHRA; Edgar T. Collins, Annual Report, Operations and Training Divisions, G-3, W.D.G.S., FY 1932, AGO 319.12 (6-30-82), RG 407.

30. William Lassiter to Commandant, 14th Naval District, 26 Mar. 1931, JB 303, Series 494, Box 14, E 284, RG 165. Report of a Board of Officers, Apr. 1931, 145.93-149, AFHRA; Geoffrey P. Baldwin, The Defense of Hawaii, 28 Mar. 1928, CAWC 1927–28, F 349-54, AWCCA; Edward R. Stone to C/S, Sub: Proposed Air Attack on Naval Blue Air Base at Molokai during Grand Joint Army and Navy Exercise No. 3, 3 Oct. 1925, WPD 1678-57, RG 165; John L. Hines, "Grand Joint Army and Navy Exercise No. 3," 26 June 1925, Lecture, F 294-7, AWCCA.

31. Willis H. Hale to Executive, Sub: Air Garrison for Hawaiian Department, 4 June 1931, 167.6-34, AFHRA.

32. Edward M. Markham, Report on Defensive Features of the Hawaiian Islands, 10 Jan. 1938, WPD 3878, RG 165. Conn, Engelman, and Fairchild, Guarding the United States, pp. 154–55.

33. Charles D. Herron, Surmises on Insular Operations, 12 Nov. 1940; George C. Marshall to Charles D. Herron, 28 Nov. 1940, both in WPD 3878, RG 165.

34. Blumenson, Patton, p. 136; Reynolds, Admiral John H. Towers, pp. 237–38; Toland, Infamy, pp. 250–51; Slackman, Target: Pearl Harbor, pp. 10–11.

35. Malin Craig and Frank Schofield, Report of the Chief Umpires, Grand Joint Exercise No. 4, 18 Feb. 1932, F 500, Box 14, E 284, RG 165. History of the Hawaiian Department Primary Tactical Plan; Secret Report of Army Participation in Grand Joint Exercise No. 4, Hawaii, Feb. 1932, by Major General Malin Craig, Commanding General, BLUE Expeditionary Forces, 15 Mar. 1932, Box 5, HDR; Briant H. Wells to AG, Sub: Report of Formal Tactical Inspection, HD, 1931, 29 Nov. 1932, AGO 333.3 HD (11-24-33), RG 407.

36. Craig and Schofield, Report of the Chief Umpires. Maxwell Kirby to Benjamin D. Foulois, 19 Feb. 1932, AGO 353.5, PF HD, RG 18; Maurer, Aviation in the U.S. Army, pp. 251–52.

37. Gerald C. Brant to CG, HD, Sub: Minor Joint Army and Navy Exercise, 8 Nov. 1932, 167.6-34, AFHRA. Joseph P. Tracy to AG, Sub: Anti-aircraft Defense of Pearl Harbor, 20 Oct. 1931, WPD 3583, RG 165.

38. Cited in History of the Hawaiian Department Primary Tactical Plan, p. 36, 1940, Box 2, HDR, RG 338.

39. Hugh A. Drum to AG, Sub: Defensive Consideration, HD, 25 May 1937, Box 21, Drum Papers. Hugh A. Drum to James G. Harbord, 3 May 1941, Box 9, Drum Papers; Report of 18th Composite Wing, AAC, Concurrent Exercise, Hawaiian Department, 1937, 248.2125-7A, AFHRA; Notes, Re—Joint Exercises, 1937; Ammunition Chart—18th Composite Wing, 3 Feb. 1937, both filed in AGO 381.1, E 6036, RG 395.

40. War Plans Study, Sub: Defense Mission—Hawaiian Department, 9 Dec. 1935, WPD 3878, RG 165.

41. William Lassiter to Commandant, 14th Naval District, 26 Mar. 1931, F 494, Box 14, E 284, RG 165; HD, Estimate of the Situation, Joint Defense Plan, Hawaiian Theatre, 1935, Box 10, E 6051, RG 165; Basic Agreement Hawaiian Department and 14th Naval District, Joint Defense Plan, Hawaiian Theatre, 1938, Box 14, F 6051, RG 165.

42. Prange, *Pearl Harbor*, pp. 420–21, 622–23; Sherman Miles to Walter Krueger, Sub: Interview with General Drum, 13 Sept. 1937, WPD 3878-7, RG 165.

43. Edward M. Lewis to AG, Sub: Annual Report, HD, FY 1926, 30 June 1926, AGO 319.12 HD (6-30-26), RG 407.

44. Robert J. Brown, Reasons Ford's Island Should Be Retained by the Army, 1927, AGO 321.9, PF HD, RG 18. Emphasis omitted.

45. Hugh A. Drum to Douglas MacArthur, 12 June 1935, Box 9, Drum Papers. Hugh A. Drum to Malin Craig, 12 Feb. 1936, Box 9, Drum Papers. War Plans Study, Sub: Defense Mission—Hawaiian Department, 9 Dec. 1935, WPD 3878, RG 165; Fox Conner to AG, Sub: New Army Airdrome Site, 8 May 1929, AGO 580.2, Oahu, RG 407; George R. Marvell, Commandant to SN, Sub: New Army Airdrome, 8 Mar. 1929, ACO 580.2, CF Oahu, RG 407.

46. James A. Ulio to CG, HD, Memo: 1937 Estimate of the Situation, 6 Mar. 1936; Thomas D. Osborne to C/S Sub: Mission, United States Forces, Hawaiian Islands, 5 Aug. 1936, both in Box 13, E 6051, RG 395.

47. Gerald C. Brant to CG, HD, Sub: 18th Wing Participation in Part Four of Hawaiian Tactical Exercise No. 2, 23 Feb. 1934, 145.98-149, AFHRA; Hugh A. Drum to AG, Sub: Army Participation in Fleet Maneuvers, 15 May 1935, Box 21, Drum Papers.

48. Ryan Oral History, pp. 114–17. The Hawaiian Air Force was created in 1940.

49. John Curry to CG, HD, Sub: Strength of the Air Service in the Hawaiian Department, 16 Mar. 1920, Early Aviation in Hawaii Folder, 15th Air Base Wing History Office. John H. Howard to Mason Patrick, 15 Nov. 1926, AGO 319.2, PF HD, RG 18.

50. John P. Smith, Statistical Data . . . from the Military Point of View, [1921], F Wood-Forbes, Box 82, McCoy Papers. Mason Patrick to WPD, Sub: Increase in Air Service Garrison in the Philippine Islands, 18 Oct. 1921, AGO 381, SCF 1918–35, E 167, RG 18; Orange Efforts in a Blue-Orange Conflict, from an Orange Viewpoint, Outline of Course to G-3, CAWC 1921–22, Box 15, AWCIR, RG 165. On prewar U.S. plans to bomb Japan, see Sherry, *Rise of American Air Power*, pp. 100–115.

51. Walter H. Frank to AG, 5 Jan. 1924, 660.2 PD (7-23-23), RG 407. JB, Sub: Report on Results of Aviation and Ordnance Tests Held during June and July, 1921, and Conclusions Reached, 18 Aug. 1921, JB 349, Series 159, F 159, E 258, RG 165.

52. J. C. McDonnell, Plan of the Third Pursuit Squadron on the Outbreak of Hostilities, 9 Jan. 1924, Box 42, Mitchell Papers. Critique, Joint Army-Navy War Game, 20 Mar. 1926, Command Course, Vol. 6, CAWC 1925–26, AWCCA.

53. William Mitchell, "Report of Inspection of United States Possessions in the Pacific and Java, Singapore, India, Siam, China and Japan by Brigadier General Wm. Mitchell, Assistant Chief of Air Service, Oct. 24, 1924," p. 18, Air Corps Library Collection, RG 18. Burke Davis, *Billy Mitchell Affair*, pp. 163, 173, 182; Alfred F. Hurley, *Billy Mitchell*, pp. 87–88; Brune, *Origins*, pp. 93–99.

54. Mitchell, "Report of Inspection," pp. 10, 51–69.

55. William Mitchell, "Recommendations for Training Air Service Units now in the Hawaiian Department," 1923, Box 42, Mitchell Papers. Mitchell made a similar inspection of the Philippines and predicted bombers flying from Taiwan via intermediate airbases would first destroy U.S. air, then oil supplies at Cavite, docks at Manila, and then "reduce Corregidor by an aeronautical siege"; see William Mitchell, "Preliminary Report of Inspection of Air Service Activities in the Philippine Islands by Gen. William Mitchell," 1924, Box 42, Mitchell Papers.

56. Mitchell, "Report of Inspection," p. 11. Mitchell, "Recommendations for Training."

57. Charles P. Summerall to Mason Patrick, 27 Dec. 1923, AGO 321.9, PF HD, RG 18.

58. Mason Patrick to Charles P. Summerall, 26 Jan. 1924, 167.6-34, AFHRA.

59. Hugh A. Drum to C/S, HD, Sub: Recent W.D. Instructions, 14 Aug. 1936, Box 13, E 6051, RG 395. Emphasis in original.

60. Hugh A. Drum to C/S, Sub: Estimate of the Situation, 30 Oct. 1936, E 6051, RG 395. Conn, Engelman, and Fairchild, *Guarding the United States*, pp. 153–55.

61. HD, Estimate of the Situation, Joint Defense Plan, Hawaiian Theater, 1936, F 107, Box 53, RG 407; Hugh A. Drum to Douglas MacArthur, 12 June 1935, Box 9, Drum Papers.

62. Stanley D. Embick to C/S, Sub: Defense Mission, Hawaiian Department, 28 Mar. 1936, WPD 3878, RG 165.

63. War Plans Study, Sub: Defense Mission—Hawaiian Department, 9 Dec. 1935, WPD 3878, RG 165. Memorandum for W.P.D. Files, 4 Dec. 1935, WPD 3878, RG 165; Thomas D. Osborne to C/S Sub: Mission, United States Forces, Hawaiian Islands, 5 Aug. 1936, E 6051, RG 395.

64. Hugh A. Drum to Malin Craig, 4 Mar. 1936, Box 9, Drum Papers. Underwood, "Army Air Corps," pp. 134–35.

65. H. H. Arnold to Walter H. Frank, 9 Sept. 1940, 145.93-150, AFHRA. Conn, Engelman, and Fairchild, *Guarding the United States*, pp. 156–57.

66. George V. Strong to Chief, AC, Sub: Estimates for Aviation Reinforcement for the Philippine Department, 23 Feb. 1940, 145.93-161, AFHRA.

67. [George C. Marshall], Memo for General Arnold, 16 July 1941, cited in Marshall, *Papers of George Catlett Marshall*, 2:567–68.

68. Stimson and Bundy, *On Active Service*, p. 388.

69. Memorandum from Robert L. Sherrod to David W. Hulburd Jr., 15 Nov. 1941, cited in Marshall, *Papers of George Catlett Marshall*, 2:676–79.

70. Otto G. Trunk to AC/S, WPD, Sub: Estimate for Aviation Reinforcements for the Philippine Department, 26 Feb. 1940, 145.93-161, AFHRA; Harris Oral History, p. 58.

71. Bartsch, *Doomed from the Start*, p. 41. Anderson Oral History, p. 138; Conn, Engelman, and Fairchild, *Guarding the United States*, pp. 166–67.

Chapter Ten

1. 31st Infantry Organization Day Pamphlet, 1934, Hooper Papers.

2. JB, Sub: Military Value of the Philippine Islands to the United States, 23 Oct. 1931, JB 305, Serial 499, AGO 093.5, CF, RG 407. JANPC to JB, Sub: Independence of the Philippine Islands: Effect of Withdrawal of Military Forces, 28 Feb. 1934, F 525, Box 16, E 284, RG 165; J. H. Cunningham, Memo: Policy in Philippine Islands, 24 Feb. 1934, F 525, Box 16, E 284, RG 165.

3. PD, First Phase Plan Orange, 1933, F 245X, SPWPC, E 365, RG 407; PD Plan, First Phase—Orange, 1936, F 200X, SPWPC, E 365, RG 407.

4. G-2 Appendix, PD, First Phase Plan Orange, 1934, F 189, SPWPC, E 365, RG 407. Parker Oral History, p. 37.

5. ASP Orange (1936), F 235, SPWPC, E 365, RG 407. Joint Army and Navy BWPO, 1938, F 223, SPWPC, E 365, RG 407.

6. Robert S. Thomas, The Army Force Required to Insure the Retention of the Manila Bay Region in the Event of an Orange War, 1 Mar. 1932, F 387-74, AWCCA; Friend, *Between Two Empires*, pp. 161–62.

7. Samuel T. Mackall, The Defense of Hawaii, pp. 3–4, 14 Mar. 1929, F 357-56, AWCCA. For a similar view of Hawaii's dual purpose, see Report of Committee No. 8, Critical Areas—Coast Defense, AWC G-3 Course 1933–34, F 403-8A, AWCCA.

8. War Plans Study, Sub: Defense Mission—Hawaiian Department, 9 Dec. 1935, WPD 3878, RG 165.

9. Basic Project for Defense of Oahu, 1924, Box 1, E 6051, RG 395.

10. JB, Sub: Changes in Joint BWPO, 9 Dec. 1934, JB 325, Series 594, F 542, Box 18, E 284, RG 165.

11. JB to SW, Sub: Mission, United States Forces, Hawaiian Islands, 19 May 1936, WPD 3878, RG 165.

12. HD, Estimate of the Situation, Army Operating Defense Plan, Hawaiian Coastal Frontier, 1939, F 132, Box 55, RG 407; Conn, Engleman, and Fairchild, *Guarding the United States*, p. 151; Prange, *Pearl Harbor*, pp. 322–23, 382–88.

13. Basic Document, Joint Defense Plan, Hawaiian Theater, 1933, F 115, SPWPC, E 365, RG 407.

14. History of the Hawaiian Department Primary Tactical Plan, 1940, Box 2, HDR; G-3 Annex, Joint Defense Plan, Hawaiian Theater, Basic Document, 1933, E 6051, RG 395.

15. Geoffrey P. Baldwin, The Defense of Hawaii, 28 Mar. 1928, F 349-54, AWCCA. G-3, HD to C/S, HD, 2 Mar. 1932, R 206, HDR; Marginalia on Sherman Miles to C/S, HD, Hostile Overland Advances, 12 Nov. 1929, enclosed in HD, Primary Tactical Plan, 1930, E 6051, RG 395.

16. "Report on Night Firing Problems Involving Firing of Infantry Weapons from Boats at Sea," 17 Aug. 1931, Machine Guns, U.S. Card, AWCCLC. William Lassiter to AG, Sub: Annual Report, FY 1931, AGO 319.12 (8-22-31) HD, RG 407; August W. Dannemiller, "A Study of the Military Topography of the Island of Oahu, T.H.," Individual Research Paper, No. 112, 1931, CARL; Briant H. Wells to CG, HD, 8 June 1931, R 206, HDR; Briant H. Wells to AG, Sub: Annual Report, FY 1932, 16 July 1932, AGO 319.12 (7-16-32) HD, RG 407; HD, AG Memo, 5 Nov. 1932, R 256, HDR; HD, Training Memos, 1930–40, E 6044, RG 395.

17. Joint Defense Plan, Hawaiian Theater, Estimate of the Situation, Hawaiian Department, 1935 E 6051, RG 395.

18. Malin Craig and Frank Schofield, Report of the Chief Umpires: Grand Joint Exercise No. 4, 18 Feb. 1932, F 500, Box 14, E 284, RG 165; Briant H. Wells to AG, Sub: Report of Formal Tactical Inspection, HD, 1931, 29 Nov. 1932, AGO 333.3 HD (11-24-33), RG 407; Charles E. Kilbourne to C/S, Sub: Infantry reserves, Hawaiian Department, 9 Nov. 1934, WPD 3615-2, RG 165; Cooper, "Military Career of General Holland M. Smith," pp. 103–4.

19. Warren T. Hannum to District Corps Area, Sub: Description of Construction of a 16-inch Gun Battery, 25 Nov. 1935, F A52-87, AGO 662 (Oahu), Box 92, RG 77; Dorrance, *Fort Kamehameha*, pp. 84–91.

20. Baldwin, Defense of Hawaii, pp. 10–11. This debate over artillery is extensively covered in Secret and Confidential File No. 1, F A 42-87, AGO 662 (Oahu), Box 92, RG 77; Stanley Embick to C/S, Sub: Location of the Guns, Magazines, Power Plant and Switchboard and Plotting Rooms for the Two 16-inch Guns to be Emplaced on Oahu, 22 Oct. 1928, WPD 2011-7, RG 165.

21. HD, Estimate of the Situation, Joint Defense Plan, Hawaiian Theater, 1935, E 6051, RG 395. Briant H. Wells to AG, Sub: Minor Joint Exercise No. 5, 7 Feb. 1934, 145.98-149, AFHRA.

22. W. E. Cole to CG, HD, 16 June 1932, R 206, HDR; R. E. Fraile to AG, Sub: Flying Hours for Cooperative Missions, 15 June 1935, AGO 353, PF HD, RG 18; Charles D. Herron, Report of Department Maneuvers, Hawaiian Department, Apr.–May 1940, Box 2, HDR; Dorrance, *Fort Kamehameha*, pp. 92–100.

23. J. L. Parkinson to CG, HD, Sub: Annual Inspections, Schofield Barracks, Including Wheeler Field, FY 1937, 29 July 1937, AGO 333.1, Box 25, E 11, RG 159. Edward M. Markham, Report on Defensive Features of the Hawaiian Islands, 10 Jan. 1938, WPD 3878, RG 165; HD, Training Memos, E 6044, RG 395; Memoir, p. 31, Larsen Papers; Interview,

pp. 77–78, Collins Papers. For documentation on the construction of Hawaii's military roads, see Section D—Hawaiian Roads, WPD 901-63 to 901-115, RG 165; Rader, "Works Progress Administration."

24. Charles E. Kilbourne to AG, Sub: First Phase Plan Orange, Philippine Department, 1933, 17 Nov. 1933, WPD 3251-14, RG 165.

25. Douglas MacArthur to SW, Oct. 1931, AGO 093.5 PI (10-2-31), CF, RG 407.

26. George S. Simonds to AC/S, G-4, Sub: Possible Reduction in the Philippine Garrison, 16 July 1930, WPD 3251-7, RG 165.

27. CNO [Willian V. Pratt] to Commander in Chief, Asiatic Fleet, 18 Mar. 1933, F 525, Box 16, E 284, RG 165.

28. Philippine Defense Project: Basic Document, 1931, F 333, SPWPC, E 365, RG 407.

29. Ewing E. Booth to AG, 1 Oct. 1932, Sub: 1932, Philippine Defense Project, AGO 660.2 PD (10-1-32), RG 407.

30. Army and Navy Joint Defense Plan for Philippine Island Coastal Frontier, 1932, F 244X, SPWPC, E 365, RG 407.

31. Stanley D. Embick to CG, PD, Sub: Military Policy of the U.S. in Philippine Islands, AGO 093.5 PI (10-2-31), RG 407. For similar sentiments, see Louis J. Van Shaick to George Van Shaick, 4 Feb. 1933, F Confidential: Puerto Rico and Philippine Islands, Box 3, E 207, RG 107.

32. Ewing E. Booth to AG, 25 Apr. 1933, endorsement on Stanley D. Embick to CG, PD, Sub: Military Policy of the U.S. in Philippine Islands, AGO 093.5 PI (10-2-31), RG 407.

33. Johnson Hagood to Ewing E. Booth, 23 Jan. 1932, F 5, Box 186, Hagood Papers. PD, First Phase Plan Orange, F 199X, 1933, SPWPC, E 365, RG 407.

34. Extract from letter by Gen. Parker, 28 Mar. 1935, enclosed in PD, First Phase Plan Orange, 1933, F 199X, 1933, SPWPC, E 365, RG 407. Collins, *Lightning Joe*, pp. 65–71.

35. Charles. E. Kilbourne to C/S, Sub: First Phase Plan Orange, Philippine Department, 1933, 25 Oct. 1933, WPD 3251-14, RG 165.

36. Charles E. Kilbourne to C/S, Sub: Military Policy of the United States in the Philippine Islands, 12 June 1933, WPD 3251-15, RG 165.

37. F. B. Upham and Frank Parker to CNO and C/S, 1 Mar. 1934, F 533, Box 16, E 284, RG 165.

38. G-2 Appendix, PD, First Phase Plan Orange, 1934, F 189, SPWPC, E 365, RG 407; D. Clayton James, *Years of MacArthur*, pp. 583–84.

39. G-3 Estimate of the Situation, PD, First Phase Plan Orange, 1934, F 171, SPWPC, E 365, RG 407.

40. F. B. Upham and Frank Parker to CNO and C/S, 1 Mar. 1934, F 533, Box 16, E 284, RG 165. Frank Parker to AG, 17 Aug. 1934, AGO 93.5 PI (10-2-31), RG 407; Frank Parker, Personal and Confidential Memorandum for the Secretary of War, 1935, Box 176, E 207, RG 107.

41. Kilbourne to C/S, Sub: Military Policy in the Philippine Islands.

42. JANPC to JB, Sub: Inadequacy of Present Military and Naval Forces, Philippine Area, to Carry Out Assigned Missions in Event of an Orange War, 9 May 1934, F 525, Box 16, E 284, RG 165.

43. JB, Sub: Inadequacy of Present Military and Naval Forces, Philippine Area, to Carry Out Assigned Missions in Event of an Orange War, 30 June 1934, B 325, Serial 533, Box 16, E 284, RG 165.

44. Stanley D. Embick, Military Aspects of the Situation That Would Result from the Retention by the United States of a Military (Including Naval) Commitment in the Philippine Islands. Appendix A—Defense of the Philippine Islands by the United States, 2 Dec. 1935, F Philippine Islands—Secret, Box 3, E 207, RG 107.

45. Lucius R. Holbrook to Malin Craig, 6 Aug. 1936, AGO 660.2 PD (7-16-36), RG 407. Emphasis in original.

46. Douglas MacArthur to Frederick H. Payne, 8 Oct. 1936, F 11, Box 1, RG 190, MacArthur Papers. The Craig-MacArthur relationship is explored in D. Clayton James, *Years of MacArthur*, pp. 449–50, 493–94, 502–5, 521–22.

47. Douglas MacArthur to Hugh A. Drum, 25 July 1936, Box 9, Drum Papers.

48. Ibid. Douglas MacArthur to Malin Craig, 9 July 1936, AGO 093.5 PD, RG 407.

49. Lucius R. Holbrook to Malin Craig, 16 July 1936, AGO 660.2 PD (7-16-36), RG 407.

50. Douglas MacArthur to Hugh A. Drum, 25 July 1936, MacArthur File, Box 9, Drum Papers.

51. Douglas MacArthur to Bonner Fellers, 1 June 1939, F 10, Box 2, RG 1, MacArthur Papers. Friend, *Between Two Empires*, p. 162.

52. Lucius R. Holbrook to Malin Craig, 27 July 1936, AGO 660.2 PD (7-16-36), RG 407.

53. PD, First Phase Plan Orange, 1936, F 200X, SPWPC, E 365, RG 407. Lucius R. Holbrook to Malin Craig, 6 Aug. 1936, AGO 660.2 PD (7-16-36), RC 407.

54. G-3 Annex, PD, WPO, First Phase, 1936, F 203X, SPWPC, E 365, RG 407.

55. Lucius R. Holbrook to Malin Craig, 16 July 1936, AGO 660.2 PD (7-16-36), RG 407.

56. Lucius R. Holbrook to Malin Craig, 6 Aug. 1936, AGO 660.2 PD (7-16-36), RG 407.

57. J. H. Cunningham, Memo for Colonel Kreuger, Sub: Philippine Defense Policy and Defense Project, 14 July 1936, WPD 3251-17, RG 165.

58. Malin Craig to Lucius R. Holbrook, 5 Aug. 1936, AGO 660.2 PD (7-16-36), RG 407.

59. Malin Craig to Lucius R. Holbrook, 17 Aug. 1936, AGO 660.2 PD (7-16-36), RG 407.

60. Ibid.; Malin Craig to Lucius R. Holbrook, 5 Aug. 1936, AGO 660.2 PD (7-16-36), RG 407.

61. Joint Army and Navy BWPO, (WPD WPO-1), 1938, F 223, SPWPC, E 365, RG 407. Walter Krueger to C/S, Sub: Revision of Philippine Defense Project and Data Concerning Philippine Reserves, 9 Oct. 1937, AGO 660.2 PD (7-16-36), RG 407.

62. Walter Krueger to C/S, Sub: Defense Reserves in the Philippine Department, 16 Feb. 1938, AGO 660.2 PD (7-16-36), RG 407.

63. Army and Navy Joint Defense Plan for Philippine Islands Coastal Frontier, 1938, F 328; Philippine Defense Project, 1938, F 331, both in SPWPC, E 365, RG 407

64. G-3 Annex, PD, Plan-Orange, 1940, F 326, Box 89, RG 407. PD, Plan-Orange, 1940, F 326, SPWPC, E 365, RG 407.

65. The argument that in 1941 MacArthur substituted an ambitious plan to defend the entire archipelago for the existing Orange plan that called for the defense of Manila Bay appeared in the U.S. Army's official history and has been accepted by virtually all subsequent scholars; see Louis Morton, *Fall of the Philippines*, pp. 60–71. A recent study credits Philippine Department commander George S. Grunert as the author of the plan to defend all of Luzon; see Meixsel, "Major General George S. Grunert."

66. PD, BWPO, 1929, F 206X, SPWPC, E 365, RG 407. John J. Pershing to William M. Wright, 23 May 1922, AGO 320.2 PD (5-19-22), RG 407.

67. James H. Tierney, The Defense of the Philippine Islands, 1 Apr. 1928, F 349-33, AWCCA; PD, WPO, First Phase, 1934, F 198X, SPWPC, E 365, RG 407.

68. AG to CG, PD, Sub: Future Military Policy in the Philippines, 10 Dec. 1934, AGO 093.5 PI (10-2-31), RG 407. Charles E. Kilbourne to C/S, Sub: Provisions of the Philippine Independence Act Affecting Our Future Military Policy in the Philippines, 23 July 1934, AGO 093.5 PI (10-2-31), RG 407.

69. Frank Parker to Regino G. Padua, 13 Sept. 1934, F 279, Vol. 4, Parker Papers; Stanley D. Embick, Sub: Military System for the Philippine State, 2 Dec. 1935, F 573, Box 17, E 284, RG 165; Map Study No. 3: Philippine Department. Situation and Requirements, 13–21

Feb. 1936, WPD Course, Vol. 1, CAWC 1935–36, AWCCA; Petillo, *Douglas MacArthur*, pp. 181–82. The most thorough accounts of the Commonwealth Army are Jose, *The Philippine Army, 1935–1942*, and Meixsel, "An Army for Independence?" For other accounts, see Friend, *Between Two Empires*, pp. 163–64, 192–94; D. Clayton James, *Years of MacArthur*, esp. pp. 480–552; Petillo, *Douglas MacArthur*, pp. 177–95; Louis Morton, *Fall of the Philippines*, pp. 12–13.

70. *Report on National Defense in the Philippines*, p. 20, copy in F 3, Box 2, RG 1, MacArthur Papers. Dwight D. Eisenhower, Memorandum to President Quezon, 22 June 1942, F Manuel Quezon, Box 94, Prepresidential Papers, Eisenhower Papers; Jose, *Philippine Army*, pp. 25–43; Petillo, *Douglas MacArthur*, pp. 177–80; D. Clayton James, *Years of MacArthur*, pp. 479–509.

71. Petillo, *Douglas MacArthur*, pp. 173, 184–86.

72. D. Clayton James, *Years of MacArthur*, p. 533.

73. Dwight D. Eisenhower's Philippine Diary, 2 Feb. 1936, Box 1, Kevin McCann Papers, Eisenhower Library. On relations between the Philippine Department and MacArthur's staff, see Interview with Colonel Frederick A. Ward, 1966, AUD-146, RG 32, MacArthur Papers; F. J. Monaghan to Creed F. Cox, 27 Oct. 1937, AGO 093.5 PI, RG 407; Friend, *Between Two Empires*, pp. 192–94; D. Clayton James, *Years of Macarthur*, pp. 535–42; Petillo, *Douglas MacArthur*, pp. 193–95.

74. Eisenhower's Philippine Diary, 29 May 1936. Interview with General Hugh A. Parker by Dr. Maclyn P. Burg, 16 March 1972, pp. 11, 45, Oral History No. 326, Eisenhower Library. D. Clayton James, *Years of MacArthur*, pp. 557–60.

75. Eisenhower's Philippine Diary, 6 Feb. 1936.

76. Jose, *Philippine Army*, p. 127.

77. Ibid, pp. 138–45; Lim, *To Inspire and Lead*, pp. 35–40, 87–91, 115.

78. MacArthur, *Reminiscences*, p. 119. Lucius R. Holbrook to Malin Craig, 16 July 1936, AGO 660.2 PD (7-16-36), RG 407; Eisenhower's Philippine Diary, 15 Feb. 1936; James B. Ord to Dwight D. Eisenhower, 27 July 1937, Box 1, RG 1, MacArthur Papers.

79. George P. Tyner to C/S, Sub: Additional Equipment for Loan to the Philippine Army for Mobilization Purposes, 14 Oct. 1938, AGO 093.5 PI, RG 407. An extensive correspondence dealing with MacArthur's requests can be found in: Sub: Policy for Furnishing Supplies and Equipment to the Philippine Army, AGO 093.5 PI, RG 407.

80. Cordell Hull to Henry H. Woodring, 18 Sept. 1936, AGO 093.5 PI, RG 407.

81. Charles Burnett, "The Philippine Islands," 9 Feb. 1939, Lecture, Analytical Studies Course, CAWC 1938–39, AWCIR, RG 165. Stanley D. Embick, Sub: Military System for the Philippine State, 2 Dec. 1935, F 573, Box 17, E 284, RG 165; Malin Craig to Douglas MacArthur, 4 Aug. 1936, AGO 093.5 PI, RG 407.

82. William L. Osborne to J. K. Evans, Sub: Special Report on the Philippine Army, 2 Dec. 1942, F 6000, E 77, RG 165.

83. G-3 Estimate of the Situation, PD, First Phase Plan Orange, 1934, F 171, SPWPC, E 365, RG 407; Army and Navy Joint Defense Plan for Philippine Islands Coastal Frontier, 1938, F 328, SPWPC, E 365, RG 407. After 1934 the Philippine Department was organized into five distinct commands: the Harbor Defenses of Manila and Subic Bays had 103 officers and 2,799 men (1,524 Americans and 1,275 Filipinos); the Air Corps (60 officers and 623 men, all American); the Philippine Division (255 officers, 4,992 men, a majority of officers were American); the all-American 31st Infantry Regiment (54 officers and 1,113 men); and the departmental staff and service units, with 1,016 officers and men.

84. "Monkeys Have No Tails," Vol. 5, pp. 52–53, Ivins Papers.

85. Inspection of Fort Stotsenburg, P.I., including Clark Field, 31 Oct. 1935, AGO 333.1, Box 134, RG 159.

86. F. B. Upham and Frank Parker to CNO and C/S, 1 Mar. 1934; Charles E. Kilbourne

to Charles P. Summerall, 1930, AGO 660.2 PD (5-31-30), RG 407; HDMSB, Estimate of the Situation, PD, First Phase Plan Orange, 1934, F 198, Box 167, RG 407; HDMSB, Medical Plan, PD, First Phase Plan Orange, 1936, F 176, Box 65, RG 407.

87. Stanley D. Embick to CG, PD, Sub: Military Policy of the U.S. in Philippine Islands, AGO 093.5 PD (10-2-31), RG 407. Fred W. Sladen to AG, 26 Mar. 1928, AGO 660.2 PD (12-2-27), RG 407; Johnson Hagood to William Lassiter, 20 May 1928, F 5, Box 186, Hagood Papers; JANPC to JB, Sub: Independence of the Philippine Islands: Effect of Withdrawal of Military Forces, 28 Feb. 1934, F 525, Box 16, E 284, RG 165; Walter Krueger, Memorandum: Our Policy in the Philippines, 28 Oct. 1935, F 573, Box 17, E 284, RG 165.

88. Interview, p. 44, Almond Papers.

89. Lucius R. Holbrook to Malin Craig, 21 July 1936, AGO 353 PD (12-18-34), RG 407; "Story of a Soldier," pp. 123–24, Koch Papers; J. Lawton Collins, "The 1936 March of the Philippine Division" [n.d.], F Background Materials, Box 51, Collins Papers; Collins, *Lightning Joe*, pp. 70–71.

90. GCM, Memo for General Arnold, 16 July 1941, cited in Marshall, *Papers of George Catlett Marshall*, 2:567–68.

91. Chynoweth, *Bellamy Park*, p. 195. Emphasis in original. Louis Morton, *Fall of the Philippines*, pp. 31–50; Watson, *Chief of Staff*, pp. 412–52.

92. Jonathan M. Wainwright to My darling Freeda, 28 May 1941, Wainwright Papers. Schultz, *Hero of Bataan*, pp. 50–51; Louis Morton, *Fall of the Philippines*, pp. 21–30.

93. Ewing E. Booth to Hugh A. Drum, 2 Jan. 1942, Box 9, Drum Papers.

BIBLIOGRAPHY

U.S. Government Record Groups, National Archives, Washington, D.C.

RG 18—Records of the Army Air Force
RG 38—Records of the Office of the Chief of Naval Operations
RG 45—Naval Records Collection of the Office of Naval Records and Library
RG 77—Records of the Office of the Chief of Engineers
RG 80—General Records of the Department of the Navy, 1798–1947
RG 94—Records of the Adjutant General's Office, 1780–1917
RG 107—Records of the Office of the Secretary of War
RG 111—Records of the Office of the Chief Signal Officer
RG 112—Records of the Office of the Surgeon General of the Army
RG 127—Records of the United States Marine Corps
RG 153—Records of the Office of the Judge Advocate General (Army)
RG 159—Records of the Office of Inspector General
RG 165—Records of the War Department General and Special Staffs
RG 338—Records of U.S. Army Commands, 1942–
RG 350—Records of the Bureau of Insular Affairs
RG 393—Records of United States Army Continental Commands, 1821–1920
RG 395—Records of the United States Army Overseas Operations and Commands, 1898–1942
RG 407—Records of the Adjutant General's Office, 1917–

Microfilm Collections, National Archives, Washington, D.C.

M 254—Philippine Insurgent Records, 1896–1901, with Associated Records of the U.S. War Department, 1900–1906
M 719—John R. M. Taylor, "History of the Philippine Insurrection against the United States, 1898–1903: A Compilation of Documents and Introduction"
M 1023—Record Cards to the Correspondence of the War College Division, Related General Staff, and Adjutant General's Office, 1902–19
M 1064—Letters Received by the Commission Branch of the Adjutant General's Office, 1863–70
M 1421—Records of the Joint Board, 1903–47

State Archives

Hawaii State Archives, Honolulu, Hawaii
    Correspondence of the Governors, 1900–1941
Texas State Archives, Austin, Tex.

Manuscript Collections

Combined Arms Research Library, U.S. Army Command and General Staff College, Ft.
    Leavenworth, Kans.
Duke University Library, Special Collections, Durham, N.C.
    Robert L. Eichelberger Papers
    Lymon W. V. Kennon Papers
Dwight D. Eisenhower Library, Abilene, Kans.
    J. Lawton Collins Papers
    Dwight D. Eisenhower Papers, Prepresidential, 1916–52
    Charles H. Gerhardt Memoirs
    Leland S. Hobbs Papers
    Courtney H. Hodges Papers
    Kevin McCann Papers
    Floyd L. Parks Papers
Fifteenth Air Base Wing History Office, Hickam Air Force Base, Hawaii
    Kenneth L. Bayley, "Life at Hickam, 1940." Transcript.
Hawaiian Historical Society, Honolulu, Hi.
    John W. Waldron Papers
Library of Congress Manuscripts Division, Washington, D.C.
    Henry T. Allen Papers
    Robert L. Bullard Papers
    William H. Carter Papers
    Henry C. Corbin Papers
    W. Cameron Forbes Papers
    Benjamin F. Foulois Papers
    James G. Harbord Papers
    John L. Hines Papers
    Frank McCoy Papers
    Merrill Family Papers
    William Mitchell Papers
    George V. H. Mosely Papers
    George S. Patton Papers
    John J. Pershing Papers
    Charles D. Rhodes Papers
    Riggs Family Papers
    Theodore Roosevelt Papers
    Elihu Root Papers
    Charles P. Summerall Papers
    William H. Taft Papers
    Leonard Wood Papers
MacArthur Memorial, Norfolk, Va.
    Harold G. Howard Papers
    Douglas MacArthur Papers

Massachusetts Historical Society, Boston, Mass.
  Francis W. Carpenter Papers
  Clarence R. Edwards Papers
New York Public Library, Rare Books and Manuscript Division, New York, N.Y.
  Francis V. Greene Papers
South Carolina Historical Society, Charleston, S.C.
  Johnson Hagood Papers
Southern Historical Collections, University of North Carolina, Chapel Hill, N.C.
  Frank Parker Papers
U.S. Air Force Historical Research Agency, Maxwell Air Force Base, Montgomery, Ala.
  Samuel E. Anderson Oral History, K239.0512-905
  Gordon H. Austin Oral History, K239.0512-1325
  Glenn O. Barcus Oral History, K239.0512-908
  Gordon A. Blake Oral History, K239.0512-1562
  Cecil E. Combs Oral History, K239.0152-1344
  Orval R. Cook Oral History, K239.0152-740
  Harold C. Davidson Oral History, K239.0152-817
  Leighton I. Davis Oral History, K239.0152-668
  Matthew K. Deichelmann Oral History, K239.0152-897
  Harold K. Donnelly Oral History, K239.0152-1589
  Eugene L. Eubank Oral History, K239.0512-1345
  Norris B. Harbold Oral History, K239.0152-1760
  Joseph Harmon Papers
  Hunter Harris Oral History, K239.0152-811
  Albert F. Hegenberger Oral History, K239.0152-854
  Bruce K. Holloway Oral History, K239.0152-95
  Joseph H. Nazarro Oral History, K239.0152-1189
  Lauris Norstad Oral History, K239.0152-1116
  William O. Ryan Oral History, K239.0512-980
  Thomas D. White Papers
U.S. Army Military History Institute, Carlisle Barracks, Pa.
  Edward M. Almond Papers
  Lorenzo Alvarado Papers
  Army War College Curriculum Archives
  James C. Barr Questionnaire, 4th Cavalry Box, Spanish-American War Survey
  William and James Belote Collection
  Biographical File: Philippines
  Tasker H. Bliss Papers
  Edward Bowser Papers
  William E. Carraway Papers
  Bradford G. Chynoweth Papers
  Charles G. Clifton Papers, 43rd Infantry Box, Spanish-American War Survey
  Homer Cook Questionnaire, 1st Cavalry Box, Spanish-American War Survey
  Anton Cesar Cron Papers
  Walter S. Cutler Papers
  Joseph R. Darnell Papers
  Hugh A. Drum Papers
  Ira C. Eaker Papers.
  E. Carl Englehardt Papers
  Albert C. Gardner Papers, 1st Cavalry Box, Spanish-American War Survey

George Grunert Papers
Hagood Family Papers
Eli and Charles Helmick Papers
Guy V. Henry Papers
Marvin C. Hepler Papers
Sidney R. Hinds Papers
Horace B. Hobbs Papers
Edward L. Hooper Papers
Howell-Taylor Papers
Charles F. Ivins Papers
Alan W. Jones Papers
Arthur L. Koch Papers
Peter Konrad Questionnaire, 5th Infantry Box, Spanish-American War Survey
Stanley R. Larsen Papers
Samuel Lyon Papers
Clenard McLaughlin Papers
Robert W. Mearns Papers
Stephen C. Mills Papers
William H. Montgomery Papers
John E. Olson Papers
Oscar S. Reeder Papers
Lewis S. Sorley Papers
Matthew F. Steele Papers
Johnathan M. Wainwright Papers
Williams Family Papers
Stuart Yeo Papers
Samuel B. M. Young Papers
U.S. Military Academy, Special Collections, West Point, N.Y.
Ola Walter Bell Papers
Bernard A. Byrne Papers
Frank William Gilbreath Papers
Campbell Blackshear Hodges Papers
Francis J. Kernan Papers
Walter Krueger Papers
John H. Parker Papers
Charles D. Rhodes Papers
William Ross Scott Papers

Government Documents

Annual Report of the War Department, 1897–1941.
Hagood, Johnson. *Circular Relative to Pay of Officers and Enlisted Men of the Army.* Washington, D.C.: Government Publishing Office, 1907.
Military Information Division. Adjutant General's Office. *The Hawaiian Islands: Report on the Physical Features, Ports of Landing, Supplies, Climate, Diseases, Etc. Compiled from the Best Available Sources for the Information of the Army.* Washington, D.C.: Government Printing Office, 1893.
U.S. Congress. House. *Sale of Beer and Light Wines in Post Exchanges.* H. Doc. 252, 57th Cong., 2nd sess., 1903.
——. Committee on Military Affairs. *Hearings before the House Committee on Military Af-*

fairs, to Increase the Efficiency of the Army. 2 vols. Washington, D.C.: Government Printing Office, 1916.

U.S. Congress. Senate. Committee on Military Affairs. *Hearings before the Committee of Military Affairs on the Sales of Intoxicating Liquors at the Army Canteens.* Washington, D.C.: Government Printing Office, 1899.

———. Committee on Military Affairs. *Hearings before the Committee of Military Affairs (Senate), on the Army Appropriations Act, 1906–7.* Washington, D.C.: Government Printing Office, 1906.

———. Committee on Military Affairs, *Hearings on the Army Appropriations Bill, 1908 (HR 17288).* Washington, D.C.: Government Printing Office, 1908.

———. Committee on Military Affairs. *Hearings before the Senate Committee on Military Affairs on Bill S.8129, to Increase the Efficiency of the Army.* Washington, D.C.: Government Printing Office, 1910.

———. Committee on Military Affairs, *Hearings before the Senate Committee on Military Affairs Relating to Various Army Matters.* Washington, D.C.: Government Printing Office, 1910.

———. Committee on the Philippines. *Affairs in the Philippines. Hearings before the Committee on the Philippines of the United States Senate.* Sen. Doc. 331, 57th Congress, 1st sess., 1902.

U.S. War Department. *Report of the Secretary of War, 1907.* Washington, D.C.: Government Publishing Office, 1908.

Published Manuscript Collections

Strategical Planning in the Navy: Its Evolution and Execution, 1891–1945. Washington, D.C.: Scholarly Resources, 1977.

U.S. Military Intelligence Reports: Japan, 1918–1941. Frederick, Md.: University Publications of America, 1986.

Newspapers

Army and Navy Journal
Honolulu Advertiser
Honolulu Star Bulletin
Manila Times
Pacific Commercial Advertiser (Honolulu)
Paradise of the Pacific (Honolulu)
Philippines Free Press (Manila)

Books

Abrahamson, James L. *America Arms for a New Century: The Making of a Great Military Power.* New York: Free Press, 1981.

Achútegui, Pedro S., and Miguel A. Bernad. *Aguinaldo and the Revolution of 1896: A Documentary History.* Manila: Ateneo de Manila Press, 1972.

Allen, Francis J. *The Concrete Battleship: Fort Drum, El Fraile Island, Manila Bay.* Missoula, Mont.: Pictoral Histories Publishing Co, 1989.

Allen, Gwenfread. *Hawaii's War Years, 1941–1945.* Honolulu: University of Hawaii Press, 1950.

Anderson, William H. *The Philippine Problem.* New York: G. P. Putnam's Sons, 1939.

Armstrong, David A. *Bullets and Bureaucrats: The Machine Gun and the United States Army, 1861–1916*. Westport, Conn.: Greenwood Press, 1982.

Bacevich, Andrew J. *Diplomat in Khaki: Major General Frank Ross McCoy and American Foreign Policy, 1898–1949*. Lawrence: University Press of Kansas, 1989.

Baclagon, Uldarico. *Philippine Campaigns*. Manila: Liwayway Publications, 1952.

Bailey, Beth, and David Farber. *The First Strange Place: The Alchemy of Race and Sex in World War II Hawaii*. New York: Free Press, 1992.

Baldwin, Alice B., ed. *Memoirs of the Late Frank D. Baldwin, Major-General, U.S.A.* Los Angeles: Wetzel Publishing, 1929.

Barber, Joseph. *Hawaii: Restless Rampart*. Indianapolis: Bobbs-Merrill, 1941.

Barrows, David P. *History of the Philippines*. New York: World Book, 1926.

Bartlett, Merril L. *Assault from the Sea: Essays on the History of Amphibious Warfare*. Annapolis, Md.: Naval Institute Press, 1983.

Bartsch, William H. *Doomed at the Start: American Pursuit Pilots in the Philippines, 1941–1942*. College Station: Texas A&M University Press, 1992.

Beale, Howard K. *Theodore Roosevelt and the Rise of America to World Power*. Baltimore: Johns Hopkins University Press, 1956.

Beckett, Ian F. W., ed. *The Roots of Counter-Insurgency: Armies and Guerrilla Warfare, 1900–1945*. London: Blandford Press, 1988.

Belote, James H., and William M. Belote. *Corregidor: The Saga of a Fortress*. New York: Harper and Row, 1967.

Betts, Raymond F. *Assimilation and Association in French Colonial Theory, 1890–1914*. New York: Columbia University Press, 1961.

Bisbee, William H. *Through Four American Wars*. Boston: Meador Publishing, 1931.

Blount, James H. *The American Occupation of the Philippines, 1898–1912*. New York: G. P. Putnam's Sons, 1912.

Blumenson, Martin. *Patton: The Man Behind the Legend*. New York: William Morrow, 1985.

———. *The Patton Papers, 1885–1940*. Boston: Houghton Mifflin, 1972.

Bond, Brian. *British Military Policy between the Two World Wars*. Oxford: Clarendon Press, 1980.

Booth, Ewing E. *My Observations and Experiences in the United States Army*. N.p., 1944.

Bordwell, Percy. *The Law of War between Belligerents: A History and Commentary*. Chicago: Callahan, 1908.

Borg, Dorthy, and Sumpei Okamoto, eds. *Pearl Harbor As History: Japanese-American Relations, 1931–1941*. New York: Columbia University Press, 1973.

Bradford, James C., ed. *Crucible of Empire: The Spanish-American War and Its Aftermath*. Annapolis, Md.: Naval Institute Press, 1993.

Braisted, William R. *The United States Navy in the Pacific, 1897–1909*. Austin: University of Texas Press, 1958.

———. *The United States Navy in the Pacific, 1909–1922*. Austin: University of Texas Press, 1971.

Brands, H. W. *Bound to Empire: The United States and the Philippines*. New York: Oxford University Press, 1992.

Brereton, Lewis H. *The Brereton Diaries: The War in the Air in the Pacific, Middle East and Europe*. New York: William Morrow, 1946.

Brown, John C. *Diary of a Soldier in the Philippines*. Portland, Ore.: n.p., 1901.

Brown, Richard C. *Social Attitudes of American Generals, 1898–1940*. New York: Arno Press, 1979.

Browning, Robert S. *Two If by Sea: The Development of American Coastal Defense Policy*. Westport, Conn.: Greenwood Press, 1983.

Brune, Lester H. *The Origins of American National Security Policy: Sea Power, Air Power, and Foreign Policy, 1900–1941.* Manhattan, Kans.: MA/AH Publishing, 1981.

Buck, Beaumont B. *Memories of Peace and War.* San Antonio: Naylor, 1935.

Buckley, Thomas H. *The United States and the Washington Conference, 1921–1922.* Knoxville: University of Tennessee Press, 1970.

Butt, Archibald. *The Letters of Archie Butt.* Edited by Lawrence F. Abbott. Garden City, N.Y.: Doubleday, Page, 1924.

Byrd, Martha. *Chennault: Giving Wings to the Tiger.* Tuscaloosa: University of Alabama Press, 1987.

Callaway, Helen. *Gender, Culture and Empire: European Women in Colonial Nigeria.* Urbana: University of Illinois Press, 1987.

Callwell, Charles E. *Small Wars: Their Principles and Practice.* 3rd ed. London: Harrison and Sons, 1906.

Carter, William H. *The American Army.* Indianapolis: Bobbs-Merrill, 1915.

——. *The Life of Lieutenant General Chaffee.* Chicago: University of Chicago Press, 1917

Challener, Richard D. *Admirals, Generals, and American Foreign Policy, 1898–1914.* Princeton: Princeton University Press, 1973.

Chamberlain, Elinor. *The Far Command.* New York: Ballantine Books, 1952.

Chandler, Melbourne C. *Of Garryown in Glory: The History of the Seventh United States Cavalry Regiment.* Annandale, Md.: Turnpike Press, 1960.

Che Man, W. K. *Muslim Separatism: The Moros of Southern Philippines and the Malays of Southern Thailand.* Singapore: Oxford University Press, 1990.

Chennault, Claire L. *Way of a Fighter.* New York: G. P. Putnam's Sons, 1949.

Chwialkowski, Robert. *In Caesar's Shadow: The Life of General Robert Eichelberger.* Westport, Conn.: Greenwood Press, 1993.

Chynoweth, Bradford Grethen. *Bellamy Park.* Hicksville, N.Y.: Exposition Press, 1975.

Clark, Maurine. *Captain's Bride, General's Lady: The Memoirs of Mrs. Mark W. Clark.* New York: McGraw-Hill, 1956.

Clary, David A. *Fortress America: The Corps of Engineers, Hampton Roads, and United States Coastal Defense.* Charlottesville: University Press of Virginia, 1990.

Clinard, Outen J. *Japan's Influence on Amercan Naval Power, 1897–1917.* Berkeley: University of California Press, 1947

Cline, Ray S. *The War Department. Washington Command Post: The Operations Division.* Washington, D.C.: Center of Military History, 1990.

Cloman, Sydney A. *Myself and a Few Moros.* Garden City, N.Y.: Doubleday, Page, 1923.

Coffman, Edward M. *The Old Army: A Portrait of the American Army in Peacetime, 1784–1898.* New York: Oxford University Press, 1986.

Cohen, Elliot A. *Citizens and Soldiers: The Dilemmas of Military Service.* Ithaca: Cornell University Press, 1985.

Cohen, Warren I. *Empire without Tears: America's Foreign Relations, 1921–1933.* Philadelphia: Temple University Press, 1987.

Collins, J. Lawton. *Lightning Joe.* Baton Rouge: Louisiana State University Press, 1979.

Colquhoun, Archibald R. *The Mastery of the Pacific.* New York: Macmillan, 1904. Reprint. New York: Arno Press and New York Times, 1970.

Conn, Stetson, Rose C. Engelman, and Byron Fairchild. *Guarding the United States and Its Outposts.* Washington, D.C.: Historical Division, Department of the Army, 1964.

Conner, Virginia. *What Father Forbad.* Philadelphia: Dorrance, 1951.

Coolidge, Archibald C. *The United States As a World Power.* New York: Macmillan, 1910.

Cosmas, Graham A. *An Army for Empire: The United States Army in the Spanish-American War.* Columbia: University of Missouri Press, 1971.

Costello, John. *Days of Infamy: MacArthur, Roosevelt, Churchill, the Shocking Truth Re-*

vealed: How Their Secret Deals and Strategic Blunders Caused Disasters at Pearl Harbor and the Philippines. New York: Pocket Books, 1994.

Craven, Frank W., and James L. Cate, eds. *The Army Air Forces in World War II*. Vol. 1, *Plans and Operations January 1939 to August 1942*. Chicago: University of Chicago Press, 1948.

Crow, Carl. *America and the Philippines*. Garden City, N.Y.: Doubleday, 1914.

Cruikshank, Bruce. *Samar: 1768–1898*. Manila: Historical Conservation Society, 1985.

Cruz, Romeo V. *America's Colonial Desk in the Philippines*. Quezon City: University of the Philippines Press, 1974.

Darcy, Ted. *Army Aviation in Hawaii*. Kailua, Hi.: N.p., 1991.

Dauncey, Campbell. *The Philippines*. Boston: J. B. Millet, 1910.

Davis, Burke. *The Billy Mitchell Affair*. New York: Random House, 1967.

Davis, Oscar King. *Our Conquests in the Pacific*. New York: Frederick A. Stokes, 1899.

Daws, Gavan. *Shoal of Time: A History of the Hawaiian Islands*. New York: Macmillan, 1968.

Dennett, Tyler. *Roosevelt and the Russo-Japanese War*. New York: Doubleday, Page, 1925. Reprint. Gloucester: Peter Smith, 1959.

Dingman, Roger. *Power in the Pacific: The Origins of Naval Arms Limitation, 1914–1922*. Chicago: University of Chicago Press, 1976.

Dixon, Joe E., ed. *The American Military and the Far East: Proceedings of the Ninth Military History Symposium*. Washington, D.C.: U.S. Air Force Academy, 1980.

Dobbs, Horace P. *Kris and Krag: Adventures among the Moros of the Southern Philippines*. N.p., 1962.

Dorrance, William H. *Fort Kamehameha: The Story of the Harbor Defenses of Pearl Harbor*. Shippensburg, Pa.: White Mane Publishing, 1992.

Dowart, Jeffrey M. *The Office of Naval Intelligence: The Birth of America's First Intelligence Agency, 1865–1918*. Annapolis, Md.: U.S. Naval Institute Press, 1979.

Dower, John W. *War without Mercy: Race and Power in the Pacific War*. New York: Pantheon, 1986.

Dudden, Arthur P. *The American Pacific: From the Old China Trade to the Present*. New York: Oxford University Press, 1992.

Dunlay, Thomas D. *Wolves for the Blue Soldiers: Indian Scouts and Auxiliaries with the United States Army*. Lincoln: University of Nebraska Press, 1982.

Ellis, L. Ethan. *Republican Foreign Policy, 1921–1933*. New Brunswick, N.J.: Rutgers University Press, 1968.

Esthus, Raymond. *Theodore Roosevelt and the International Rivalries*. Waltham, Mass.: Ginn-Blaisdell, 1970.

Fairbairn, Geoffrey. *Revolutionary Guerrilla Warfare: The Countryside Version*. Harmondsworth: Penguin Books, 1974.

Fitzpatrick, Ernest H. *The Coming Conflict of Nations or the Japanese-American War*. Springfield, Ill.: H. W. Rokker, 1909.

Fletcher, Marvin. *The Peacetime Army, 1900–1941: A Research Guide*. Westport, Conn.: Greenwood Press, 1988.

Forbes, W. Cameron. *The Philippine Islands*. Cambridge, Mass.: Riverside Press, 1928.

Friend, Theodore. *Between Two Empires: The Ordeal of the Philippines, 1929–1946*. New Haven: Yale University Press, 1965.

Futrell, Robert F. *Ideas, Concepts, Doctrine: A History of Basic Thinking in the United States Air Force*. Maxwell Air Force Base, Ala.: Air University Press, 1974.

Ganoe, William A. *The History of the United States Army*. New York: D. Appleton-Century, 1942.

Gates, John M. *Schoolbooks and Krags: The United States Army in the Philippines, 1898–1902*. Westport, Conn.: Greenwood Press, 1973.

Geffen, William, ed. *Command and Commanders in Modern Warfare*. 2nd ed. Washington, D.C.: Government Printing Office, 1971.

Gibson, Arrell M. *Yankees in Paradise: The Pacific Basin Frontier*. Albuquerque: University of New Mexico Press, 1993.

Gleeck, Lewis E., Jr. *The Manila Americans (1901–1964)*. Manila: Carmelo and Bauermann, 1977.

Griffith, Robert K. *Men Wanted for the U.S. Army: America's Experience with an All-Volunteer Army between the Wars*. Westport, Conn.: Greenwood Press, 1982.

Griswold, A. Whitney. *The Far Eastern Policy of the United States*. New York: Harcourt, Brace, 1938.

Grunder, Garel A., and William E. Livezey. *The Philippines and the United States*. Norman: University of Oklahoma Press, 1951.

Gwynn, Charles W. *Imperial Policing*. London: Macmillan, 1934.

Hagan, Kenneth R., and William R. Roberts, eds. *Against All Enemies: Interpretations of American Military History from Colonial Times to the Present*. Westport, Conn.: Greenwood Press, 1986.

Hagedorn, Hermann. *Leonard Wood: A Biography*. 2 vols. New York: Harper Bros., 1931.

Hagood, Johnson. *We Can Defend America*. Garden City, N.Y.: Doubleday, Doran, 1937.

Hammond, Paul Y. *Organizing for Defense: The American Military Establishment in the Twentieth Century*. Princeton: Princeton University Press, 1961.

Harrison, Francis B. *The Corner-Stone of Philippine Independence: A Narrative of Seven Years*. New York: Century, 1922.

Hawaiian Department. *Digest of Information—The Hawaiian Department and the Territory of Hawaii*. Honolulu: Army Printing Office, 1930.

Headrick, Daniel R. *The Tools of Empire: Technology and European Imperialism in the Nineteenth Century*. New York: Oxford University Press, 1981.

Hewes, James E. *From Root to McNamara: Army Organization and Administration, 1900–1963*. Washington, D.C.: U.S. Army Center of Military History, 1975.

Hicks, John D. *Republican Ascendancy, 1921–1933*. New York: Harper and Brothers, 1960.

Higham, Robin, and Carol Brandt, eds. *The United States Army in Peacetime: Essays in Honor of the Bicentennial, 1775–1975*. Manhattan, Kans.: MA/AH Publishing, 1975.

Hogg, Ian. *The History of Fortification*. New York: St. Martin's Press, 1981.

Holley, I. B. *General John M. Palmer, Citizen Soldiers, and the Army of a Democracy*. Westport, Conn.: Greenwood Press, 1982.

Honolulu Social Survey. *Report of the Committee on the Social Evil*. Honolulu: Honolulu Star-Bulletin, 1914.

Huidekoper, Frederic L. *The Military Unpreparedness of the United States: A History of American Land Forces from Colonial Times until June 1, 1915*. New York: Macmillan, 1915.

Hunt, George A. *History of the Twenty-Seventh Infantry*. Honolulu: Honolulu Star-Bulletin, 1931.

Hurley, Alfred F. *Billy Mitchell: Crusader for Air Power*. Rev. ed. Bloomington: Indiana University Press, 1975.

Hurley, Victor. *Swish of the Kris: The Story of the Moros*. New York: E. P. Dutton, 1936.

Ileto, Renaldo C. *Payson and Revolution: Popular Movements in the Philippines, 1840–1910*. Manila: Ateneo de Manila Press, 1979.

Iriye, Akira. *Across the Pacific: An Inner History of American–East Asian Relations*. New York: Harcourt, Brace and World, 1967.

——. *Pacific Estrangement: Japanese and American Expansion, 1897–1911*. Cambridge, Mass.: Harvard University Press, 1972.

——, ed. *Mutual Images: Essays in American-Japanese Relations*. Cambridge, Mass.: Harvard University Press, 1975.

Israel, Jerry, ed. *Building the Organizational Society: Essays on Associational Activities in Modern America*. New York: Free Press, 1972.

Jackson, William. *Withdrawal from Empire: A Military View*. New York: St. Martin's Press, 1986.

Jaher, Frederic C. *Doubters and Dissenters: Cataclysimic Thought in America, 1865–1918*. New York: Free Press of Glencoe, 1964.

James, D. Clayton. *The Years of MacArthur*. Vol. 1, *1880–1941*. Boston: Houghton Mifflin, 1970.

James, Lawrence. *Imperial Rearguard: Wars of Empire, 1919–85*. London: Brassey's Defense Publishers, 1988.

——. *The Savage Wars: British Campaigns in Africa, 1870–1920*. New York: St. Martin's Press, 1985.

Jensen, Irene K. *The Chinese in the Philippines during the American Regime: 1898–1946*. San Francisco: R and E Research Associates, 1975.

Jensen, Joan M. *Army Surveillance in America, 1775–1980*. New Haven: Yale University Press, 1991.

Jessup, Philip C. *Elihu Root*. New York: Dodd, Mead, 1938.

Joesting, Edward. *Hawaii: An Uncommon History*. New York: W. W. Norton, 1972.

Johnston, Robert M. *Arms and the Race: The Foundations of Army Reform*. New York: Century, 1915.

Jones, James. *From Here to Eternity*. New York: Charles Scribner's Sons, 1951.

Jose, Ricardo T. *The Philippine Army, 1935–1942*. Quezon City: Ateneo de Manila Press, 1992.

Kalaw, Maximo M. *The Development of Philippine Politics, 1872–1920*. Manila: Escolta, 1927.

Karnow, Stanley. *In Our Image: America's Empire in the Philippines*. New York: Random House, 1989.

Kerrick, Harrison S. *Military and Naval America*. Garden City, N.Y.: Doubleday, 1916.

Killigrew, John W. *The Impact of the Great Depression on the Army*. New York: Garland Press, 1979.

King, Charles. *A Conquering Corps Badge and Other Stories of the Philippines*. Milwaukee: L. A. Rhoades, 1902.

——. *Found in the Philippines*. New York: Hurst, 1899.

Kuykendall, Ralph S. *The Hawaiian Kingdom*. Vol. 2, *Twenty Critical Years: 1854–1874*. Honolulu: University of Hawaii Press, 1966.

Kuykendall, Ralph S., and A. Grove Day. *Hawaii: A History from Polynesian Kingdom to American State*. Rev. ed. Englewood Cliffs, N.J.: Prentice-Hall, 1961.

LaFeber, Walter. *The New Empire: An Interpretation of American Expansion, 1860–1898*. Ithaca: Cornell University Press, 1963.

Lane, Jack C. *Armed Progressive: General Leonard Wood*. San Rafael, Calif.: Presidio Press, 1978.

Lea, Homer R. *The Valor of Ignorance*. 1909. Reprint. New York: Harper and Brothers Publishers, 1942.

LeRoy, James A. *The Americans in the Philippines*. 2 Vols. Boston: Houghton Mifflin, 1915.

Lewis, Emmanuel R. *Seacoast Fortifications of the United States: An Introductory History*. 1970. Reprint. Annapolis, Md.: Leeward Publications, 1979.

Lim, Vicente. *To Inspire and Lead: The Letters of Gen. Vicente Lim, 1938–1942*. Edited by Adelaida Perez. Manila: N.p., 1980.

Linn, Brian M. *The U.S. Army and Counterinsurgency in the Philippine War, 1899–1902*. Chapel Hill: University of North Carolina Press, 1989.

MacArthur, Douglas. *Reminiscences*. New York: Crest, 1965.

McFarland, Keith D. *Henry H. Woodring: A Political Biography of FDR's Controversial Secretary of War*. Lawrence: University Press of Kansas, 1975.

Mahan, Alfred Thayer. *The Influence of Seapower upon History, 1660–1783*. 1890. Reprint. New York: Hill and Wang, 1957.

Major, John. *Prize Possession: The United States and the Panama Canal, 1903–1979*. New York: Cambridge University Press, 1993.

Majul, Cesar A. *Muslims in the Philippines*. Quezon City: University of the Philippines Press, 1973.

Malcolm, George A. *The Commonwealth of the Philippines*. New York: D. Appleton-Century, 1936.

Manchester, William. *American Caesar*. Boston: Little, Brown, 1978.

Marshall, George C. *The Papers of George Catlett Marshall*. Vol. 1, *"The Soldierly Spirit,"* December 1889–June 1939. Edited by Larry I. Bland and Sharon R. Ritenour. Baltimore: Johns Hopkins University Press, 1981.

———. *The Papers of George Catlett Marshall*. Vol. 2, *"We Cannot Delay,"* July 1, 1939–December 6, 1941. Edited by Larry I. Bland, Sharon R. Ritenour, and Clarence E. Wunderlin Jr. Baltimore: Johns Hopkins University Press, 1986.

Matloff, Morris, and Edwin M. Snell. *The War Department: Strategic Planning for Coalition Warfare, 1941–1942*. Washington, D.C.: Office of the Chief of Military History, 1953.

Maurer, Maurer. *Aviation in the U.S. Army, 1919–1939*. Washington, D.C.: Office of Air Force History, 1987.

Maus, L. Mervin. *An Army Officer on Leave in Japan*. Chicago: A. C. McClurg, 1911.

May, Ernest R. *Imperial Democracy: The Emergence of America As a Great Power*. New York: Harcourt Brace and World, 1961.

———, ed. *Knowing One's Enemies: Intelligence Assessment before the Two World Wars*. Princeton: Princeton University Press, 1986.

May, Glenn A. *Battle for Batangas: A Philippine Province at War*. New Haven: Yale University Press, 1991.

———. *Social Engineering in the Philippines: The Aims, Executions, and Impact of American Colonial Policy, 1900–1913*. Westport, Conn.: Greenwood Press, 1980.

Mayo, Kathleen. *The Isles of Fear: The Truth about the Philippines*. New York: Harcourt, Brace, 1924.

Millard, Thomas F. *America and the Far Eastern Question*. New York: Moffat, Yard, 1909.

Miller, Edward S. *War Plan Orange: The U.S. Strategy to Defeat Japan, 1897–1945*. Annapolis, Md.: Naval Institute Press, 1991.

Millett, Allan R. *The General: Robert L. Bullard and Officership in the United States Army, 1881–1925*. Westport, Conn.: Greenwood Press, 1975.

———. *Semper Fidelis: The History of the United States Marine Corps*. New York: Free Press, 1980.

Millett, Allan R., and Peter Maslowski. *For the Common Defense: A Military History of the United States of America*. New York: Free Press, 1984.

Millis, Walter. *American Military Thought*. Indianapolis: Bobbs-Merril, 1962.

Minger, Ralph E. *William Howard Taft and United States Foreign Policy: The Apprenticeship Years, 1900–1908*. Urbana: University of Illinois Press, 1975.

Morton, Louis. *The Fall of the Philippines*. Washington, D.C.: Office of the Chief of Military History, 1953.
——. *Strategy and Command: The First Two Years*. Washington, D.C.: Office of the Chief of Military History, 1966.
Nedbalek, Lani. *Wahiawa: From Dream to Community*. Mililani, Hi.: Wonderview Press, 1984.
Neu, Charles E. *An Uncertain Friendship: Theodore Roosevelt and Japan, 1906–1909*. Cambridge, Mass.: Harvard University Press, 1967.
Noble, Dennis L. *The Eagle and the Dragon: The U.S. Military in China, 1901–1937*. Westport, Conn.: Greenwood Press, 1991.
Okihiro, Gary Y. *Cane Fires: The Anti-Japanese Movement in Hawaii, 1865–1945*. Philadelphia: Temple University Press, 1991.
Onorato, Michael P. *Leonard Wood and the Philippine Cabinet Crisis of 1923*. Manila: University of Manila Press, 1967.
Osborne, Thomas J. *"Empire Can Wait": American Opposition to Hawaiian Annexation, 1893–1898*. Kent, Ohio: Kent State University Press, 1981.
Palmer, John M. *America in Arms: The Experience of the United States with Military Organization*. New Haven: Yale University Press, 1941.
Paret, Peter, Gordon A. Craig, and Felix Gilbert, eds. *Makers of Modern Strategy from Machiavelli to the Nuclear Age*. Princeton: Princeton University Press, 1986.
Parker, James. *The Old Army: Memories, 1872–1918*. Philadelphia: Dorrance, 1929.
Perez, Adelaida, ed. *To Inspire and Lead: The Letters of Gen. Vicente Lim, 1938–1942*. Manila: N.p., 1980.
Petillo, Carol M. *Douglas MacArthur: The Philippine Years*. Bloomington: Indiana University Press, 1981.
Pogue, Forrest C. *George C. Marshall: Education of a General, 1880–1939*. New York: Viking Press, 1963.
Porteus, Stanley D. *A Century of Social Thinking in Hawaii*. Palo Alto, Calif.: Pacific Books, 1962.
Prange, Gordon W., with Donald M. Goldstein and Katherine V. Dillon. *At Dawn We Slept: The Untold Story of Pearl Harbor*. New York: McGraw-Hill, 1981.
——. *Pearl Harbor: The Verdict of History*. New York: McGraw-Hill, 1986.
Puleston, W. D. *The Armed Forces of the Pacific: A Comparison of the Military and Naval Power of the United States and Japan*. New Haven: Yale University Press, 1941.
Putnam, Israel. *Daniel Everton, Volunteer-Regular: A Romance of the Philippines*. New York: Funk and Wagnalls, 1902.
Quezon, Manuel L. *The Good Fight*. New York: D. Appleton-Century, 1946.
Reardon, Carol. *Scholars and Soldiers: The U.S. Army and the Uses of Military History, 1865–1920*. Lawrence: University Press of Kansas, 1990.
Remembering Kakaako: 1910–1959. Honolulu: Ethnic Studies Oral History Project, University of Hawaii at Manoa, 1978.
Reynolds, Clark. *Admiral John H. Towers: The Struggle for Naval Air Supremacy*. Annapolis, Md.: Naval Institute Press, 1991.
Rickey, Don. *Forty Miles a Day on Beans and Hay: The Enlisted Soldier Fighting the Indian Wars*. Norman: University of Oklahoma Press, 1963.
Roberts, William R., and Jack Sweetman, eds. *New Interpretations in Naval History: Selected Papers from the Ninth Naval History Symposium*. Annapolis, Md.: Naval Institute Press, 1991.
Rogers, Paul. *The Good Years: MacArthur and Sutherland*. New York: Praeger Publishers, 1990.
Roosevelt, Nicholas. *The Restless Pacific*. New York: Charles Scribner's Sons, 1928.

Root, Elihu. *The Military and Colonial Policy of the United States: Addresses and Reports by Elihu Root*. Edited by Robert Bacon and James B. Scott. Cambridge, Mass.: Harvard University Press, 1916.

Roth, Russell. *Muddy Glory: America's "Indian Wars" in the Philippines, 1899–1935*. West Hanover, Mass.: Christopher Publishing House, 1981.

Ryan, Gary D., and Timothy K. Nenninger, eds. *Soldiers and Civilians: The U.S. Army and the American People*. Washington, D.C.: National Archives Trust Fund Board, 1987.

Schultz, Duane. *Hero of Bataan: The Story of Johnathan M. Wainwright*. New York: St. Martin's Press, 1981.

Scott, Hugh L. *Some Memories of a Soldier*. New York: Century, 1928.

Seone, Consuelo A., and Robert L. Nieman. *Beyond the Ranges*. New York: Robert Speller and Sons, 1960.

Sexton, William T. *Soldiers in the Sun: An Adventure in Imperialism*. Harrisburg, Pa.: Military Service Publishing, 1939.

Shea, Nancy. *The Army Wife*. New York: Harper and Brothers, 1941.

Sherry, Michael S. *The Rise of American Airpower: The Creation of Armageddon*. New Haven: Yale University Press, 1987.

Shunk, Caroline S. *An Army Woman in the Philippines: Extracts from Letters of an Army Officer's Wife Describing Her Personal Experiences in the Philippine Islands*. Kansas City, Mo.: Franklin Hudson, 1914.

Sills, David L., ed. *International Encyclopedia of the Social Sciences*. New York: Macmillan, 1968.

Slackman, Michael. *Target: Pearl Harbor*. Honolulu: University of Hawaii Press and Arizona Memorial Museum Association, 1990.

Smith, Cornelius C. *Don't Settle for Second: Life and Times of Cornelius C. Smith*. San Rafael, Calif.: Presidio Press, 1977.

Smythe, Donald. *Guerrilla Warrior: The Early Life of John J. Pershing*. New York: Charles Scribner's Sons, 1973.

Spector, Ronald. *Admiral of the New Empire: The Life and Career of George Dewey*. Baton Rouge: Louisiana State University Press, 1974.

Stephan, John J. *Hawaii under the Rising Sun: Japan's Plans for Conquest after Pearl Harbor*. Honolulu: University of Hawaii Press, 1984.

Sternberg, David J. *The Philippines: A Singular and a Plural Place*. 2nd ed. Boulder, Colo.: Westview Press, 1990.

Stimson, Henry L., and McGeorge Bundy. *On Active Service in Peace and War*. New York: Harper Brothers, 1948.

Stratemeyer, Edward. *The Campaign of the Jungle, or, Under Lawton through Luzon*. Boston: Lee and Shepard, 1900.

——. *Under MacArthur in Luzon, or, Last Battles in the Philippines*. Boston: Lee and Shepard, 1901.

Sturtevant, David R. *Popular Uprisings in the Philippines, 1840–1940*. Ithaca: Cornell University Press, 1976.

Tabrah, Ruth. *Hawaii: A Bicentennial History*. New York: W. W. Norton, 1980.

Tate, Merze. *Hawaii: Reciprocity or Annexation*. East Lansing: Michigan State University Press, 1968.

Thrupp, Sylvia L., ed. *Millennial Dreams in Action: Studies in Revolutionary Religious Movements*. New York: Schocken Books, 1970.

Toland, John. *Infamy: Pearl Harbor and Its Aftermath*. New York: Doubleday, 1982.

Trani, Eugene P., and David L. Wilson. *The Presidency of Warren G. Harding*. Lawrence: Regents Press of Kansas, 1977.

Trask, David F. *The War with Spain in 1898*. New York: Macmillan, 1981.

Truscott, Lucian K. *The Twilight of the U.S. Cavalry: Life in the Old Army, 1917–1942*. Lawrence: University Press of Kansas, 1989.

Twichell, Heath, Jr. *Allen: The Biography of an Army Officer, 1859–1930*. New Brunswick, N.J.: Rutgers University Press, 1974.

Upton, Emory. *The Armies of Asia and Europe*. 1878. Reprint. Westport, Conn.: Greenwood Press, 1968.

Vander Meulen, Jacob A. *The Politics of Aircraft: Building an American Military Industry*. Lawrence: University Press of Kansas, 1991.

Vandiver, Frank E. *Black Jack: The Life and Times of John J. Pershing*. 2 vols. College Station: Texas A&M Press, 1977.

Waikiki, 1900–1985. 5 vols. Honolulu: Oral History Project, Social Science Research Institute, University of Hawaii at Manoa, 1985.

Wakukawa, Ernest H. *A History of the Japanese People in Hawaii*. Honolulu: Tokyo Shoin, 1938.

Wagner, Arthur L. *The Service of Security and Information*. Washington, D.C.: James J. Chapman, 1893.

Watson, Mark S. *Chief of Staff: Prewar Plans and Preparations*. Washington, D.C.: Historical Division, Department of the Army, 1950.

Weigley, Russell F. *The American Way of War: A History of United States Military Stategy and Policy*. 1973. Reprint. Bloomington: Indiana University Press, 1977.

——. *History of the U.S. Army*. 1967. Reprint. Bloomington: Indiana University Press, 1984.

——. *Towards an American Army: Military Thought from Washington to Marshall*. New York: Columbia University Press, 1962.

Welch, Richard E. *Reponse to Imperialism: The United States and the Philippine-American War, 1899–1902*. Chapel Hill: University of North Carolina Press, 1979.

Wernstedt, Frederick L., and J. E. Spencer. *The Philippine Island World: A Physical, Cultural, and Regional Geography*. Berkeley: University of California Press, 1967.

Wheeler, Gerald E. *Prelude to Pearl Harbor: The United States Navy and the Far East, 1921–1931*. Columbia: University of Missouri Press, 1963.

White, John R. *Bullets and Bolos: Fifteen Years in the Philippine Islands*. New York: Century, 1928.

Willeford, Charles. *Something about a Soldier*. New York: Random House, 1986.

Winslow, Anne G. *Fort DeRussy Days: Letters of a Malahini Army Wife, 1908–1911*. Edited by M. Winslow Chapman. Honolulu: Folk Press, 1988.

Woodruff, Charles E. *The Effects of Tropical Light on White Men*. New York: Rebman, 1905.

Wooster, Robert. *The Military and United States Indian Policy, 1865–1903*. New Haven: Yale University Press, 1988.

——. *Nelson A. Miles and the Twilight of the Frontier Army*. Lincoln: University of Nebraska Press, 1993.

Worcester, Dean. *The Philippines Past and Present*. New York: Macmillan, 1930.

Young, Kenneth R. *The General's General: The Life and Times of Arthur MacArthur*. Boulder, Colo.: Westview Press, 1994.

Articles

Abbot, Henry L. "The Recent Japanese Manoevers." *Journal of the Military Service Institute of the United States* 11 (September 1890): 748–50.

Adams, Will. "The Education of Trooper Brown." *Century* 74 (May 1907): 10–18.

Albert, Allen B. "The Roosevelt of the Army." *Munsey's Magazine* 36 (October 1906): 53–57.

"The American Army." *Outlook* 74 (11 July 1903): 643–45.

Archer, Elizabeth S. "Home Economics in the Philippines." *Infantry Journal* 28 (January 1926): 52–59.

Archer, William. "Will Japan Ever Fight the United States." *McClure's* 40 (February 1912): 38–45.

Arens, Richard. "The Early Pulahan Movement in Samar." *Leyte-Samar Studies* 11 (1977): 57–109.

Astin, Joseph A. "Soldiering in the Hawaiian Islands." *Infantry Journal* 24 (April 1924): 449–56.

Bacon, Alexander S. "Is Our Army Degenerate?" *The Forum* 27 (March 1899): 11–23.

Bacevich, Andrew J. "Disagreeable Work: Pacifying the Moros, 1903–1906." *Military Review* 40 (June 1982): 49–61.

——. "Family Matters: American Civilian and Military Elites in the Progressive Era." *Armed Forces and Society* 8 (Spring 1982): 405–18.

Bailey, Thomas A. "The United States and Hawaii during the Spanish-American War." *American Historical Review* 36 (April 1931): 552–60.

Ballou, Sidney. "Naval Defense of the Pacific." *The Navy* (March 1911): 28–35.

Baltzell, George F. "Our Present Drill Regulations." *Journal of U.S. Infantry Association* 6 (July 1909): 37–43.

Bateman, C. C. "Military Roadmaking in Mindanao." *Journal of the Military Service Institute of the United States* 33 (September–October 1903): 190–99.

——. "The Military Taming of the Moro." *Journal of the Military Service Institute of the United States* 34 (March–April 1904): 259–66.

Belote, W. M. "The Rock in the 'Tween War Years." *Bulletin of the American Historical Collection* 19 (January–March 1991): 26–43.

Benjamin, Anna N. "Some Filipino Characteristics." *Outlook* 68 (31 August 1901): 1003–8.

Birkhimer, William E. "Land Defenses of Manila Bay, May 1, 1898." *Journal of the U.S. Artillery* 15 (January–February 1902): 16–21.

Bjornstad, Alfred W. "The Military Necessities of the United States and the Best Provisions for Meeting Them." *Journal of the Military Service Institute of the United States* 42 (May–June 1908): 335–61.

Blount, James H. "Army Morals and the Canteen." *North American Review* 193 (March 1911): 409–21.

Boardman, Mabel T. "A Woman's Impressions of the Philippines." *Outlook* 82 (24 February 1906): 443–44.

Bogart, Charles H. "The Doomed Philippine Island Inland Seas Project." *Periodical* 14 (March 1986): 37–44.

Boies, H. M. "The Defense of Free People in the Light of the Spanish War." *Journal of the Military Service Institute of the United States* 24 (January 1899): 15–27.

Boughton, Daniel H. "The Study of Law at the Infantry and Cavalry School." *Journal of the Military Service Institute of the United States* 38 (March–April 1906): 264–71.

Boyd, Charles T. "A Country Fair in Moroland." *Century* 82 (September 1911): 681–85.

Braisted, William R. "The Washington Conference, 1921–22: Naval Rivalry, East Asian Stability, and the Road to Pearl Harbor." *Diplomacy and Statecraft* 4 (November 1993): 102–23.

Breedan, James O. "The Army and Public Health." In *The United States Army in Peacetime: Essays in Honor of the Bicentennial, 1775–1975*, edited by Robin Higham and Carol Brandt, pp. 83–106. Manhattan, Kans.: MA/AH Publishing, 1975.

Brownell, Atherton. "Impressions of Manila." *Munsey's Magazine* 35 (April 1906): 53–60.
———. "Turning Savages into Citizens." *Outlook* 96 (24 December 1910): 921–31.
Bullard, Robert L. "Among the Savage Moros." *Metropolitan Magazine* 34 (June 1906): 262–79.
———. "The Army in Cuba." *Journal of the Military Science Institute of the United States* 41 (September–October 1907): 152–57.
———. "The Citizen Soldier—The Volunteer." *Journal of the Military Service Institute of the United States* 39 (September–October 1906): 153–67.
———. "The Hard-Pressed Regular Army." *National Guard Magazine* (October 1907): 214–15.
———. "Military Pacification." *Journal of the Military Science Institute of the United States* 46 (January–February 1910): 1–24.
———. "Preparing Our Moros for Government." *Atlantic Monthly* (March 1906): 385–94.
———. "Road Building among the Moros." *Atlantic Monthly* (December 1903): 818–26.
———. "Small Maneuvers." *Journal of the Military Service Institute of the United States* 2 (April 1906): 57–67.
Butt, Archibald. "The Problem of Army Transportation." *Cosmopolitan* 30 (November 1900): 87–92.
Carter, William H. "Elihu Root: His Services as Secretary of War." *North American Review* 178 (January 1904): 110–21.
———. "A General Staff for the Army." *North American Review* 175 (October 1902): 558–65.
———. "Interdependence of Political and Military Policies." *North American Review* 194 (December 1910): 837–47.
———. "Military Preparedness." *North American Review* 191 (May 1910): 636–43.
———. "The War Department: The Military Administration." *Scribners* 33 (June 1903): 661–73.
Chester, James. "The Great Lesson of the Boer War." *Journal of the Military Service Institute of the United States* 32 (January–February 1903): 1–7.
———. "Musings of a Superannuated Soldier." *Journal of the Military Service Institute of the United States* 47 (November–December 1910): 387–97.
Christian, Francis L. "Harbor Defenses of Honolulu." *Coast Artillery Journal* 72 (June 1930): 483–84.
Church, William C. "Increasing Desertions and the Army Canteen." *North American Review* 177 (December 1903): 855–63.
Churchill, Marlborough. "The Military Intelligence Division, General Staff." *Journal of the U.S. Artillery* 52 (April 1920): 293–315.
Clodfelter, Mark. "Pinpointing Devastation: American Air Campaign Planning before Pearl Harbor." *Journal of Military History* 58 (January 1994): 75–102.
Cloke, H. E. "A Trip to Hawaii." *Coast Artillery Journal* 72 (June 1930): 475–83.
Coffman, Edward M. "The American 15th Infantry Regiment in China, 1912–1938: A Vignette of Social History." *Journal of Military History* 58 (January 1994): 57–74.
"Conditions in the Philippines." *Infantry Journal* 28 (April 1926): 436–37.
Conger, M. G. "The Sergeant's Valet." *Munsey's Magazine* 30 (October 1903): 94–99.
Cooke, Philip St.J. "Our Army and Navy." *Journal of the Military Service Institute of the United States* 8 (December 1887): 426–30.
Crane, Charles J. "Fighting Tactics of Filipinos." *Journal of the Military Service Institute of the United States* 31 (July 1902): 496–506.
———. "The Filipinos War contribution." *Journal of the Military Service Institute of the United States* 30 (September 1901): 270–74.
———. "Our New Infantry Drill Regulations." *Journal of the Military Service Institute of the United States* 36 (March–April 1905): 238–42.

——. "Paragraphs 93, 97 and 88 of General Orders 100." *Journal of the Military Service Institute of the United States* 32 (March–April 1903): 254–56.

——. "Who Burned Iloilo, Panay, and Why Were Conditions in Negros More Favorable to Us?" *Journal of the Military Service Institute of the United States* 30 (March 1902): 232–39.

Crowl, Philip A. "Alfred Thayer Mahan: The Naval Historian." In *Makers of Modern Strategy from Machiavelli to the Nuclear Age*, edited by Peter Paret, Gordon A. Craig, and Felix Gilbert, pp. 444–77. Princeton: Princeton University Press, 1986.

Cruikshank, Bruce. "Pilgrimage and Rebellion on Samar, 1884–1886." *Wisconsin Papers on Southeast Asia*. Madison: Center for Southeast Asian Studies, 1979.

Cullen, E. J. "The Function and Use of Railway Artillery." *Journal of the United States Artillery* 53 (September 1920): 271–89.

Cullinane, Michael. "Quezon and Harry Bandholtz." *Bulletin of the American Historical Collection* 9 (January–March 1981): 79–90.

Dannemiller, Augustus W. "Education of Army Children." *Infantry Journal* 23 (August 1923): 151–54.

Davis, Henry C. "Advance Base Training." *United States Naval Institute Proceedings* 37 (March 1911): 95–99.

——. "Battle under the New Conditions." *Journal of the Military Service Institute of the United States* 23 (September 1898): 249–67.

——. "Joint Exercises." *Journal of the Military Service Institute of the United States* 28 (November–December 1907): 286–90.

Davis, Oscar. "The Moros in Peace and War." *Munsey's Magazine* 27 (August 1902): 787–92.

Dean, John M. "Hawaii and the Philippines." *Chautauquan* (December 1903): 351–54.

deCamp, J. T. "Hawaii Thrilled by Night Bombing." *Coast Artillery Journal* 72 (January 1930): 41–48.

Dienstbach, Carl, and T. R. MacMechen. "The Aërial Battleship." *McClure's* 22 (August 1909): 343–54.

Doeppers, Daniel F. "The Philippine Revolution and the Geography of Schism." *Geographical Review* 66 (April 1976): 158–77.

Driggs, L. L. "The American Aldershot." *Munsey's Magazine* 29 (April 1903): 134–36.

Drysdale, Walter S. "The Infantry at Caloocan." *Infantry Journal* 28 (April 1926): 421–25.

Edwards, Arthur M. "The Proposed Garrison Ration." *Journal of the Military Service Institute of the United States* 41 (November–December 1907): 327–36.

Ellis, Wilmot E. "The Military Necessities of the United States and the Best Provisions for Meeting Them." *Journal of the Military Service Institute of the United States* 43 (July–August 1908): 1–24.

——. "What Is the Cause of the Falling Off in Enlisted Strength of the Army and Navy and What Means Should Be Taken to Remedy It." *Journal of the Military Service Institute of the United States* 44 (March–April 1909): 167–83.

Ely, Hanson E. "The Military Policy of the United States." *Journal of the Military Service Institute of the United States* 45 (May June 1907): 384–94.

Evans, Robert K. "Infantry Fire in Battle." *Journal of the United States Artillery* 31 (May–June 1909): 279–306.

——. "The Organization and Functions of a Bureau of Military Intelligence." *Journal of the Military Service Institute of the United States* 32 (May–June 1903): 318–43.

Farrell, John T. "An Abandoned Approach to Philippine History: John R. M. Taylor and the Philippine Insurgent Records." *Catholic Historical Review* 39 (January 1954): 385–407.

Fenn, C. C. "Polo for Infantry." *Infantry Journal* 23 (August 1923): 149–50.

Fitch, George H. "The New Pacific Empire." *World's Work* 3 (January 1902): 1591–97.

Flint, Roy K. "The United States Army on the Pacific Frontier, 1899–1939." In *The American Military and the Far East: Proceedings of the Ninth Military History Symposium*, edited by Joe E. Dixon, pp. 139–59. Washington, D.C.: U.S. Air Force Academy, 1980.

Foote, Stephen M. "Based on Present Conditions and Past Experience, How Should Our Volunteer Armies Be Raised, Organized, Trained, and Mobilized for Future Wars." *Journal of the Military Service Institute of the United States* 22 (January 1898): 1–49.

——. "The Military Necessities of the United States and the Best Provisions for Meeting Them." *Journal of the Military Service Institute of the United States* 43 (September–October 1908): 171–88.

Frisbee, John L. "Warrior, Prophet, Martyr." *Air Force Magazine* (September 1985): 158–66.

Fry, George T. "Our Land Forces for National Defense." *Infantry Journal* 11 (January–February 1915): 460–69.

Ganley, Eugene F. "Mountain Chase." *Military Affairs* 34 (February 1961): 203–10.

Gates, John M. "Indians and Insurrectos: The U.S. Army's Experience with Insurgency." *Parameters* 12 (March 1983): 59–68.

——. "The Official Historian and the Well-Placed Critic: James A. LeRoy's Assessment of John R. M. Taylor's *The Philippine Insurrection against the United States.*" *Public Historian* 7 (Summer 1985): 57–67.

——. "The Pacification of the Philippines." In *The American Military and the Far East: Proceedings of the Ninth Military History Symposium*, edited by Joe E. Dixon, pp. 79–91. Washington, D.C.: U.S. Air Force Academy, 1980.

Geere, Frank. "Our Military Individualism: The Relation of American Character to It, and the Importance of Its Effective Development." *Journal of the Military Service Institute of the United States* 39 (September–October 1906): 208–18.

Gibbon, John. "The Danger to Our Country from the Lack of Preparation for War." *Journal of the Military Service Institute of the United States* 11 (January 1890): 16–28.

Gibbs, David. "Soldier Schools in the Philippines." *Outlook* 74 (30 May 1903): 277–79.

Gillett, Mary C. "Medical Care and Evacuation during the Philippine Insurrection, 1899–1901." *Journal of the History of Medicine and Allied Sciences* 42 (April 1987): 169–85.

——. "U.S. Army Medical Officers and Public Health in the Philippines in the Wake of the Spanish-American War, 1898–1905." *Bulletin of the History of Medicine* 64 (1990): 567–87.

Gillette, Cassius E. "An American Uniform for the United States Army." *Journal of the Military Service Institute of the United States* 37 (July–August 1905): 63–80.

Gilmore, Russell. "The New Courage: Rifles and Soldier Individualism, 1876–1918." *Military Affairs* 30 (October 1976): 97–102.

Glassford, W. A. "Preparation for Defense." *Journal of the Military Service Institute of the United States* 45 (July–August 1909): 68–81.

Gleeck, Lewis E. "American Club Life in Old Manila." *Bulletin of the American Historical Collection* 4 (October 1975): 26–39.

Glenn, Edwin F. "Some Things Our Infantry Requires." *Journal of the U.S. Infantry Association* 4 (July 1907): 117–33.

Goodrich, Walter R. "Fort Kamehameha and Fort Weaver." *Coast Artillery Journal* 72 (June 1930): 485–86.

Gordon, W. H. "Training of New Regiments." *Infantry Journal* 11 (November–December 1911): 360–81.

Gray, David. "The Recantation of an Anti-Imperialist." *Outlook* 77 (20 August 1904): 931–34.

Green, Fred M. "Coast Artillery Life in the Philippines." *Journal of the U.S. Artillery* 56 (May 1922): 444–47.

Greene, Fred. "The Military View of American National Policy, 1904–1910." *American Historical Review* 46 (January 1961): 354–77.

Greer, Richard A. "Collarbone and the Social Evil." *Hawaiian Journal of History* 7 (1973): 3–17.

Hackett, Carl. "How the Soldier Goes to War." *Munsey's Magazine* 27 (September 1902): 903–7.

Hagood, Johnson. "The United States in the Next War." *Journal of the U.S. Artillery* 53 (July 1920): 1–8.

Hamilton, Allen L. "Military Strategists and the Annexation of Hawaii." *Journal of the West* 15 (April 1976): 81–91.

Hamilton, Louis M. "Jungle Tactics." *Journal of the Military Service Institute of the United States* 37 (July–August 1905): 23–28.

Hanna, Matthew E. "Increasing the Efficiency of the Cuban Army." *Journal of the Military Service Institute of the United States* 35 (July–August 1904): 28–36.

——. "Our Army a School." *Journal of the Military Service Institute of the United States* 41 (September–October 1907): 143–51.

Hauser, William L. "The Peacetime Army: Retrospect and Prospect." In *The United States Army in Peacetime: Essays in Honor of the Bicentennial, 1775–1975*, edited by Robin Higham and Carol Brandt, pp. 207–31. Manhattan, Kans.: MA/AH Publishing, 1975.

"The Hawaiian Islands: With Maps and Charts." *Journal of the U.S. Cavalry Association* 6 (June 1893): 215–16.

Helmick, Eli A. "How May Public Opinion concerning the Army and Navy Be So Educated As to Secure to the Soldier and Sailor in Uniform the Consideration Ordinarily Accorded to the Civilian." *Journal of the Military Services Institute of the United States* 42 (January–February 1908): 1–12.

Hersey, Henry B. "The Menace of Aerial Warfare." *Century* 77 (February 1909): 627–30.

Hickman, Edwin A. "Remarks on the Last Days of the Insurrection in Southern Luzon." *Journal of the United States Cavalry Association* 14 (October 1903): 297–308.

Higday, Hamilton M. "A Day in the Regular Army: The Life of a Private Cavalryman from Reveille to Taps in a Western Military Post." *World's Work* 5 (January 1903): 3007–12.

Hogan, Frank J. "The Sultan of Sulu." *Everybody's Magazine* 10 (May 1904): 636–41.

Holmes, J. M. "War and Civilization." *Infantry Journal* 11 (November–December 1914): 317–31.

Holt, Daniel D. "An Unlikely Partnership and Service: Dwight Eisenhower, Mark Clark, and the Philippines." *Kansas History* 13 (Autumn 1985): 149–65.

Hopper, James. "Kling." *Everybody's Magazine* 18 (June 1908): 769–74.

Horan, John P. "A Week at Kilauea." *Infantry Journal* 22 (January 1923): 31–40.

Hori, Joan. "Japanese Prostitution in Hawaii during the Immigration Period." *Hawaii Journal of History* 15 (1981): 113–24.

Horn, Tiemann N. "Recent Methods and Lessons in Regard to Field Artillery Taught by the Russo-Japanese War." *Journal of the United States Artillery* 30 (November–December 1908): 251–62.

Howard, Oliver O. "Is Cruelty Inseparable from War." *Independent* 54 (15 May 1902): 1161–62.

Howland, H. S. "Field Service in Mindanao." *Journal of the U.S Infantry Association* 2 (October 1905): 36–80.

Hunt, Michael H. "Resistance and Collaboration in the American Empire, 1898–1903: An Overview." *Pacific Historical Review* 48 (November 1979): 467–71.

Hunter, Charles H. "Murder, Rape, and Carpetbaggers." *Pacific Northwest Quarterly* (July 1967): 151–54.

Ide, Henry C. "Philippine Problems." *North American Review* 186 (December 1907): 510–24.

"Information on Philippine Service." *Infantry Journal* 30 (April 1927): 428–33.

"Insular Notes." *Journal of the Military Service Institute of the United States* 22 (November 1901): 448.

Iriye, Akira. "Japan as a Competitor, 1895–1917." In *Mutual Images: Essays in American-Japanese Relations,* edited by Akira Iriye, pp. 73–99. Cambridge, Mass.: Harvard University Press, 1975.

James, William. "The Moral Equivalent of War." *Journal of the Military Service Institute of the United States* 47 (November–December 1910): 405–16.

J.C.B. "The Hawaiian Islands. With Maps and Charts." *Journal of the Military Services Institute of the United States* 14 (May 1893): 682–83.

Johnson, Hugh. "The Lamb Rampant." *Everybody's Magazine* 18 (March 1908): 291–301.

Johnston, Robert M. "The Imperial Future of the United States." *Infantry Journal* 10 (November–December 1913): 311–17.

Johnston, William H. "Comment: A Filipino Army." *Journal of the U.S. Infantry Association* 6 (September 1910): 281–85.

———. "First Battalion, Philippine Scouts." *Journal of the U.S. Infantry Association* 1 (April 1905): 28–39.

———. "Philippine Infantry, A Plea for our Little Brown Soldiers." *Journal of the U.S. Infantry Association* 4 (May 1908): 861–74.

Jose, Ricardo T. "Before the Storm: The Commonwealth Army, Background and Development." *Bulletin of the American Historical Collection* 12 (October–December 1984): 22–47.

———. "The Philippine National Guard in World War I." *Philippine Studies* 36 (1988): 275–99.

Kahn, David. "The United States Views Germany and Japan in 1941." In *Knowing One's Enemies: Intelligence Assessment before the Two World Wars,* edited by Ernest May, pp. 476–501. Princeton: Princeton University Press, 1986.

Karsten, Peter. "Armed Progressives: The Military Reorganizes for the American Century." In *Building the Organizational Society: Essays on Associational Activities in Modern America,* edited by Jerry Israel, pp. 197–232. New York: Free Press, 1972.

Kelley, R. H. "Recruiting." *Infantry Journal* 11 (July–August 1914): 54–60.

Kernan, Francis J. "Field Training for the United States Army." *Journal of the Military Service Institute of the United States* 38 (May–June 1906): 379–91.

———. "What Does the Infantry Want?" *Journal of the United States Infantry Association* 4 (July 1907): 110–16.

Kerrick, Harrison S. "Our Military Resources vs. Our Military Power—National Assurance vs. National Insurance." *Journal of the Military Service Institute of the United States* 54 (May–June 1914): 293–316.

———. "What Is the Cause of the Falling Off in Enlisted Strength of the Army and Navy and What Means Should Be Taken to Remedy It." *Journal of the Military Service Institute of the United States* 44 (May–June 1909): 370–93.

Killingray, David. "The Idea of a British Imperial African Army." *Journal of African History* 20 (1979): 421–36.

———. "A Swift Agent of Government: Air Power in British Colonial Africa, 1916–1939." *Journal of African History* 25 (1984): 429–44.

King, Campbell. "The Peace Training of Armies." *Journal of the U.S. Infantry Association* 4 (July 1907): 88–109.

King, Charles. "The American Soldier." *The World To-day* 7 (November 1904): 1401–8.

Krausz, Sigmund. "The Porto Rican Provisional Regiment of Infantry." *Journal of the Military Science Institute of the United States* 38 (July–August 1905): 43–51.

Landor, A. Henry S. "The American Soldier As He Is." *North American Review* 178 (June 1904): 897–903.

Latham, George E. "The Brain of the Army." *Munsey's Magazine* 29 (September 1903): 900–903.

Linn, Brian M. "Intelligence and Low-Intensity Conflict in the Philippine War." *Intelligence and National Security* 6 (1991): 90–114.

———. "The Struggle for Samar." In *Crucible of Empire: The Spanish-American War and Its Aftermath*, edited by James C. Bradford, pp. 158–82. Annapolis, Md.: Naval Institute Press, 1993.

———. "We Will Go Heavily Armed: The Marines' Small War on Samar, 1901–1902." In *New Interpretations in Naval History: Selected Papers from the Ninth Naval History Symposium*, edited by William R. Roberts and Jack Sweetman, pp. 273–92. Annapolis, Md.: Naval Institute Press, 1991.

Livermore, William R. "Field and Siege Operations in the Far East." *Journal of the Military Service Institute of the United States* 36 (May–June 1905): 421–41.

Lynch, George A. "National Defense." *Infantry Journal* 10 (March–April 1914): 627–43.

McArthur, J. C. "Jungle Warfare in Panama." *Infantry Journal* 10 (May–June 1914): 855–60.

McClernand, Edward J. "Mounted Troops." *Journal of the Military Service Institute of the United States* 34 (March–April 1904): 227–41.

———. "Our Philippine Problem." *Journal of the Military Service Institute of the United States* 22 (November 1901): 327–32.

McCoy, Alfred W. "Baylan: Animist Religion and Philippine Peasant Ideology." *Philippine Quarterly of Culture and Society* 10 (1982): 141–94.

McLachlan, James. "Defenselessness of the Pacific Coast." *Infantry Journal* 7 (July 1910): 1–32.

Maguire, T. Miller. "Guerrilla or Partisan Warfare." *Journal of the Military Service Institute of the United States* 22 (July 1901): 86–92.

Malone, Paul B. "The Capture of New York." *Century* 85 (April 1913): 927–33.

Mastura, Michael O. "The American Presence in Mindanao: The Eventful Years in Cotabato." *Mindanao Journal* 8 (June 1981–July 1982): 31–32.

May, Glenn A. "Why the United States Won the Philippine-American War, 1899–1902." *Pacific Historical Review* 52 (November 1983): 353–77.

Meixsel, Richard B. "Major General George Grunert, WPO-3, and the Philippine Army, 1940–1941." *Journal of Military History* 59 (April 1995): 303–24.

Menoher, Charles T. "The Hawaiian Division." *Infantry Journal* 24 (April 1924): 376–78.

Merrill, Dana T. "Infantry Attack." *Journal of the United States Infantry Association* 6 (March 1910): 633–54.

———. "Infantry Training." *Infantry Journal* 9 (July–August 1912): 59–70.

Metcalf, H. B. "The Hawaiian Islands: The Paradise of the Pacific." *Pacific Monthly* 4 (May 1900): 2–6.

"Military Marriages." *The Independent* 47 (6 October 1904): 811–12.

Millard, Bailey. "The Shame of Our Army." *Cosmopolitan* 49 (September 1910): 411–20.

———. "The Story of a Deserter." *Cosmopolitan* 50 (January 1911): 274–82.

Mills, A. L. "The Organized Militia." *Infantry Journal* 11 (September–October 1914): 153–71.

Miwa, Kimitada. "Japanese Images of War with the United States." In *Mutual Images: Essays in American-Japanese Relations*, edited by Akira Iriye, pp. 115–37. Cambridge, Mass.: Harvard University Press, 1975.

Monroe, William H. "War and Peace: The Military Point of View." *North American Review* 192 (August 1910): 233–34.

Morrison, J. F. "The Proper Organization for Our Philippine Troops." *Journal of the United States Infantry Association* 2 (January 1906): 54–65.

——. "Some Notes on the Japanese Infantry." *Journal of the U.S. Infantry Association* 2 (January 1906): 20–29.

Morton, Charles J. "Machine Guns in Our Army." *Journal of the U.S. Infantry Association* 1 (July 1902): 21–32.

——. "Reflections of an Inspector." *Journal of the U.S. Infantry Association* 4 (January 1908): 545–61.

Morton, Louis. "Military and Naval Preparation for the Defense of the Philippines during the War Scare of 1907." *Military Affairs* 13 (Summer 1949): 95–104.

——. "War Plan Orange: Evolution of a Strategy." *World Politics* 11 (January 1959): 220–50.

Moseley, George V. H. "A Colonial Army." *Journal of the Military Service Institute of the United States* 34 (March–April 1904): 242–51.

Munro, John N. "The Philippine Native Scouts." *Journal of the United States Infantry Association* 2 (July 1905): 178–90.

Munson, Edward L. "The Ideal Ration for an Army in the Tropics." *Journal of the Military Service Institute of the United States* 36 (May 1905): 309–46.

Naylor, E. H. "As in Time of War." *Outlook* 95 (27 August 1910): 976.

Ness, Gayl D., and William Stall. "Western Imperialist Armies in Asia." *Comparative Studies in Society and History* 19 (January 1977): 2–29.

Nixon, Courtland. "Colonial Protection: A Mobile Army for the First Line of Action." *Journal of the Military Service Institute of the United States* 42 (March–April 1908): 294–99.

Nockolds, Coleman, "Tropical Diseases of Army Animals." *Journal of the Military Service Institute of the United States* 32 (March–April 1903): 286–92.

Paine, G. H. "Polo in the Philippines." *Infantry Journal* 30 (April 1927): 417–18.

Palmer, Frederick. "The Last of the Little Fights." *Munsey's Magazine* 27 (September 1902): 943–48.

——. "White Man and Brown Man in the Philippines." *Scribners Magazine* 27 (January–June 1900): 73–86.

Parker, James. "The Knell of the Volley." *Journal of the Military Service Institute of the United States* 30 (March 1902): 256–58.

——. "Mounted and Dismounted Action of Cavalry." *Journal of the Military Service Institute of the United States* 39 (November–December 1906): 381–87.

——. "Some Random Notes on the Fighting in the Philippines." *Journal of the Military Service Institute of the United States* 27 (March 1900): 317–40.

Parker, John H. "What Shall We Do with the Phillippines?" *Forum* 32 (February 1902): 662–70.

Pearce, E. D'A. "The Coast Artillery in the Philippines." *Coast Artillery Journal* 72 (February 1930): 134–40.

Pettit, James L. "How Far Does Democracy Affect the Organization and Discipline of Our Armies and How Can Its Influence Be Most Effectually Utilized." *Journal of the Military Service Institute of the United States* 38 (January–February 1906): 1–38.

Pierce, P. E. "The Squad Formation: Its Advantages as Illustrated by an Infantry Company in the Philippines." *Journal of the Military Service Institute of the United States* 30 (May 1902): 409–17.

Pope, Steven W. "An Army of Athletes: Playing Fields, Battlefields, and the American Military Sporting Experience, 1890–1920." *Journal of Military History* 59 (July 1995): 435–56.

Porch, Douglas. "Bugeaud, Galliéni, Lyautey: The Development of French Colonial Warfare." In *Makers of Modern Strategy from Machiavelli to the Nuclear Age*, edited by Peter Paret, Gordon A. Craig, and Felix Gilbert, pp. 376–407. Princeton: Princeton University Press, 1986.

Powell, J. W. "The Utilization of Native Troops in Our Foreign Relations." *Journal of the Military Service Institute of the United States* 30 (January 1902): 23–41.

Prentice, James. "The Effect of Air Service on the Tactics of Coast Defense." *Journal of the U.S. Artillery* 52 (February 1920): 97–106.

Pritchett, H. H. "The Army Canteen: From the Standpoint of the Man in the Ranks." *Outlook* 80 (15 July 1905): 676–79.

Prouty, S. M. "Philippine Service." *Infantry Journal* 22 (January 1923): 58–61.

Rader, Frank J. "The Works Progress Administration and Hawaiian Preparedness, 1935–1940." *Military Affairs* 41 (1978): 12–17.

Ransom, Edward. "Nelson A. Miles As Commanding General, 1895–1903." *Military Affairs* 29 (1966): 173–83.

Reade, Philip. "The Cargador in Mindanao." *Journal of the Military Service Institute of the United States* 37 (July–August 1905): 114–20.

Reeves, J. H. "The Hawaiian Islands." *Journal of the U.S. Cavalry Association* 11 (March 1898): 171–208.

Reichmann, Carl. "In Pace Para Bellum." *Journal of the U.S. Infantry Association* 2 (January 1906): 3–19.

Rhodes, Charles D. "Cavalry Expansion." *Journal of the Military Service Institute of the United States* 43 (November–December 1908): 452–60.

———. "The Experiences of Our Army since the Outbreak of the War with Spain: What Practical Use Has Been Made of Them and How May They Be Further Utilized to Improve Its Fighting Efficiency." *Journal of the Military Service Institute of the United States* 36 (March–April 1905): 197–223.

———. "How Best to Instruct Officers of Our Army in Tactics." *Journal of the Military Service Institute of the United States* 43 (September–October 1908): 202–21.

———. "The Utilization of Native Troops in Our Foreign Relations." *Journal of the Military Service Institute of the United States* 30 (January 1902): 1–22.

Richard, B. H. "The Question of Guam." *Military Historian and Economist* 1 (January 1916): 63–69.

Richards, Jeffrey. "Popular Imperialism and the Image of the Army in Juvenile Literature." In *Popular Imperialism and the Military, 1850–1950*, edited by John M. MacKenzie, pp. 80–107. Manchester: Manchester University Press, 1992.

Roberts, William R. "Reform and Revitalization, 1890–1903." In *Against All Enemies: Interpretations of American Military History from Colonial Times to the Present*, edited by Kenneth J. Hagan and William R. Roberts, pp. 197–218. Westport, Conn.: Greenwood Press, 1986.

Russel, Florence K. "Tales of a Tawi Tawi Garrison." *Everybody's Magazine* 9 (August 1903): 210–17.

Ruth, H. S. "Chemical Warfare against a Semi-Civilized Enemy with Particular Reference to Its Use against the Moros." *Chemical Warfare* 16 (January 1930): 12–13.

Saeki, Shoichi. "Images of the United States as a Hypothetical Enemy." In *Mutual Images: Essays in American-Japanese Relations*, edited by Akira Iriye, pp. 100–14. Cambridge, Mass.: Harvard University Press, 1975.

Saltzman, C. McK. "How May Public Opinion concerning the Army and Navy Be So Educated As to Secure to the Soldier and Sailor in Uniform the Consideration Ordinarily Accorded to the Civilian." *Journal of the Military Service Institute of the United States* 42 (January–February 1908): 13–21.

"Sand-30." [pseud.] "Trench, Parapet, or 'the Open.'" *Journal of the Military Service Institute of the United States* 32 (July 1902): 471–86.

Sanford, Wayne L. "Battle of Bud Dajo: 6 March 1906." *Indiana Military History Journal* 7 (May 1982): 4–20.

Sanger, J. P. "Artillery in the East." *Journal of the Military Services Institute of the United States* 1 (1880): 225–54.

Sapp, Burt. "Reminiscences of Mindanao Days." *Military Engineer* 23 (May–June 1931): 269–70.

Schaffer, Ronald. "General Stanley D. Embick: Military Dissenter." *Military Affairs* 37 (October 1973): 89–95.

Schofield, John M. "Notes on 'The Legitimate in War.'" *Journal of the Military Service Institute of the United States* 2 (1881): 1–10.

Seaman, Louis L. "A Crisis in the History of the American Army." *North American Review* 187 (May 1908): 748–57.

———. "Native Troops for Our Colonial Possessions." *North American Review* 171 (December 1900): 847–60.

———. "The U.S. Army Ration, and Its Adaptability for Use in Tropical Climates." *Journal of the Military Services Institute of the United States* 24 (May 1899): 375–97.

Sharpe, A. C. "The Campaign at Dinaluphin." *Journal of the Military Service Institute of the United States* 47 (July–August 1910): 13–24.

Shiner, John F. "The Air Corps, the Navy, and Coast Defense, 1919–1941." *Military Affairs* (October 1981): 113–20.

Sibert, W. L. "Military Occupation of Northern Luzon." *Journal of the Military Service Institute of the United States* 30 (May 1902): 404–8.

Sigerfoos, Edward. "Are Members of the Military Forces in the Philippines Entitled to a Trial by Jury." *Journal of the Military Service Institute of the United States* 43 (September–October 1908): 222–33.

Sixsmith, E. K. G. "Kitchener and the Guerrillas in the Boer War." *Army Quarterly and Defense Journal* 104 (January 1974): 203–14.

Slocum, S. L. "The Annexation of Hawaii: Some of Its Military and Economic Advantages." *Journal of the U.S. Cavalry Association* 11 (March 1898): 209–18.

Smith, Herbert E. "The Soldier in the Philippines." *Infantry Journal* 30 (April 1927): 375–79.

Smith, Roy C. "The Army and Navy Maneuvers As Viewed from Afloat." *Journal of the U.S. Artillery* 19 (March–April 1903): 146–60.

Sothern, Richard J. "Athletics in the Philipines." *Infantry Journal* 30 (April 1927): 387–94.

Starr, R. E. "Fort Shafter." *Coast Artillery Journal* 72 (June 1930): 486–88.

Steadman, Edward C. "The Prince of the Power of the Air." *Century* 76 (May 1908): 18–26.

Steele, Matthew F. "The Conduct of War." *Journal of the Military Service Institute of the United States* 42 (January–February 1908): 22–31.

Stone, J. Hamilton. "Our Troops in the Tropics: From the Surgeon's Standpoint." *Journal of the Military Service Institute of the United States* 36 (May 1900): 358–69.

Sumida, Jon T. "Sir John Fisher and the *Dreadnought*: The Sources of Naval Mythology." *Journal of Military History* 59 (October 1995): 619–637.

Swanson, Maynard. "The Sanitation Syndrome: Bubonic Plague and Urban Native Policy in the Cape Colony, 1900–1909." *Journal of African History* 18 (1977): 387–410.

Swift, Eben. "Military Education of Officers in Times of Peace." *Journal of the U.S. Artillery* 33 (May–June 1910): 285–96.

———. "Peon or Soldier." *Journal of the Military Service Institute of the United States* 30 (March 1902): 225–231.

Talmon, Yonina. "Millenarism." In *International Encyclopedia of the Social Sciences*, edited by Davil L. Sills, 10:349–62. New York: Macmillan, 1968.

Tan, Samuel K. "Sulu under American Military Occupation, 1899–1913." *Philippine Social Science and Humanities Review* 32 (1967): 1–187.

———. "Sulu under the Eagle's Shadow." *Mindanao Journal* 8 (June 1981–July 1982): 55–80.

Taylor, John R. M. "A Filipino Army." *Journal of the U.S. Infantry Association* 5 (May 1909): 893–908.

Terami-Wada, Motoe. "A Japanese Takeover of the Philippines." *Bulletin of the American Historical Collection* 13 (January–March 1985): 7–28.

———. "Kerayuki-san of Manila: 1890–1920." *Philippine Studies* 34 (1986): 287–316.

Tuttle, H. E. "Camp Stotsenburg, Pampanga." *Infantry Journal* 30 (April 1927): 350–52.

Vaile, Robert B. "Living with the Filipinos." *World's Work* 4 (June 1902): 2238–39.

Van Deusen, George W. "Which Are More Needed for Our Future Protection, More War-Ships or Better Coast Defenses." *Journal of the Military Services Institute of the United States* 15 (September 1894): 986–93.

Von Schiebrand, Wolf. "The Coming Supremacy of the Pacific." *Pacific Monthly* 15 (January 1906): 98–101.

Wagner, Arthur L. "The Military Necessities of the United States and the Best Provisions for Meeting Them." *Journal of the Military Service Institute of the United States* 5 (September 1884): 237–71.

Walworth, Frederick. "The Pacification of Cebu." *Everybody's Magazine* 10 (January 1904): 43–50.

Ward, John M. "The Utilization of Native Troops in Our Foreign Relations." *Journal of the Military Service Institute of the United States* 31 (November 1902): 793–805.

Weckerling, John. "The Natives of Northern Luzon." *Infantry Journal* 28 (February 1926): 141–44.

———. "Our Own Simla." *Infantry Journal* 28 (June 1926): 656–58.

Weigley, Russell F. "The Elihu Root Reforms and the Progressive Era." In *Command and Commanders in Modern Warfare*, edited by William Geffen, pp. 11–27. 2nd ed. Washington, D.C.: Government Printing Office, 1971.

———. "The Long Death of the Indian-Fighting Army." In *Soldiers and Civilians: The U.S. Army and the American People*, edited by Gary D. Ryan and Timothy K. Nenninger, pp. 27–39. Washington, D.C.: National Archives Trust Fund Board, 1987.

———. "The Role of the War Department and the Army." In *Pearl Harbor As History: Japanese American Relations, 1931–1941*, edited by Dorthy Borg and Sumpei Okamoto, pp. 165–88. New York: Columbia University Press, 1973.

Welch, Richard E. "American Atrocities in the Philippines: The Challenge and the Response." *Pacific Historical Review* 43 (May 1974): 233–53.

Wheeler, Gerald. "Republican Philippine Policy, 1921–1933." *Pacific Historical Review* 28 (November 1959): 377–90.

White, Charles. "Strategic Importance of Hawaii." *Infantry Journal* 23 (July 1923): 30–35.

Wildrick, Meade. "Coast Artillery in Hawaii." *Infantry Journal* 24 (April 1924): 422–24.

Williams, Dion. "Blue Marine Corps Expeditionary Force: Joint Army and Navy Exercises, 1925." *Marine Corps Gazette* 10 (September 1925): 76–88.

———. "The Defense of Our New Naval Stations." *United States Naval Institute Proceedings* 28 (June 1902): 181–94.

Williams, James T. "The Recent Army and Navy Maneuvers." *World To-Day* 5 (October 1903): 1333–37.

Williams, S. L. "The Governor of Paragua." *Munsey's Magazine* (May 1905): 136–38.

Wise, Hugh D. "Drill, Tactics, and Study." *Infantry Journal* 10 (January–February 1914): 511–16.

——. "Notes on Field Service in Samar." *Journal of the U.S. Infantry Association* 4 (July 1907): 3–58.

Wisser, John P. "Combined Army and Navy Operations." *Journal of the Military Service Institute of the United States* 30 (September 1902): 637–45.

Wood, Leonard. "Why We Have No Army." *McClure's* 38 (April 1912): 677–83.

Wood, S. A. "The Racial Problem in Hawaii." *Infantry Journal* 24 (April 1924): 425–34.

Woodruff, Charles E. "The Normal Malay and the Criminal Responsibility of Insane Malays." *Journal of the U.S. Cavalry Association* 16 (January 1906): 494–517.

Dissertations and Theses

Ames, Frank S. "A History of the Hawaii National Guard in Peace and War, 1923–1948." M.S. thesis, University of Hawaii, 1954.

Atwater, William F. "United States Army and Navy Development of Joint Landing Operations, 1898–1942." Ph.D. diss., Duke University, 1986.

Carpenter, Susan G. "Toward the Development of Philippine National Security Capability, 1920–1940: With a Special Reference to the Commonwealth Period." Ph.D. diss., New York University, 1976.

Coats, George Y. "The Philippine Constabulary: 1901–1917." Ph.D. diss., Ohio State University, 1968.

Cooper, Norman V. "The Military Career of General Holland M. Smith, U.S.M.C." Ph.D. diss., University of Alabama, 1974.

De Bevoise, Ken. "The Compromised Host: The Epidemilogical Context of the Philippine-American War." Ph.D. diss., University of Oregon, 1986.

Dwan, John E. "Franklin D. Roosevelt and the Revolution in the Strategy of National Security." Ph.D. diss., Yale University, 1954.

Fairfull, Thomas M. "General Nelson A. Miles and His Charges of Army Brutality in the Philippine Insurrection: Humanitarian Concern or Political Ambition?" M.A. thesis: Duke University, 1972.

Gole, Henry G. "War Planning at the Army War College, 1934–1940: The Road to Rainbow." Ph.D. diss., Temple University, 1991.

Gott, Camillus. "William Cameron Forbes and the Philippines, 1904–1946." Ph.D. diss., Indiana University, 1974.

Gowing, Peter. "Mandate in Moroland: The American Government of Muslim Filipinos, 1899–1920." D.S.S. diss., Syracuse University, 1968.

Guerrero, Milagros C. "Luzon at War: Contradictions in Philippine Society, 1898–1902." Ph.D. diss., University of Michigan, 1977.

Hamburger, Kenneth E. "The Technology, Doctrine and Politics of U.S. Coast Defenses, 1880–1945: A Case Study in U.S. Defense Planning." Ph.D. diss., Duke University, 1975.

Johnson, David E. "Fast Tanks and Heavy Bombers: The United States Army and the Development of Armor and Aviation Technologies, 1917 to 1945." Ph.D. diss., Duke University, 1990.

Jornacion, George W. "The Time of Eagles: United States Army Officers and the Pacification of the Philippine Moros, 1899–1913." Ph.D. diss., University of Maine, 1973.

Masse, Eugene H. "Francis Burton Harrison, Governor General of the Philippine Islands, 1913–1921." Ph.D. diss., Catholic University of America, 1971.

McGinty, Patrick E. "Intelligence and the Spanish-American War." Ph.D. diss., Georgetown University, 1983.

Meixsel, Richard B. "An Army for Independence? The American Roots of the Philippine Army." Ph.D. diss., Ohio State University, 1993.

——. "United States Army Policy in the Philippine Islands, 1902–1922." M.A. thesis, University of Georgia, 1988.

Miller, Robert A. "The U.S. Army during the 1930's." Ph.D. diss., Princeton University, 1973.

Osterhoudt, Henry J. "The Evolution of U.S. Army Assault Tactics, 1778–1919: The Search for Sound Doctrine." Ph.D. diss., Duke University, 1986.

Powers, Thomas L. "The U.S. Army and the Washington Conference, 1921–1922." Ph.D. diss., University of Georgia, 1978.

Raines, Edgar F., Jr. "Major General J. Franklin Bell and Military Reform: The Chief of Staff Years, 1906–1910." Ph.D. diss., University of Wisconsin, 1976.

Reed, John S. "Burden and Honor: The United States Volunteers in the Southern Philippines, 1899–1901." Ph.D. diss., University of Southern California, 1994.

Roberts, William F. "Loyalty and Expertise: The Transformation of the Nineteenth-Century American General Staff and the Creation of the Modern Military Establishment." Ph.D. diss., Johns Hopkins University, 1980.

Thompson, Wayne S. "Governors of the Moro Province: Wood, Bliss, and Pershing in the Southern Philippines, 1903–1913." Ph.D. diss., University of California–San Diego, 1975.

Underwood, Jeffrey S. "The Army Air Corps under Franklin D. Roosevelt: The Influence of Airpower on the Roosevelt Administration, 1933–1941." Ph.D. diss., Louisiana State University, 1988.

Wakefield, Charles L. "A History of the Hawaii National Guard." M.A. Thesis, University of Hawaii, 1934.

Williams, Vernon L. "The U.S. Navy in the Philippine Insurrection and Subsequent Native Unrest, 1898–1906." Ph.D. diss., Texas A&M University, 1985.

Woolard, James R. "The Philippine Scouts: The Development of America's Colonial Army." Ph.D. diss., Ohio State University, 1975.

Zais, Barrie M. "The Struggle for a Twentieth Century Army: Investigation and Reform of the United States Army after the Spanish-American War, 1898–1903." Ph.D. diss., Duke University, 1981.

—in Philippines: Drum, 70, 92, 233; Frank, 70, 92, 233; Hughes, 70, 92; Santiago, 70; William McKinley, 68, 70, 73, 103, 118, 121, 125, 148; Wint, 70, 243. *See also* Corregidor; Manila Bay; Stotsenburg
Foulois, Benjamin, 35, 36
From Here to Eternity, 51, 117, 130, 136
Funston, Frederick, 57, 89–90, 107, 124
Fuqua, Stephen O., 122

Ganoe, William, 16
Gardener, Cornelius, 18
General Headquarters (Air Force), 212–13, 216
General Orders: No. 100, 13; No. 152, 26; No. 8, 63
General Staff, 5, 52, 53, 54, 55, 61, 62, 64, 82, 85, 86, 94, 107–8, 146, 156, 165, 167–68, 175–76, 178, 183, 187, 188, 203, 234, 236
George, Harold H., 218
Glenn, Edwin F., 17–18, 21
Gole, Henry, 171, 178
Grafton, Homer, 27
Great Britain, 6, 35, 47, 52, 53, 57, 92, 119, 124, 145, 148, 165, 166, 170–71, 194, 217, 221, 251. *See also* Plans: Red-Orange
Guam, 89, 168, 170, 171, 177
Gulick, John W., 172

Haan, William G., 188, 192, 194, 196, 226
Hagood, Johnson, 104, 108, 123–24, 190–91, 200, 202, 227, 235, 243, 251
Hall, Harrison, 93
Hannum, Warren, 96
Harbold, Norris, 206
Hare-Hawes-Cutting Act, 177
Harris, Hunter, 205
Harrison, Francis B., 111, 120, 145, 150, 185
Hawaii: strategic value of, xii, 6–8, 80, 82, 87–88, 95, 109, 147, 173, 186, 194, 219, 221–22, 246; annexation, 6–7, 8–9; army views of inhabitants, 7, 8, 122–23, 152, 159; manpower in, 8, 53, 64, 82, 86, 146–50, 152–57, 194, 195, 197–98, 221, 223–24, 250–51; 1898 expedition to, 8–9; community relations, 9, 110, 111–12, 115, 120, 121–23, 124–26, 136, 250; living con-

ditions in, 71–72, 115–21; defense of, 80–82, 85, 87–88, 92–97, 104, 108, 153, 166–67, 173, 175, 194–99, 214, 221–22, 246, 248; internal threat to, 82, 85, 88, 95, 104–6, 110, 145, 159–63, 181, 194, 195, 206, 221–22, 249–50; war scares in, 85, 107, 248; threat from air attack, 180, 196, 208–10, 213, 214, 222, 246, 248; aviation in, 196, 203, 205–6, 207, 208–13, 214–17; and chemical warfare, 198, 214; interservice relations, 198–200, 204, 210–13, 246
Hawaii, Republic of, 7, 8, 54
Hawaiian Department, 71, 109, 110, 117, 130, 167, 197, 206, 212, 214, 221–22; mission, 215–16, 221–22, 246, 248
Hawaiian Division, 71, 135, 201, 222, 224, 225, 291 (n. 1)
Hawaii National Guard, 59–60, 82, 84, 149, 154–56; in World War I, 109–12
Health: disease, 9, 10, 11, 16, 59, 74–75, 102; army preventative measures, 75, 122, 128–30, 219, 250; venereal disease, 127–30
Helmick, Eli, 37
Henderson, Robert, 172
Henty, G. A., 57
Herron, Charles D., 156, 208–9, 210, 223, 251
Heuer, William H., 80–82, 94
Hodges, Campbell B., 61
Holbrook, Lucius R., 231; and Holbrook plan, 232–38, 242, 244, 245, 246
Holbrook, Willard A., 126
Holloway, Bruce, 206
Homosexuality, 130–33
Honolulu: army garrison at, 9; army views of, 68; activities in, 68, 115, 118, 124–26, 134; defense of, 80–81, 125–26, 195–97, 214, 248, 268 (n. 5), 271 (n. 54); police, 135–36
Hoover, Herbert, 175, 177
Howell, D. L., 135
Hurley, Patrick, 174

Ide, Henry C., 32
Intelligence, 44; and Military Information Division, 7, 47, 85; and internal security, 157, 250
Internal security, xiii, 157, 250; in Philip-

pines, 84–85, 104, 106–7, 157–58; in
Hawaii, 85, 88, 104–6, 158–62
Interservice relations, xiii, 89–90, 113, 169,
200; differing strategic views, 5, 88–90;
cooperation, 13, 33, 92, 94, 99, 179;
rivalry, 82–84, 86–87, 97, 117, 180, 181,
199, 204, 210–13, 246; joint army-navy
maneuvers, 103, 198–99, 204, 209–10,
213. *See also* Joint Army and Navy
Board
Ivins, Charles F., 51, 66, 69

Japan: as threat to Pacific possessions, xi,
xiv, 49, 84–85, 88, 145, 165, 169–71, 174,
177, 180, 187–98, 199–200, 208, 214, 220,
222, 228–29, 232–34, 243, 244, 247–49,
251; military views of, 6, 88, 177–78, 220,
229; war scares about, 71, 85–88, 97, 104,
106–8, 248; in World War I, 112, 160,
165; aircraft carrier attack on Hawaii,
208–10, 213, 222, 246, 247. *See also*
Plans: Orange
Japanese in Hawaii, xiii, 104, 123, 159–60,
163; as source of manpower, xiii, 111–12,
122, 149, 152–57, 251; as internal threat,
82, 88, 95, 104–6, 110, 145, 159–63, 181,
195, 206, 221–22, 250; army views of, 122,
123, 152–53, 156–57
Johnson, Hugh, 56
Johnston, William H., 48, 101
Joint Army and Navy Board, 54, 167, 171,
211, 288 (n. 9); and Hawaii, 81, 89, 96,
208, 211–13, 221–22; and Philippines,
83, 86–87, 186, 187, 190, 220–21, 230–31,
235–36; and 1907 War Scare, 85–86,
108; Planning Committee, 169, 173, 175,
187, 204; and Pacific strategy, 169–75,
180, 204, 230–31
Jones, James, 51, 130
Jones, T. W., 85
Jones Act, 101, 109, 145, 185, 238
Judd, Charles, 122
Judd, Lawrence M., 123

Keeney, Robert W., 117–18
Kellog, E. S., 99–100
Kernan, Francis J., 186
Kilbourne, Charles E., 48, 175, 177, 228–30
King, Charles, 57
Koch, Arthur, 69, 72, 76

Krogstad, Arnold, 208
Krueger, Walter, 179–83, 231, 234, 236

Ladrones (brigands), 19, 24, 28, 42; in
Cavite, 28–30, 42, 44
Landers, H. L., 122
Langfitt, William C., 80
Langhorne, George T., 46
Larsen, Stanley G., 66, 117
Lassiter, William, 48, 155, 195, 208, 222,
223, 251; and Philippines, 151, 189–92,
193, 200, 208, 245
Lea, Homer, 88
Lee, John C. H., 124
Lee, Raymond, 200
Lewis, Edward M., 153
Leyte: Pulahan campaign on, 30, 33–34,
47
Liggett, Hunter, 48, 101; and Liggett
Board, 98–100, 113
Lim, Vicente, 124, 186, 239, 241
Luke Air Field. *See* Air Fields

MacArthur, Arthur: strategic views of, 6,
20–21, 82, 110, 166; in Philippine War,
12–14; and Taft, 18–19
MacArthur, Douglas, xii, xiv, 67, 148, 215,
217, 251; romantic view of Philippines,
65; and 1929 Philippine Defense Plan,
151–52, 192–94, 196–97, 202, 225–26, 228,
233–34, 238–39, 251; alters Orange plans,
174–77, 178–79, 183, 228, 232, 234–36,
238, 245; as chief of staff, 174–77, 207,
213, 220, 225–26, 239; as USAFFE commander, 182, 218, 244–46; plans defense
of Philippines, 225, 231–32, 234, 236, 238,
245, 251; as military advisor in Philippines, 231, 234, 235, 237, 239–42
McFarlane, Munro, 82
Maciejowski, Walter, 118, 136
Mackall, Samuel T., 221
Mackenzie, Alexander, 81
McKinley, William, 7, 8, 10, 13, 18, 20, 51,
52
McKinley, William E. W., 23
McKinley, Fort William. *See* Forts
Macomb, Montgomery M., 96; and
Macomb Boards, 95–97, 106, 166–67;
and defense of Philippines, 100, 102,
107–8

Cavalry, 63; 7th Infantry, 60; 8th Cavalry, 63; 8th Infantry, 63; 9th Cavalry, 59, 66, 68, 127; 10th Cavalry, 60, 119; 12th Infantry, 34; 12th Medical Regiment, 148; 13th Infantry, 63; 14th Cavalry, 56; 14th Infantry, 34; 15th Cavalry, 63; 15th Infantry, 63, 70, 116, 230; 19th Infantry, 72; 21st Infantry, 34; 23rd Brigade, 244; 23rd Infantry, 59; 23rd Squadron, 206; 24th Division, 224; 24th Field Artillery, 244; 24th Infantry, 33, 34, 60, 63; 25th Division, 224; 25th Infantry, 60, 61, 68, 121; 27th Infantry, 116, 201; 28th Squadron, 205; 31st Infantry, 64, 66, 70, 73, 118, 125, 127, 130, 177, 201, 219, 227, 243; 35th Infantry, 117; 35th Pursuit Group, 217; 45th Regiment, 244; 51st Scout Company, 41; 52nd Scout Company, 41; 57th Infantry, 148; 64th Coast Artillery, 224; 298th Infantry, 149; 299th Infantry, 149; Hawaiian Separate Coast Artillery Brigade, 224

Paine, G. H., 121
Palmer, John M., 62, 63, 64, 96–98, 105, 146, 166, 169
Parker, Frank, 229–30, 237, 239, 243
Parker, James, 55
Parker, John H., 15, 21
Parks, Floyd, 120
Patrick, Mason, 214–15
Patton, George S., 161–62
Pearl Harbor: Japanese attack on, xi, 212, 213, 247; strategic value of, 6–7, 80, 89, 90, 215–16, 222–24; defense of, 80–81, 84, 86, 90, 92, 104, 108, 173, 195–97, 199, 209–10, 211–12, 213, 215, 221, 224, 247, 248, 268 (n. 5), 271 (n. 54); naval base at, 87, 123, 212; threat of air attack on, 207, 208–13, 214–15
Pershing, John J., 129; in Moro conflicts, 35, 36, 38, 40–42, 48, 200; training program of, 103; as chief of staff, 146–47, 238
Pettit, James L., 56
Philippine (Commonwealth) Army, 162, 182, 220, 232–33, 235, 237, 238, 240–42, 245, 247, 251
Philippine Commission, 14, 37, 52; and army relations with, 18–19, 25–28
Philippine Commonwealth, 158, 177, 220, 231–32, 233, 235, 239–41

Philippine Constabulary, 14, 19, 24, 25, 26, 27, 29, 32–33, 39, 40, 41, 48, 84, 107, 109, 124, 150, 157, 158
Philippine Defense Act, 234, 239–40
Philippine Defense Board, 98–100, 113
Philippine Department, 64, 148, 150, 157, 167, 204, 206, 231, 257 (n. 12), 291–92 (n. 1); independence of commanders in, 15, 42–43, 96, 98, 108, 167, 168–69, 183, 189, 190, 193, 219, 225, 232, 234–38, 246; mission, 99–102, 157, 170, 173, 187, 220, 230, 235, 236, 237, 249; defense plans, 187–94, 226, 231–32, 240. *See* Carabao Army
Philippine Division, 107, 190, 191, 200, 237, 239, 244, 245, 257 (n. 12), 291–92 (n. 1)
Philippine Islands: strategic value of, xii, 20–21, 82–83, 98–100, 109, 147, 170–72, 174–75, 178–80, 185–87, 189, 194, 217, 219–21, 224, 225, 226–32, 236, 243–44, 249; internal threat to, xiii, 82, 104, 106–7, 124, 145, 157–58, 249–50; manpower in, 8, 15, 53, 60–64, 98, 102, 109, 146–47, 150–52, 188, 191–93, 200, 219, 226, 227, 235, 239, 242–45, 244–45; civil-military relations, 12–13, 18–19, 23, 24–28, 28–30, 45–46, 110, 115, 194, 240; pacification campaigns in, 25–49, 80, 249, 250; living conditions in, 65, 69, 72–73, 115–21; as base for attacks on Japan, 82, 214, 217, 225, 244–45; defense of, 82–84, 91–93, 97–103, 151–52, 171–78, 187–94, 197–98, 203, 207–8, 220–21, 225–46 passim, 249; independence of, 98, 101, 104, 109, 124, 145, 175, 177, 185–86, 191–92, 220, 227, 229, 230, 231, 235, 236, 239, 242, 243, 251; effects of World War I on, 109–11; athletics in, 115, 116, 120–21, 245; aviation and, 183, 191, 192, 197, 203–5, 206, 207–8, 214, 216–18; neutrality of, 235, 239, 242
Philippine National Guard, 110–11, 112, 145, 151, 239
Philippine Scouts, 19, 25, 32, 42, 45, 59, 103, 145, 158, 181, 251; and civil government, 26–28, 103; in Pulahan campaign, 31–34; in Moro campaigns, 41, 59; army views of, 48–49, 59, 148–49, 220; manpower, 109, 149, 191, 241; effect

of World War I on, 109–10; athletics in, 117; social relations of, 123, 126; mutiny of, 148–49, 157; as internal security threat, 158; and Philippine Army, 237, 239, 241. *See also* Carabao Army; Pacific Army units

Philippines Division, 28, 61, 257 (n. 12)

Philippine War, 11–14; effect on U.S. Army, 16–18, 56–59

Pilar, Pio del, 45

Pineapple Army, 65, 185, 188, 202, 221, 225, 246

Pinkham, Lucius, 110

Plans and projects, xiv, 167–69, 188–89, 192, 194, 195–96, 202, 225, 233–34; for Philippine defense, 82–83, 85–86, 88, 126, 151, 152, 158, 160, 172–77, 180–81, 187–94, 197–98, 220–21, 225–46 passim; Orange, 85–86, 88, 105, 151, 152, 161, 162, 167, 169, 170, 172–76, 178–83, 185, 187–94, 196–98, 221, 225, 226–31, 232–36, 237, 251; for Hawaiian defense, 88, 105, 153, 160–62, 166, 173, 194–200, 211–12, 221–24; Brown, 126, 158, 160; Red-Orange, 153, 165, 182, 194; White, 158, 160; Rainbow, 182

Police, Military, 68, 128, 130, 131, 133, 135; and Honolulu Police, 135–36

Poore, Benjamin A., 88

Posts: selection of, 69–73, 116. *See also* Air Fields; Camps; Forts

Pratt, William V., 175, 207, 215, 226

Prostitution, 68, 115, 119, 127–29

Public opinion: and Philippine War, 16–18, 46, 52, 57; and army, 46–47, 57, 121; and Philippine defense, 100, 177, 187, 189, 227, 231, 247

Public works, 10, 12–13, 20, 25, 33, 37, 40, 45, 122, 219, 225, 250

Pulahan campaign, 31–34, 43–45, 46, 47, 48, 61, 69, 75, 120

Pulahanes, 28, 49; on Samar, 28, 29, 30–34, 42, 44; on Leyte, 33–34, 61

Quezon, Manuel, 110–11, 186, 239–41

Reeder, Oscar, 75

Reeves, J. H., 8

Rhodes, Charles D., 58, 166

Richardson, Robert C., 151

Rodgers, W. L., 87; and War College committee, 87–88, 93, 95, 104–5

Roosevelt, Franklin D., xi, 177, 182, 236, 242

Roosevelt, Theodore, 6, 23, 25, 37, 38, 39, 57, 58, 87, 90, 109, 113, 128

Root, Elihu, 25, 202; reforms of, 52–56, 58, 59, 62, 79, 80, 86, 91

Ruckman, John W., 92

Russo-Japanese War, 84, 86, 87

Sakay, Macario, 29

Samar: in Philippine War, 14, 17; and Pulahan campaign on, 30–34, 37, 44, 47, 48

Schofield, John M., 6, 8, 106

Schofield Barracks, 68, 71–72, 76, 94, 95, 105, 120, 122, 124, 125, 159, 195, 196, 199, 201, 214; athletics at, 116–17; facilities at, 118–21, 225; stockade at, 135–36

Schuyler, Walter S., 105

Scott, Hugh L., 35, 52, 66, 93

Seaman, Louis L., 59

Seone, Consuelo, 105

Sexton, William T., 15

Shanks, David, 29–30

Shea, Nancy, 123

Sheriden, J. M., 24

Sherman, William T., 6, 106

Sherrod, Robert, 217

Short, Walter C., 157

Shunk, Caroline, 72–73

Sibley, Frederick W., 30

Slackman, Michael, 162

Slocum, S. L., 8

Smith, Jacob H., 14, 30

Smith, John P., 214

Spanish-American War, 5, 8, 9, 11

Steele, Matthew F., 166

Steever, Edgar Z., 40, 46

Stimson, Henry L., 55, 61, 62, 182, 191, 217, 244, 246

Storey, J. P., 88, 104

Stotsenburg, Fort, 69, 70, 72–73, 121, 123–24, 193, 203, 227, 243. *See also* Air Fields—in Philippines: Clark

Strategy: and Pacific, 80, 89–91, 147, 170–74, 177, 180–81, 216, 246. *See also* Plans; Tactics

Stratemeyer, Edward, 57

Subic Bay, 70, 235, 243; defense of, 70, 108, 220, 236, 238; controversy over base at, 82–84, 86–87, 97
Sulu. *See* Moros
Summerall, Charles P., 48, 191–92; in Hawaii, 122, 152–53, 155, 159, 161, 214–15; 1924 defense plan, 153, 195–97, 199, 202, 222, 251
Surigao expedition, 46
Sutherland, J. M., 75

Tactics, xii–xiii, 79; Filipino, 11–13; in pacification campaigns, 11–13, 15, 17, 38, 42–48; concentration of population, 14, 29, 44, 105–6; Pulahan, 31; Moro, 36; coast defense, 80–81, 83, 91–94, 98, 108, 188, 190–99, 194, 196, 197, 224; projected Japanese, 85, 88, 95, 191, 192, 196, 197, 198, 199–200, 207–9, 214, 220, 222; mobile and beach defense, 88, 96–97, 99, 166, 188, 191–92, 195–97, 219, 223, 226–27, 232–33, 237–38, 244, 248; citadel defense, 91–93, 95–102, 166, 208, 227–28, 248; Positive System of Coast Defense, 188, 192, 194–96, 224; for chemical warfare, 191, 193, 196, 197–98, 199, 207, 214; for antiaircraft, 207, 224; aerial, 207–9, 216
Taft, William H., 120; and Arthur Mac-Arthur, 18–19; and views of postwar violence, 23–25; use of Scouts, 27; and use of army, 29; as secretary of war, 47, 55, 57, 83–84, 86; and use of black troops, 60–61; as governor, 120. *See also* National Coast Defense Board
Taylor, James S., 74
Taylor, John R. M., 47
Tierney, James H., 239
Transports, 67–68, 76–77, 119, 172, 245
Tydings-McDuffie Act, 177, 180, 220, 232, 233

U.S. Army: and Pacific strategy, xii, 20–21, 79–80, 89–91, 147, 170–72, 179–83; and views on Pacific, 5, 6, 87–88, 248; missions of, 5, 79–80, 146, 249; and civic projects, 10, 12–13, 20, 25, 33, 37, 40, 45, 122, 219, 225; and Philippine War, 11–15; casualties in, 16, 34, 39, 41, 43, 247; pacification operations of, 25–49; impact

of Root reforms on, 52–59, 62; Coast Artillery, 57, 63, 92, 96; impact of overseas rotation, 60–64, 66–67; and views of Japanese threat, 85–86, 88, 165, 177–78, 220, 229, 251; and views of war, 106; athletics in, 116–17, 120–21. *See also* General Staff; Interservice relations; Joint Army and Navy Board; Pacific Army units; War College, U.S. Army; War Plans Division
U.S. Army Forces in Far East, 182–83, 244, 245
U.S. Navy, xiii, 5, 33, 80; and Pearl Harbor, 81, 87, 212–13; and Philippines, 82–84, 85, 86–87, 99–100, 101, 174–75, 177, 179, 191–93, 209, 214; General Board, 83–86; views of Japanese threat, 85–86, 165; views of Pacific defense, 89–90, 169, 173, 178–81; joint army-navy maneuvers, 103, 198–99, 204, 209–10, 213. *See also* Interservice relations; Joint Army and Navy Board
Upham, F. B., 230
Upton, Emory, 6, 55

Van Deusen, George W., 5

Wainwright, Jonathan M. , 245
War College, U.S. Army, 52, 53, 54, 85–86, 88, 93, 95, 96, 100–101, 105, 149, 172, 177–78, 182, 194, 239, 242
War Plans Division, 146, 155, 156, 166–67, 168, 169, 172, 175–76, 178–80, 181, 188, 190, 194–95, 211, 215–16, 217, 221, 225, 228, 230–31, 234, 236, 287 (n. 2)
Washington Naval Conference, 167–68, 170–71, 173, 177, 186, 197, 204, 220, 243
Wells, Briant H., 48, 172, 186; in Hawaii, 122–23, 124, 155–56, 161, 209, 222, 223, 251
Wheaton, Loyd, 15
Wheeler, Erasmus, 96
White, John R., 124
Willeford, Charles, 65
Williams, Constant, 127
Wilson, Woodrow, 98, 110
Women: and interracial unions, 60–61, 65, 115, 124, 126–27; U.S. Army and, 65, 72–73, 118, 119, 121, 123, 124, 125–26; as wives, 67, 68, 71, 72–74, 107, 117, 120,

121, 123; clubs for, 69, 121, 123; and
racism, 123–24, 126
Wood, Leonard, xii, 24, 166, 251; and
Moros, 35, 37–39, 45, 46, 48; as commander in Philippines, 39, 61, 70, 83,
85, 86, 87, 91, 99, 103, 104, 108, 116, 129;
as chief of staff, 56, 90, 91, 98, 99, 103,
104; as governor general, 150, 157, 186,
191
Wood, S. A., 123

Wood-Forbes Mission, 186
Woodruff, Charles E., 24, 74
World War I, 48, 109, 244; effects of, 74,
76, 109–12, 145, 147, 165–66, 188, 191,
194, 195, 197–98, 201, 202, 203, 224
Wotherspoon, William W., 86, 113
Wright, Luke E., 18, 25, 30

Yarnell, Harry E., 169
Young, Samuel B. M., 58